Study Edition

my REFLECTIONS on CIVICS

re•flec'tion (ri-FLEK-shuhn) ▶ noun
1. a thought, idea, or opinion formed or a remark made as a result of meditation **2.** consideration of some subject matter, idea, or purpose **3.** an instance of reflecting; especially: the return of light or sound waves from a surface **4.** the production of an image by or as if by a mirror **5.** something produced by reflecting, as **a**: an image given back by a reflecting surface **b**: an effect produced by an influence

Use the study edition to record your thoughts, ideas, and opinions and make connections between the essential questions and yourself, your community, and the world.

 McGraw Hill

McGraw-Hill
networks™
A Social Studies Learning System

Cover Photo Credit: Radius Images/Corbis

connected.mcgraw-hill.com

The McGraw-Hill Companies

 Education

Copyright © 2013 by The McGraw-Hill Companies, Inc.

Send all inquiries to:
McGraw-Hill Education
8787 Orion Place
Columbus, OH 43240

ISBN: 978-0-07-661730-2
MHID: 0-07-661730-0

Printed in the United States of America.

6 7 8 9 ROV 16 15 14

How will YOU use *My Reflections on Civics*?

The *My Reflections on Civics Florida Study Edition* was created as a study edition just for you. Using this interactive textbook along with your full student edition and **netw⊙rks** will empower you to learn civics in a whole new way.

You will be able to write directly in this book! You can take notes, interact with what you read, and reflect on what you learn.

As a result, you will be able to make connections between civics and your life, your community, and your world today.

Show Your Skill

1. Make Inferences
Why was it difficult to pass laws under the Articles of Confederation?

Dig into the text and show what you know!

Think Critically

2. Infer How have the courts interpreted the Second Amendment?

Analyze what you read!

Mark the Text

3. Underline the three non-legislative powers of Congress.

Finally—a book you can write in!

Take the Challenge

4. Write a proposal for a new amendment. With your class acting as Congress, propose your change to the Constitution and see if it passes.

Create a unique project or do some learning on your own!

Keep Going! ▶▶

Make the Most of the *My Reflections* Activities!

Does civics matter to you today? Is it relevant to your daily life? Yes, it is!

The ideas and events you learn about in civics help you understand people, the government, and economics. As a result, you are better equipped to understand your life and the world today.

The "My Reflections" activities at the end of each chapter were created to help you make connections between the past and the present. Each activity allows you to reflect on what you have learned and how that relates to you, your community, and even the world.

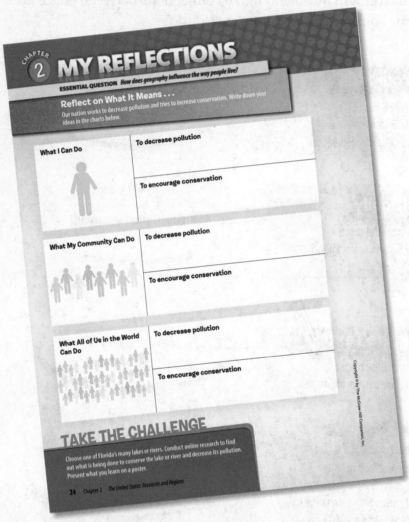

Have fun with *My Reflections on Civics* You never know . . . you might just love civics by the time you're finished.

FLORIDA *Study Edition*

Contents

Due **I'm Finished**

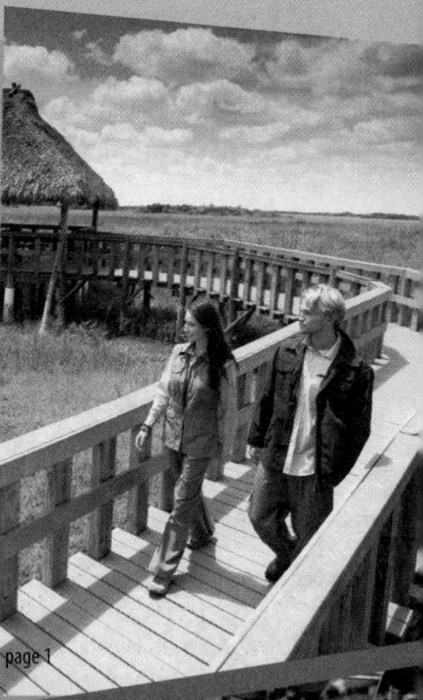

page 1

page 25

page 86

netw⦿rks
*Interact with your
Florida Study Edition Online!*

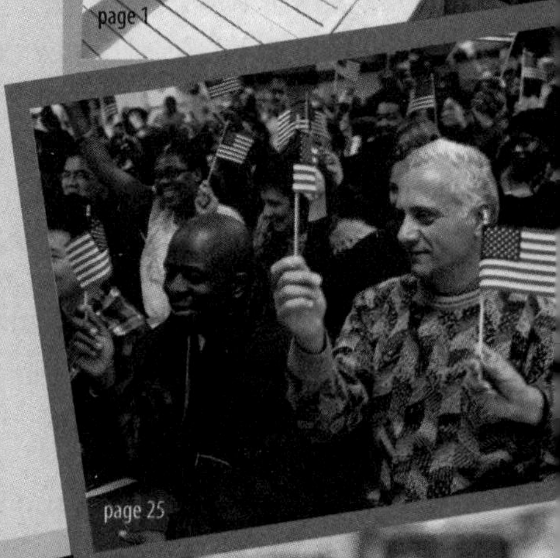

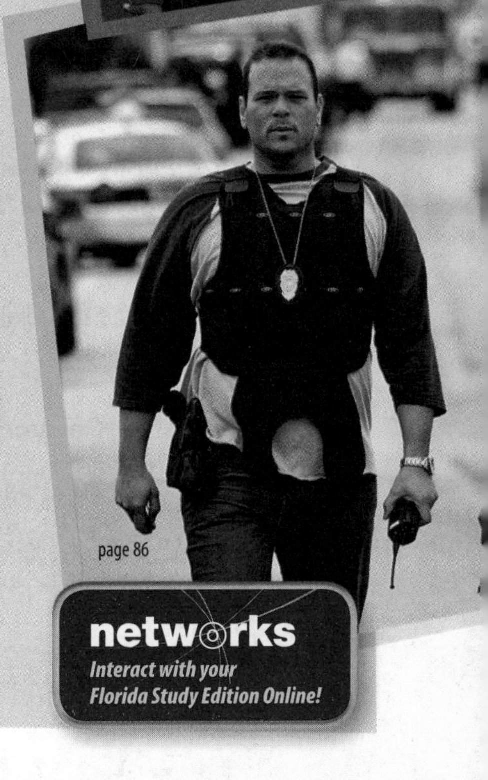

page 113

page 133

page 156

networks
Interact with your
Florida Study Edition Online!

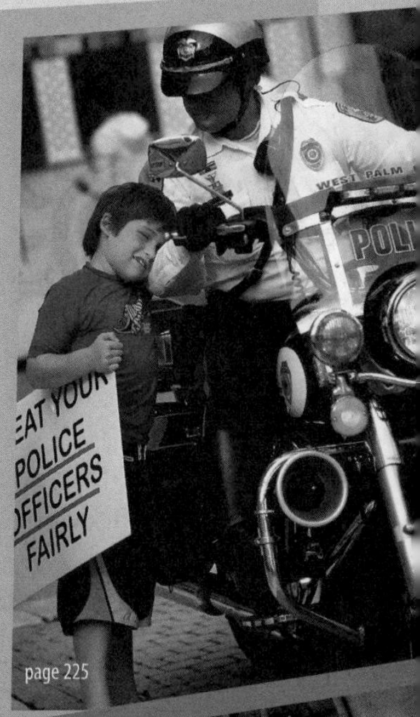

page 225

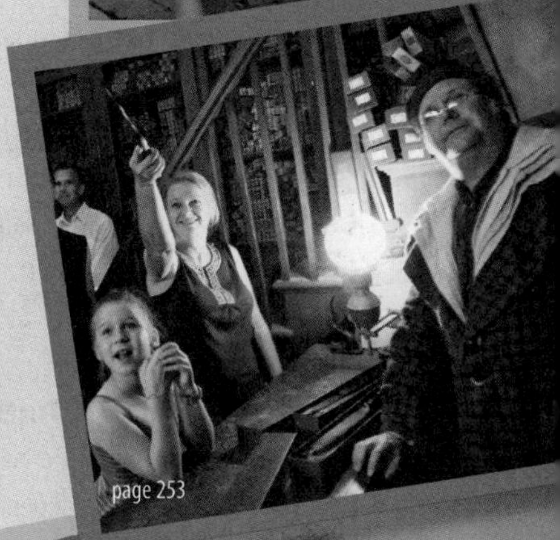
page 253

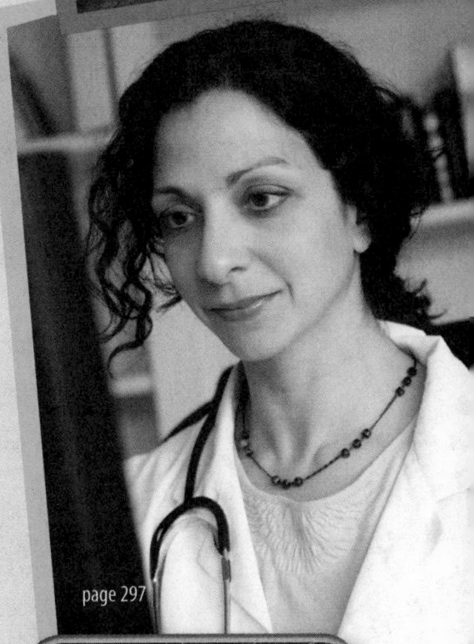
page 297

networks
Interact with your Florida Study Edition Online!

page 320

page 347

page 73

networks
Interact with your
Florida Study Edition Online!

THE UNITED STATES: LOCATION AND LANDS

NGSSS

SS.7.G.2.2 Locate major physical landmarks that are emblematic of the United States. Remarks/Examples: Examples are Grand Canyon, Mt. Denali, Everglades, Great Salt Lake, Mississippi River, Great Plains.

ESSENTIAL QUESTIONS *How do people determine location and boundaries? How does geography influence the way people live?*

American naturalist John Muir traveled to many places in the United States. He preferred to hike, or walk, in order to see and experience the features of each place he visited. Muir's first long trip took place in 1867 when he walked more than 1,000 miles (1,610 km) from Indiana to Florida.

*"*Fresh beauty opens one's eyes wherever it is really seen. . . . It is a good thing, therefore, to make short excursions now and then to the bottom of the sea among the dulse [seaweed] and coral, or up among the clouds on mountain-tops . . . to learn something of what is going on in those out-of-the-way places.*"*

JOHN MUIR

short excursion

Based on what you read, what do you think an *excursion* is?

_____

_____

DBQ BREAKING IT DOWN

Rewrite Muir's statement in your own words. Do you agree with what he is saying?

_____

_____

McGraw-Hill
netw⊙rks™
There's More Online!

The United States: Location and Lands   Chapter 1   **1**

PHOTO: Aurora Open/Corey Rich/Getty Images

LESSON 1 — LOCATION

Essential Question
How do people determine location and boundaries?

Guiding Questions
1. How might you describe the location of the United States in the world?
2. What political features make up the United States?

NGSSS
SS.7.G.1.1 Locate the fifty states and their capital cities in addition to the nation's capital on a map.

SS.7.G.1.2 Locate on a world map the territories and protectorates of the United States of America. Remarks/Examples: Examples are American Samoa, Guam, Puerto Rico, U.S. Virgin Islands.

SS.7.G.1.3 Interpret maps to identify geopolitical divisions and boundaries of places in North America.

SS.7.G.2.3 Explain how major physical characteristics, natural resources, climate, and absolute and relative location have influenced settlement, economies, and intergovernmental relations in North America.

Terms to Know

hemisphere
one of the halves into which the globe is divided

continent
one of seven large masses of land on Earth

nation
an area of land with boundaries and a government

border
a political boundary separating nations

state
a political unit within a nation with clear borders and a government

capital
the seat of government

territory
an area of land held by a national government; also known as a possession

protectorate
small country controlled and protected by a larger country

commonwealth
a type of U.S. territory with its own constitution but with a government that is granted power by the U.S. Congress and that is subject to U.S. laws

It Matters Because

Knowing our location in the world helps us understand how the United States relates to other nations.

If you could travel to visit any spot in the world, how would you describe where that place is located?

What Do You Know?

Directions: In the first column, answer the questions based on what you know before you study. After this lesson, complete the last column.

Before the Lesson		After the Lesson
	Where is the United States located?	
	Into what political units is the United States divided?	

Where Is the United States?

Suppose someone new moved to your street. To tell your neighbor how to find the school, you could say that it is near the park. This would be using the school's relative location. Relative location is based on nearby landmarks. If you give the school's address, you are using absolute location. Absolute location is an exact location on a map.

Every place on Earth has a unique location. This means that no other place can occupy the exact same spot. Geographers often use natural features like mountains and oceans to describe this unique location. They might say that Florida lies between the Atlantic Ocean and the Gulf of Mexico.

Geographers also use lines of latitude and longitude. These lines do not exist in the real world. They are drawn on maps and globes. Latitude is the distance to the north or south of the Equator. The Equator is located at 0° latitude. Longitude is the distance to the east or west of the Prime Meridian. The Prime Meridian is located at 0° longitude. It runs through the Royal Observatory in Greenwich, England.

Geographers use these latitude and longitude lines to divide Earth into **hemispheres.** Each hemisphere is one of the halves into which the globe is divided. There are four hemispheres. The Equator divides the Northern from the Southern Hemisphere. The Prime Meridian and the 180° longitude line divide the Western from the Eastern Hemisphere. The part of Earth east of the Prime Meridian to 180° is the Eastern Hemisphere. The part of Earth west of the Prime Meridian to 180° is the Western Hemisphere.

Think Critically

1. Contrast What is the difference between latitude lines and longitude lines?

_____

_____

_____

_____

_____

_____

Mark the Text

2. Maps Put an "X" on the maps to show where you live. On what hemispheres do you live?

_____

_____

Where in the World?

The Hemispheres

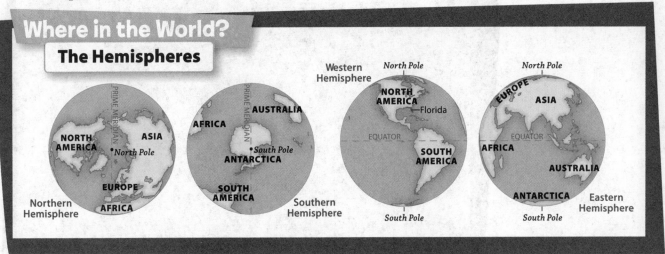

3. Describe List at least three physical features that form boundaries of the mainland United States.

_____

_____

_____

_____

_____

_____

4. Classify Information Which of the following is part of the North American continent? (circle one)

Colombia

Greenland

Hawaii

Each hemisphere includes large masses of land called **continents.** There are seven continents on Earth. They are Africa, Antarctica, Asia, Australia, Europe, North America, and South America.

North America is bounded on the west by the Pacific Ocean. It is bounded on the east by the Atlantic Ocean. To the north lies the Arctic Ocean and to the south lies the Gulf of Mexico. The Gulf of Mexico extends to the Caribbean Sea.

The Caribbean Sea includes many small islands, such as the islands of the Bahamas and Cuba. The islands of the Caribbean are also part of North America. Like the United States, these islands are nations. A **nation** is an area of land with boundaries and a government. It can be any size. The boundaries that separate nations are called **borders.**

The United States lies in the middle of North America. The continent also includes the countries to the north and south of the United States, Canada, and Mexico. The St. Lawrence River and the Great Lakes make up part of the border between the United States and Canada. The Rio Grande makes up much of the border between the United States and Mexico.

North America also includes Central America. This is a strip of land south of Mexico. Northeast of Canada lies Greenland. It, too, is part of North America. To the west of Canada lies Alaska. It is one of the 50 states of the United States. The only state that is not in North America is Hawaii. Hawaii is a chain of islands and lies in the Pacific Ocean.

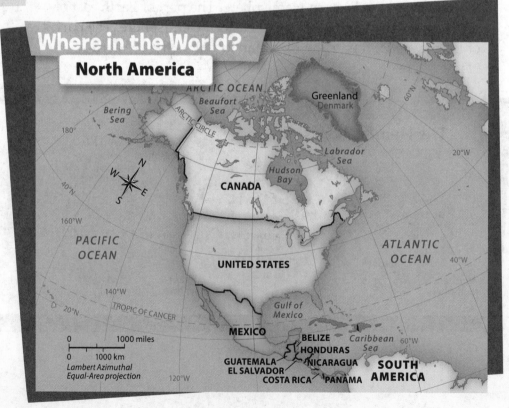

Where in the World?

North America

Where in the World?

United States: Political

CANADA

○ National capital

Wash. · Montana · N. Dak. · Minn. · Wis. · Mich. · Vt. · N.H. · Maine · N.Y. · Mass. · R.I. · Conn. · N.J. · Pa. · Ohio · Ind. · Ill. · W. Va. · Va. · Del. · Md. · Washington, D.C.

Oregon · Idaho · Wyoming · S. Dak. · Iowa · Nebraska · Ky. · N.C.

Nevada · Utah · Colorado · Kansas · Mo. · Tenn. · S.C.

PACIFIC OCEAN · California · Arizona · New Mexico · Okla. · Ark. · Miss. · Ala. · Ga. · ATLANTIC OCEAN

Texas · La. · Fla.

RUSSIA · ARCTIC OCEAN · Bering Sea · Alaska · CAN. · PACIFIC OCEAN

PACIFIC OCEAN · 0 500 mi · 0 500 km · Hawaii · 0 200 mi · 0 200 km · MEXICO

Gulf of Mexico · 0 400 miles · 0 400 km · Albers Equal-Area projection

What Are the United States?

Fifty states make up the United States. A **state** is a political unit within a nation. States have set borders and their own governments. They are also subject to the national government.

The states come in a range of shapes and sizes. Alaska is huge, while Rhode Island is small. Kansas is surrounded by land; Hawaii is surrounded by water. Florida is a peninsula. A peninsula is land that is almost completely surrounded by water but is still connected to the mainland.

The United States also includes a special area called the District of Columbia, or Washington, D.C. It is the capital of the nation and is located between Maryland and Virginia. A **capital** is the seat of government. Each state also has a capital. The federal government is headquartered in Washington, D.C.

Show Your Skill

5. Compare and Contrast
Choose two states and compare and contrast their locations, shape, or size.

_____

_____

_____

_____

Mark the Text ✏

6. Map Circle the states that border Florida.

The capital of Florida is Tallahassee. The capitol consists of an older building that was built in 1845 and a newer section that was built in the 1970s.

7. Summarize Briefly summarize the citizenship of people living in Puerto Rico and those living on the Northern Mariana Islands.

_____

_____

_____

_____

_____

8. Compare and Contrast How are states and territories alike and different?

_____

_____

_____

_____

_____

_____

_____

_____

9. Choose one United States territory. Learn five fascinating facts about it to share with the class.

Where in the World?

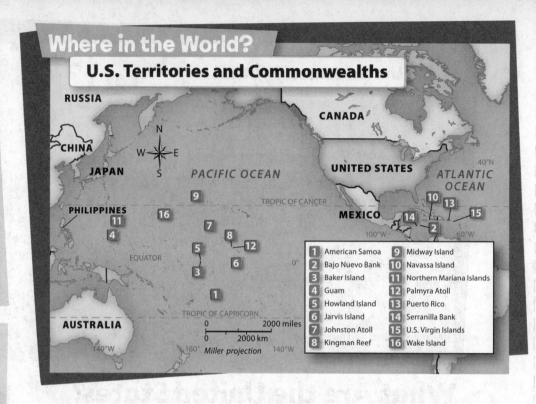

U.S. Territories and Commonwealths

1	American Samoa	9	Midway Island
2	Bajo Nuevo Bank	10	Navassa Island
3	Baker Island	11	Northern Mariana Islands
4	Guam	12	Palmyra Atoll
5	Howland Island	13	Puerto Rico
6	Jarvis Island	14	Serranilla Bank
7	Johnston Atoll	15	U.S. Virgin Islands
8	Kingman Reef	16	Wake Island

The United States also holds several territories. A **territory** is not a state. A territory is subject to the U.S. government, but has looser ties to the nation than the states have. Many U.S. territories were acquired as a result of wars. These include the U.S. Virgin Islands in the Caribbean, Guam, American Samoa, Wake Island, and the Midway Islands in the Pacific.

At one time the United States also had **protectorates.** These were small countries that the United States protected from rival nations. Cuba, Haiti, and Panama in the Caribbean were once protectorates. So were Hawaii and the Philippines in the Pacific.

Two U.S. territories are called commonwealths. They are Puerto Rico and the Northern Mariana Islands. A **commonwealth** is a territory that has its own constitution and a government that gets its powers from the U.S. Congress. American laws apply in a commonwealth. The people living in a commonwealth are U.S. citizens. They do not pay federal income tax. However, they also cannot vote in national elections. Each commonwealth has one delegate in the U.S. Congress, but this delegate cannot vote.

The United States also operates hundreds of military bases around the world. People living on these bases follow American laws rather than those of the country in which they are located.

 NGSSS Check List some examples of types of borders between states and nations. SS.7.G.1.3

_____

_____

LANDFORMS, WATERWAYS, AND CLIMATES

NGSSS

SS.7.G.2.2 Locate major physical landmarks that are emblematic of the United States. *Remarks/Examples:* Examples are Grand Canyon, Mt. Denali, Everglades, Great Salt Lake, Mississippi River, Great Plains.

SS.7.G.2.3 Explain how major physical characteristics, natural resources, climate, and absolute and relative location have influenced settlement, economies, and intergovernmental relations in North America.

Essential Question
How does geography influence the way people live?

Guiding Questions
1. What are the major landforms of the United States?
2. What important waterways are found in the United States?
3. How does climate vary throughout the United States?

Terms to Know

landform
a natural feature on Earth's surface

lowland
flat land at or near sea level

highland
an area of high ground that is above sea level

plain
a region of flat land with few trees

wetland
a large area where the soil is wet most of the time

plateau
a large, flat highland area

tributary
a river that feeds into a larger river

canal
a human-made waterway

climate
weather patterns in a place over time

It Matters Because

The ways in which people live and work in the United States are affected by the land, water, and weather in their regions.

Compared to living in Florida, how do you think your daily life would be different if you lived in Alaska?

What Do You Know?

Directions: Choose any four of the words below and write a sentence or two about the geography of Florida. When you finish the lesson, write another sentence using four different words from the list.

water	flat	river	ocean	hill	lake
weather	east	shape	near	border	
build	beach	open	forest		

Major Landforms

The United States is a vast country. From east to west and north to south it includes many different types of landforms. A **landform** is a natural feature on Earth's surface. Earth has two main types of land. They are lowlands and highlands. **Lowlands** are flat lands at or near sea level. **Highlands** are areas of high ground that are above sea level.

The middle of the United States has two large lowland areas. The eastern part of the lowland area is called the central lowlands. They stretch to the east from the Mississippi River to the Appalachian Mountains and are good for farming.

The western part of the lowland area is called the Great Plains. **Plains** are regions of flat land with few trees. The Great Plains are rolling grasslands called prairies. Farmers raise wheat and cattle in the region. The Great Plains have rich soil and reach to the west from the Mississippi River to the Rocky Mountains. North to south they stretch from Canada to Mexico.

Lowlands are also found along the Atlantic and Gulf coasts. The Atlantic coastal plains become woodlands toward the east. In the southeast, woodlands give way to wetlands. A **wetland** is a large area where the soil is wet most of the time.

The Florida Everglades are a wetland. Everglades National Park's swamps and marshes cover more than 2,000 square miles from south-central Florida to the Gulf of Mexico. Swamps have trees, while marshes have grasses. The Everglades are home to many special plants and animals.

The Florida Everglades by the Numbers	
1	foot deep in most places
6	million people in South Florida rely on the Everglades for drinking water
40–65	inches of rain per year
67	threatened or endangered species live there
350	bird species live there
1,000	plant species live there

Florida has dozens of islands that lie near the Atlantic and Gulf coasts. Florida's Gulf coast is dotted with tiny islands. Its Atlantic coast has sandbars and barrier islands. One group of islands located to the south is called the Florida Keys.

The United States also has large highland areas. In the east, the Appalachian Mountains stretch from eastern Canada to Alabama. They are the oldest mountain range in North America. Wind and weather have worn the mountains down to rounded peaks. The Appalachians include smaller ranges such as the White Mountains and Blue Ridge Mountains. The states of Arkansas and Missouri feature the Ozark Plateau. A **plateau** is a large, flat highland area.

To the west of the Great Plains, a series of highlands run from north to south. The Rocky Mountains are the longest mountain range in North America. They reach from Alaska to Mexico. Near the Pacific coast are the Alaska Range, the Coast Ranges, the Cascade Range, and the Sierra Nevada. The Alaska Range features the majestic Mount McKinley, also known as Denali, the highest mountain in North America.

Among the highlands are pockets of dry lowlands. They include the Great Basin, the Mojave Desert, and Death Valley. The Grand Canyon is located in the Colorado Plateau. It is one of North America's most distinct features. A canyon is a deep valley with steep rock sides. It is formed by a river.

Major Waterways

Oceans and rivers have always been important for the United States. People traveled the Pacific and Atlantic Oceans to reach this country. American port cities grew as immigrants settled near harbors. Rivers have been used as routes for transportation, farming, and other activities. Large inland port cities grew up along them.

The Mississippi River is the longest river in the United States. It begins in Minnesota and flows south for some 2,300 miles to the Gulf of Mexico. The Mississippi has several major tributaries including the Ohio, the Tennessee, and the Missouri Rivers. A **tributary** is a river that feeds into a larger river. The Mississippi and its tributaries are important trade routes. Ships use these rivers to move products between inland port cities and to foreign ports.

There are other important U.S. rivers. They provide water for people, animals, and plants. In the dry Southwest, which goes from the Rocky Mountains to Mexico, the Colorado River is the main source of fresh water. The Hudson River goes from the Adirondack Mountains to New York City and was very important in the settlement of the Northeast.

Think Critically

3. Contrast In what ways is a plateau different from a plain?

_____

_____

_____

_____

Show Your Skill

4. Classify Information What are the names of some specific lowland features that are found among the highlands of the country?

_____

_____

_____

Think Critically

5. Evaluate What do you think is the most important river in the United States? Explain your answer.

_____

_____

_____

_____

The Mississippi River is used to carry grain grown in the Midwest to storage facilities like this one in Louisiana.

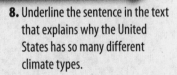

PHOTO: Glow Images/SuperStock

Think Critically

6. Explain How do waterways link cities on the Great Lakes with ports in Europe or Asia?

_____

_____

_____

_____

Show Your Skill

7. Identify the Main Idea Summarize the main uses for lakes and rivers in the United States.

_____

_____

_____

_____

_____

Mark the Text

8. Underline the sentence in the text that explains why the United States has so many different climate types.

The United States has many large lakes. The Great Lakes are among the world's largest freshwater lakes. They include Lakes Superior, Michigan, Huron, Erie, and Ontario. These lakes flow into the St. Lawrence River, which empties into the Atlantic Ocean. Ships use the St. Lawrence Seaway, a system of canals, to transport goods between Great Lakes cities and the world. A **canal** is a human-made waterway.

Lake Michigan links to the Mississippi River through canals and other rivers. This makes travel between the Atlantic Ocean and the Mississippi possible—down through the St. Lawrence Seaway, through Lakes Ontario, Erie, and Huron, to Lake Michigan. Another route is up through the Hudson River to the Erie Canal and into the Great Lakes. This system forms one of the world's largest inland waterways. It connects the northern Atlantic Ocean to the Mississippi River, the interior United States, and the Gulf of Mexico.

Another major lake is the Great Salt Lake in Utah. It is the largest inland body of salt water in the Western Hemisphere. Many states throughout the nation have lakes that provide fresh water, fish, and recreation. Florida alone has thousands of lakes. Lake Okeechobee in south-central Florida is the state's largest and the nation's seventh-largest freshwater lake.

Climate

What is the weather like where you live? Is it usually warm or cold? Is it rainy or snowy? The answers to these questions describe the climate. **Climate** is the pattern of weather in a place over time. Climate is affected by elevation, nearby oceans and lakes, landforms, and distance from the Equator.

Climate in the United States varies because the nation is so large. Most of the country has a temperate climate. This means that temperature, rainfall, and snowfall are moderate. The southeastern region, for example, gets plenty of rainfall and is generally warm to hot and moist.

The region from New England to the Great Lakes and into the Midwest has cool, wet weather. Winters are cold with plenty of snow. Summers are mild. Along the West Coast from Washington to central California, the weather is affected by moist ocean winds. This keeps temperatures moderate and rainfall plentiful. In Southern California, summers are warm and dry and winters are mild and rainy.

Some parts of the United States have more extreme climates. In Alaska, the winters are long and very cold, and heavy snows are frequent. Summers are short and cool. The West and Southwest have dry climates with little rain or snow. Daytime temperatures for much of the year are warm to hot, but nights can be very cold.

The higher altitudes of the Rocky Mountains have a different weather pattern than some other areas of the West. Generally, the higher a place is above sea level, the colder it is. The Rocky Mountains have cool summers and cold winters and heavy snows.

Hawaii and southern Florida have tropical climates with warm temperatures year-round and a lot of rain. The climate of North and Central Florida is humid subtropical. Winds off the warm waters of the Gulf Stream keep the temperature moderate most of the year. The rainy season runs from June to September. There are more tornadoes per square mile in Florida than in any other state, but they are weaker than those that occur in the Midwest or Great Plains. Most are waterspouts and relatively harmless. Florida is called the thunderstorm capital of the United States and has more lightning strikes than any other state.

NGSSS Check How have landforms in the central United States affected how people make a living? SS.7.G.2.3

_____

_____

_____

How do tributaries increase the economic benefits of rivers? SS.7.G.2.3

_____

_____

_____

Show Your Skill

9. Identify the Main Idea What kind of climate does most of the United States have?

_____

_____

_____

_____

Think Critically

10. Explain How does altitude affect temperature?

_____

_____

_____

_____

Take the Challenge

11. Research information on extreme weather in the United States. Write five questions and answers to contribute to a class game show about the country's weather.

MY REFLECTIONS

ESSENTIAL QUESTION *How does geography influence the way people live?*

Reflect on What It Means . . .

The Florida Everglades. The Blue Ridge Mountains. The Mississippi River. These are just a few of the many natural wonders in the United States.

Think about all of the amazing natural places in the country. Then complete the tables below. For the pictures, you can draw a sketch or glue a printed picture.

A natural wonder that I have always wanted to see:	Name:	Picture:
	Description:	

A natural wonder that my community is proud of:	Name:	Picture:
	Description:	

A natural wonder in Florida I wish everyone around the world could see:	Name:	Picture:
	Description:	

TAKE THE CHALLENGE

Think about where you are right now. In how many ways could you describe your location? You might say you are in a home or a school, in a city, in a country, next to a friend, on a planet, or under the sky. Write out as many different ways as you can to describe where you are.

THE UNITED STATES: RESOURCES AND REGIONS

NGSSS

SS.7.G.2.3 Explain how major physical characteristics, natural resources, climate, and absolute and relative location have influenced settlement, economies, and intergovernmental relations in North America.

ESSENTIAL QUESTIONS *How does geography influence the way people live? What defines a region?*

Every region of the United States is unique. What image comes to mind when you hear the word *Florida?* What images do you think come to mind for people who do not live here? Water is a vital part of the state's ecosystem and industry.

> "Water is Florida's lifeblood. It quenches our thirst, powers our economy and draws visitors. It is fickle. Abundant one year. Scarce another. Yet, everything that is Florida is defined by the quality of its water resources—and deserves all the protection we can provide."
>
> FLORIDA DEPARTMENT OF ENVIRONMENTAL PROTECTION

fickle

Read the word *fickle* in context. What do you think it means?

_____

powers

How do you think water *powers* Florida's economy?

_____

_____

DBQ BREAKING IT DOWN

Something that is called a *lifeblood* is absolutely necessary for life. Do you agree that water is absolutely necessary for life in Florida? Why or why not?

_____

_____

_____

McGraw-Hill
networks™
There's More Online!

TEXT: Florida Department of Environmental Protection (DEP). http://www.protectingourwater.org/florida_water_story/
PHOTO: Rich Reid/National Georgraphic/Getty Images

NATURAL RESOURCES

NGSSS

SS.7.G.2.3 Explain how major physical characteristics, natural resources, climate, and absolute and relative location have influenced settlement, economies, and intergovernmental relations in North America.

SS.7.G.3.1 Use maps to describe the location, abundance, and variety of natural resources in North America.

Essential Question

How does geography influence the way people live?

Guiding Questions

1. How do renewable and nonrenewable natural resources supply human needs?
2. What natural resources in the United States are limited in supply?
3. What important natural resources are renewable?
4. Why is it important to conserve as well as use natural resources?

Terms to Know

environment
the air, water, and land that surround a person

natural resource
something found in nature that people use

nonrenewable
resource that cannot be replaced within a lifetime

renewable
resource that can be replaced within a reasonable time

mineral
natural material found in the earth that does not come from plants or animals

fossil fuel
fuel made from the breakdown of plants and animals; used to produce energy

pollution
material that dirties the air, water, or soil

conservation
planned and careful use of natural resources

It Matters Because

The natural resources found in the United States determine the economic activities of people throughout the nation.

What resources from nature do you use every day? Try to list at least five resources.

What Do You Know?

Directions: In the first column, answer the questions based on what you know before you study. After this lesson, complete the last column.

Before the Lesson		After the Lesson
	What are natural resources and how are they used?	
	What is meant by the term *nonrenewable resource*?	
	What are environmentally friendly energy sources?	
	How does human activity affect the environment?	

Types of Resources

Many things that we all need and use come from nature and the environment around us. The **environment** is the air, water, and land in a place. Materials from nature that people use are called **natural resources.** Some examples of natural resources are the land we grow food on and the oil and gas we use in our homes and cars.

Natural resources can be nonrenewable or renewable. **Nonrenewable** resources are those that cannot be replaced within our lifetimes. Examples include iron ore, gold, and oil. **Renewable** resources are those that cannot be used up or that can be replaced within a reasonable amount of time. They include things like sun, wind, water, and forests.

Nonrenewable resources include minerals. **Minerals** are things in nature that do not come from plants or animals. They can take thousands of years to form. Workers extract, or take, minerals from mines and quarries. Minerals are used to make things like computer chips and steel.

We need energy to run cars, heat homes, and light cities. Energy refers to power such as heat and electricity. People today rely mainly on oil, natural gas, and coal for energy. These are all nonrenewable resources. Oil, natural gas, and coal are fossil fuels. **Fossil fuels** are made when the remains of living things break down. Like minerals, it takes thousands of years for fossil fuels to form.

Our country also has many renewable resources, including land, water, the wind, the sun, lumber (wood), and fish. Many people today believe that it is important to find ways to get energy from these renewable sources.

Think Critically

1. **Synthesize** Complete the following sentence.

   Mountains, oceans, and deserts

   are all things that might be found

   in a person's _____.

2. **Explain** How do fossil fuels form?

   _____

   _____

   _____

3. **Contrast** What is the difference between renewable and nonrenewable resources?

   _____

   _____

   _____

   _____

   _____

   _____

Mark the Text

4. **Graphic Organizer** Complete the graphic organizer by filling in some specific resources found in the United States.

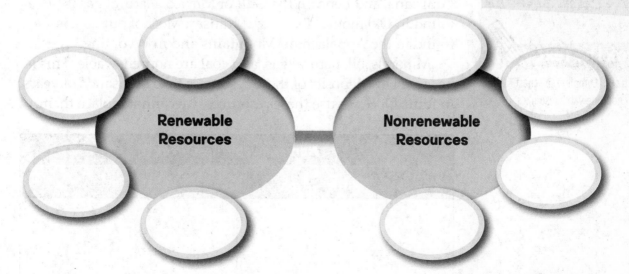

Renewable Resources — Nonrenewable Resources

Natural Resources

Locating Nonrenewable Resources

Show Your Skill

5. Make Predictions What problems might occur if we use up a nonrenewable energy resource?

_____

_____

_____

_____

_____

Mark the Text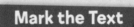

6. Chart Complete the chart of nonrenewable resources.

Minerals are found in many parts of the United States. Copper is mined in the West. Gold is found mainly in Alaska and Nevada. Iron ore and limestone come from the Great Lakes area in the Midwest. Florida also has limestone. Zinc is found in Alaska, Tennessee, and Missouri. Most granite is quarried in Vermont and New Hampshire.

Fossil fuels are also found in various parts of the country. Oil has been found in Alaska, California, Oklahoma, Texas, Louisiana, and beneath the Gulf of Mexico. Natural gas is found in Oklahoma, Texas, and Kansas. Most of our coal is found in the Appalachian Mountains and in Wyoming.

Minerals, oil, natural gas, and coal are nonrenewable. This is because new deposits of these resources take thousands of years to form. Once we use these resources, we cannot replace them.

Nonrenewable Resources	
Minerals	**Fossil Fuels**

Using Renewable Resources

The United States has a wealth of natural resources. Many natural resources are renewable. Land, water, the wind, the sun, lumber, and fish are some of the United States' most important renewable resources.

Almost half of our land is used to grow crops and to raise animals. Major crops include corn, wheat, and cotton. Farmers also grow vegetables and fruits, and raise livestock such as poultry and swine. Cattle and sheep graze on open land in the western half of the country.

Water is another major resource. Our rivers and lakes provide water for drinking, farming, and other needs. Water can be also used to produce energy. The motion of water through hydroelectric dams produces electricity. Large dams can make enough energy for thousands of buildings.

The United States has also begun using wind to make energy. Wind farms, or large groupings of wind turbines, generate electricity in 36 states.

Solar power is electricity produced from the light of the sun. Many homes and businesses now use solar power. Some people believe that solar power will become a major industry.

Forests cover about one-third of the nation, so the supply of lumber, or wood, is large. Lumber is used for many things, including heating, building, and making paper.

Fish and other sea animals are another renewable resource. Many areas along the coasts are fished. In fact, high demand for fish has led to overfishing in some places. Overfished species can die out.

Loss of Wetlands: The Everglades

Everglades in 1911

Tampa
St. Petersburg
ATLANTIC OCEAN
Lake Okeechobee
Cape Coral
Fort Lauderdale
Gulf of Mexico
Cape Romano
Hialeah
Miami
Key Largo
Florida Bay
Florida Keys
Straits of Florida
0 50 miles
0 50 km
Albers Equal-Area projection

Everglades in 1990

Tampa
St. Petersburg
ATLANTIC OCEAN
Lake Okeechobee
Cape Coral
Fort Lauderdale
Gulf of Mexico
Cape Romano
Hialeah
Miami
Key Largo
Florida Bay
Florida Keys
Straits of Florida
0 50 miles
0 50 km
Albers Equal-Area projection

Think Critically

7. Describe How does a hydroelectric dam use a renewable resource?

_____
_____
_____
_____
_____

Show Your Skill

8. Compare and Contrast What is the difference between solar power and wind power? How are they similar?

_____
_____
_____
_____
_____
_____

Think Critically

9. Synthesize If renewable resources are renewed in a reasonable length of time, why do we still need to conserve them?

_____
_____
_____
_____
_____
_____

Consequences of Human Activity

Many human activities can cause pollution. **Pollution** refers to things that make the air, water, and soil dirty. Burning fossil fuels in vehicles and factories pollutes the air. Dumping industrial waste pollutes the water and soil. Urban sprawl, or the spread of cities, can cause many kinds of pollution and destroy wildlife habitat. Pollution damages the environment. This in turn harms people.

One way to prevent or reduce pollution is through conservation. **Conservation** is the planned and careful use of natural resources. In 1935 the federal government began setting aside land for conservation. No one was allowed to build, mine, or drill on this land. Since then, states have set aside large areas of land for conservation as well. The goal of conservation is to preserve our natural resources so there will be enough for future Americans.

Members of the Florida Fish and Wildlife Conservation Commission examine green sea turtles before releasing them to the wild. The turtles were treated for "cold stunning" after cold temperatures hit the area.

PHOTO: HO/Reuters/CORBIS

 NGSSS Check How do natural resources influence the way we live? SS.7.G.2.3

_____

_____

NGSSS

SS.7.G.2.1 Locate major cultural landmarks that are emblematic of the United States. Remarks/Examples: Examples are Statue of Liberty, White House, Mount Rushmore, Capitol, Empire State Building, Gateway Arch, Independence Hall, Alamo, Hoover Dam.

SS.7.G.2.2 Locate major physical landmarks that are emblematic of the United States. Remarks/Examples: Examples are Grand Canyon, Mt. Denali, Everglades, Great Salt Lake, Mississippi River, Great Plains.

SS.7.G.2.3 Explain how major physical characteristics, natural resources, climate, and absolute and relative location have influenced settlement, economies, and inter-governmental relations in North America.

SS.7.G.2.4 Describe current major cultural regions of North America. Remarks/Examples: Examples are the South, Rust-belt, Silicon Valley.

Essential Question
What defines a region?

Guiding Questions
1. How has the geography of the Northeast influenced its economy?
2. How have recent population trends changed the South?
3. How has the geography of the Midwest shaped its development?
4. In what ways is the Interior West diverse?
5. Which parts of its economy make the Pacific region unique?

Terms to Know

urban
thickly settled

Latino
a person with a Spanish-speaking background or with roots in Latin America

trade
the buying and selling of goods and services

service sector
the part of the economy that produces services rather than goods

aerospace
industry that develops aircraft, spacecraft, missiles, and satellites

textile
yarn or thread and the cloth that is woven from them

rural
less populated; having more open countryside than cities and towns

It Matters Because

People's jobs and lifestyles are closely connected to the region of the country in which they live.

Describe the region of the country where you live. What makes it unique?

Where in the World?
Regions of the United States

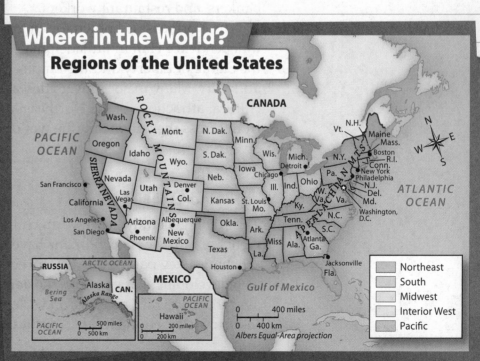

Albers Equal-Area projection

Northeast
South
Midwest
Interior West
Pacific

Copyright © by The McGraw-Hill Companies, Inc.

<table>
<tr><td>

Mark the Text

1. Underline the five major regions of the United States.

Show Your Skill

2. **Generalize** The economy of the Northeast is largely based on what two major areas of activity?

_____

_____

Think Critically

3. **Contrast** How does the service sector differ from industries that make goods such as computers?

_____

_____

_____

_____

_____

_____

</td></tr>
</table>

The Northeast

Our nation can be divided into five major regions. They are the Northeast, the South, the Midwest, the Interior West, and the Pacific. Each region has its own geographic features, economy, and culture.

The Northeast is the smallest geographic region. It is mostly **urban.** This means that there are many cities and towns with many people. In fact, it is the most densely populated of the five regions. Many people in the Northeast have European backgrounds. Others are African American, Asian, and Latino. **Latino** describes people with Spanish-speaking backgrounds, or whose roots are in Latin America.

At first the early settlers in the Northeast tried farming. They soon found that the soil was rocky and the winters were cold. They also found farming in the mountains difficult. Instead the settlers turned to fishing and to shipping. The region's long coastlines and rivers helped settlers build these industries. The long coastlines and rivers also made trade easier, and trade grew. **Trade** is the buying and selling of goods and services.

Today the Northeast still relies on industry and trade. The region has many industries such as computers, communications, research, and publishing.

In recent years the service sector has grown in the region. The **service sector** produces services rather than goods. Services are jobs done by one person for another in exchange for payment. Examples of people in service jobs include nurses, bankers, and restaurant workers.

The Northeast is known for historic sites such as Independence Hall in Philadelphia. National landmarks include the Statue of Liberty and the Empire State Building in New York City. Many major universities, art museums, and other cultural attractions of the Northeast draw students and visitors from across the nation and the world.

The South

The South generally has a warm climate, rich soil, and gets plenty of rain. These conditions have made farming and ranching a key part of the region's economy. New industries are also developing. For example, the **aerospace** industry develops aircraft, spacecraft, missiles, and satellites. Much of this industry is based in Florida. **Textiles,** or cloth production, is also a major part of the economy. Manufacturing and service industries are important as well.

The population of the South has grown and changed. Many retired people choose the South for their homes. Latinos and Haitians have also moved to this region.

Like the Northeast, the South has a rich history. Early U.S. leaders such as George Washington and Thomas Jefferson were Southerners. More recent leaders from the region include presidents such as Jimmy Carter, George H.W. Bush, Bill Clinton, and George W. Bush. Texas is the home of the Alamo, the site where a famous battle for Texas's independence from Mexico took place.

The South has large **rural** areas. A rural area has fewer cities and towns. Rural areas generally have a lower population than urban areas. Much of the land in the South is forests, farmland, and plains. The Florida Everglades is a huge wetland area.

The South also has growing urban areas. Some of the large cities in this region are Atlanta, Miami, Dallas, Houston, and New Orleans. One famous city in the region is the nation's capital, Washington, D.C. It lies between Maryland and Virginia. The White House and the Capitol are among the capital's most famous sites.

Major Crops and Natural Resources			
South		**Midwest**	
• citrus fruits	• soybeans	• wheat	• vegetables
• cotton	• coal	• corn	• iron ore
• rice	• oil	• oats	• coal
• tobacco	• natural gas	• soybeans	• lead
• nuts		• fruits	• zinc

The Midwest

The Midwest is known for the Great Plains and the Great Lakes. The Great Plains have flat, fertile land. Farmers raise crops and produce pork, beef, and dairy products. The Great Plains are often called the nation's breadbasket because so much grain is grown there.

Mount Rushmore in South Dakota is also found in this region. The St. Louis Gateway Arch in Missouri celebrates the city's role as gateway to the West.

Think Critically

4. Contrast Most of the Northeast is densely populated and

_____ , while the South

is more _____ .

5. Compare What parts of the economies of the Northeast and the South are similar?

_____

_____

_____

_____

Mark the Text

6. Chart Circle items in the chart that are common to both the South and the Midwest regions.

Think Critically

7. Explain The Great Plains is sometimes called a breadbasket. Why is that an appropriate name?

_____

_____

_____

8. Describe How would you describe the geography of the Interior West?

_____

_____

_____

Show Your Skill

9. Explain What are some of the ethnic groups that make up the population of the Interior West?

_____

_____

The Midwest became a center for U.S. manufacturing during the 1900s. Easy access to coal and iron ore and shipping on rivers and on the Great Lakes made this possible. Late in the 1900s, however, the region's manufacturers fell on hard times. Many factories closed or left the region.

This sharp decline in the economy and loss of jobs led people to call the region the Rust Belt. Some industries have recovered. The automobile industry, however, is still troubled. It has suffered from a downturn in the economy.

Many African Americans, Latinos, and Asian Americans live in the Midwest. Experts approximate that African Americans make up 80 percent of the population of Detroit, Michigan.

The Interior West

The Interior West has a diverse geography, population, and economy. It has both high mountains and miles of desert. Many of its people have Native American, Spanish, or Mexican roots. It has fewer people than any other region, yet it is home to some big cities.

Farming, mining, and manufacturing are all important to the region's economy. Research and development and tourism are also key growth areas.

Visitors to the region can enjoy Arizona's Grand Canyon and Utah's Great Salt Lake. The Hoover Dam on the Arizona-Nevada border is 726 feet (221 meters) high. It provides electricity, water for crops, and drinking water.

The Grand Canyon is over 250 miles long. It was formed by the erosion caused by the Colorado River, which flows through the canyon.

The Pacific

The states in this region border the Pacific Ocean. The areas along the coast often have plenty of rain. This is especially true in Washington, Oregon, and northern California. The Pacific region has several major mountain ranges. The Alaska Range includes Mount McKinley, the highest peak in North America. This peak is sometimes called Denali. The Pacific region also is dotted with volcanoes. The state of Hawaii is made of a chain of volcanic islands.

The Pacific region has many valuable natural resources. They include gold, lead, copper, and oil. The timber industry in Oregon and Washington contributes to the economy of those areas. Good soil has made farming important to the region. California grows more than half the fruits and vegetables in the nation.

The Pacific region also has computer and electronics industries. They are centered in Silicon Valley near San Francisco. Los Angeles is the center of the film industry. Other important industries include tourism, lumbering, fishing, livestock, oil, plastics, and satellite communications.

The people of Oregon and Washington have mostly European backgrounds. The region's other states are home to many Native Americans, Latinos, and Asian Americans.

NGSSS Check How has the geography of the Midwest influenced its development? SS.7.G.2.3

_____

_____

_____

In what ways is the Interior West diverse? SS.7.G.2.4

_____

_____

_____

Write one geographic feature or landmark for each of the regions.

Northeast _____

South _____

Midwest _____

Interior West _____

The Pacific _____

Think Critically

10. Explain What is Silicon Valley?

_____

_____

_____

_____

11. Summarize What are some main industries of the Pacific region?

_____

_____

_____

_____

_____

_____

_____

Take the Challenge

12. Work with a small group to plan a fictional trip to one of the U.S. regions. What cities, natural wonders, and landmarks would you want to visit? Present the plans to the class using images and maps to make it more interesting.

CHAPTER 2

MY REFLECTIONS

ESSENTIAL QUESTION *How does geography influence the way people live?*

Reflect on What It Means . . .

Our nation works to decrease pollution and tries to increase conservation. Write down your ideas in the charts below.

| What I Can Do  | To decrease pollution |
| | To encourage conservation |

| What My Community Can Do  | To decrease pollution |
| | To encourage conservation |

| What All of Us in the World Can Do  | To decrease pollution |
| | To encourage conservation |

TAKE THE CHALLENGE

Choose one of Florida's many lakes or rivers. Conduct online research to find out what is being done to conserve the lake or river and decrease its pollution. Present what you learn on a poster.

AMERICANS, CITIZENSHIP, AND GOVERNMENTS

NGSSS

SS.7.G.4.1 Use geographic terms and tools to explain cultural diffusion throughout North America.

SS.7.C.2.1 Define the term "citizen," and identify legal means of becoming a United States citizen.

SS.7.C.2.2 Evaluate the obligations citizens have to obey laws, pay taxes, defend the nation, and serve on juries.

SS.7.C.3.1 Compare different forms of government (direct democracy, representative democracy, socialism, communism, monarchy, oligarchy, autocracy).

ESSENTIAL QUESTION • *What are the characteristics that make up a culture? • What is a citizen? • Why do people create, structure, and change governments?*

What is a citizen? People from other countries can become citizens, or official members, of the United States. One of the things they must do is swear an oath:

PHOTO: Andrew Lichtenstein/Corbis

Copyright © by The McGraw-Hill Companies, Inc.

> *"I hereby declare, on oath, that I absolutely and entirely renounce and abjure all allegiance and fidelity to any foreign prince, potentate, state or sovereignty . . . that I will support and defend the Constitution and laws of the United States of America against all enemies, foreign and domestic . . ."*
>
> OATH OF ALLEGIANCE

renounce and abjure

Renounce and *abjure* mean "to reject." What is the point of this part of the oath?

_____

_____

_____

DBQ BREAKING IT DOWN

Why do you think people take an oath to support the Constitution instead of the country or the president?

_____

_____

_____

_____

Do you think every American should take this oath? Explain your answer.

_____

_____

_____

_____

McGraw-Hill
networks™
There's More Online!

1 BEING AN AMERICAN

NGSSS

SS .7.G.4.1 Use geographic terms and tools to explain cultural diffusion throughout North America.

Essential Question
What are the characteristics that make up a culture?

Guiding Questions
1. From what areas did early Americans come?
2. What do Americans value?

Terms to Know

immigrant
a person who moves permanently to a new country

ethnic group
a group of people who have the same race, culture, or nationality

values
the principles or beliefs people use to make judgments and decisions

institution
an important practice, relationship, or organization

popular sovereignty
idea that government gets its power from the people

It Matters Because

The United States is enriched by its diversity and unified by its shared values.

As Americans we celebrate our unity and also celebrate our diversity. Why are they both strengths of our country?

_____

_____

_____

_____

_____

What Do You Know?

Directions: In the first column, answer the questions based on what you know before you study. After this lesson, complete the last column.

Before the Lesson		After the Lesson
	How has immigration to the United States changed over time?	
	What shared values unite Americans?	

A Diverse Population

Almost all of the people in the United States come from families who once lived in another country. This is why the United States is called a nation of **immigrants.** Immigrants are people who come from other lands to live in a new country. Once they arrived in the United States, these immigrants worked together to build a nation.

The first people to live in North America came from Asia thousands of years ago. They slowly spread across the land. These early Americans developed many different languages and distinct, or separate, cultures. Today they are called Native Americans.

Other people began moving to North America, beginning in the 1500s. The first European settlers were Spanish. They settled in what is now Florida and the Southwest. Spanish-speaking people also settled in the present-day states of Texas and California. In the 1600s, the French settled mainly in what is now Canada. The English came to live on the east coast of North America. They were soon joined by other Europeans.

Some people did not come to North America of their own free will. Many Africans were captured in their homelands and sold into slavery. Hundreds of thousands were brought to the United States. Congress ended the slave trade in 1807. By then, there were about 500,000 enslaved Africans in this country.

Between 1830 and 1930 about 40 million immigrants came to the United States. During the 1800s many were from northern and western Europe. They were trying to escape hardship and disease. Then gold was discovered in California in 1848. Many immigrants came hoping to get rich. Thousands were from China.

Immigration changed in the late 1800s. The new immigrants were from a different part of Europe. They came from southern and eastern Europe. This included countries such as Italy, Greece, Poland, and Russia.

Immigration changed again in the later 1900s. A larger share of immigrants began to arrive from Asia and Latin America.

These immigrants are walking off the barge and onto Ellis Island. They are carrying all of their belongings.

Think Critically

1. Contrast What was different about the way many Africans came to the United States?

_____

_____

_____

2. Describe How did immigration begin to change in the 1890s?

_____

_____

_____

_____

_____

_____

Take the Challenge

3. Research how and when your family came to the United States. Try to find places on a world map where your ancestors might have lived.

4. Describe What are some of the changes in the way people live in the United States now compared to a hundred years ago?

_____

_____

_____

_____

_____

5. Categorize Latinos are an example of a(n) (circle one)

blue-collar group.

ethnic group.

European group.

Show Your Skill

6. Interpret Graphs Write one fact you learned from the graph.

_____

_____

_____

_____

People have also moved around within the United States. In the mid-1800s, people began moving from the country to the city. After the Civil War, many African Americans moved to cities in the North. They hoped to find jobs and a better life.

By the 1920s, more than half of all Americans lived in towns or cities. Many were blue-collar workers. This meant they worked in factories. People who worked in offices, stores, and other businesses were called white-collar workers.

Today, work has changed. More women work than ever before. Many people work from home. At the same time, the number of factory jobs has decreased. More people earn a living by providing services. This means they do things such as provide health care, teach, or offer other services to people.

The people who make up the United States today come from many different ethnic groups. An **ethnic group** is a group of people who share the traits of a race, culture, or national background. Latinos are one ethnic group. Their heritage traces back to Latin America. African Americans are another ethnic group. The graph below shows different ethnic groups in the United States. White Americans form the largest group. The others are called minority groups.

Americans also practice many different religions. Most belong to a Christian church, but millions also follow Judaism, Buddhism, Islam, or another religion.

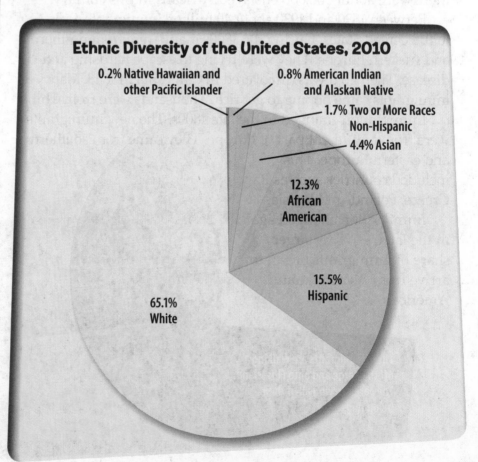

Ethnic Diversity of the United States, 2010

0.2% Native Hawaiian and other Pacific Islander

0.8% American Indian and Alaskan Native

1.7% Two or More Races Non-Hispanic

4.4% Asian

12.3% African American

15.5% Hispanic

65.1% White

Values and Institutions

Each person has his or her own values. **Values** are the principles or beliefs people use to make judgments and decisions. The people of the United States have many shared values. These shared values help unite the American people. They include values such as freedom, justice, and democracy.

The Declaration of Independence states some of these values. It says that everyone is equal and has a right to freedom. It also says that everyone has the right to life and to seek happiness.

People express their values through the institutions they create. An **institution** can be many things. It can be an important custom or relationship. An institution can also be an organization. The family is the most important institution in the United States. It is the center of social life. Families teach children values. Schools and religions also teach values. Clubs and volunteer groups bring together people with shared values.

Government institutions are also based on American values. For example, freedom. Americans value the right to make their own choices without arbitrary meddling by the government. *Arbitrary* means unrestrained. American government is based on the idea of **popular sovereignty.** This is the idea that the government gets its power from the people. The people choose their leaders.

The Constitution is also based on American values. One important idea is that the power of government should be limited. To achieve this, the government is divided into three parts. No one part can have more power than the others. The Bill of Rights limits the government's power over the individual.

Types of Institutions in the United States	
• _____	• _____
• Schools	• _____
• Religious groups	• Government institutions

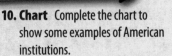 **NGSSS Check** Which group first settled North America? Where did they come from? SS.7.G.4.1

_____

_____

Show Your Skill

7. Identify the Main Idea
In the United States, the people choose their leaders. What American value does this fact reflect?

_____

_____

Think Critically

8. Explain Why is the family an important institution?

_____

_____

_____

9. Infer List two American documents that reflect important American values.

_____

_____

Mark the Text

10. Chart Complete the chart to show some examples of American institutions.

BECOMING A CITIZEN

 NGSSS

SS.7.C.2.1 Define the term "citizen," and identify legal means of becoming a United States citizen.

Essential Question

What is a citizen?

Guiding Questions

1. How does a person become a citizen of the United States?
2. In what ways can a foreign person enter the United States?

Terms to Know

government
the ruling authority for a group of people

citizen
a person who is loyal to a government and is protected by that government

civics
the study of the rights and duties of citizens

citizenship
the rights and duties of citizens

naturalization
a legal process to become a citizen

alien
a person who lives in a country in which he or she was not born

refugee
a person who flees his or her country to escape danger

It Matters Because

In the United States there are two ways to become a citizen.

What does citizenship mean to you?

What Do You Know?

Directions: In the first column, circle "True" if you think the statement is true and "False" if you think it is false based on what you know before you read the lesson. After this lesson, complete the last column.

Before the Lesson			After the Lesson	
True	False	Only people born in the United States are citizens.	True	False
True	False	The government establishes rules for citizenship.	True	False
True	False	A naturalized citizen has the same rights as other citizens.	True	False
True	False	A person can be a citizen of two countries.	True	False
True	False	You do not become a citizen until you are 18 years old.	True	False

What Is Civics?

Government is the ruling power for a group of people. A **citizen** is a person who is loyal to a government and is protected by that government. The study of the rights and duties of citizens is called **civics.** For government to work well, citizens must understand their rights and duties.

The idea of citizenship is very old. **Citizenship** is the rights and duties of citizens. It began in ancient Greece and Rome. At that time, citizenship was only for men who owned property. Their duties included paying taxes and serving in the armed forces.

In the 1700s, new ideas arose about citizenship and government. Citizenship came to mean "belonging to a nation." People came to believe that governments got their power from the people. This idea is known as "consent of the governed."

The Growth of American Citizenship

1776
Only white men who own property are allowed to vote.

1868
African American men become citizens through the 14th Amendment.

1920
Women gain the right to vote through the 19th Amendment.

1924
All Native Americans are granted citizenship.

Today citizenship in the United States is not based on how much land a person owns. It is also not based on gender, race, or religion. Instead it is based on birth. People who are citizens because they were born in the United States or have parents who were born in the United States are called natural-born citizens.

A person is an American citizen if he or she was born in any one of these places:

- in any of the 50 states or in the District of Columbia
- in an American territory
- on a U.S. military base in another country

Even if a person's parents are not citizens of the United States, he or she is still a citizen if born on American soil.

Show Your Skill

1. Interpret Diagrams How did the concept of citizenship change in 1868?

_____

_____

Mark the Text

2. Circle the phrase in the text that explains what citizenship is based on today.

Think Critically

3. Infer Is every baby born in Florida an American citizen? Explain.

_____

_____

_____

A person who is born in another country can be an American citizen if

1. both parents are U.S. citizens, or if

2. one parent is a U.S. citizen who has lived in the United States.

A person can also be a citizen of both the United States and another country. This is known as dual citizenship.

A person can still become an American citizen even if he or she is not a natural-born citizen. To do so, he or she must complete the **naturalization** process. Naturalization is a legal process to become a citizen. Immigrants who want to become citizens must meet five requirements. They must

1. be at least 18 years old,

2. have been a legal permanent resident for five years,

3. be able to read, write, and speak English,

4. be of good moral character, and

5. show that they understand U.S. civics.

There are four main steps to the naturalization process. They are shown in the box below.

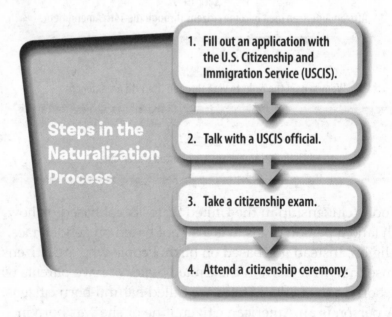

Steps in the Naturalization Process

1. Fill out an application with the U.S. Citizenship and Immigration Service (USCIS).

2. Talk with a USCIS official.

3. Take a citizenship exam.

4. Attend a citizenship ceremony.

When the applicant meets with a USCIS official, the official makes sure the person meets all the requirements. The exam tests whether the applicant can read, write, and speak English. It also asks questions about U.S. history and government. At the citizenship ceremony, applicants swear their loyalty to the United States. They also promise to obey the Constitution and the laws. After taking this oath and signing a paper, they are citizens.

A person can lose his or her citizenship. This can happen in three ways.

1. Expatriation If a person gives allegiance to another country, such as by becoming a naturalized citizen of another country.

2. Denaturalization If a person is found to have lied on his or her citizenship application, he or she loses citizenship and can be deported. To be deported is to be sent out of the country.

3. Being convicted of certain crimes If a person is convicted of treason, rebelling against the government, or using violence to try to overthrow the government, he or she can lose citizenship.

Only the federal government can grant citizenship or take it away. The states can deny some privileges of citizenship. They can prevent a person from voting, for example. But states cannot take away citizenship itself.

Foreign-Born Residents

Many people who live in the United States are not citizens. People who were born in another country and who have not been naturalized are called **aliens.** There are three kinds of aliens: legal aliens, refugees, and illegal aliens.

Legal aliens can be either resident aliens or nonresident aliens. A resident alien is a person who lives permanently in the United States. They may stay as long as they wish. A nonresident alien is a person who is planning to stay in this country for only a certain length of time. A reporter from Mexico who is covering a U.S. election would be a nonresident alien.

Legal aliens have some rights. They can hold jobs, own property, and attend public schools. They have some duties, such as paying taxes. But they do not have the right to vote or hold public office. They also cannot work in government jobs or serve on juries.

Think Critically

7. Conclude Why do you think only the national government can take away someone's citizenship?

_____

_____

Show Your Skill

8. Compare and Contrast What is the difference between a resident alien and a nonresident alien? How are they related?

_____

_____

_____

_____

_____

_____

_____

Mark the Text

9. Graphic Organizer Complete the graphic organizer to show the types of aliens in the United States.

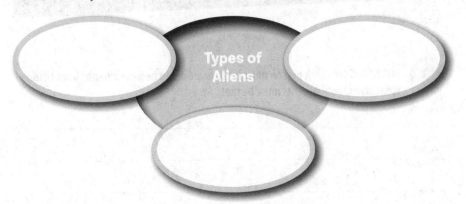

Types of Aliens

10. Predict Outcomes Suppose an illegal alien feels that he or she needs a job that pays a higher wage. What can he or she do?

_____

_____

_____

_____

_____

_____

_____

_____

Think Critically

11. Contrast How do the rights of legal aliens differ from those of U.S. citizens?

_____

_____

_____

A **refugee** is a person who leaves his or her country to escape danger, such as an earthquake or a war. Our government protects some refugees.

The United States allows only about one million people to enter the country each year. Top priority goes to relatives of U.S. citizens and people with job skills that we need in the United States. About another million people enter or stay in the country illegally each year. Some come as visitors and then never leave. Others secretly cross the borders from Canada or Mexico.

Close to 12 million people live in the United States illegally today. Most came in search of a better life. But living as an illegal alien is hard. It is against the law to hire illegal aliens, so most end up working for low pay and without benefits. They live in fear that they will be discovered and sent out of the country.

These refugees are trying to escape a repressive government in Haiti. The Coast Guard interviews some of the refugees off the coast of Ft. Lauderdale.

 NGSSS Check A person must be 18 years old to become a naturalized citizen. What other requirements must be met? SS.7.C.2.1

_____

_____

_____

PHOTO: Alasair Worden/US Coast Guard/Time Life Pictures/Getty Images

3 DUTIES AND RESPONSIBILITIES OF AMERICAN CITIZENS

NGSSS

SS.7.C.2.2 Evaluate the obligations citizens have to obey laws, pay taxes, defend the nation, and serve on juries.

Essential Question
What is a citizen?

Guiding Questions
1. What are the duties of American citizens?
2. What are American citizens' responsibilities?
3. How can citizens make their community a better place to live?

Terms to Know

responsibility
an obligation that we meet of our own free will

duty
a thing we are required to perform

tolerance
respecting and accepting others

welfare
health, wealth, and happiness

volunteerism
giving one's time and services to others without expecting payment

It Matters Because

Democracy depends on citizens fulfilling their duties and acting responsibly.

What does it reveal about a person who does the right thing even when no one notices?

_____

_____

_____

_____

What Do You Know?

Directions: Use no more than three words to tell what you know about each of these terms. After you finish the lesson, adjust any of your descriptions if needed.

volunteer
_____

responsible
_____

respect
_____

citizen
_____

community
_____

Think Critically

1. Categorize Is paying taxes a responsibility or a duty? Explain.

_____

_____

_____

Show Your Skill

2. Predict Outcomes If the military did not have enough volunteers to fight a war against an attacker, what would the government have to do?

_____

_____

_____

3. Make a Connection What duties of citizenship do you take on now?

_____

_____

_____

Duties of Citizens

A community can be a neighborhood, town, school, workplace, state, country, or even the world. We all play a part in making our communities safe and successful. We all have responsibilities. **Responsibilities** are things we should do. They are obligations we meet of our own free will. No law requires us to meet our responsibilities. Duties are different from responsibilities. **Duties** are things that we have to do. If we ignore or forget our duties, we may have to pay a fine or even go to jail.

Citizens have many duties. The most important is to obey the law. Laws are rules that help people live together in peace. Laws keep order in society by letting people know which actions are acceptable and which are not. It is important for people to obey the law so that communities can keep order and protect our health, safety, and property.

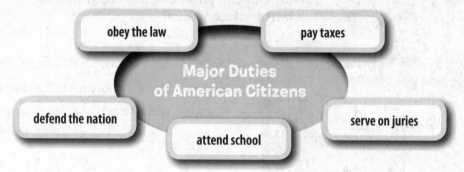

Citizens are also required to pay taxes. Taxes keep the government running. They allow the federal government to pay its employees, defend the country, and help those in need. Taxes allow state and local governments to run the schools, pave roads, and hire firefighters. There are different kinds of taxes. The main kinds are income, property, and sales taxes.

Most male citizens aged 18 to 25 must register with the Selective Service System (SSS). In the case of a war or a major national emergency, the government may draft men from the SSS list. To draft means to call into military service. We have not had a draft in this country since 1973. This is because we have had enough volunteers to meet our defense needs.

Another duty is serving on juries. The Constitution guarantees any person accused of a crime the right to trial by jury. A jury is a group of citizens who listen to the facts of a case and decide whether the accused person is innocent or guilty. Every adult citizen must be prepared to serve on a jury. An accused person also has the right to call witnesses. If a citizen is called as a witness, he or she has a duty to respond.

Attending school is also a duty. Most states require children aged 7 to 16 to go to school. Schools teach the knowledge needed to be good citizens. They also prepare students to be skilled workers who can provide for themselves and help keep the economy strong.

Responsibilities of Citizens

For society to work, every citizen must do his or her own part. Every citizen must also help others. The first responsibility of citizens is to be informed and active. Government decisions affect your life. You will have less money to spend if the state legislature decides to raise the sales tax. You will have to get up earlier if the local school board decides to extend the school day. You have a responsibility to know what the government is doing so that you can voice your opinion about these matters.

Remember that government in this country gets its power from the people. This means that you have a responsibility to make sure the government is working properly. You can do this by contacting elected officials and by voting.

All citizens who are at least 18 years old have the right to vote. Voting gives you the chance to help shape the future of your community, state, and nation. To vote well you must study the candidates and the issues. You must also keep track of what your elected officials are doing. If you do not like how they are performing, you can vote against them in the next election. Voting is a peaceful way to hand power from one group to another.

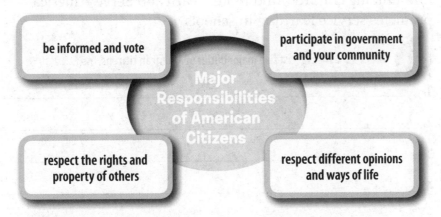

be informed and vote

participate in government and your community

Major Responsibilities of American Citizens

respect the rights and property of others

respect different opinions and ways of life

Society runs smoothly when people respect one another's rights and property. Respecting others' opinions and ways of life is also important. The United States is a nation of many diverse people. Everyone has a right to his or her own opinions and beliefs. For all these different people to get along, citizens must respect and accept others. This is called **tolerance.**

4. Explain Why is attending school considered a duty?

_____

_____

5. Summarize Why is it important to stay informed about what the government is doing?

_____

_____

_____

_____

Show Your Skill

6. Draw Conclusions Why is tolerance an important responsibility of citizenship?

_____

_____

_____

_____

_____

_____

7. Formulate Questions Write two questions you would ask a volunteer to better understand why he or she volunteers.

_____

_____

_____

_____

8. Work with a partner to prepare a 15-second commercial for a volunteer organization that helps a cause you support. Perform the commercial for the class.

Being Involved

Good citizens care about the welfare of others. **Welfare** includes people's health, wealth, and happiness. One way to help others is to volunteer. Volunteering makes our communities better places to live. It also helps us learn useful skills.

Giving your time and services to others without expecting payment is called **volunteerism.** Millions of people in this country volunteer every day. Without their help, the needs of many people would not be met.

These students volunteer to serve lunch to people in need. The students are not only helping others, but they are also learning work skills themselves.

Some people choose to support causes by giving money. Americans give more than $300 billion to charities every year. Much of this money comes from small donations from ordinary citizens.

The federal government supports volunteerism through many agencies. The Corporation for National and Community Service provides training and manages AmeriCorps, Senior Corps, and Learn and Serve America. AmeriCorps provides 75,000 Americans work in education, public safety, health, and the environment. Senior Corps provides Americans aged 55 or older a chance to help their communities by serving as foster grandparents, assisting the disabled, building houses, immunizing children, and more. Learn and Serve America promotes service learning in schools.

 NGSSS Check List five major duties of American citizens. SS.7.C.2.2

1. _____

2. _____

3. _____

4. _____

5. _____

List three major responsibilities of American citizens.

1. _____

2. _____

3. _____

LESSON

4 FORMS OF GOVERNMENT

NGSSS

SS .7.C.3.1 Compare different forms of government (direct democracy, representative democracy, socialism, communism, monarchy, oligarchy, autocracy).

Essential Question
Why do people create, structure, and change governments?

Guiding Questions
1. What is the purpose of government?
2. What are the types of government?

Terms to Know

public policy
the decisions and actions a government takes to solve problems

representative democracy
a government in which people choose leaders to represent them

constitutional monarchy
a government in which the power of the monarch is limited by a constitution

majority rule
democratic principle that says a majority of the people has the power to make laws binding on all the people

authoritarian regime
a government in which one person or a small group holds all the power

totalitarian
a system in which government controls people's lives

ideology
a set of ideas about life and society

It Matters Because

People form governments to establish order, provide security, and accomplish common goals.

What would your community be like without any government for a week?

What Do You Know?

Directions: You already know a lot about government. What kinds of governments are there? What do governments do? In the space below, list words you already know that relate to government. When you finish the lesson, add more words that you learn.

Show Your Skill

1. Classify Information
What three types of services do governments provide?

_____

_____

_____

Think Critically

2. Evaluate What government function do you think is the most important? Give two reasons for your answer.

_____

_____

_____

_____

_____

_____

The Importance of Government

A government is the ruling power for a community. Any group that can make and carry out laws and decisions for those living in a community is a government.

Government is important. It helps people to live together peacefully. Governments do many things. The most important purpose is to make rules for how people should act so they can live together peacefully. These rules are called laws. Laws help prevent conflict. They also help resolve conflict when it does occur. To resolve means to find a solution. Governments use police officers and courts to enforce the law.

Governments also keep the nation safe. They set up armed forces to guard the people from enemies.

Governments provide many other services. They run libraries, schools, hospitals, and parks. They build and repair streets and bridges. They collect garbage and deliver the mail. Some services are meant to keep people healthy and safe. These services include police and fire protection and licensing doctors. The government ensures the safety of food, medicines, and a long list of other products.

Functions of Government	
Keep Order	**Provide Services**
• Pass and enforce laws to prevent crime, resolve conflict	• Protect public health
• Establish courts	• Protect public safety
	• Protect public welfare
Provide Security	**Guide the Community**
• Establish armed forces	• Develop public policy
• Protect citizens from foreign attacks	• Manage the economy
	• Conduct foreign relations

Governments also help the poor and those who are out of work. They supply housing, health care, and special programs for people with disabilities.

Governments guide the community by making public policy. **Public policy** means the decisions and actions a government takes to solve problems. Putting public policies to work takes money. Since governments have limited funds, they must plan carefully.

Governments also guide the community by working with other nations. Trade and travel are two areas where governments must work together to help their citizens.

The United States has a federal system of government. This means that power is divided between the national government and the states. The states then give some power to local governments.

The national government makes and enforces laws for the entire country. It also sets the rules for citizenship. State and local laws cannot go against the laws of the federal government.

Each state has its own government. These governments make laws and create public policy for the people of their state. States do things such as make marriage laws, run schools, and hold elections. They protect public health and safety and build roads and bridges. States also can set up local governments.

Local governments are found in counties, cities, and towns. They help the local community by setting up police and fire departments and local courts. They light the streets and maintain parks. Like state governments, local governments cannot do anything that goes against the laws or authority of the federal government.

The Types of Government

Nations have different forms of government. Not all nations are governed like the United States. But despite their differences, many countries do have a detailed, written plan of government called a constitution.

Democracy began in ancient Greece more than 2,500 years ago. The Greek city of Athens had a direct democracy. This meant that all male citizens met to discuss and vote on issues.

Today's nations are too large for direct democracy to work. Instead, many countries have **representative democracies.** This means the people choose leaders to represent them. The United States is the world's oldest representative democracy.

Government employees like this person fighting a forest fire near Taylor, Florida, protect and serve the citizens.

3. Contrast What is the difference between state and federal governments?

_____

_____

_____

_____

_____

_____

_____

Show Your Skill

4. Draw Conclusions Why is direct democracy impractical in the United States today?

_____

_____

_____

_____

5. Compare What is similar about republics and constitutional monarchies?

_____

_____

_____

6. Summarize Why is the concept of majority rule so important in a democracy?

_____

_____

_____

_____

_____

Take the Challenge

7. Work in a small group and research the types of governments in ten countries. Make a graph to show the types of governments they have.

There are two types of representative democracies. They are republics and constitutional monarchies. The United States is a republic. In a republic, citizens play a part in choosing the head of government.

The second type is a **constitutional monarchy.** In a monarchy the head of government is not chosen by the people. Instead, a king or queen inherits this position. The power of most monarchs today is limited by a constitution. For this reason, these governments are called constitutional monarchies. The monarch has mostly ceremonial and social duties. Real power is found in an elected lawmaking body. The members of that body choose a leader called a prime minister.

Democracy works by **majority rule.** This means that citizens agree that they will abide by what most people want. At the same time, members of the minority keep their rights as citizens.

The government in power is called a regime. In a democracy, the people rule. In **authoritarian regimes** one person or a small group holds all the power. They do not answer to the people.

Monarchs with unlimited, or absolute, power are one kind of authoritarian government. A more common kind is a dictatorship. Dictators also have absolute power. They usually take over the government by force. To stay in power, dictators often rely on the army. Elections usually are not allowed. People do not have freedom and they cannot criticize the government.

Many dictators force the people to accept **totalitarian** rule. This means that the government controls people's lives. It decides what factories and farms will produce. It tells people what they can believe and what groups they can join.

Totalitarian leaders often have an **ideology** that they expect people to obey. An ideology is a strict idea about life and society. To enforce their ideas, these leaders control the media. They use fear, violence, and propaganda. Propaganda is information used to support a cause or to damage someone else's cause.

NGSSS Check Compare two types of governments you have learned about in this lesson. SS.7.C.3.1

_____

_____

_____

_____

_____

ESSENTIAL QUESTION *What is a citizen?*

Reflect on What It Means . . .

For generations, people from all over the world have come to America and have worked to become citizens of the United States. Some people take their citizenship for granted.

How might you, your community, and the country as a whole celebrate the honor of being citizens? Jot down your ideas below.

My Celebration

My Community's Celebration

Keep Going! ▶▶

My Country's Celebration

TAKE THE CHALLENGE

With your teacher's help, find someone in your community who immigrated to the United States. Find out what drew him or her to this country.

THE AMERICAN COLONIES AND THEIR GOVERNMENT

NGSSS

SS.7.C.1.3 Describe how English policies and responses to colonial concerns led to the writing of the Declaration of Independence.

ESSENTIAL QUESTIONS *How does geography influence the development of communities? Why do people create, structure, and change governments?*

Richard Henry Lee was a delegate to the Second Constitutional Convention. He introduced a resolution at the Convention that would change the world. Read this excerpt from it:

> " That these United Colonies are, and of right ought to be, free and independent States . . . And that all political connection between them and the State of Greater Britain is, and ought to be, totally dissolved. "
>
> RICHARD HENRY LEE

United Colonies

What are the *United Colonies* today?

_____

_____

dissolved

What are some synonyms for *dissolved*?

_____

_____

DBQ BREAKING IT DOWN

Lee uses the phrase "are, and of right ought to be" when referring to independence. What is the difference in meaning between "are" or "is" and "ought to be"?

_____

_____

Why do you think Lee uses these phrases?

_____

_____

_____

McGraw-Hill
networks™
There's More Online!

INFLUENCES ON AMERICAN COLONIAL GOVERNMENT

NGSSS

SS.7.C.1.1 Recognize how Enlightenment ideas including Montesquieu's view of separation of power and John Locke's theories related to natural law and how Locke's social contract influenced the Founding Fathers.

SS.7.C.1.2 Trace the impact that the Magna Carta, English Bill of Rights, Mayflower Compact, and Thomas Paine's "Common Sense" had on colonists' views of government.

Essential Questions

How does geography influence the development of communities? Why do people create, structure, and change governments?

Guiding Questions

1. What ancient principles, traditions, and events have shaped the system of government we have today?
2. How did Europe's Enlightenment influence ideas about government in what became the United States?
3. How were the first English colonies in America shaped by earlier ideas about democracy and government?

Terms to Know

democracy
rule by the people

direct democracy
a system in which the people govern themselves

representative democracy
a system in which the people choose leaders to govern

republic
a country with a representative democracy

limited government
the idea that the power of a government can be limited

legislature
a group of representatives that makes laws

natural rights
rights that government cannot take away

social contract
an agreement in which the people agree to give up some freedom in exchange for the government's protection of people's rights

It Matters Because

Ancient peoples and the great thinkers of the Enlightenment influenced how the Founders shaped our government in ways that still affect us today.

The following list gives examples of ancient or Enlightenment influences on the U.S. government. Which one affects your life the most? Circle your answer and then use the space provided to explain.

town hall meetings   **freedom to assemble**

freedom of the press   **freedom of speech**

freedom to practice religion **democratic elections**

_____

_____

What Do You Know?

Directions: Use the table below to answer the questions based on what you know "Now." After the lesson, write in the "Later" column to complete the table.

Now		Later
	What is a democracy?	
	Why do people need government?	

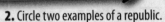

networks Read Chapter 4 Lesson 1 in your textbook or online.

The Foundations of Democracy

A **democracy** is a type of government in which the people rule. This is different from a government in which one person has all the power. This type of ruler is called a monarch.

The Jewish religion gave the world some of its first democratic ideas. Since ancient times, Judaism has taught that every person has worth. This belief is one of the basic ideas of democracy.

Our government today was influenced by ancient Greece and Rome. In ancient Greece, the people of Athens created the world's first direct democracy in the 400s B.C. In a **direct democracy,** the people govern themselves. Direct democracy works when the population is small. In Athens, all free men over 18 years old were citizens. They could take part in the assembly, which made decisions for the community. In places with large populations, an assembly of all citizens would be too big. People would choose leaders to govern. This is called **representative democracy.**

When a country has a representative democracy, it is called a republic. The United States is a **republic.** The world's first republic was ancient Rome. In 509 B.C., the Romans overthrew their king and set up a republic. A senate ran the government. Its members were chosen from Rome's wealthy upper class. The Roman republic helped shape the American government today.

After the Roman Empire ended, kings and lords ruled most of Europe for 700 years. Lords were noblemen that usually inherited land and wealth. As these rulers became more powerful, some nobles rebelled. In England they made King John sign a document called the Magna Carta (Latin term for "Great Charter"). The graphic organizer below lists important points from the Magna Carta.

> **Made it illegal for the king to tax the nobles without their permission**

> **Gave landowners the right to equal treatment under law**

Magna Carta, 1215

> **Gave landowners the right to trial by their peers**

> **Gave nobles the right to rebel if the king broke his agreement**

The Magna Carta put forth the idea of **limited government.** This meant that a ruler or government was no longer all-powerful.

Think Critically

1. Contrast What is the difference between a direct democracy and a representative democracy?

_____

_____

_____

_____

Mark the Text ✏️

2. Circle two examples of a republic.

Show Your Skill

3. Interpret Charts What were the main points of the Magna Carta?

_____

_____

_____

_____

Think Critically

4. Explain How did the Magna Carta establish the principle of limited government? Give some examples.

_____

_____

_____

_____

Mark the Text

5. Circle the name of the group that makes laws such as Parliament.

Show Your Skill

6. Identify Cause and Effect
What effect did the Glorious Revolution have on government?

_____

_____

_____

_____

By the late 1300s, England had a group of nobles that advised the king. It was called Parliament. In addition to giving the king advice, Parliament made laws. A group of representatives that makes laws is called a **legislature.** Many kings did not want Parliament's help. In 1625 King Charles I dismissed Parliament and ruled alone. In 1628, however, he called back Parliament. Its members forced him to sign the Petition of Right, which limited the power of England's kings.

The English Parliament decided to make changes to their government. In 1688 Parliament forced King James II from the throne of England. It asked James's daughter Mary and her husband William to rule instead. This event became known as the Glorious Revolution.

Parliament created a set of rules for the government called the English Bill of Rights. William and Mary had to accept the English Bill of Rights before they took power. These rules listed certain rights of English citizens and said that kings could not take them away. The Glorious Revolution and the English Bill of Rights changed English government forever. The events also received much notice in the English colonies in North America.

William and Mary served as co-monarchs after King James II was forced off the throne in the Glorious Revolution.

Influence of the Enlightenment

The problems between the monarchy and Parliament created new ideas about government. These ideas were part of a movement in Europe known as the Enlightenment.

New discoveries in science led some to believe that God had created a universe governed by laws. These laws of nature could be discovered using human reason, or careful thought. This change in how some people saw their world was called the Enlightenment.

Enlightenment thinkers wanted to apply the laws of nature to people and societies. These ideas changed how people thought of government in Europe and in the Americas.

The Glorious Revolution also let Enlightenment thinkers share their ideas more freely. One important Enlightenment thinker was John Locke. Locke influenced how the settlers in North America thought of government. Locke said that people form governments to protect their natural rights. **Natural rights** are rights that everyone should have. These include the right to life, the right to freedom, and the right to own property. Locke argued that an agreement existed between government and the people. Locke called this agreement the **social contract.** According to the social contract, the people agreed to give up some freedom and be ruled by government. In return, the government agreed to protect the people's rights. If it did not do that, the contract was broken. If the contract was broken, then the people could choose new leaders.

The First Colonial Governments

During the 1600s, people from England traveled to North America and set up colonies. A *colony* is a settlement controlled by another country. The early colonists were loyal to England. They had a strong belief in democracy and representative government. They brought these ideas to America.

The first permanent English settlement in North America was Jamestown. The Virginia Company set it up in 1607. At first, the Virginia Company appointed officials to run Jamestown. To convince more people to come to Jamestown, the company began to let the colonists make their own laws. Beginning in 1619 the colonists elected leaders called *burgesses* to represent them. This group was called the House of Burgesses. Jamestown's House of Burgesses was the first representative government in the colonies.

Think Critically

7. **Summarize** Describe John Locke's ideas about the social contract.

_____

_____

_____

_____

_____

Mark the Text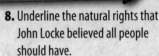

8. Underline the natural rights that John Locke believed all people should have.

The Pilgrims wrote an agreement on rules for their new colony. The agreement, known as the Mayflower Compact, was signed on the ship during the journey to North America.

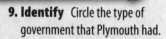

Mark the Text

9. Identify Circle the type of government that Plymouth had.

Take the Challenge

10. Write a journal entry from the point of view of an early settler in Jamestown or Plymouth. Describe your ideas on government.

In 1620 a group of people called Pilgrims sailed to North America. The Pilgrims wanted the freedom to practice their religion. Their small ship was called the *Mayflower*. The ship landed in what is now Massachusetts. There was no English government in this part of North America. The men on the ship decided to make a list of rules for the colony. It was called the Mayflower Compact. A compact is a written agreement. The Mayflower Compact set up a direct democracy in the new colony of Plymouth.

 NGSSS Check What were three important influences on the growth of democracy in America? SS.7.C.1.1

1. _____

2. _____

3. _____

NGSSS

SS.7.C.1.3 Describe how English policies and responses to colonial concerns led to the writing of the Declaration of Independence.

Essential Questions
How does geography influence the development of communities?
Why do people create, structure, and change governments?

Guiding Questions
1. Why did people settle in England's colonies in America?
2. How was life in the colonies shaped by where people lived?
3. What factors weakened the ties between England and its colonies?

Terms to Know

indentured servant
a person who agreed to work for someone else for a certain length of time, in return for passage on a ship, food, shelter, and clothing

dissenter
someone who does not agree with official or common views

economy
wealth and resources; way of producing goods

cash crop
crops grown in large amounts to be sold

plantation
large farms where crops are grown for sale

It Matters Because

The reasons early settlers came to America and the economies and government that grew helped to shape the new United States and continue to influence American culture today.

You live in a community that is already established. Look at the list of characteristics below and circle the ones that you think make a good community.

safety	freedom	cultural diversity
natural resources	workers	education

What Do You Know?

Directions: Fill in the blanks to complete the sentences.

Settlers came to America for many reasons. Some were looking

for _____. Others wanted to practice their

_____ freely. The land and climate of the region

affected the _____ of the colonies. The English

colonists brought new ideas about _____. These

ideas and their distance from _____ helped them

to think differently about government.

Mark the Text

1. Underline the two major reasons that people came to America.

Show Your Skill

2. **Interpret Charts** Were the founders of Rhode Island dissenters? Why or why not?

_____

_____

_____

_____

Think Critically

3. **Explain** Why did some people come to the colonies as indentured servants?

_____

_____

_____

_____

Settling the English Colonies

Colonists came to North America from many parts of Europe. Settlers traveled across the ocean from England, Scotland, Ireland, and Wales. The Dutch and the Swedes also started colonies along the Atlantic Coast.

People came to America for many reasons. Most of the colonists came to America for land or jobs. Even those who could not afford the cost of the trip to America could come by agreeing to be indentured servants. An **indentured servant** had to work for another colonist for a certain length of time. In return, the colonist paid for the indentured servant's trip to the colonies. They were also given food, shelter, and clothing when they reached America. The servants worked from four to seven years, and after that they were free to work for themselves.

In Europe, some people were being treated harshly because of their religious beliefs. Many of these people came to America for the right to worship in their own way. That is why the Pilgrims left England. Another group started the Massachusetts Bay Colony near Plymouth. They were called Puritans. The Puritans were dissenters. A **dissenter** is a person who is against official or common views.

Reasons People Settled in the Colonies	
Economic Opportunity	**Religious Freedom**
Food and shelter in return for work	Puritans fled harsh treatment (*Plymouth*)
Earn a living by farming land, working at other jobs (*Jamestown, others*)	People wanted to worship in their own way (*Massachusetts Bay Colony; colonies of Rhode Island, Connecticut*)

The Puritans wanted freedom to worship in their own way, but they did not allow others to do so. Some people were forced to leave the Massachusetts Bay Colony because of their religious views. These people started the colonies of Rhode Island and Connecticut. In 1639 the people of Connecticut produced America's first written constitution. They called it the Fundamental Orders of Connecticut. It created an assembly of elected representatives from each town. These leaders passed laws for the colony. The colonists also elected their own governor and judges.

Colonial Economy, 1750

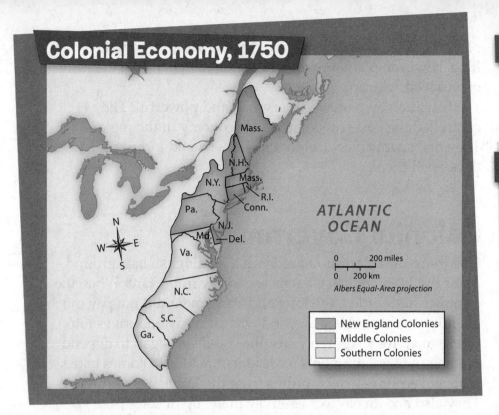

Mass.

N.H.

N.Y.   Mass.

R.I.

Pa.   Conn.

N.J.

Md.   Del.

Va.

N.C.

S.C.

Ga.

ATLANTIC
OCEAN

0   200 miles
0   200 km
Albers Equal-Area projection

New England Colonies
Middle Colonies
Southern Colonies

Colonial Life

By 1733, England had 13 colonies along the Atlantic Coast of North America. The land and the climate were different among the colonies from north to south. These differences affected each colony's **economy,** or way of producing goods, and their way of life.

In New England, most people lived in towns. The cold climate and rocky soil made it hard to farm. Farms were small and were located near towns. Many New Englanders worked as shopkeepers or in other small businesses. The region's forests provided wood for shipbuilding. Fishermen worked on boats in the Atlantic Ocean. Colonists hunted and trapped. They sold the furs to Native Americans and also shipped furs overseas.

In the Middle Colonies, the climate and soil were better for farming. Farmers raised wheat and other **cash crops.** Cash crops are crops that are grown in large amounts. They were sold instead of being saved to feed the farmers' families. Cash crops were often sold overseas. This trade helped make New York City and Philadelphia busy port cities. The Middle Colonies were also rich in natural resources such as lumber, metals, and harbors. Because of this, sawmills, mines, ironworks, and other businesses grew.

The Southern Colonies had warm weather, a long growing season, and rich soil. This meant that crops grew well in these colonies. Tobacco and rice, especially, thrived along the coast. They were the cash crops of the region. Large farms called **plantations** developed. Many workers were needed on these

Mark the Text

4. Circle the products that helped make New York and Philadelphia busy port cities.

Show Your Skill

5. **Compare and Contrast** How did the farms of the Southern Colonies compare to those of the New England Colonies?

_____

_____

_____

_____

Think Critically

6. **Explain** Why did the Southern Colonies need lots of workers?

_____

_____

_____

Think Critically

7. Explain Who controlled the elected assemblies in the Southern Colonies, and why?

_____

_____

_____

Think Critically

9. Evaluate How did the distance between England and America influence colonists' ideas about leadership?

_____

_____

_____

_____

_____

Take the Challenge

10. Perform a skit in a small group to show how the English government treated the colonies from the early 1600s to the mid-1600s.

plantations. At first indentured servants did the work. Over time, however, plantation owners came to depend on the labor of enslaved Africans.

Plantation owners were very rich and powerful. They controlled the government and the economy in the region. They had so much control that few towns and industries developed there.

Colonial Government

One thing the colonists shared was their English background. Their rights as English citizens were very important. When the colonists first settled, the king and Parliament did not pay much attention to them. Also, England was far away. Messages took weeks to arrive. Over the years, the colonists began to depend on their own governments for leadership. Most colonies had a royal governor who took orders from the English government. They also had an elected assembly made up of colonists.

English leaders believed the colonies were supposed to make money for England. In the 1650s, Parliament began passing laws to control how the colonies traded. In colonies south of New England, few people lived along the coast. Ships could load and unload goods without being seen. Because of this the laws were hard to enforce, and the colonists often ignored them.

As time went on, the colonial assemblies grew strong and made local laws. They could also tax the colonists and decide how that tax money would be spent. They used these powers to make the royal governor weaker.

By the mid-1700s, the colonists were used to governing themselves. Most agreed with John Locke's idea that government should protect the people's rights. The colonists thought it was unfair when the royal governors did things to benefit, or help, England instead of the colonies. Many colonists also began to think that they did not have as many rights as people in England did. Over time, the colonists came to see themselves as Americans rather than as English citizens.

NGSSS Check How did the colonial assemblies grow strong? SS.7.C.1.3

_____

_____

_____

NGSSS

SS.7.C.1.3 Describe how English policies and responses to colonial concerns led to the writing of the Declaration of Independence.

SS.7.C.1.4 Analyze the ideas (natural rights, role of the government) and complaints set forth in the Declaration of Independence.

LESSON

3 DISAGREEMENTS WITH GREAT BRITAIN

Essential Question

Why do people create, structure, and change governments?

Guiding Questions

1. What events and movements affected colonial attitudes?
2. What events increased colonists' anger toward British rule?
3. What ideas about government influenced the Declaration of Independence?

Terms to Know

liberty
personal freedom

proclamation
official announcement

boycott
refuse to buy or use

repeal
to cancel

duty
a tax on imported goods

smuggling
moving goods illegally in or out of a country

delegate
representative

It Matters Because

The events that led American colonists to declare independence affected the choices they made about a new government.

The principles laid out in the Declaration of Independence are still ones that we are working on today.

"We hold these truths to be self-evident, that all men are created equal, that they are endowed by their Creator with certain unalienable Rights, that among these are Life, Liberty and the pursuit of Happiness."

What Do You Know?

Directions: Write what you know now in the "Now" column. After this lesson, complete the last column by writing your answers in the "Later" column.

Now		Later
	What changed the colonists' ideas about Britain?	
	Why were colonists angry with the British?	
	Why was the Declaration of Independence written?	

Mark the Text ✏️

1. **Identify** Underline the words that help determine the meaning of the word *authority*.

Think Critically

2. **Identify Cause and Effect** What effect did the French and Indian War have on the colonies?

_____

_____

_____

_____

_____

Take the Challenge

3. Write a letter from the point of view of a colonist who wants to move to western lands after the French and Indian War.

Social and Political Changes in the Colonies

In the 1740s, a religious movement called the Great Awakening began in the colonies. Colonists began to question the traditional religious authority of the church. Enlightenment thinkers urged people to question political authority. The Great Awakening and the Enlightenment made people in the colonies want more **liberty,** or personal freedom. More and more colonists believed that they should have the same rights as people in Great Britain.

The colonists thought that Parliament should protect the rights of British people from the king. Yet the king and Parliament made the laws for the colonists. The colonists thought they should be able to choose their own leaders. The royal governors did what the king wanted, not what the colonists wanted.

The colonies began to get bigger. By the 1750s, British colonists were moving west into places that France said it already owned. Soon people from Great Britain and France began to fight over the land. In 1754 French soldiers joined with some Native American groups. Together, they tried to make the British colonists leave the land west of the Appalachian Mountains. Britain sent troops to the colonies. The conflict was called the French and Indian War.

The British won the French and Indian War in 1763. Now the British controlled French lands as far west as the Mississippi River. The colonists wanted to move onto those lands. The shaded area on the map below shows the land that the British won from France.

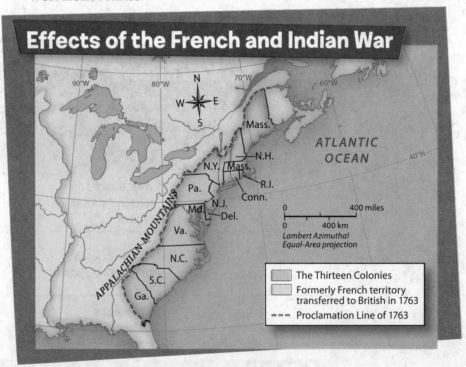

Effects of the French and Indian War

Map legend:
- The Thirteen Colonies
- Formerly French territory transferred to British in 1763
- Proclamation Line of 1763

King George did not want the colonists to move onto the lands won from France because he did not want fighting with Native Americans to start again. He made it against the law to move there. He let the colonists know about this in a new law called the Proclamation of 1763. A **proclamation** is an official announcement. The colonists were angry; they thought that Great Britain was trying to limit their growth.

King George also decided that the colonists should help pay for the war. Fighting the French and Indian War had cost a lot of money and Great Britain was in debt. In 1765 Parliament passed the Stamp Act to help raise money to help pay for the war. This law made the colonists buy and place tax stamps on all official documents. These stamps had to be put on many kinds of documents, even on newspapers.

The colonists were angry about the new laws. The colonists did not think Parliament had the right to tax them. To show this, they **boycotted** British goods. This meant that they refused to buy them. Colonial leaders organized a Stamp Act Congress to write a protest to Parliament and the king. Finally Parliament **repealed,** or canceled, the Stamp Act.

affix the STAMP.

This is the Place to

The *Pennsylvania Journal and Advertiser* published this skull and bones to protest the Stamp Act.

PHOTO: Bettmann/CORBIS

Mark the Text ✎

4. The colonists' refusal to buy British goods was called a

_____.

Show Your Skill

5. Interpret Charts Which British law was related to the housing of soldiers?

_____

Colonial Dissatisfaction Grows

A year later, Parliament began to tax the colonists again. One type of tax was a duty. A **duty** is a tax on imported goods. The chart below outlines these taxes.

Great Britain Taxes the Colonies		
Act	**Year Passed**	**What It Did**
Sugar Act	1764	Set duties on sugar imports from countries other than Great Britain
Stamp Act	1765	Placed a tax on legal papers, newspapers, and other documents
Townshend Acts	1767	Placed duties on goods the colonists imported to the colonies
Tea Act	1773	Made British tea cheaper than other tea sold in the colonies. British tea grown in India did not have to pay the import duty, but other tea did.
Coercive Acts	1774	Passed several laws to punish the colonists for resisting British authority
Quartering Act	1774	Required the colonists to give food, housing, and other help to British troops

Show Your Skill

6. Draw Conclusions Why did the colonists dislike the Tea Act?

_____

_____

_____

_____

_____

Think Critically

7. Analyze Why did the colonists refer to the Coercive Acts as the Intolerable Acts?

_____

_____

_____

Mark the Text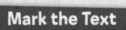

8. Underline the words in the paragraph that help you determine the meaning of *debate*.

One of the Townshend Acts gave British officials the power to search any business or home. Officers searched for goods on which the import duty had not been paid. The searches were meant to help stop smuggling by the colonists. **Smuggling** is moving goods illegally in or out of a country.

These searches angered the colonists. Nearly 20 years later, Americans remembered them when they added a protection against "unreasonable searches and seizures" to the United States Constitution.

The Tea Act also angered the colonists. It hurt the business of colonial tea merchants. The colonists responded to the act by boarding British ships in Boston harbor. They dumped the ships' cargoes of tea into the water. This came to be called the Boston Tea Party.

Parliament passed laws called the Coercive Acts to punish the colonists for the Boston Tea Party. These acts took away some of the colonists' basic rights. They were so harsh that the colonists called them the Intolerable Acts. Some of these laws violated the English Bill of Rights—rights that the colonists believed in strongly.

Steps Toward Independence

Anger about the Coercive Acts made the colonies join together. They wanted the British government to change the laws. In 1774 **delegates,** or representatives, from 12 colonies met in Philadelphia. This meeting was called the First Continental Congress. The delegates decided to send a letter to the king asking him to change the laws. They also agreed to boycott British goods and stop all trade with Great Britain.

King George refused to do as the colonists asked. He sent more soldiers to the colonies. In 1775 fighting broke out in Massachusetts between British soldiers and armed colonists. Delegates from the colonies met again to debate what to do next. This meeting was called the Second Continental Congress. The discussion lasted for months. Some delegates wanted independence, but others did not.

Support for independence was growing. In January 1776, Thomas Paine published a pamphlet called *Common Sense*. In it, he explained why he felt that America needed to be independent. Paine used some of John Locke's ideas to make his case.

Common Sense was so popular that 500,000 copies were sold. By the spring of 1776, more than half of the delegates to the Second Continental Congress also wanted independence.

The Congress decided it was time to tell the world why the colonies wanted to be free from Great Britain's control. A group of delegates worked together on an announcement. Thomas Jefferson, a delegate from Virginia, did most of the writing. The document was called the Declaration of Independence.

Enlightenment thinking, along with ancient Greek ideas about democracy, influenced Jefferson's writing. Voltaire believed that people had a right to liberty. Jean-Jacques Rousseau wrote that if a government did not protect its people's freedom, it should not exist.

John Locke's ideas about natural rights and the social contract were Jefferson's main guide. In the Declaration of Independence, Thomas Jefferson wrote, "all men are created equal." He also said that they had God-given rights. Jefferson pointed out that Great Britain had broken the social contract. This gave the colonists the right to rebel.

The Second Continental Congress approved the Declaration on July 4, 1776. No other government in the world was based on the ideas of natural rights and the social contract. Since 1776, many nations have used the Declaration as an example to follow.

Show Your Skill

9. Use Time Lines Fill in the blanks to complete the time line.

Mark the Text

10. Whose writings had the greatest influence on the Declaration of Independence? Underline the person's name.

First Steps Toward Independence

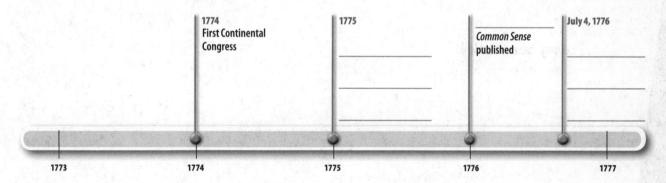

1774
First Continental
Congress

1775

Common Sense published

July 4, 1776

1773   1774   1775   1776   1777

NGSSS Check List three reasons why the colonists became angry with Parliament and the king. SS.7.C.1.3

1. _____

2. _____

3. _____

Reflect on What It Means . . .

In the "Concord Hymn," Emerson wrote about the first battle of the American Revolution. The bridge he refers to is the Old North Bridge that crosses the "flood" of the Concord River in Concord, Massachusetts. Here, the battle for independence began. Think about how disagreements with Britain and dissatisfaction with the government led to "the shot heard round the world." Write about what the Declaration of Independence means to you, your community, and the world.

"By the rude bridge that arched the flood,
Their flag to April's breeze unfurled,
Here once the embattled farmers stood,
And fired the shot heard round the world"
—Ralph Waldo Emerson, "Concord Hymn"

What the Declaration of Independence Means . . .

. . . to me

. . . to my community

. . . to the world

TAKE THE CHALLENGE

Emerson wrote the poem to accompany the placement of a stone monument at the site. Read the entire poem. Then write a summary of what it means.

THE CONSTITUTION

NGSSS

SS.7.C.1.7 Describe how the Constitution limits the powers of government through separation of powers and checks and balances.

ESSENTIAL QUESTION • *Why do people create, structure, and change governments?* • *How do societies balance individual and community rights?* • *How does social change influence government?*

Authors often use an introduction to explain the purpose of what they are writing. The Preamble to the U.S. Constitution is the introduction to the document that outlines the principles and structure of the government of the United States.

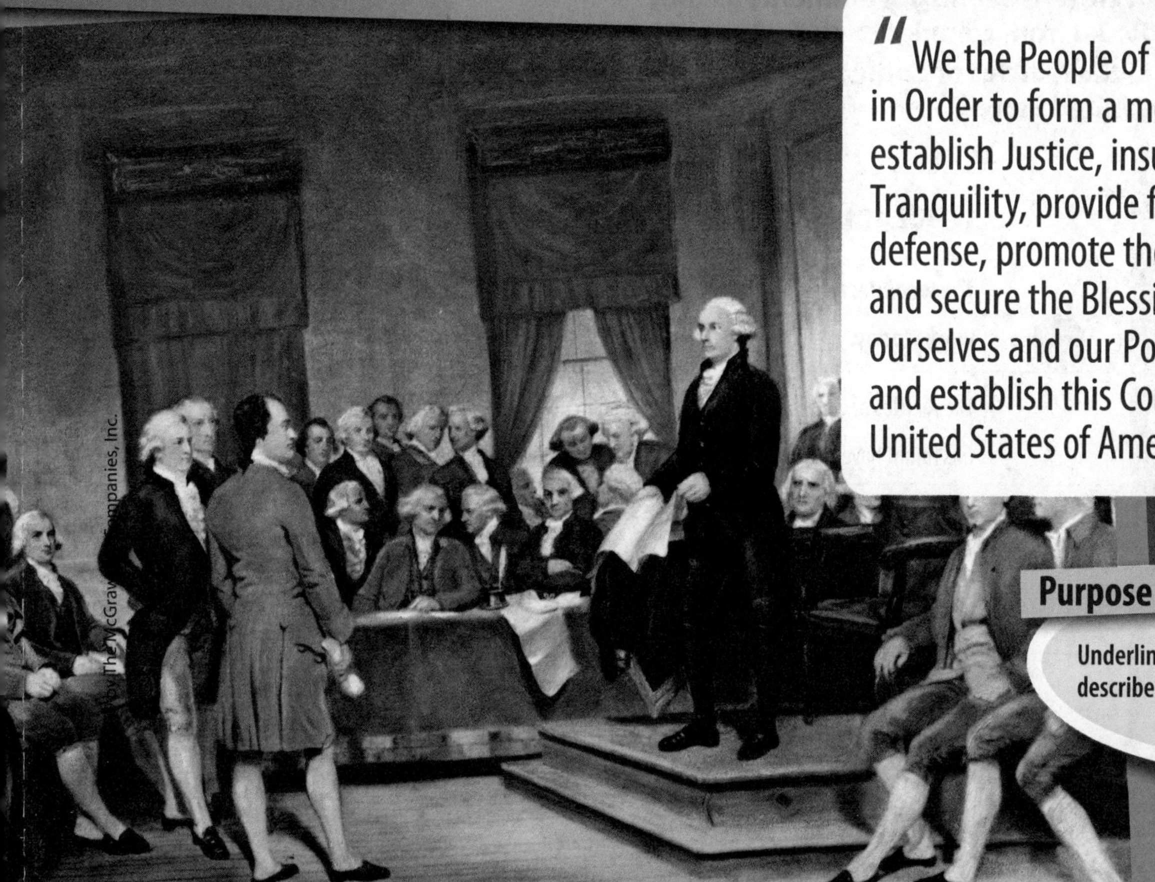

" We the People of the United States, in Order to form a more perfect Union, establish Justice, insure domestic Tranquility, provide for the common defense, promote the general Welfare, and secure the Blessings of Liberty to ourselves and our Posterity, do ordain and establish this Constitution for the United States of America. "

Purpose

Underline the phrases that describe the document's purpose.

DBQ BREAKING IT DOWN

Pick one of the phrases you underlined and explain what it means.

_____

_____

_____

Today, we are *the Posterity* described in the Preamble. Posterity means all future generations. In what ways do you think you enjoy *the Blessings of Liberty*?

_____

_____

_____

McGraw-Hill
netw rks™
There's More Online!

NGSSS

SS.7.C.1.5 Identify how the weaknesses of the Articles of Confederation led to the writing of the Constitution.

Essential Question

Why do people create, structure, and change governments?

Guiding Questions

1. How did citizens set up governments as they transitioned from colonies to states?
2. How did the Articles of Confederation create problems for the United States?

Terms to Know

constitution
a detailed, written plan for government

bicameral
divided into two parts, or houses

confederation
a group that comes together for a common purpose

Articles of Confederation
the first plan of government for the United States

ratify
to approve

ordinance
a law

Ordinance of 1785
law that set rules for surveying and selling land in the Northwest Territory

Northwest Ordinance
law that set rules for governing the new territory

Shays's Rebellion
armed uprising in which farmers attacked a federal building in Massachusetts

It Matters Because

The weaknesses of the first U.S. government shaped the way our government works today.

The Articles of Confederation withheld certain powers from Congress. How do you think this might have caused problems for the federal government?

What Do You Know?

Directions: Use the table below to answer the questions based on what you know now in the "Now" column. After the lesson, complete the table with your answers in the "Later" column.

Now		Later
	How were state governments different from colonies?	
	Why did the Articles of Confederation not work?	

State Constitutions

By 1776, American colonists were planning for independence. They knew that freedom from Great Britain would mean an end to colonial charters. The colonists would need to form new governments. New Hampshire led the way. In January 1776, its leaders wrote the first state constitution. A **constitution** is a detailed, written plan for government. Within a few years the other states had done the same.

The state governments were all very much alike. Each one had a legislature to make laws. Most of the state legislatures were **bicameral.** This means they were divided into two parts, called houses. Each state had a governor. The governor's job was to carry out the laws. Each state also had courts. Court judges decided how to apply the laws in cases of lawbreaking.

Most state constitutions also included a bill of rights. This is a list of the basic freedoms that belong to every citizen. A bill of rights guarantees that the government will protect the rights of its citizens. Some of these rights can be traced back to the Magna Carta and the English Bill of Rights.

The Articles of Confederation

Each state was ready to govern itself when independence was declared. However, the states also needed to join together. They could not win a war against Britain with thirteen small armies. They needed one strong army under a single command.

In 1777 the Second Continental Congress wrote a plan to unite the states. It called for the states to form a confederation. A **confederation** is a group that comes together for a common purpose. The plan was called the **Articles of Confederation.** By 1781, all 13 states had ratified the Articles. To **ratify** means to approve.

This document is the Articles of Confederation, which was the states' first federal constitution.

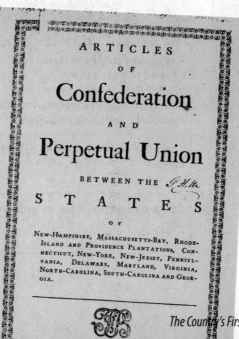

Think Critically

1. Explain Why did the colonies write state constitutions, beginning in 1776?

_____

_____

_____

_____

2. Compare How were the state governments alike?

_____

_____

_____

_____

Mark the Text

3. Identify Underline the meaning of *constitution*.

Take the Challenge

4. With a small group, model what a *confederation* is and explain the purpose of the Confederation Congress.

The Articles of Confederation set up a national legislature. It was called the Confederation Congress. It had one house, and each state had one vote. The legislature controlled the army and had the power to deal with foreign countries for the United States.

The Confederation Congress did have one success. It passed laws, called **ordinances,** which helped settle the Northwest Territory. This was an area, or region, that would later become Ohio, Indiana, Illinois, Michigan, Wisconsin, and part of Minnesota.

The first law was the **Ordinance of 1785.** It set up rules for measuring and selling the land. It divided land into townships six miles square. The second law was called the **Northwest Ordinance.** It was passed in 1787. The Northwest Ordinance set up a plan for governing the new territory. It created a way for new states to join the Union. It also made slavery against the law in the Northwest Territory. These ordinances would have a major impact, or effect, on the future settlement of the West.

However, the Articles of Confederation also withheld some important powers from Congress. Congress could not enforce its own laws. It did not have the power to tax. Its voting rules made it hard to get anything done. As a result, Congress was weak and states could ignore its laws.

In 1783 the powers in the Articles helped the United States become an independent nation. However, the new nation was in trouble. Congress was in debt and it could not collect taxes. The state governments were also in debt. They taxed the people heavily. The state governments also taxed goods imported from other states and countries. These taxes hurt trade. As trade slowed, merchants, workers, and farmers all suffered.

| Weaknesses of the Articles of Confederation ||
Weakness	Result
The approval of nine states was needed to pass a law.	It was very hard to pass laws.
Changing the Articles required the approval of all thirteen states.	It was virtually impossible to change the powers of Congress.
Congress had no power to collect taxes.	The government did not have enough money. It could ask the states for money, but not demand it.
Congress had no power to enforce laws.	Congress relied on the states to carry out its laws. It could not force the states to do so.

During Shays's Rebellion, fights broke out like this one, which ultimately showed the weaknesses of the federal government under the Articles of Confederation.

PHOTO: Bettmann/CORBIS

The Confederation Congress did not have the power to fix these problems. Americans became fearful that the government could not protect them. In Massachusetts, a farmer named Daniel Shays owed money because of heavy taxes. The state court threatened to take his farm away. In response, Shays led an army of farmers in an attack on a federal building that held weapons. The uprising became known as **Shays's Rebellion.**

Shays's Rebellion scared the whole country. People started to wonder if the government was too weak to keep law and order. Leaders began to call for a stronger national government. In 1787 twelve states sent delegates to a meeting in Philadelphia. A delegate is someone who represents others. The task of the delegates was to change the Articles of Confederation and make them stronger.

Mark the Text

9. Diagram Fill in the effect in the chart below.

Think Critically

10. Explain Why did Daniel Shays try to attack a federal building that held weapons?

_____

_____

_____

_____

Cause

Shays's Rebellion

Effect

_____

_____

_____

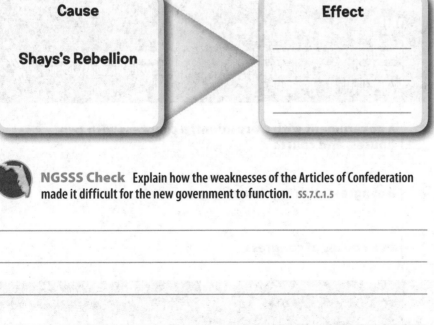

NGSSS Check Explain how the weaknesses of the Articles of Confederation made it difficult for the new government to function. **SS.7.C.1.5**

_____

_____

_____

_____

LESSON 2
CREATING A NEW CONSTITUTION

NGSSS

SS.7.C.1.5 Identify how the weaknesses of the Articles of Confederation led to the writing of the Constitution.

SS.7.C.1.8 Explain the viewpoints of the Federalists and the Anti-Federalists regarding the ratification of the Constitution and inclusion of a bill of rights.

Essential Question

Why do people create, structure, and change governments?

Guiding Questions

1. Why did American leaders decide to create a new plan of government?
2. Why were compromises made at the Constitutional Convention?
3. How did Federalist and Anti-Federalist viewpoints differ?

Terms to Know

Constitutional Convention
meeting at which the United States Constitution was written

Great Compromise
agreement that settled the question of representation in Congress

Three-Fifths Compromise
agreement that settled the question of representation of enslaved people in Congress

Electoral College
group of electors who choose the president and vice-president

Federalist
person who wanted to ratify the Constitution

federalism
system in which power is divided between the federal and state governments

The Federalist Papers
essays supporting the Constitution

Anti-Federalist
person who was against ratifying the Constitution

It Matters Because

In creating the Constitution, the basis for our government today, the Framers reached important compromises that had lasting legacies. A compromise involves each side giving up something that it wants in order to reach an agreement.

List an example of a time when you made a compromise with a friend. Explain what you and your friend gave up to satisfy the other person.

_____

_____

_____

What Do You Know?

Directions: The delegates at the Constitutional Convention agreed on what became known as the Great Compromise. Place a check mark next to the plan that you think became the Great Compromise.

☐ **a government with a president, a congress with two houses, and courts**

☐ **a congress with one house**

☐ **two houses of congress**

The Constitutional Convention

On May 25, 1787, a convention began in Philadelphia. A convention is a large, formal meeting. The purpose of this convention was to change the Articles of Confederation to make the national government stronger.

Fifty-five delegates attended. Many of them had been leaders in government. Most were well educated and wealthy. They included lawyers, merchants, and planters. Only Rhode Island did not send delegates. That state did not want a stronger central government. Also, there were no women, African Americans, or Native Americans at the convention. These groups were not allowed to have a part in politics at that time.

As the convention process began, the delegates made some decisions. They chose General George Washington to lead the convention. He was greatly respected for his leadership during the American Revolution.

The public would not be allowed at the meeting. The doors were guarded and the windows were kept shut, despite the hot weather. This would allow delegates to talk freely. James Madison of Virginia kept a journal, however. This is how we know today what went on at the convention.

The delegates also decided that the Articles of Confederation could not be fixed. The Articles were too weak and flawed. They decided instead to start over. They would write a whole new plan of government. The United States Constitution was the result of their work. The meeting came to be known as the **Constitutional Convention.**

Compromising for a Constitution

When the delegates began their work, the Virginia delegates introduced a plan. It was called the Virginia Plan, and it was written by James Madison.

Show Your Skill

1. Make a Connection Why do you think it would be important for the delegates to talk freely?

_____

_____

_____

Think Critically

2. Explain Why did the delegates decide not to revise the Articles of Confederation?

_____

_____

_____

Take the Challenge

3. With your class, take a side in the debate about whether the Articles of Confederation should be replaced or revised. Support your argument.

In an artist's portrayal of the Constitutional Convention, delegates debated what the new form of government would be and what plan would be adopted.

4. Identify Circle the proposed plan for government that favored states with large populations.

5. Identify Underline the proposed plan that favored small states.

Show Your Skill

6. Draw Conclusions Why was reaching a compromise so important?

_____

_____

_____

_____

The Virginia Plan called for a government with a president, a Congress with two houses, and courts. It was very similar to our government today. The number of representatives in both houses of Congress would be based on each state's population. This would give large states more votes—and more power—than small states.

Delegates from smaller states did not like the Virginia Plan. They thought that a Congress controlled by large states would ignore their interests. The small states introduced their own plan called the New Jersey Plan. It called for a Congress with one house. Each state would have one vote so all states had equal power. This plan thought a committee named by Congress should carry out the laws instead of a president.

There was much debate; large and small states could not agree. Finally, Roger Sherman of Connecticut came up with a compromise. A compromise is an agreement between opposing sides. Each side gives up something but gains something else.

Sherman's plan called for two houses of Congress—a Senate and a House of Representatives. In the Senate, each state would have two members. The small states liked this. It gave them equal power in the Senate. In the House, the number of members for each state would be based on population. The large states liked this. It gave them more power in the House. The plan was one that both sides could accept. It has come to be known as the **Great Compromise.**

Disagreements came up between Northern and Southern delegates about representation in Congress. Many enslaved people lived in the South. There were more than 550,000 enslaved people in 1787. The Southern states wanted to count them as part of their populations. This would give them more seats in the House of Representatives. In Congress, a member has a "seat" so the number of members are counted as seats. The Northern states were against this. They did not want to give Southern states more power.

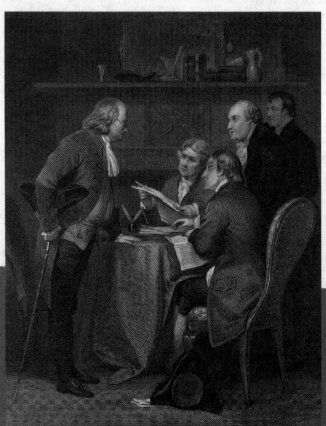

Roger Sherman (standing in the background) was an influential voice in the development of our nation's government. He also helped draft the Declaration of Independence, shown here.

PHOTO: Stock Montage/Archive Photos/Getty Image

The delegates came up with a plan called the **Three-Fifths Compromise.** They decided that every five enslaved people would equal three free people. This meant that three-fifths of the enslaved population of a state would count toward seats in Congress.

Northern and Southern delegates also compromised on trade. They agreed to give Congress the power to make laws regulating trade. This included trade between states and trade with other countries. This pleased the Northern delegates because trade was important to their economy.

However, the delegates did not allow Congress to tax exports. Exports are goods sold to other countries. Nor could Congress try to end the slave trade before 1808. This pleased the Southern delegates. The Southern economy depended on exports of tobacco and rice grown with the hard work of enslaved laborers.

Another compromise settled a debate over how to choose the president. Some delegates thought the state legislatures should elect the president. Others thought the people should have this right. They decided on an **Electoral College.** This is a special group of electors. They would be chosen by state legislatures to elect the president and vice president. The Electoral College is still in use today. However, the voters of each state now choose the electors.

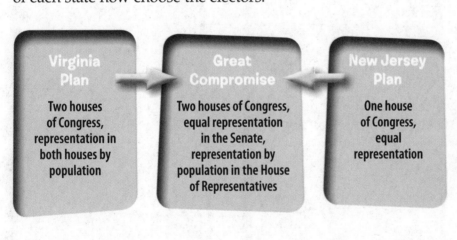

Virginia Plan	Great Compromise	New Jersey Plan
Two houses of Congress, representation in both houses by population	Two houses of Congress, equal representation in the Senate, representation by population in the House of Representatives	One house of Congress, equal representation

Federalists and Anti-Federalists

It took the delegates almost four months to write the Constitution. They signed the finished document on September 17, 1787. Now it was up to the states to approve it. At least nine states had to ratify the Constitution for it to become the law of the land.

Americans had differing views of the Constitution. Those who supported it were known as **Federalists.** They believed the Constitution would create a system in which power is divided between the federal, or national, government and the states. Such a system is called **federalism.**

7. Interpret Diagrams In the Great Compromise, what did small states and large states give up?

_____

_____

_____

_____

Think Critically

8. Analyze What does the Three-Fifths Compromise say about how most Americans viewed enslaved people at this time in history?

_____

_____

_____

_____

Mark the Text

9. Identify Circle the two issues about which the Northern and Southern delegates debated and eventually compromised.

10. Evaluate What was the significance of the Federalist Papers?

_____

_____

_____

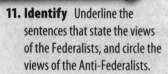

Mark the Text

11. Identify Underline the sentences that state the views of the Federalists, and circle the views of the Anti-Federalists.

12. Chart In each column of the chart, summarize the central view of each side.

James Madison, Alexander Hamilton, and John Jay were leaders of the Federalists. They argued that the nation needed a strong central government to survive. They wrote essays in defense of the Constitution. These essays are known as **the Federalist Papers.**

People who opposed the Constitution were called **Anti-Federalists.** They argued that a strong central government would ignore the rights of the states. They also thought it would favor wealthy people and ignore the common people. They pointed out that the Constitution had no bill of rights to protect citizens. Many states said they would not ratify it without a bill of rights.

Federalist leaders agreed. They promised to add a bill of rights if the Constitution was adopted. That promise helped win people over. In June of 1788, New Hampshire became the ninth state to ratify, and the Constitution took effect. By May of 1790, the other four states had also ratified. The thirteen states were now a nation—the United States of America.

Federalists	Anti-Federalists

NGSSS Check How did ideas of the Federalists and the Anti-Federalists differ?
SS.7.C.1.8

_____

_____

_____

NGSSS

SS.7.C.1.6 Interpret the intentions of the Preamble of the Constitution.

SS.7.C.1.7 Describe how the Constitution limits the powers of government through separation of powers and checks and balances.

SS.7.C.3.3 Illustrate the structure and function (three branches of government established in Articles I, II, and III with corresponding powers) of government in the United States as established in the Constitution.

SS.7.C.3.5 Explain the Constitutional amendment process.

THE STRUCTURE OF THE CONSTITUTION

Essential Question

Why do people create, structure, and change governments?

Guiding Questions

1. How does the U.S. Constitution organize the government?
2. In what ways can the Constitution be changed?

Terms to Know

Preamble
introduction to the U.S. Constitution

article
section of the Constitution describing the structure of government

legislative branch
the part of government that makes laws

executive branch
the part of government that enforces the law

judicial branch
the part of government that interprets the law

interpret
to decide what something means

amendment
any change in the Constitution

It Matters Because

The U.S. Constitution sets up the structure of our government and the basic laws of our nation.

Circle the purposes of government from the Preamble to the Constitution that you think are the most important.

to unite the states	**to defend the country from attack**
to make sure people are treated equally	**to help the people live healthy and happy lives**
to keep peace and order and protect citizens	**to guarantee people's basic rights**

What Do You Know?

Directions: The U.S. government is divided into three branches. Read the following statements about the three branches. If you believe the statement is true, circle T. If you believe the statement is false, circle F.

Statement	True/False	
The Constitution divides the government into three branches.	T	F
The judicial branch makes the laws.	T	F
One branch of government is responsible for interpreting the laws.	T	F
The legislative branch defends the Constitution.	T	F
The branches use a system of checks and balances.	T	F

Mark the Text

1. Underline the part of the Constitution that states its purposes.

Think Critically

2. **Analyze** Why do the articles need to describe how the government should be set up?

_____

_____

_____

_____

_____

Take the Challenge

3. Write a proposal for a new amendment. With your class acting as Congress, propose your change to the Constitution and see if it passes.

Mark the Text

4. **Graphic Organizer** Write a sentence in each box describing the powers of each branch.

The Parts of the Constitution

The U.S. Constitution is more than a plan of government. It is the highest law of the land. It is a symbol of our nation and its values of freedom and fairness.

The Constitution has three main parts. It has a preamble, articles, and amendments.

The first part is the **Preamble** (PREE•am•buhl). The Preamble states the purposes of the Constitution. It is one sentence long. It begins with these famous words: "We the People of the United States . . . ." It ends with these words: ". . . do ordain and establish this Constitution for the United States of America." These words make clear that the power of government comes from the people.

The Preamble lists six purposes of the government. They are

- to unite the states
- to make sure people are treated equally
- to keep peace and order and protect citizens
- to defend the country from attack
- to help the people live healthy and happy lives
- to guarantee people's basic rights

The second part of the Constitution is made up of the articles. There are seven **articles,** or sections. They describe how the government is to be set up. The government is divided into three parts called branches. Each branch has different powers.

Article I describes the **legislative branch,** or Congress. This branch has the power to make laws. It describes how members will be chosen and what rules Congress has to follow when making laws.

Article II describes the **executive branch.** This branch carries out the laws and makes sure laws are obeyed. The president and vice president head the executive branch. This article explains how these leaders are elected and how they can be removed from office. It also lists the president's powers, which includes leading the armed forces.

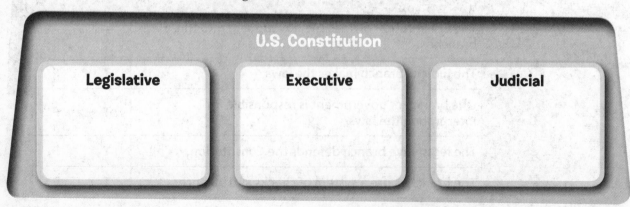

U.S. Constitution

| Legislative | Executive | Judicial |

Article III describes the **judicial branch.** This branch is made up of the Supreme Court and lower courts. The Supreme Court is the head of the judicial branch. The courts **interpret** laws, or decide what laws mean, and make sure laws are enforced fairly. This article also describes the kind of cases the courts may hear.

The rest of the articles cover other matters. They explain the relationship between the states and the federal government. They also tell how the Constitution can be changed.

The last part of the Constitution is made up of the **amendments.** These are changes that have been added over time. There are 27 amendments in all. The first ten amendments are the Bill of Rights. They were added soon after ratification.

Amending and Interpreting the Constitution

The writers of the Constitution knew that changing even a small detail of the Constitution would have a major effect on the government. However, they wanted to make sure it could be changed when the people demanded it. They did not want change to be too easy, but they did want it to be possible.

They created a process for amending, or changing, the Constitution. The process has two steps: First, an amendment must be proposed, and then it must be ratified.

An amendment may be proposed either by a two-thirds vote of Congress, or by a national convention called by two-thirds of state governments.

To ratify an amendment, three-fourths of the states must vote to approve it. Of the thousands of amendments proposed, only 27 have ever been passed. These amendments are called "formal" amendments because they are officially part of the Constitution. However, certain actions by the president have led to informal, or unofficial, amendments. For example, in 1841 William Henry Harrison became the first president to die in office. Vice-President John Tyler assumed, or accepted, the powers of the president as authorized by the Constitution.

William Henry Harrison was the first president to die in office. At that time, the Constitution did not address what to do when a president died. In 1967, the Twenty-fifth amendment was ratified and established the line of succession for the presidency.

Think Critically

5. Analyze Why do you think the writers of the Constitution made it difficult to amend?

_____

_____

_____

_____

_____

Mark the Text

6. Circle the proportion of states that must approve an amendment in order for it to be ratified.

Show Your Skill

7. Identify the Main Idea List three ways our interpretations of the Constitution can change.

_____

_____

_____

Think Critically

8. Summarize How can Congress change the Constitution? Are these types of changes formal or informal?

_____

_____

_____

_____

Think Critically

10. Infer What might bring about new interpretations of the Constitution?

_____

_____

_____

Take the Challenge

11. How can citizens take part in the amendment process? Make a poster to encourage citizens to do their part and debate the amendment that you proposed earlier in the lesson.

The Constitution, however, did not say if Tyler automatically became president or if he was just acting as president until the next election. Tyler took the presidential oath. This meant he was president, not just acting president. His action became an informal amendment. It was the way things were done for more than a hundred years. In 1967 the Twenty-fifth Amendment was ratified. It made Tyler's action a formal part of the Constitution.

The Amendment Process

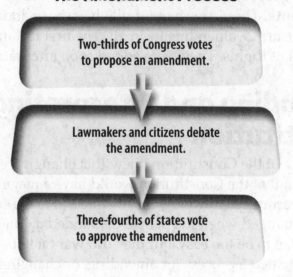

Two-thirds of Congress votes to propose an amendment.

Lawmakers and citizens debate the amendment.

Three-fourths of states vote to approve the amendment.

The writers of the Constitution knew that the world would change. So, they wanted the Constitution to be as general as possible. They were very specific about some things but left others open to interpretation. That is, people have to decide what certain things mean. For example, the Constitution gives Congress the power to make all laws that are "necessary and proper." This allows Congress to use powers that are not directly written in the Constitution. These are called "implied powers." Regulating, or controlling, air pollution is an example of an implied power.

The Supreme Court is the final judge of what the Constitution means. However, the Court's interpretations can change. Congress and the president also sometimes change the way they interpret their powers. Changing customs can also bring about new interpretations of the Constitution.

NGSSS Check How can an amendment to the Constitution be proposed? **SS.7.C.3.5**

_____

_____

_____

4 PRINCIPLES OF THE CONSTITUTION

NGSSS

SS.7.C.1.9 Define the rule of law and recognize its influence on the development of the American legal, political, and governmental systems.

Essential Questions

How do societies balance individual and community rights?
How does social change influence the government?

Guiding Questions

1. What are the principles of United States government?
2. How is power distributed under federalism?

Terms to Know

popular sovereignty
the people's right to rule

limited government
the idea that the government can only do what the people allow it to do

rule of law
the idea that the law applies to everyone

separation of powers
the division of the government into three branches

checks and balances
the ways that each branch of government limits the power of the other two branches

enumerated powers
the powers given to the federal government under the Constitution

reserved powers
the powers set aside for the states

concurrent powers
the powers that both federal and state governments may exercise

supremacy clause
the part of the Constitution that puts federal law over state law, and the Constitution over both

It Matters Because

Every aspect of our lives is affected by the principles set down in the Constitution by the first American leaders.

The term *popular sovereignty* was first used around 1848. In a new U.S. territory people would cast their vote to determine whether slavery would be allowed or not. Today, the term relates more to the idea that government comes from the will of the people. Write an example of how people today use popular sovereignty, as guaranteed by the Constitution.

_____

_____

What Do You Know?

Directions: Write a description or draw a sketch to show an example of the following terms.

Term	Description
Checks and balances	
Rule of law	

PHOTO: Comstock Images / Alamy

Copyright © by The McGraw-Hill Companies, Inc.

Show Your Skill

1. Identify the Main Idea
How is the will of the people, or popular sovereignty, most strongly expressed, according to the Constitution?

_____

_____

_____

Think Critically

2. Summarize In your own words, what is the rule of law?

_____

_____

_____

Major Principles of Government

Principles are basic beliefs that guide people's lives. Principles can also guide governments. The United States Constitution contains five basic principles. They are the base on which our government is built.

These five principles of the U.S. government are the following:

- Popular sovereignty
- Limited government and the rule of law
- Separation of powers
- Checks and balances
- Federalism

Popular sovereignty (SAH•vuhrn•tee) is the idea that the power of government comes from the people. *Sovereignty* means "the right to rule." *Popular* means "of the people." So popular sovereignty is "the people's right to rule."

The Constitution ensures, or guarantees, popular sovereignty by giving citizens the right to vote. The will of the people, or what they want, is shown in whom they elect. The people elect members of Congress to represent them. The people vote for a president to lead them. All elected officials have to answer to the people who put them in positions of power. Otherwise, the people will vote for someone else next time.

Limited government is the idea that the government can do only what the people allow it to do. The writers of the Constitution did not want the government to have too much power. So they put specific limits in the Constitution. The Constitution states what the federal government and the states may and may not do.

Under the Constitution, the government is also limited by the **rule of law.** This means that the law applies to everyone. It applies even to those who govern. No one, even the president, is above the law.

The Constitution limits power in another way, too. It divides the government into three branches. This is called **separation of powers.** The Constitution assigns each branch its own tasks. Each branch has some power, but no branch has all the power.

The separation of powers is a delicate balance in which each branch of government must have defined powers and tasks.

Even so, the writers of the Constitution feared that one branch could still control the other two. So, they put **checks and balances** into the Constitution. Different tasks are assigned to different branches of government. These are ways that each branch can limit the power of the other two branches.

A good example of checks and balances is how laws are made. The Constitution says that a bill passed by Congress must be signed by the president to become law. The president can also veto, or refuse, to sign, a bill. This veto is a check on legislative power. However, Congress can override the veto if two-thirds of its members vote to do so. This is a check on executive power. There are many checks and balances in the Constitution. They allow the branches of government to challenge each other's power.

Five Principles of American Government

United States Constitution

Federalism

Our federal system also limits the power of government. Under this system, power is divided between the national government and the states. Some powers are also shared.

The Constitution gives certain powers to the national government. These are called **enumerated powers.** *Enumerated* means "listed" or "spelled out." For example, the national government can set up post offices and print money.

Other powers are set aside, or reserved, for the states. These are called **reserved powers.** For example, the states can set up and oversee school systems.

Some powers belong to both levels of government. These are called **concurrent powers.** They include the power to collect taxes and to set up courts and prisons.

3. Analyze Why did the writers of the Constitution create checks and balances?

_____

_____

_____

Mark the Text

4. Circle the term that describes the powers given to the national government by the Constitution. Underline the term for powers that are reserved for states.

Take the Challenge

5. As a class, put the system of checks and balances to work! Brainstorm ideas for a new law. Using what you know about how checks and balances work, decide who will represent each branch of government.

Federal and State Powers

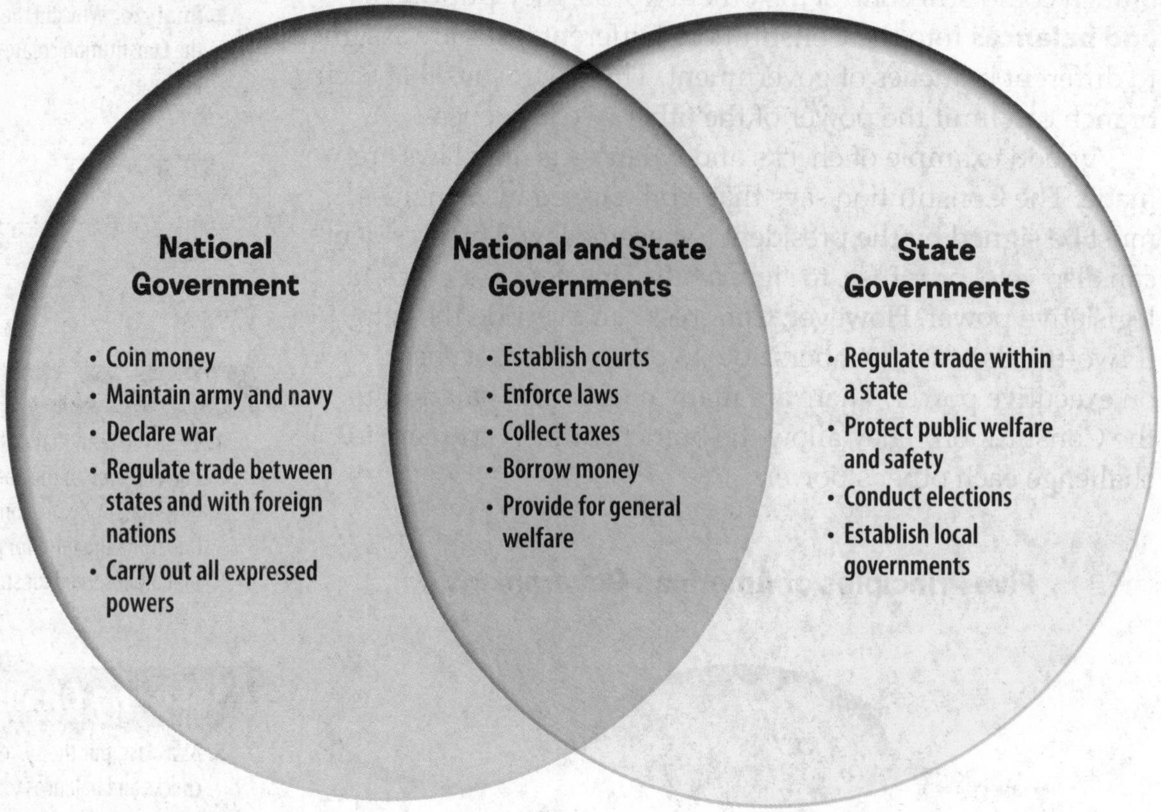

National Government

- Coin money
- Maintain army and navy
- Declare war
- Regulate trade between states and with foreign nations
- Carry out all expressed powers

National and State Governments

- Establish courts
- Enforce laws
- Collect taxes
- Borrow money
- Provide for general welfare

State Governments

- Regulate trade within a state
- Protect public welfare and safety
- Conduct elections
- Establish local governments

Think Critically

6. Infer Which has the highest authority—state law, federal law, or the Constitution?

_____

Show Your Skill

7. Interpret Diagrams Which powers shown in the diagram are concurrent powers?

_____

_____

_____

_____

In a federal system, a state may sometimes pass a law that conflicts with, or is different from, a federal law. The writers of the Constitution knew this might happen. So they included a statement called the **supremacy clause.** It says that the Constitution and other laws and treaties made by the national government "shall be the supreme Law of the Land." This means that federal law has authority over state law. The Constitution has authority over both.

 NGSSS Check List the five principles that guide the United States government. SS.7.C.1.9

_____

_____

ESSENTIAL QUESTION *Why do people create, structure, and change governments?*

Reflect on What It Means . . .

The Constitution is a living document. It was designed to be flexible to accommodate change. Think about what the Constitution means and how it is important to you, your community, and the world.

Blog About It!

Blog is short for "web log." A blog is an online journal where the owner of the blog can share thoughts about a topic. Visitors to the blog leave comments. Blogs can lead to fascinating discussions and a lot of learning.

Suppose you want to start blogging on your own blog. Write three blog entries about the Constitution, each of which has been started for you on the next page. Use this space below to jot down ideas before you write the blogs.

Keep Going! ➤

The U.S. Constitution is important to me...

The U.S. Constitution is important to my community...

The U.S. Constitution is important to the world...

TAKE THE CHALLENGE

Work with a teacher or another adult to find a real blog about the Constitution. What do you like about it? How is it alike or different from yours?

THE BILL OF RIGHTS

NGSSS

SS7.C.2.4 Evaluate rights contained in the Bill of Rights and other amendments to the Constitution.

SS.7.C.2.5 Distinguish how the Constitution safeguards and limits individual rights.

ESSENTIAL QUESTION *How do societies balance individual and community rights?*

Long before he was president, Thomas Jefferson was an outspoken supporter of personal freedom. Read this excerpt from a letter he wrote to a friend.

" . . .[W]ere it left to me to decide whether we should have a government without newspapers, or newspapers without a government, I should not hesitate a moment to prefer the latter. "

THOMAS JEFFERSON

hesitate
Write another word (synonym) for *hesitate* below.

_____
_____

latter
What might the term *latter* mean here?

_____
_____

DBQ BREAKING IT DOWN

Is Jefferson saying he would rather have government or newspapers? What is the relationship between government and newspapers?

_____
_____

Besides newspapers, where can you read the news today? List examples below.

_____
_____

McGraw-Hill
netw⦿rks™
There's More Online!

PHOTO: SuperStock/Getty Images

THE FIRST AMENDMENT

NGSSS

SS7.C.2.4 Evaluate rights contained in the Bill of Rights and other amendments to the Constitution.

SS.7.C.2.5 Distinguish how the Constitution safeguards and limits individual rights.

SS.7.C.3.6 Evaluate Constitutional rights and their impact on individuals and society

LESSON 1

Essential Question
How do societies balance individual and community rights?

Guiding Questions
1. Which individual rights are protected by the First Amendment?
2. Why are limits placed on individual rights?

Terms to Know

civil liberties
basic freedoms that all citizens have

free speech
the right to express ideas without fear of punishment by the government

censorship
telling the press what to print or broadcast

petition
a written request

slander
telling lies about someone

libel
printing lies about someone

It Matters Because

The rights granted under the First Amendment are among our most basic freedoms.

The basic freedoms described in the First Amendment are listed below. Which is most important to you today? Circle your answer below and then use the space provided to explain.

freedom of religion

freedom of assembly

freedom of speech

freedom to petition (to make a request of) government

freedom of the press

_____

_____

What Do You Know?

Directions: Read each statement. If you agree with the statement, circle the A. If you disagree with the statement, circle the D. Be ready to explain your choices.

Before You Read Agree/Disagree		Statement	After You Read Agree/Disagree	
A	D	1. The Florida Legislature can outlaw religious practices that voters don't like.	A	D
A	D	2. The police chief can have a person arrested for disagreeing with the government.	A	D
A	D	3. The editor of a major newspaper must obey the governor of Florida if the governor requests a news story to be shut down.	A	D
A	D	4. You have the right to send a letter to leaders in your government asking them to change a law you disagree with.	A	D

Guaranteeing Civil Liberties

The first 10 amendments to the Constitution are known as the Bill of Rights. The Bill of Rights lists the basic freedoms that all citizens of the United States have. These freedoms are also called **civil liberties.** "Civil" means relating to citizens. So civil liberties are those liberties relating to people. Protecting civil liberties is one of the most important parts of a democracy. Having civil liberties gives citizens the power to have their own beliefs. They also give citizens the power to express themselves to others and the government. The Bill of Rights states that the government may not take away our civil liberties.

The First Amendment in the Bill of Rights protects five basic freedoms.

1. Freedom of Religion The First Amendment protects religious freedom in two ways. It says that the government may not set up or support an official religion for the country. It also says that people are free to worship in any way they choose.

2. Freedom of Speech **Free speech** means being able to say what we think without fear of being punished by the government. The First Amendment gives us the right to express ideas even if they offend other people. Not all free speech is expressed in words. It also protects the right to express yourself in music, art, and dress.

3. Freedom of the Press "The press" means sources of news and information. It includes books, newspapers, and magazines. It also includes radio, television, and the Internet. The First Amendment forbids government **censorship** of the press. This means that the government cannot tell the press what it can or cannot print or broadcast. A free press is important in a democracy. It helps keep the government honest by telling the people about mistakes or misuse of power.

4. Freedom of Assembly This is the right to gather in groups. Meetings, parades, and protests are all forms of assembly. We have the right to assemble for any reason, as long as the assemblies are peaceful. We also have the right to associate with, or join, any group we want.

5. Freedom to petition the government A **petition** is a formal request. It may be a statement signed by many people. It may also be a simple letter from one person. A petition is a way to tell the government what you think.

Mark the Text

1. As you read this section, underline the five civil liberties protected by the First Amendment.

Show Your Skill

2. Identify the Main Idea What different kinds of media make up the press?

_____

_____

_____

_____

_____

Think Critically

3. Explain Why is a free press important to democracy?

_____

_____

_____

Think Critically

4. Contrast What is the difference between slander and libel?

_____

_____

_____

Show Your Skill

5. Make Inferences What do you think might happen if there were no limits on civil liberties?

_____

_____

_____

_____

_____

_____

Take the Challenge

6. With a small group, act out an example of limits on civil liberty to another small group. Have the other group members guess which limits you are showing.

These citizens in Miami peacefully protest the governor's budget proposals, a right that is guaranteed by the Constitution.

Limits on Civil Liberty

The First Amendment does not allow Americans to do and say whatever they want to. Each person's rights must be balanced against the rights of others. That means that acting on your rights should not harm others or the community. Communities also have rights. In order to protect the rights of everyone, the government places limits on our civil liberties.

For example, free speech gives you the right to criticize public figures. It does not give you the right to tell lies about them. Spreading lies is a crime. If the lies are spoken, the crime is called **slander.** If the lies are printed, the crime is called **libel.**

Other restrictions, or limits, on civil liberties protect public safety. For example, no one has the right to say or write anything that directly leads someone to commit a crime. Another example is that people have the right to march in protest, but not to riot.

People must use their civil liberties in a responsible way. That means respecting the rights of others. For example, you can listen to whatever music you want—but not so loud that you disturb your neighbors. When one person's rights come into conflict with the rights of the community, the community often comes first.

 NGSSS Check Identify two ways the Constitution limits individual rights.
SS.7.C.2.5

_____

_____

_____

PHOTO: Joe Raedle/Getty Images

NGSSS

SS.7.C.2.4 Evaluate rights contained in the Bill of rights and other amendments to the Constitution.

LESSON 2
OTHER BILL OF RIGHTS PROTECTIONS

Essential Question
How do societies balance individual and community rights?

Guiding Questions
1. How does the Bill of Rights protect the rights of the accused?
2. What other protections does the Bill of Rights offer?

Terms to Know

the accused
person(s) charged with a crime

search warrant
court order to search a suspect's property

probable cause
valid reason

due process
legal steps that must be followed

eminent domain
the government's power to take private property

indictment
formal charge by a grand jury

double jeopardy
being tried twice for the same crime

self-incrimination
testifying against oneself

bail
money that an accused person pays to remain free while waiting for a trial

It Matters Because

Other parts of the Bill of Rights provide important protections.

The Second Amendment of the Bill of Rights says that citizens have the right to "keep and bear arms." What do you think this means?

What Do You Know?

Directions: Use the table below to answer the questions based on what you know "Now." After the lesson, complete the "Later" column.

	Now	Later
What rights do people accused of a crime have?		
What is one way that the U.S. Constitution limits the power of the federal government?		

Show Your Skill

1. In your own words, define *due process.*

_____

_____

_____

_____

_____

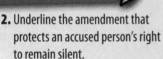

Mark the Text

2. Underline the amendment that protects an accused person's right to remain silent.

Rights of the Accused

An important part of democracy is protecting the rights of people accused of crimes. The Fourth, Fifth, Sixth, and Eighth Amendments protect the rights of the **accused**—people charged with crimes. These amendments guarantee their right to fair legal treatment.

The Fourth Amendment has to do with searches. It says that no law officer can search a person's home or property without a search warrant. A **search warrant** is a court order. It allows the police to search property to look for evidence from a crime. To get a search warrant, the police must convince a judge that they have **probable cause** to suspect a person of a crime. Probable cause means to have a valid reason.

The Fifth Amendment protects many rights. It protects every citizen's right to due process of the law. **Due process** refers to the legal steps that must be followed before the government can take away a person's life, freedom, or property. For example, the government cannot take a person's house without paying a fair price for it. The government has the power to take away property to be used for the public if it pays for the property. This power is called **eminent domain.** The Fifth Amendment limits this power.

The Fifth Amendment also says:

- No one can be tried for a serious crime without an indictment. An **indictment** is a formal charge from a grand jury. This is a group of citizens that looks at evidence to decide if a person may have carried out a crime.

- No one can be put on trial twice for the same crime. This is called **double jeopardy.**

- No one can be forced to testify against himself or herself. This is called **self-incrimination.**

These St. Petersburg police officers walk away after a shoot-out between a suspect and police who were serving a search warrant.

The Sixth Amendment guarantees other rights to accused persons.

- They must be told the charges against them.
- They must be allowed a speedy and fair trial.
- They have the right to a public trial by a jury, or to be tried by a judge if they wish.
- They have the right to hear, question, and call witnesses.
- They have the right to a lawyer.

The Eighth Amendment says that bail may not be set too high. **Bail** is a type of security deposit. It is money that an accused person pays to remain free while waiting for trial. The Eighth Amendment also forbids "cruel and unusual" punishment. The question of what punishments are cruel and unusual is a matter of debate.

Think Critically

3. Summarize What four rights are protected by the Sixth Amendment?

_____

_____

_____

_____

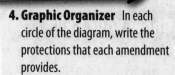

Mark the Text

4. Graphic Organizer In each circle of the diagram, write the protections that each amendment provides.

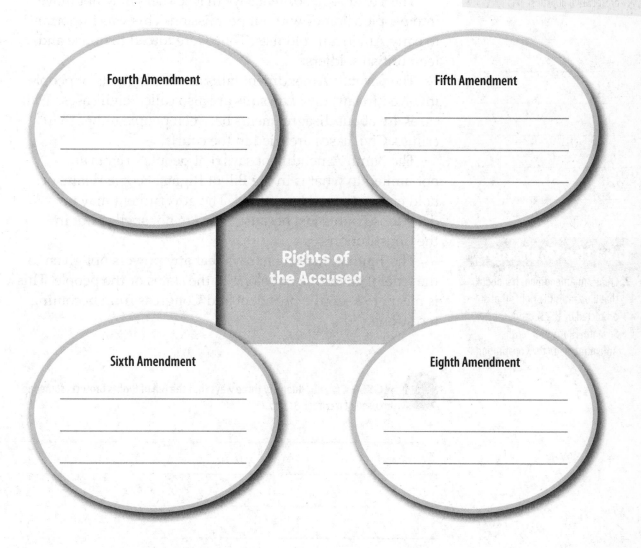

Fourth Amendment

_____

_____

_____

Fifth Amendment

_____

_____

_____

Rights of the Accused

Sixth Amendment

_____

_____

_____

Eighth Amendment

_____

_____

_____

5. Infer How have the courts interpreted the Second Amendment?

_____

_____

_____

_____

_____

6. Draw Conclusions In what way does the Ninth Amendment protect civil liberties?

_____

_____

_____

_____

_____

_____

7. Create an Amendment handbook that illustrates the rights that are protected by the Second, Third, Seventh, Ninth, and Tenth Amendments to the Constitution.

Additional Protections

The Second, Third, Seventh, Ninth, and Tenth Amendments protect other rights of American citizens.

The Second Amendment states that people have the right to "keep and bear arms." People do not agree about the exact meaning of that phrase. The courts have ruled that the government cannot stop people from owning guns. It can pass laws to control the way guns are licensed and sold.

Chief Judge Belvin Perry, Jr., speaks during a civil case at the Orange County Courthouse in Orlando.

The Third Amendment says that soldiers may not move into people's homes without permission. This was important to early American colonists. They were forced to house and feed British soldiers.

The Seventh Amendment talks about the rights of people involved in lawsuits. Lawsuits are also called civil cases. Civil cases are about disagreements between people rather than crimes. Civil cases are tried in the courts.

The Ninth Amendment says that people's rights are not limited to what is in the Bill of Rights. People retain, or hold on to, other rights as well. The government may not deny those rights just because they are not spelled out in the Constitution.

The Tenth Amendment says that any powers not given to the federal government belong to the states or the people. This is meant to keep the president and Congress from becoming too strong.

NGSSS Check Identify three ways that the Bill of Rights protects someone accused of a crime. SS.7.C.2.4

_____

_____

_____

_____

PHOTO: Red Huber/Orlando Sentinel/MCT via Getty Images

FURTHERING CIVIL LIBERTIES

NGSSS

SS7.C.2.4 Evaluate rights contained in the Bill of Rights and other amendments to the Constitution.

Essential Question

How do societies balance individual and community rights?

Guiding Questions

1. How were civil rights extended following the Civil War?
2. In what ways have twentieth-century amendments affected voting rights and changed the election process?

Terms to Know

black codes
state laws that limited the rights of African Americans

suffrage
the right to vote

poll tax
fee that is charged for voting

It Matters Because

Voting is the way the people in a democracy make their wishes known.

In the United States, elections are held to fill positions in local, state, and the national government. Does your school hold elections for student groups such as student council? Use the space below to brainstorm a list of current or past elected officials that you can recall.

National Government: **Local Government:**

Florida Government: **Your School:**

What Do You Know?

Directions: Use what you know to complete the paragraph below.

In a _____, leaders are elected by the

_____ and must answer to them. All genuine

democracies have free, fair, and competitive

_____. Everyone's _____ must

carry the same weight. This principle is often expressed

as "one person, one _____."

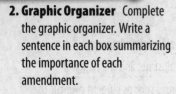

1. Draw Conclusions Why was the Fourteenth Amendment needed?

_____

_____

_____

_____

_____

_____

Mark the Text

2. Graphic Organizer Complete the graphic organizer. Write a sentence in each box summarizing the importance of each amendment.

Civil War Amendments

Before Reconstruction, the Bill of Rights was meant to protect citizens from the power of the federal government. It did not apply to state governments. Because of this, states could and often did pass laws that denied people's rights. For example, women and African Americans could not vote in most states. Slavery was legal in southern states. Enslaved African Americans had almost no rights at all and were often treated as property.

After the Civil War, three new amendments were added to the Constitution. They extended civil liberties to African Americans. The first was the Thirteenth Amendment. It made slavery illegal.

Though slavery was against the law, many states still would not give African Americans basic rights. Many southern states passed laws called **black codes.** Black codes put strict limits on where freed slaves could live and what jobs they could do. The Fourteenth Amendment was passed to protect the rights of the newly freed slaves.

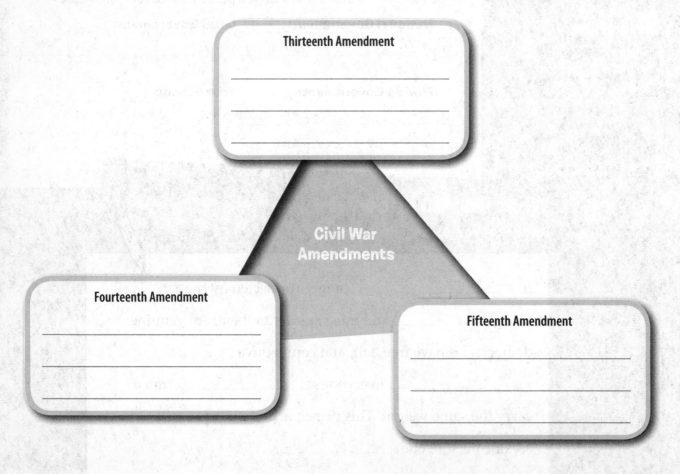

Thirteenth Amendment

_____

_____

_____

Civil War Amendments

Fourteenth Amendment

_____

_____

_____

Fifteenth Amendment

_____

_____

_____

The Fourteenth Amendment struck down the black codes. It said that all people "born or naturalized in the United States" were citizens. That included most African Americans. It said the states had to give all citizens "equal protection of the laws." It also said that the states must guarantee due process to all citizens.

Since that time, the "equal protection" part of the Fourteenth Amendment has helped women and other groups gain equal rights. The Supreme Court has also said that the "due process" part of the amendment makes the Bill of Rights binding on the states. This is known as the incorporation doctrine. It means that American citizens in every state have the same basic rights.

The last Civil War amendment was the Fifteenth Amendment. It extended **suffrage,** or the right to vote, to African Americans. However, it applied only to men. State laws still kept women from voting in most elections until 1920.

Electoral Process and Voting Rights

The Constitution was amended several more times in the 1900s. Some new amendments extended the right to vote to more people. Others changed the way we elect government leaders. These changes helped put more power in the hands of the people.

The Seventeenth Amendment changed the way U.S. senators are chosen. It was passed in 1913. Until then, members of the Senate were chosen by the legislatures of their states. The Seventeenth Amendment allowed people to elect their senators directly.

In Coral Gables, supporters rally for Democratic presidential hopeful Senator Hillary Clinton during a campaign stop on May 21, 2008.

PHOTO: Joe Raedle/Getty Images

Copyright © by The McGraw-Hill Companies, Inc.

5. Explain What groups gained the right to vote by constitutional amendment in the 1900s?

_____

_____

_____

Mark the Text

6. Chart For each amendment, check the column that shows whether it extended voting rights or changed the electoral process.

Take the Challenge

7. Write a proposal for a new amendment that would affect voting rights or the electoral process.

The Nineteenth Amendment gave women the right to vote. The question of woman suffrage had always been left up to the states. Most states did not allow it. This changed in 1920 when the Nineteenth Amendment passed. It gives women the right to vote in all elections.

The Twenty-third Amendment was added in 1961. It gave voting rights to people living in Washington, D.C. "D.C." stands for the District of Columbia. Because this area is not part of any state, its residents could not vote in national elections. The Twenty-third Amendment gave them the right to vote for president and vice-president. But even today they do not have representatives in Congress.

The Twenty-fourth Amendment was added in 1964. It eliminated **poll taxes.** A poll tax is a fee that is charged for voting. Southern states used poll taxes to keep poor people from voting. This kept most African Americans away from the polls. It also affected poor whites.

In 1971 the Twenty-sixth Amendment lowered the voting age to 18 years of age. Before then, most states had set the minimum age for voting at 21.

	Voting Rights	Electoral Process
17th Amendment		X
19th Amendment		
23rd Amendment		
24th Amendment		
26th Amendment		

NGSSS Check Name two ways that the Civil War amendments added to individual freedoms. SS.7.C.2.4

_____

_____

_____

_____

MY REFLECTIONS

ESSENTIAL QUESTION *How do communities balance individual and community rights?*

Reflect on What It Means . . .

Communities often have to balance their needs with those of individuals in the community. For example, if a community wants to build a library on land that is already being used for a park, it may upset some people in the community.

Search newspapers, magazines, or news Web sites for stories that relate to what you have learned about individual and community rights.

To My Community

Find a headline about an event in your community or another community in Florida. The event should relate to balancing individual or community rights. Write the headline below, or cut it out of the newspaper or a magazine and paste it below.

To the World

Find a headline about individual or community rights in a different country. Write it below, or cut it out of a newspaper or magazine and paste it below.

Keep Going! ➤

What It Means To Me

How has the need to balance individual and community rights affected you? Use the space below to write a news headline about your own life that shows how you balance your rights with the rights of those around you. Then, write a short news story that describes the event in more detail.

TAKE THE CHALLENGE

As a class, create the front page of a newspaper or news Web site that combines the best headlines you found on your own. Give your newspaper or site a name. Publish it on your teacher's Web site or blog.

THE LEGISLATIVE BRANCH

NGSSS

SS.7.C.3.8 Analyze the structure, functions, and processes of the legislative, executive, and judicial branches.

ESSENTIAL QUESTION *Why do people create, structure, and change governments?*

The Constitution requires that top government officials "shall be bound by oath or affirmation, to support this Constitution." This is the oath that members of Congress take:

" I, [name], do solemnly swear (or affirm) that I will support and defend the Constitution of the United States against all enemies, foreign and domestic; that I will bear true faith and allegiance to the same; . . . and that I will well and faithfully discharge the duties of the office on which I am about to enter. So help me God. "

—OATH OF OFFICE, U.S. HOUSE OR SENATE

support and defend

In what ways do you think members of Congress might support and defend the U.S. Constitution?

_____

_____

_____

bear true faith and allegiance

Does this mean the same thing as *swearing to* or *affirming* something?

_____

DBQ BREAKING IT DOWN

Who might be a foreign enemy of the Constitution? Who might be a domestic enemy?

_____

_____

_____

Would you be willing to take this oath? Why or why not?

_____

_____

_____

McGraw-Hill
networks™
There's More Online!

PHOTO: Scott J. Ferrell/Congressional Quarterly/Alamy

NGSSS

SS.7.C.3.3 Illustrate the structure and function (three branches of government established in Articles I, II, and III with corresponding powers) of government in the United States as established in the Constitution.

SS.7.C.3.8 Analyze the structure, functions, and processes of the legislative, executive, and judicial branches.

STRUCTURE OF CONGRESS

Essential Question

Why do people create, structure, and change governments?

Guiding Questions

1. Why is Congress composed of a House of Representatives and a Senate?
2. Why are members of Congress assigned to work on committees?

Terms to Know

Senate
the upper house of the United States Congress

House of Representatives
the lower house of the United States Congress

constituent
a voter that a member of Congress represents

census
a count of the population

gerrymander
to draw congressional district lines to favor one party

majority party
party that holds the most seats

minority party
party that does not hold the majority

seniority
years of service

It Matters Because

Congress makes the federal laws that affect all Americans.

You are not old enough to exercise your right to vote. Yet Congress still takes actions that affect your life today and the world you will live in as an adult. What would you want Congress to know about your hopes for the future? What do you want Congress to do to make your future better? Write your responses below.

What Do You Know?

Directions: Use the table below to answer the questions based on what you know now in the "Now" column. After the lesson, complete the table by writing the answers in the "Later" column.

Now		Later
	How big is Congress?	
	How does Congress do its work?	

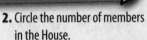 **network** Read Chapter 7 Lesson 1 in your textbook or online.

The Two Houses of Congress

Article I of the Constitution describes the United States Congress. It says that Congress should have two parts. These parts are called the Senate and the House of Representatives. The **Senate** has equal representation, two senators for each state. The **House of Representatives** has proportional representation. Each state has one or more representatives, depending on its population.

Each member of Congress is elected by his or her **constituents** to make laws for the country. A constituent (kuhn•STIHCH•wuhnt) is a person represented by a legislator.

Members of Congress gather in the U.S. Capitol, in Washington, D.C. A Congress lasts for a term, or period of time, of two years. Each Congress is numbered. The First Congress met from 1789 to 1791, and the 112th Congress met from 2011 to 2013.

Each term of Congress is divided into two meetings called sessions. A joint session occurs when the House and Senate meet together. Congress may also hold a special session during a crisis.

Today, there are 435 members in the House of Representatives. The number of representatives for each state is based on how many people live in that state. To find this number, a **census,** or population count, is taken every ten years. Congress uses the count to adjust the number of representatives each state has in the House.

Representatives serve for two years. They can be reelected at the end of that time and can serve an unlimited number of terms.

Think Critically

1. Contrast How is representation in the House and Senate different?

_____

_____

_____

Mark the Text

2. Circle the number of members in the House.

Show Your Skill

3. Draw Conclusions Why do you think a senator serves a longer term than a representative?

_____

_____

_____

_____

In Immokalee, Florida, a 2010 census worker records data from a local family.

Think Critically

5. Why do you think the Speaker of the House is next in line to become president in the event of the death of both the president and vice president?

_____

_____

_____

Take the Challenge

6. Draw an example of gerrymandering, using the political cartoon in your textbook as a model. Be creative. Think of a different way to illustrate the term.

Each state is divided into congressional districts. One representative is elected from each district. The law says that each district must include about the same number of voters. Sometimes state lawmakers **gerrymander** districts, however. That means the district lines are drawn to help one party gain voting strength. If most of a state's representatives are Republican, they can draw the lines to make oddly shaped districts that have more Republican than Democratic voters.

There are 100 members, two from each of the 50 states, in the Senate. Each senator represents the entire state, not just one district. Senators serve a six-year term. Like representatives, they can be reelected when their term ends.

In both the House and the Senate, the **majority party** is the party that holds more than half of the seats. The other party is called the **minority party.**

When a term begins, the House and the Senate each choose leaders. The table below shows the most important leaders in Congress.

Congressional Leaders	
House of Representatives	**Senate**
Speaker of the House	President of the Senate president pro tempore
Majority floor leader Minority floor leader Party whips	Majority floor leader Minority floor leader Party whips

The Speaker of the House has great power. She or he leads House sessions and heads the majority party. The Speaker also guides proposed laws through the House and leads debates. If anything happens to both the president and vice president, the Speaker is next in line to become president.

The Senate does not have a Speaker. The vice president of the United States has the title of President of the Senate. He or she can only vote to break a tie, however.

The president pro tempore (proh•TEHM•puh•ree) leads the Senate when the vice president is absent. He or she is from the majority party and is usually the member who has served the longest. _Pro tempore_ means "for now."

Other powerful leaders are the floor leaders. They play a large role in getting bills, or drafts of new laws, passed. The majority and minority floor leaders in each house push bills along and try to win votes.

Party "whips," or assistant leaders, help the floor leaders. They make sure legislators are present for key votes.

The Committee System

In each session, Congress looks at thousands of bills. It is a huge job. To make it easier, the work is shared between many small groups called committees. Committees do most of the work of Congress. The table below shows the three types of committees in Congress.

Types of Committees	
Type	**Definition**
standing committee	a permanent committee, such as those dealing with agriculture, commerce, and veterans' affairs
select committee	a temporary committee that deals with special issues; meets until it completes the assigned task
joint committee	a committee that includes members of both houses; meets to work on specific problems

Newly elected senators and representatives try to get put on committees that are important to the people they serve. Senators from a farming area might want to be on the agriculture committee. Those who have many factories in their districts might want to be on the labor committee.

Party leaders decide who should be on which committee. They look at members' preferences and skills. They also look at **seniority,** or years of service. Members who have served the longest usually get to sit on the most interesting committees.

The longest-serving majority committee member usually becomes the chairperson. The committee chairperson has an important job with a lot of power. Chairpersons decide when and if a committee will meet. They also decide what bills will be studied and who will serve on which subcommittees. The longest-serving committee member from the minority party leads the members of that party. He or she is called the ranking minority member.

 NGSSS Check Explain the structure and function of Congress. **SS.7.C.3.8**

_____

_____

_____

7. Analyze Which type of committee would be formed to investigate possible causes of the financial crisis in 2008?

_____

_____

Show Your Skill

8. Interpret Charts What are the three types of committees?

_____

_____

_____

 Mark the Text

9. Underline the factors that affect a member's placement on a committee.

2 POWERS OF CONGRESS

NGSSS

SS.7.C.3.3 Illustrate the structure and function (three branches of government established in Articles I, II, and III with corresponding powers) of government in the United States as established in the Constitution.

SS.7.C.3.8 Analyze the structure, functions, and processes of the legislative, executive, and judicial branches.

Essential Question

Why do people create, structure, and change governments?

Guiding Questions

1. What kinds of lawmaking powers were given to Congress by the Constitution?
2. What powers does Congress have to check the powers of the other branches of government?

Terms to Know

expressed power
a power of Congress that is listed in the Constitution

enumerated power
another name for a power of Congress that is listed in the Constitution

implied power
a power of Congress that the expressed powers point to

elastic clause
part of the Constitution that says Congress has implied powers

nonlegislative power
a power that is not related to making laws

impeach
to accuse of wrongdoing

writ of habeas corpus
an order that makes sure prisoners are told why they are being held

bill of attainder
a law that punishes a person without a trial

ex post facto law
a law that makes an act a crime after the act has been committed

It Matters Because

The Framers gave Congress many powers and also placed some limits on those powers.

The three branches of government share power. Sometimes that is no easy task.

When have you seen people share power in your family, school, or an organization?

Was it easy or not? Write your responses below.

What Do You Know?

Directions: Circle the powers that you think Congress has from the list below. At the end of the lesson, go back and check your work. Cross out the answers that are incorrect. Circle the jobs and powers that you learned about.

raise and spend money   **declare war**

interpret laws   **maintain the armed forces**

regulate commerce   **create a postal service**

Legislative Powers

The Constitution gave Congress the power to make laws for the United States government. It gave Congress other duties such as the power to coin money and regulate, or manage commerce. Commerce is the buying and selling of goods. All of Congress's duties that are actually listed in the Constitution are called **expressed powers** or **enumerated powers.** In Article I, Section 8, Clause 18, the Constitution also says that Congress has **implied powers.** These are powers that are not written in the Constitution. Instead they are implied, or pointed to, by the expressed powers. They are things that Congress needs to do to carry out its expressed powers.

Clause 18 is also called the **elastic clause.** It allows Congress to stretch its powers or do whatever is "necessary and proper" to use its expressed powers. For example, the Constitution does not say that Congress can create an air force. However, the elastic clause lets Congress do so as part of its expressed power to support an army and a navy.

Congress has many expressed and implied powers. The graphic organizer below lists some of these powers.

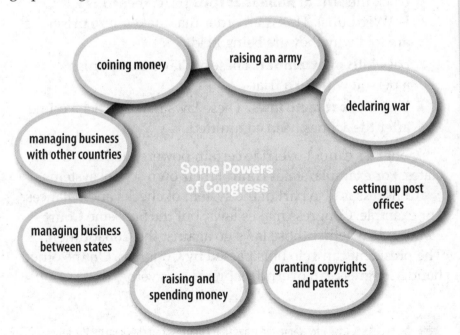

coining money

raising an army

declaring war

managing business with other countries

Some Powers of Congress

setting up post offices

managing business between states

raising and spending money

granting copyrights and patents

Other Powers and Limits

The most important job of Congress is to make laws, but it also has other duties. To do these other jobs, Congress has **nonlegislative powers.** The most important nonlegislative powers are the ones that allow Congress to check other

Think Critically

1. Contrast What is the difference between expressed and implied powers?

_____

_____

_____

_____

_____

Show Your Skill

2. Make Inferences Why is the "necessary and proper" clause also called the elastic clause?

_____

_____

_____

_____

_____

3. Interpret Charts List examples from the powers of Congress that relate to the nation's economy.

_____

_____

_____

_____

_____

_____

_____

_____

5. Summarize How does the Supreme Court check the powers of Congress?

_____

_____

_____

6. Analyze Why do you think the Constitution forbids Congress from passing ex post facto laws?

_____

_____

_____

_____

_____

_____

_____

branches of the government. Some nonlegislative powers include suggesting amendments to the Constitution, and approving or rejecting the president's choices for Supreme Court justices, federal judges, and ambassadors. The Senate also has the power to impeach federal officials.

To **impeach** means to accuse a person of doing something wrong. The House may impeach any federal official, even the president. The Senate then decides whether that person is guilty. If two-thirds of senators agree the official is guilty, they must leave office.

Only two presidents have ever been impeached. They were Andrew Johnson in 1868 and Bill Clinton in 1998. The Senate did not find them guilty so they were not removed from office.

The Constitution also lists the things that Congress may not do. Congress may not

- pass laws that go against the Constitution. A law that does not allow freedom of religion would go against the Constitution, for example.
- favor one state over another.
- tax exports.
- tax business between states.
- block the **writ of habeas corpus** (HAY•bee•uhs KAWR•puhs). This is an order that makes sure prisoners are told why they are being held.
- pass **bills of attainder.** These are laws that punish a person without a trial.
- pass **ex post facto laws.** These laws make an act a crime after the act has been committed.

Congress cannot override certain powers set aside for the states. For example, states control their own school systems.

Congress is also part of the system of checks and balances. For example, Congress makes laws, but the Supreme Court can decide whether those laws go against the Constitution. The president can veto bills passed by Congress. On the other hand, Congress can override a president's veto.

NGSSS Check Name the ways that Congress can check up on the other branches of government. SS.7.C.3.8

_____

_____

_____

_____

3 HOW CONGRESS WORKS

NGSSS

SS.7.C.3.3 Illustrate the structure and function (three branches of government established in Articles I, II, and III with corresponding powers) of government in the United States as established in the Constitution.

SS.7.C.3.8 Analyze the structure, functions, and processes of the legislative, executive, and judicial branches.

Essential Question
Why do people create, structure, and change governments?

Guiding Questions
1. What are the qualifications for becoming a member of Congress?
2. How do members of Congress exercise their responsibilities?

Terms to Know

franking privilege
the special right members of Congress have to send job-related mail without paying postage

lobbyist
a person hired to influence government decisions

casework
the work of helping people deal with the federal government

pork-barrel project
when a representative gets government money for projects in one district or state

It Matters Because

In making laws, Congress makes decisions that affect all Americans.

There are rules for who can become a member of Congress. But what are the traits that you think a person who wants to become a member of Congress should have? Which of those traits do you have? Write your responses below.

_____

_____

_____

_____

_____

What Do You Know?

Directions: Use what you know to complete the paragraph below.

The main job of Congress is to _____ laws. They also make sure that states and districts

get _____ from the federal government to pay for highways, dams, and military bases.

Members of Congress try to get _____ to make public officials aware of their needs.

Think Critically

1. **Evaluate** Do you think that the requirements for becoming a member of Congress are too strict? Explain your answer.

Show Your Skill

2. **Draw Conclusions** Why might the franking privilege help a member of Congress get reelected?

3. **Make Inferences** Based on what you know about congressional members' personal staff, who might help a representative with their casework?

Take the Challenge

4. Write a page for a day planner for a personal staff member. Include the tasks that person might do for the day.

networks™ Read Chapter 7 Lesson 3 in your textbook or online.

Qualifications and Staffing

To become a member of Congress, a person must meet certain requirements. These requirements are listed in the Constitution. They are different for members of the House and Senate. The chart below shows what they are.

Qualifications for Congress		
	Senate	House
Age	30 years old	25 years old
Residency	Live in the state you plan to represent	Live in the state you plan to represent
U.S. Citizenship	9 years	7 years

Once a person is elected to Congress, he or she has many benefits. In addition to their salary, representatives and senators also enjoy free office space, free parking, and free trips home. They receive the **franking privilege,** which means that members can send job-related mail at no cost.

Members of Congress also have immunity, or legal protection in certain situations. This is not meant to allow members of Congress to break the law. It allows them to debate and talk freely without fear.

Members of Congress have a huge workload. To get everything done, they hire people to help. They are the members' personal staff. These workers include clerks, secretaries, and special assistants.

Personal staffs work both in Washington and in the congressperson's home state. They answer questions from voters and help them deal with federal government agencies. They also research bills and talk to reporters. Another job of staff members is to meet with lobbyists. **Lobbyists** are people who represent interest groups. They contact government officials to try to influence, or shape, their policy making.

Some assistants are students. They are usually from the member's district and volunteer their time. They get to learn about Congress as they help with research, deliver messages, and do other office tasks.

Committee staff members are assistants who help keep committee work running smoothly. They schedule committee hearings. They draft, or outline, bills.

Congress also has several agencies to help with its work. These agencies include the Library of Congress, the Government Accountability Office (GAO), and the Congressional Budget Office (CBO).

The Library of Congress has a copy of every book published in the United States. Members of Congress and their staffs use these books for research. The GAO looks at federal programs and suggests ways to improve how the government spends money. The CBO helps plan the nation's budget. When Congress or the president has an idea for a new program, this office estimates, or tries to figure out, how much the program will cost.

Congress at Work

The best-known job of Congress is to make laws. That is why members of Congress are called "lawmakers." But our lawmakers also do other work. A great deal of time is spent on **casework,** or helping people deal with the federal government. Members of Congress get many requests from the voters. Voters ask for help with all sorts of things, from understanding laws to finding a late Social Security check.

Staff members spend hours each day on casework. If they cannot find answers or get results, the senator or representative will step in. Lawmakers want to help people. That is one reason they ran for office. They also know that casework does other good things, such as helping them build public support for reelection; allowing them to check up on how well the executive branch handles programs like Social Security; and providing help to citizens dealing with government agencies.

Mark the Text

6. Underline the kind of work that probably takes most of the time of a member of Congress. Circle the reason why lawmakers work so hard on casework.

Each year, Congress authorizes money to be spent on a variety of programs such as Social Security. When voters have questions about these programs, they may ask their senator or representative for help.

7. Evaluate Do you think pork-barrel projects are a good idea? Or should such projects be distributed evenly among states and districts?

_____

_____

_____

_____

_____

_____

8. Write an email to a member of Congress about an issue that you think is important and that you think he or she can help solve.

Members of Congress may meet with lobbyists, like these men here, to discuss how public works money is spent.

Members of Congress have another important job. They try to make sure that their state or district gets a fair share of federal money. This public works money is spent on projects such as highways, dams, and military bases. These projects create jobs and boost the local economy.

Executive branch agencies decide where federal money goes. But members of Congress try to sway those decisions. They also ask the voters to tell agency officials about their needs.

When a representative gets federal money mainly for one district or state, it is called a **pork-barrel project.** To understand this term, think of members of Congress dipping into the "pork barrel" (federal treasury, or money) and pulling out a piece of "fat" (a federal project for his or her district). Critics say that this is a waste of taxpayers' money. Lawmakers do not believe that bringing money to their state is doing anything wrong.

 NGSSS Check Explain what members of Congress do as part of their job. **SS.7.C.3.8**

_____

_____

_____

_____

HOW A BILL BECOMES A LAW

NGSSS

SS.7.C.3.9 Illustrate the law making process at the local, state, and federal levels.

Essential Question
Why do people create, structure, and change governments?

Guiding Questions
1. What kinds of bills come before Congress?
2. How does a bill become a law?

Terms to Know

joint resolution
a resolution passed by both houses of Congress that has the force of law if signed by the president

special-interest group
a group of people who work together for a common cause

rider
amendment to a bill that is unrelated to the subject matter of the bill

filibuster
to talk a bill to death

cloture
a vote by three-fifths of the Senate to limit debate on a bill

voice vote
a vote in which members speak their votes aloud

standing vote
a vote in which members stand to be counted for or against a bill

roll-call vote
a vote in the Senate in which senators give their vote as their name is called

pocket veto
the president does nothing to a bill for ten days. If Congress is not in session the bill is killed, if Congress is in session the bill is passed

It Matters Because

The process Congress follows to make laws is complex.

What bill would you want Congress to pass? What would the law do for your community, state, or the nation? Write your responses below.

_____

_____

_____

What Do You Know?

Directions: Sort the words below using these 3 categories: Private Bill, Public Bill, and Resolutions.

constitutional amendment   personal claim

designate money for something   taxation

farm policy   highway building

Private Bill	Public Bill	Resolutions

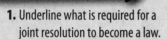
Types of Bills

During each term of Congress, more than 10,000 bills are often proposed. Only a few hundred of them actually become laws. This should tell you that it is not easy to pass a law!

There are two categories, or kinds, of bills. One is called a private bill. A private bill deals with one person or place. The other type of bill is called a public bill. It applies to the whole nation. A bill about taxes would be a public bill.

Congress also considers resolutions. These are formal statements stating lawmakers' opinions or decisions. Many resolutions do not have the power of law. A **joint resolution** is an exception, however. This type of resolution must pass both houses of Congress. If the president signs the resolution, it becomes a law. Joint resolutions can be used to propose amendments to the Constitution. They can also be used to fund special projects like natural disaster aid.

Think Critically

2. Analyze Why do you think that only a member of Congress can introduce a law?

_____

_____

_____

Take the Challenge

3. With a small group, introduce a bill and follow the steps in the lawmaking process.

From Bill to Law

Every bill starts with an idea. Ideas for bills come from citizens, the president, and special-interest groups. A **special-interest group** is a group of people who work together for a common cause.

Only a member of Congress can introduce a bill. When a bill is first read, it is given a title and a number. These show which house proposed the bill and when it was introduced. The first bill in the Senate is labeled S.1. The first bill in the House is labeled H.R.1.

PHOTO: Matthew Cavanaugh/epa/Corbis

Senators Mitch McConnell and John Warner speak to reporters about legislation that is important to citizens and special-interest groups.

These protesters hold a counter-filibuster demonstration for proposed legislation to set a time table to withdraw U.S. troops from Iraq.

Next, the bill is sent to the correct standing committee. The committee decides if the bill should be passed on to the full House or Senate for a vote. The committee can take five actions on the bill:

- pass the bill
- make changes in the bill and suggest that it be passed
- replace it with a new bill on the same subject
- ignore the bill and let it die, also called "pigeonholing"
- kill the bill by a majority vote

If a bill makes it through committee, it will be debated by the full House or Senate. Members will argue its pros and cons and amendments will be considered. The House allows amendments only if they are directly related to the subject of the bill. The Senate allows its members to attach **riders,** or completely unrelated amendments, to a bill.

In the House, there is a time limit set for how long a representative can talk about a bill. This limit is necessary because the House has so many members. Senators, however, can speak for as long as they wish. Senators sometimes use this freedom to **filibuster** a bill. Filibuster means to talk a bill to death. Senators can stop a filibuster with cloture. **Cloture** (KLOH•chuhr) is when three-fifths of the members vote to limit debate to one hour for each speaker.

After debate, it is time to vote. A majority of members must vote for a bill for it to pass. The chart on the next page shows the different ways votes are taken in each house.

Think Critically

4. Outline What four main steps are involved in passing a bill in Congress?

_____

_____

_____

_____

5. Analyze Why do you think senators attach riders to bills?

_____

_____

_____

_____

_____

_____

6. Summarize What is a conference committee?

_____

_____

_____

_____

Mark the Text

7. Chart Circle the kind of vote in which members of Congress respond verbally with their vote.

Show Your Skill

8. Make Inferences Why do you think that the lawmaking process allows the president to veto or ignore the bill even thought it has been approved by both houses of Congress?

_____

_____

_____

_____

_____

_____

Mark the Text

9. Underline the text that explains what can override a president's veto.

Voting in Congress	
House	Senate
voice vote —members say "Yea" or "No" to a bill	
standing vote—members stand to be counted for or against a bill	
recorded vote—members' votes are recorded electronically	**roll-call vote** —senators say "Aye" or "No" as their names are called

If a bill passes in one house, it is sent to the other. If a bill is defeated in either house, it dies. If both houses pass a different form of the same bill, a conference committee is formed. In this committee, members of both houses come up with one bill that everyone can agree on.

The approved bill is then sent to the president. The president can do one of three things:

1. sign the bill into law

2. veto, or refuse to sign, the bill

3. ignore the bill

An ignored bill becomes law after ten days if Congress is in session. If Congress has adjourned, the bill dies. This is called a **pocket veto.**

Congress can pass a bill over a president's veto. To do so, two-thirds of each house must vote to override the veto. This does not happen very often.

NGSSS Check Name four things that could happen to a bill when it goes to a committee for study. SS.7.C.3.9

_____

_____

_____

_____

_____

CHAPTER 7

MY REFLECTIONS

ESSENTIAL QUESTION *Why do people create, structure, and change governments?*

Reflect on What It Means . . .

Congress has a vital role in our country's lawmaking process. Yet members of Congress have many other jobs that are important to their constituents.

Plan a Web site!

Suppose you are an assistant to a senator from your state. Your latest assignment: plan a Web site that emphasizes the importance of Congress.

Your boss tells you, "I want to make sure people know why Congress is important to the community, and even to the entire world. I also want them to know that Congress is important to individuals. Use yourself as an example."

Use the planning chart below for your Web site. Fill in each box with words and ideas. If you need more space to write, use another piece of paper.

The Importance of Congress

To Me	To the Community	To the World

Keep Going!

Use the space below to sketch out the page for the Web site. Use the information from the planner on the previous page to help you.

TAKE THE CHALLENGE

Find the Web site for one of your senators or a representative. Challenge a representative to answer a tough question about your community. Maybe you would like to know what is being done to make schools better. Or perhaps you will want to demand that action is taken to improve the environment. Share your challenge—and the response from Washington—with the class.

THE EXECUTIVE BRANCH

NGSSS

SS.7.C.3.3 Illustrate the structure and function (three branches of government established in Articles I, II, and III with corresponding powers) of government in the United States as established in the Constitution.

SS.7.C.3.8 Analyze the structure, functions, and processes of the legislative, executive, and judicial branches.

ESSENTIAL QUESTION • *What is required of leaders?* • *Why do nations interact with each other?*

Barack Obama was inaugurated as the forty-fourth president of the United States on January 20, 2009. In his Inaugural Address, he called on Americans to face the challenges of that time.

> " What is required of us now is a new era of responsibility—a recognition on the part of every American that we have duties to ourselves, our nation and the world ; duties that we do not grudgingly accept , but rather seize gladly, firm in the knowledge that there is nothing so satisfying to the spirit, so defining of our character than giving our all to a difficult task. "
>
> BARACK OBAMA

grudgingly accept

What two-word phrase does Obama use that means the opposite of this one?

_____

duties to ourselves, our nation and the world

What might one such duty be?

_____

_____

DBQ BREAKING IT DOWN

When Obama refers to "our character," whose character is he referring to?

_____

_____

_____

Do you think it is "satisfying to the spirit" to give your all to a difficult task? Explain.

_____

_____

_____

PHOTO: REUTERS/Jason Reed/Corbis

THE PRESIDENT AND VICE PRESIDENT

NGSSS

SS.7.C.3.3 Illustrate the structure and function (three branches of government established in Articles I, II, and III with corresponding powers) of government in the United States as established in the Constitution.

SS.7.C.3.8 Analyze the structure, functions, and processes of the legislative, executive, and judicial branches.

Essential Question
What is required of leaders?

Guiding Questions
1. How does a citizen become president?
2. What happens if the president must step down from office?

Terms to Know

elector
member of the Electoral College that chooses the president

It Matters Because

The president and vice president are the only leaders elected by the entire nation.

The president is often seen as the "face" of the United States by the rest of the world. Which of these traits would you most want the world to see when they see our president?

Strength **Caring** **Honesty** **Intelligence**

Openness **Creativity** **Determination**

Why did you select that trait as most important?

_____

_____

What Do You Know?

Directions: In the first column, answer the questions based on what you know before you study. After this lesson, complete the last column.

Before the lesson		After the lesson
	Can any U.S. citizen be president?	
	Can the president be replaced before the end of a term?	

Office of the President

The president of the United States heads the executive branch of the national government. Because of America's strong influence in the world, the president may hold the world's most important job.

The Constitution lists three rules about who can become president. A person must be at least 35 years old and have been born in the United States. He or she must also have lived in the country for at least 14 years.

Most past presidents have been white male Protestants from states with large populations. In the past 60 years, candidates from a wider group of Americans have had a chance to be elected. In 1960, John F. Kennedy became the first Roman Catholic elected as president. In 2008, Barack Obama became the first African American president. In addition, two women have run for vice president with a major party, Geraldine Ferraro and Sarah Palin.

The election for president is held every four years. The people, however, do not directly choose the president. A group called the Electoral College elects him or her. When people vote for a president, they are actually choosing **electors.** Electors are members of the Electoral College who are selected to vote for presidential candidates in elections. The electors meet to vote for the president in December of the election year.

1. Infer Name three states with large populations.

_____

_____

_____

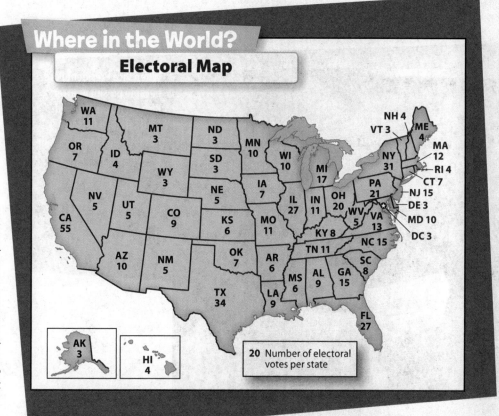

Where in the World?

Electoral Map

WA 11
OR 7
ID 4
MT 3
ND 3
SD 3
MN 10
WI 10
MI 17
NH 4
VT 3
ME 4
NY 31
MA 12
RI 4
CT 7
NJ 15
PA 21
NV 5
UT 5
WY 3
NE 5
IA 7
IL 27
IN 11
OH 20
WV 5
VA 13
DE 3
MD 10
DC 3
CA 55
CO 9
KS 6
MO 11
KY 8
NC 15
AZ 10
NM 5
OK 7
AR 6
TN 11
SC 8
MS 6
AL 9
GA 15
TX 34
LA 9
FL 27

AK 3
HI 4

20 Number of electoral votes per state

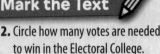

Mark the Text

2. Circle how many votes are needed to win in the Electoral College.

Show Your Skill

3. Draw Conclusions Why did Congress pass the Twenty-second Amendment?

_____

_____

There are 538 electors in the Electoral College. Each state has the same number of electors as it has members of Congress. In most states, the candidate who gets more than half of the people's votes wins all of that state's electoral votes. This is true even if the candidate wins by only a few votes. So a small number of votes can make a big difference in the outcome, or result, of an election.

To win the election, a person must get at least half of the 538 electoral votes. This means the person must get at least 270 votes. If no one person gets 270 votes, the House of Representatives must decide the election. This has only happened twice, in 1800 and in 1824. If the House votes, each state has only one vote.

The president serves a four-year term. At first, the Constitution did not limit the number of terms a president could serve. George Washington served for two terms. He set an example by refusing to run for a third term. Many years later, Franklin Roosevelt ran for president four times. He won all four elections.

Many people worried that if the number of presidential terms were not limited then one person could become too powerful. So Congress passed the Twenty-second Amendment. It was ratified in 1951. It said that a president could only serve two terms in office.

The Electoral College also chooses the vice president. The rules for becoming vice president are the same as those for the president.

When Vice President Ford became president after Richard Nixon resigned, Ford selected Nelson Rockefeller as vice president.

PHOTO: Bettman/CORNIS   Copyright © by The McGraw-Hill Companies, Inc.

The Constitution does not give the vice president much power. It says that the vice president will lead the Senate but can only vote to break a tie. The Twenty-fifth Amendment states that the vice president becomes president if the president dies, is removed from office, falls seriously ill, or resigns.

Presidential Succession

President William Henry Harrison was elected in 1840 and died in 1841. He was the first president to die in office. The Constitution says that the vice president should take on "the powers and duties" of the presidency. But no one was sure what that meant. Should the vice president stay in office as the vice president but do the president's job? Vice President John Tyler decided that he should declare himself president and take the oath of office. Then he served out the rest of Harrison's term.

In 1947, Congress passed a law called the Presidential Succession Act. *Succession* means "to follow." The law spelled out who would become president and in what order. The vice president is first, followed by the Speaker of the House, and then the president *pro tempore* of the Senate. If none of these three people can serve, the job falls to the secretary of state. The list provides 18 possible replacements for the president. The chart below displays, or shows, the first ten.

Order of Succession	
1	Vice President
2	Speaker of the House
3	President *pro tempore* of the Senate
4	Secretary of State
5	Secretary of the Treasury
6	Secretary of Defense
7	Attorney General
8	Secretary of the Interior
9	Secretary of Agriculture
10	Secretary of Commerce

Show Your Skill

4. Interpret Charts Which officer becomes president if the vice president, Speaker of the House, and president pro tempore are unable to serve?

____

____

Take the Challenge

5. What might happen if no succession plan existed? Draw a four-panel cartoon about what could happen without a succession plan.

6. Explain What problem with the vice presidency was the Twenty-fifth Amendment meant to solve?

_____

_____

_____

_____

In 1967, Congress passed the Twenty-fifth Amendment. This amendment gives the procedures to be followed if it becomes necessary for the vice president to assume the president's job. It also solved another problem. In the past, when a vice president became president, the office of vice president was left empty. The Twenty-fifth Amendment states the following:

- If the president dies or leaves office, the vice president becomes the president.
- The new president then chooses a vice president. Congress must approve this choice.
- If the president becomes seriously disabled and cannot do the job, the vice president serves as acting president. This could happen because of an event such as heart attack or stroke.

For this to happen, the vice president and a majority of the cabinet members must agree and report to Congress that the president is unable to do the job. The law also says that if the president becomes seriously ill or has to have surgery, the vice president serves as acting president until the president is able to go back to work.

NGSSS Check Name two of the qualifications that a person must have to become President of the United States. SS.7.C.3.8

_____

_____

_____

_____

If a president dies and the vice president takes over, name the two things that must happen before a new vice president can take office. SS.7.C.3.8

_____

_____

_____

_____

Describe what the Twenty-fifth Amendment does. SS.7.C.3.8

_____

_____

_____

2 THE PRESIDENT'S POWERS AND ROLES

NGSSS

SS.7.C.3.3 Illustrate the structure and function (three branches of government established in Articles I, II, and III with corresponding powers) of government in the United States as established in the Constitution.

SS.7.C.3.8 Analyze the structure, functions, and processes of the legislative, executive, and judicial branches.

Essential Question
What is required of leaders?

Guiding Questions
1. What are the duties of the president?
2. What roles does the president have?

Terms to Know

executive order
an order given by the president that has the same force as a law

pardon
presidential order that forgives a crime

reprieve
presidential order that delays punishment

amnesty
pardon for a group of people

ambassador
a person who represents the U.S. government in another country

It Matters Because

The president has many important duties that affect all Americans.

The president is the leader of our nation. What qualities do you think make

a good leader?

What Do You Know?

Directions: Choose any four of the words below and write a sentence or two about the president of the United States. When you finish the lesson, write another sentence using four different words from the list.

leader	laws	Constitution	judges	Democrat
executive	pardon	Republican	military	budget
power	Congress	treaties	elected	nation

Think Critically

1. Explain What is the veto power?

_____

_____

_____

Mark the Text

2. Underline the president's powers included in the Constitution.

Presidential Powers

The president of the United States is a symbol of the federal government and the nation. The president is the most powerful public official in the country. The president's main job is to execute, or carry out, the laws passed by Congress.

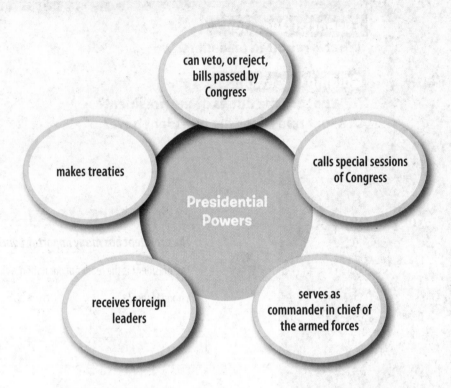

can veto, or reject, bills passed by Congress

makes treaties

Presidential Powers

calls special sessions of Congress

receives foreign leaders

serves as commander in chief of the armed forces

The legislative branch can check the president's powers. The Senate must approve any treaty and many appointments made by the president. The judicial branch can also check the president's powers. The Supreme Court has ruled that the president is not above the law, which means the president must obey the same laws as everyone else.

The Constitution also requires, or orders, the president to tell Congress how the country is doing. The president does this is by presenting the annual State of the Union message. This is a speech in which the president talks about the important issues facing the country.

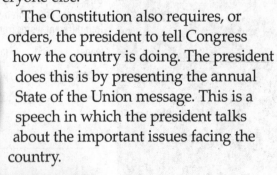

Presidential Seal

Presidential Roles

The president's main role is to carry out the nation's laws. When performing this role, the president is called the chief executive. As chief executive, the president is in charge of 15 cabinet departments and many agencies.

Presidents use executive orders to spell out the details of the laws and to put them into use. An **executive order** is a command that has the same force as a law. Presidents also use executive orders so that they can act quickly in some situations. In 1948, for example, President Harry S. Truman used an executive order to end the separation of races in the nation's military.

As chief executive, the president appoints, or chooses, justices to serve on the Supreme Court. This is an important power because Supreme Court justices serve for life. That is why presidents try to choose judges who share views similar to their own. The president also chooses judges to serve on federal courts throughout the country.

The president also has the power to grant pardons to people found guilty of federal crimes. A **pardon** forgives a crime and ends punishment. The president can also grant reprieves and amnesty. A **reprieve** delays punishment. **Amnesty** is pardon for a group of people.

The president is the country's chief diplomat. In this role, the president represents the United States government in its dealings with other countries. The president also appoints ambassadors. An **ambassador** is a person who represents the U.S. government to foreign governments.

Another role of the president is that of the head of state. As head of state, he or she represents the American people. The president greets visiting leaders from other countries. Giving out medals at ceremonies is another job of the head of state.

The president is commander in chief of the armed forces. This allows presidents to back up foreign policy decisions with force when needed. The president and Congress share the power to make war. Only Congress can declare war. Only the president has the power to order troops into battle. The War Powers Resolution puts limits on the President's power to send troops into battle. Congress passed the resolution in 1973 after the Vietnam War.

The president tries to help the economy do well. People expect the president to find solutions to problems, such as unemployment, high taxes, and rising prices.

The president is a legislative leader. The president often gives Congress ideas for new laws. He or she then works with members of Congress to get those laws passed. The president also makes speeches around the country to get citizens to support the new laws.

3. Identify Cause and Effect Why is the appointment of Supreme Court judges such an important task?

_____

_____

_____

_____

Think Critically

4. Describe What are the different ways a president deals with people convicted of federal crimes?

_____

_____

_____

_____

_____

_____

Copyright © by The McGraw-Hill Companies, Inc.

5. Infer Why might it be difficult for the president and Congress to agree when making new laws?

_____

_____

_____

_____

_____

_____

_____

Mark the Text

6. Outline Complete the outline. Give at least two details about each job. The first one has been done for you.

Take the Challenge

7. Congratulations! You've just been elected president! Make a list of the first 10 things you want to do. Make certain those are allowed by the Constitution.

Congress and the president do not always agree about which laws should be passed. Sometimes this is because the president represents the interests of the whole nation. Members of Congress represent the interests of their states or congressional districts. Those interests are not always the same as the national interests.

The president must plan the federal budget each year. He or she meets with budget officials and members of Congress to decide which programs to support and which to cut. These decisions can have a big effect on the economy.

The president is also the party leader of his or her political party. The president supports other party members that are running for office. He or she also helps the party raise money.

The President's Roles	
A. Chief Executive	**1.** carries out the nation's laws
	2. grants pardons, reprieves, and amnesty
B. Chief Diplomat	**1.** _____
	2. _____
C. Head of State	**1.** _____
	2. _____
D. Commander in Chief	**1.** _____
	2. _____
E. Economic Leader	**1.** _____
	2. _____
F. Legislative Leader	**1.** _____
	2. _____
G. Party Leader	**1.** _____
	2. _____

NGSSS Check Name three powers given to the president in the Constitution. **SS.7.C.3.3**

_____

_____

NGSSS

SS.7.C.3.3 Illustrate the structure and function (three branches of government established in Articles I, II, and III with corresponding powers) of government in the United States as established in the Constitution.

SS.7.C.3.8 Analyze the structure, functions, and processes of the legislative, executive, and judicial branches.

Essential Questions
What is required of leaders?
Why do nations interact with one another?

Guiding Questions
1. What are the goals of foreign policy?
2. What are the tools the president uses to carry out U.S. foreign policy?

Terms to Know

foreign policy
the plan a nation follows when dealing with other nations

national security
keeping the nation safe from attack

treaty
a formal agreement with another nation

executive agreement
an agreement between the president and the leader of another country

trade sanctions
stopping or slowing trade between the United States and another country

embargo
an agreement among nations to refuse to trade with a nation

It Matters Because

The president makes the key decisions about our relations with other countries.

Wars are expensive in both the cost to the economy and the cost to human lives. Sometimes we decide it is worth the cost. What do you think our country needs to decide before entering a war?

_____

_____

_____

What Do You Know?

Directions: In the first column, decide if you think the statement is true or false based on what you know before you read the lesson. After this lesson, complete the last column.

Before the lesson			After the lesson	
True	False	The president is allowed to sign treaties.	True	False
True	False	Congress approves treaties.	True	False
True	False	The only way to influence other countries is by using our military.	True	False
True	False	The main goal of our foreign policy is to win wars.	True	False
True	False	An ambassador is the leader of a foreign country.	True	False

Show Your Skill

1. Identify Cause and Effect
Why is trade so important to our economy?

_____

_____

_____

Mark the Text ✏

2. Underline the executive agencies that help the president make and carry out foreign policy.

The President and Foreign Policy

Foreign policy is the plan a nation follows when it deals with other nations. The United States has four main foreign policy targets, or goals. The most important one is **national security.** This means keeping the nation safe from attack. The second goal is to encourage trade with other countries. This is very important in today's world. Trade builds markets for U.S. goods. It also creates jobs.

A third foreign policy goal is to promote world peace. Any war, in any part of the world, can harm trade. It can also put the nation's security at risk. The fourth goal is to advance democracy around the world. Supporting basic human rights and democratic governments encourages peace.

The president directs U.S. foreign policy through the roles of commander in chief and chief diplomat. A large team of experts helps the president. These experts include people in the following executive branch agencies:

- State Department,
- Defense Department,
- National Security Council,
- Office of the Director of National Intelligence (ODNI), and
- Central Intelligence Agency (CIA).

These agencies supply the president with information for making decisions. They also help carry out American foreign policy decisions around the world.

Congress also plays a part in foreign policy. Only Congress can declare war. Congress can block some military actions

President Obama signs the New START Treaty in 2010 with Cabinet officers and lawmakers watching. This treaty was a foreign policy priority for President Obama.

One tool of foreign policy is aid and assistance. The U.S. Agency for International Development responds to disasters and other crises around the world. The agency sends people, supplies, and assistance.

through the War Powers Act. Congress also has the power to decide how much money the country should spend on defense.

The Constitution is not clear about how these branches of government should work together or which branch controls the war powers. So at various times in our country's history, control over the war powers has shifted back and forth between Congress and the president.

The president and Congress have many tools they can use to conduct foreign policy. One such tool is a treaty. A **treaty** is a formal agreement between the governments of two or more nations. The president can make a treaty, but the Senate must approve the treaty.

Another tool for making foreign policy is an executive agreement. An **executive agreement** is an agreement between the president and the leader of another country. It does not require Senate approval.

The United States also sends ambassadors to other countries. They represent the United States government. The president appoints ambassadors, but the appointments must be approved, or confirmed, by the Senate. Ambassadors are sent only to those governments the United States recognizes. The president can refuse to recognize, or accept, the government of another country.

Foreign aid is another useful tool in making foreign policy. Foreign aid is help the United States government gives to other countries. The help these countries receive can be money, food, military assistance, or supplies. The Marshall Plan is one of the nation's greatest examples of foreign aid. It was a program that helped Western Europe rebuild after World War II. The United States also sends foreign aid to countries after natural disasters.

Think Critically

3. Summarize Explain who controls the war powers.

_____

_____

_____

_____

_____

4. Synthesize Sending food to a country that has been hit by a hurricane is an example of which foreign policy tool?

_____

_____

Mark the Text

5. Circle three ways the United States uses trade as a foreign policy tool.

Take the Challenge

6. Research a recent agreement between the United States and another country. Find out if it was a treaty or an executive agreement. What countries were involved? What did the countries agree to do?

Mark the Text

7. **Graphic Organizer** Complete the web to show the foreign policy tools the nation may use.

The United States does not always agree with the way other governments treat their people or their neighbors. The president can use peaceful methods, or approaches, instead of sending in troops. One choice is to order trade sanctions. **Trade sanctions** stop or slow trade between the United States and another country. Another choice is for the United States to join an embargo. An **embargo** is an agreement among a number of nations who refuse to trade with a nation.

Congress also has a role in economic areas. It can set tariffs. Tariffs are taxes placed on goods imported from other countries. This makes the price of these goods the same as or higher than the price of similar U.S. goods. Congress also decides whether the United States should join international trade groups.

As commander in chief, the president has the power to use military force to carry out foreign policy decisions. At times, the president has used this power even when Congress has not declared war. The Vietnam War is an example of this type of foreign policy.

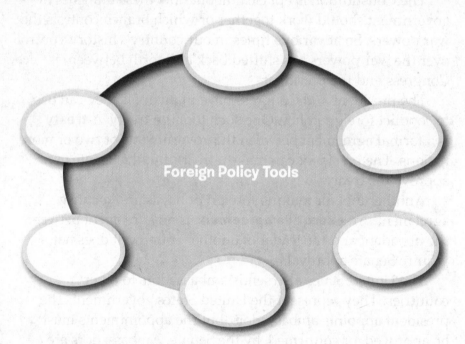

Foreign Policy Tools

 NGSSS Check Name at least two goals of America's foreign policy. SS.7.C.3.8

_____

_____

_____

_____

HOW THE EXECUTIVE BRANCH WORKS

NGSSS

SS.7.C.3.3 Illustrate the structure and function (three branches of government established in Articles I, II, and III with corresponding powers) of government in the United States as established in the Constitution.

SS.7.C.3.8 Analyze the structure, functions, and processes of the legislative, executive, and judicial branches.

Essential Question
What is required of leaders?

Guiding Questions
1. What offices make up the Executive Office of the President?
2. What role does the president's cabinet play in the government?
3. What is the federal bureaucracy?

Terms to Know

cabinet
the heads of the 15 executive departments

federal bureaucracy
the agencies below the cabinet departments in the executive branch

executive agency
a type of independent agency that deals with specific government programs

government corporation
a business operated by the government

regulatory commission
a type of independent agency that makes rules that businesses must follow

spoils system
system in which workers are given jobs in return for their political support

civil service system
system the government uses to hire workers

merit system
system in which workers are hired based on their skills and test scores

political appointee
a person appointed to a federal job by the president

It Matters Because

Decisions made by people working in the executive branch affect many areas of life.

You may not have noticed, but you interact with the government every day. Do you get mail? The government touched that. Did you pay money for something? The government touched that.

List two more ways you interact with the government in your daily life.

_____

_____

What Do You Know?

Directions: What would you like to know about people who work for the government? Write two questions you have about government workers. After you have finished the lesson, come back and see if you can answer the questions.

_____

_____

_____

_____

Think Critically

1. Evaluate Which official is the most powerful member of the White House Office?

_____

_____

Show Your Skill

2. Classify Information Which officials make up the National Security Council?

_____

_____

_____

_____

_____

_____

Executive Office Agencies

In the early days of the nation, only a few people worked in the executive branch. Today thousands of people do. Many of them work in the Executive Office of the President (EOP).

The EOP was created by President Franklin D. Roosevelt in 1939. The EOP has grown over the years and now has many different offices. The White House Office works directly for the president. It includes the president's closest advisors, called the White House staff.

The most powerful member of the White House staff is the chief of staff. This person directs the White House staff and handles the president's schedule.

The Office of Management and Budget (OMB) is another EOP agency. It works closely with the president to prepare the federal budget. It also monitors, or watches, how hundreds of government agencies spend their money.

The National Security Council (NSC) helps the president with defense and security. NSC officials include the vice president, the secretary of state, the secretary of defense, the chairman of the Joint Chiefs of Staff, the Director of National Intelligence, and the National Security Advisor.

Several other offices in the EOP help the president carry out the responsibilities of the executive branch. The Council of Economic Advisors (CEA) helps the president in his role, or job, as economic leader. The CEA is responsible for giving the president advice on economic matters, such as jobs, inflation, and trade.

President Obama meets with his cabinet and other advisors regularly.

The President's Cabinet

The executive branch also includes 15 executive departments. The president chooses the heads of these departments with the Senate's consent. This group of advisors is called the **cabinet.** The president decides when it is necessary for the cabinet to meet.

The head of the Department of Justice is called the attorney general. The other cabinet members are called secretaries. Each secretary advises the president and manages the work of his or her department. For example, the secretary of the interior manages and protects the nation's national parks.

The Department of Homeland Security is the newest cabinet department. It was created in 2002. It is responsible for keeping the nation safe from terrorist attacks.

The Constitution does not mention the cabinet. The cabinet developed when George Washington met with the heads of the first four executive departments in the new government.

Think Critically

3. Infer About what issues do you think the secretary of the treasury would advise the president?

_____

_____

_____

Show Your Skill

4. Draw Conclusions How might the work of the Department of Agriculture touch the lives of people in Florida?

_____

_____

_____

_____

_____

The Cabinet Departments	
Department of Agriculture	Department of the Interior
Department of Commerce	Department of Justice
Department of Defense	Department of Labor
Department of Education	Department of State
Department of Energy	Department of Transportation
Department of Health and Human Services	Department of the Treasury
Department of Homeland Security	Department of Veteran's Affairs
Department of Housing and Urban Development	

You may wonder how the vice president fits into the executive branch. Some vice presidents have not had much authority. Others have played key roles. This has become especially true in recent years.

The Federal Bureaucracy

The executive branch has hundreds of agencies below the cabinet departments. Together, these agencies are called the **federal bureaucracy.** The agencies of the federal bureaucracy have three main jobs. As they do these jobs, they help shape government policy.

First, the agencies must make new laws work. Congress passes laws, but it does not say how to make them work in the real world. This is the job of the executive agencies. They write specific rules so that businesses and people can follow the law.

Second, the agencies carry out the government's daily work. The federal workers deliver the mail, collect taxes, take care of the national parks, and do thousands of other jobs.

Third, the agencies regulate various kinds of businesses, services, and public utilities. These include banking, the airlines, nuclear power plants, and many others. For example, the Food and Drug Administration makes sure that food and medicine are safe for consumers.

The executive branch also includes hundreds of independent agencies. These agencies are called independent because they are not part of the cabinet. There are three types of independent agencies: (1) executive agencies, (2) government corporations, and (3) regulatory boards and commissions. **Executive agencies** work with special government programs, such as the space program. The National Aeronautics and Space Administration (NASA) is an independent executive agency.

PHOTO: Mike Theiss/Ultimate Chase/Corbis

The Kennedy Space Center in Florida is home to many NASA scientists and also attracts many tourists to the area.

Government corporations are businesses that are owned and run by the government. The United States Postal Service (USPS) is an example of a government corporation.

Regulatory commissions are also independent agencies. They make rules that businesses must follow. For example, the Federal Communications Commission (FCC) sets rules for broadcasters. Regulatory commissions are the only independent agencies that do not have to report to the president. The president appoints their members but only Congress can remove them.

The executive branch has many workers. Early in our nation's history the government used the **spoils system** to hire workers. Under the spoils system, each new president replaced the workers from the past administration with his supporters.

In 1883 Congress passed the Civil Service Reform Act. This act changed the way the government hired workers. The new system is called the **civil service system.** The government hires people based on their skills and how well they do on competitive examinations. The people who are hired become civil service workers. About 90 percent of government workers are civil service workers. The civil service system is a **merit system.** *Merit* means "ability." Civil service workers usually have permanent jobs.

Today only the top government jobs are awarded to **political appointees.** Political appointees are people chosen by the president. People in these jobs usually leave office when the president does.

Mark the Text

6. Underline the sentence that explains what makes the regulatory commissions different from the other independent agencies.

Take the Challenge

7. Work with a partner to research the names of the members of the president's cabinet. Are any of them from Florida?

NGSSS Check Name two ways that the work of the president's cabinet affects how the government runs. SS.7.C.3.3

_____

_____

_____

_____

How does a merit system improve government?

_____

_____

_____

ESSENTIAL QUESTION *What is required of leaders?*

Reflect on What It Means . . .

We see leaders on the news, in our communities, in our schools, and even as you look around you right now. Think about what makes a good leader.

To My Community

Name a leader in your community whom you admire.

_____

Now write down one thing you admire about this leader. What personal trait makes him or her an effective leader?

_____

To the World

Name a world leader whom you admire.

_____

Now write down one thing you admire about this world leader. What personal trait makes him or her an effective leader?

_____

To Me

Think about the two traits you wrote down for the leaders. What are some things that you can do to help yourself develop these traits?

_____

_____

TAKE THE CHALLENGE

Harry Truman was president of the United States from 1945 until 1953. He said, "Being a president is like riding a tiger. You have to keep on riding or be swallowed." Use electronic or print resources to find more quotes about presidential leadership. Make the quotes you selected into a book of quotations, a bulletin-board display, or a Web page.

THE JUDICIAL BRANCH

NGSSS

SS.7.C.3.3 Illustrate the structure and function (three branches of government established in Articles I, II, and III with corresponding powers) of government in the United States as established in the Constitution.

SS.7.C.3.8 Analyze the structure, functions, and processes of the legislative, executive, and judicial branches.

SS.7.C.3.11 Diagram the levels, functions, and powers of courts at the state and federal levels.

ESSENTIAL QUESTION · *How can governments ensure citizens are treated fairly?* · *Why do people create, structure, and change governments?*

Sonia Sotomayor is the first Latina and third woman to serve on the U.S. Supreme Court. During her confirmation hearing, she drew a distinct line between the judicial branch and the legislative branch:

> "I wouldn't approach the issue of judging in the way the president does. Judges can't rely on what's in their heart. They don't determine the law. Congress makes the law. The job of a judge is to apply the law."
>
> SONIA SOTOMAYOR

Copyright © by The McGraw-Hill Companies, Inc.

Judges   Congress

What branch of government does each represent? How are their jobs different?

_____

_____

_____

DBQ BREAKING IT DOWN

Why do you think Sotomayor says that judges "can't rely on what's in their heart"?

_____

_____

_____

What challenges do you think judges face? What is the best part of their job?

_____

_____

_____

PHOTO: Win McNamee/Getty Images

1 FEDERAL COURTS

NGSSS

SS.7.C.3.3 Illustrate the structure and function (three branches of government established in Articles I, II, and III with corresponding powers) of government in the United States as established in the Constitution.

SS.7.C.3.8 Analyze the structure, functions, and processes of the legislative, executive, and judicial branches.

SS.7.C.3.11 Diagram the levels, functions, and powers of courts at the state and federal levels.

Essential Question
How can governments ensure citizens are treated fairly?

Guiding Questions
1. What is the role of the federal courts?
2. What kinds of cases are heard in federal courts?

Terms to Know

dual court system
a system with both federal and state courts

jurisdiction
the authority to hear and decide a case

exclusive jurisdiction
authority of federal court alone to hear and decide cases

concurrent jurisdiction
authority of both federal and state courts to hear and decide cases

It Matters Because

The federal courts help keep order in society.

One goal of our court system is to make certain people are treated fairly.

What does fairness mean to you?

What Do You Know?

Directions: Use no more than three words to tell what you know about each of these terms. After you finish the lesson, adjust any of your descriptions if needed.

Judge

Federal Court

State Court

Civil Case

Criminal Case

networks Read Chapter 9 Lesson 1 in your textbook or online.

Role of the Federal Courts

The judicial branch is one of the three branches of the federal government. The court's two main jobs are to make sure the laws are enforced fairly and to interpret the law. Courts hear two kinds of cases, criminal and civil.

In criminal cases, people accused of crimes appear in court for trial. In a criminal trial, witnesses present evidence. A jury or judge decides whether the accused person is innocent or guilty.

In civil cases, courts use the law to settle civil disputes. In a civil dispute, both sides come before a court. Each side lays out its view. The court applies the law to the facts that have been presented. Then it decides in favor of one side or the other. A civil dispute is a conflict between

- two private parties (people, companies, or organizations)
- a private party and the government
- the U.S. government and a state or local government

Federal courts decide criminal and civil cases that involve federal laws.

The power of the federal courts comes from the Constitution. Under the Articles of Confederation, the country had no national court system. Each state had its own laws and its own courts. There was no guarantee that citizens would receive equal justice in all the states. Article III of the Constitution created a national Supreme Court and gave Congress the power to set up a system of lower courts.

Congress set up two kinds of lower federal courts: district courts and circuit courts. District courts heard minor civil and criminal cases. They served as the trial courts for specific

Mark the Text

1. A civil dispute is a conflict between two sides who feel their rights have been harmed. Underline three types of civil disputes.

Show Your Skill

2. Identify the Main Idea
What is the main goal of the federal courts?

_____

_____

_____

_____

Take the Challenge

3. Research the location of the nearest district court and the location of the nearest circuit court.

This United States district court is in Tallahassee, Florida.

Think Critically

4. Contrast What is a difference between the two court systems in our dual court system?

_____

_____

_____

_____

_____

Mark the Text

5. Diagram Fill in the diagram to show the three levels of the federal courts.

6. Underline three types of cases under the jurisdiction of the federal courts.

Think Critically

7. Interpret Use the word *jurisdiction* to write a sentence about what the federal court system does.

_____

_____

_____

_____

geographic areas. Circuit courts took more serious cases and heard appeals from the district courts. An appeal is when a person asks a higher court to review a case. In 1891, Congress made circuit courts solely courts of appeals.

The district courts at the lower level are trial courts. The circuit courts in the middle are appeals courts. The Supreme Court, the court of final appeal, is at the top.

Each state also has laws and a court system. The state courts and federal courts exist side by side. This gives our country a **dual court system.** In this kind of system, the federal courts get their powers from laws passed by Congress. The state courts get their powers from state constitutions and laws.

The federal courts exist to make certain that citizens in every state are treated the same. Each person is presumed, or thought to be, innocent until proven guilty. The goal is equal justice for all. To achieve this goal, the Constitution gives every accused person the right to a public trial. If the accused cannot pay for a lawyer, the court will provide one.

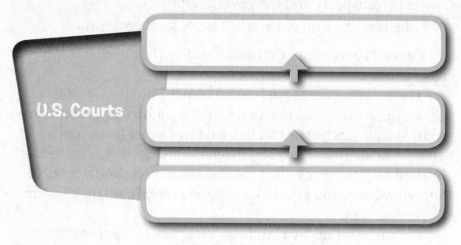

U.S. Courts

Federal Court Jurisdiction

Most court cases in this country involve state laws and are tried in state courts. The Constitution gives federal courts the power to hear certain kinds of cases, however. The authority to hear and decide a case is called **jurisdiction.** Federal courts have jurisdiction in cases that have to do with the following:

- the Constitution
- federal laws
- disputes between the states
- disputes between citizens of different states
- disputes that involve the federal government
- accidents or crimes that happen at sea
- disputes between the U.S. government and foreign governments

In most of these areas, federal courts have **exclusive jurisdiction.** This means that only federal courts can hear and decide a case. Other cases are in the jurisdiction of the state courts.

In some cases, both federal and state courts have jurisdiction. This is called **concurrent jurisdiction.** For example, this occurs when a crime breaks both federal and state laws. When this happens, either court may hold a trial.

Cases Heard

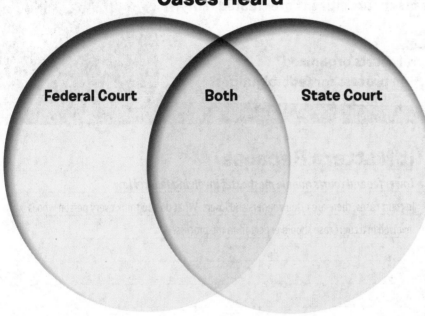

Federal Court   Both   State Court

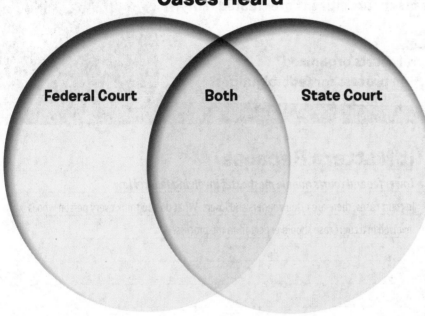

NGSSS Check In what ways are the federal and state courts the same and in what ways are they different. **SS.7.C.3.11**

SAME	DIFFERENT

Copyright © by The McGraw-Hill Companies, Inc.

8. Compare and Contrast
What is the difference between *exclusive jurisdiction and concurrent jurisdiction?*

_____
_____
_____
_____
_____
_____

Mark the Text

9. Diagram Complete the diagram. List a case that would be heard in federal court, a case that would be heard in state court, and a case that might be heard in both.

Show Your Skill

10. Classify Information What are two examples of cases where the federal courts would have exclusive jurisdiction?

_____
_____
_____
_____
_____
_____
_____
_____
_____

NGSSS

SS.7.C.3.3 Illustrate the structure and function (three branches of government established in Articles I, II, and III with corresponding powers) of government in the United States as established in the Constitution.

SS.7.C.3.8 Analyze the structure, functions, and processes of the legislative, executive, and judicial branches.

SS.7.C.3.11 Diagram the levels, functions, and powers of courts at the state and federal levels.

Essential Question
How can governments ensure citizens are treated fairly?

Guiding Questions
1. How are the federal courts organized?
2. What is the selection process for federal judges?

Terms to Know

original jurisdiction
the authority to hear cases for the first time

appellate jurisdiction
the authority to hear a case appealed from a lower court

ruling
an official decision

opinion
a detailed explanation of the legal thinking behind a court's decision in a case

precedent
a legal ruling that is used as a basis for a decision in a later, similar case

litigant
a person engaged in a lawsuit

tenure
a status that protects a person from being fired

subpoena
a court order requiring someone to appear in court

It Matters Because

Lower federal courts handle most cases involving federal law.

In court cases, there are often winners and losers. What do you think every person who is involved in a court case should expect from the process?

What Do You Know?

Directions: You may have seen courts on television or in movies. What happens in a court? Who are the people involved? Why do we have courts? In the space below, list words you already know that relate to courts. When you finish the lesson, add more words you learn.

The Lower Courts

You have learned that the federal court system has three levels. District courts are at the lowest level. These courts have what is called **original jurisdiction.** This is the authority to hear cases for the first time. Most federal cases begin in a U.S. district court.

There are 94 district courts located across 11 federal districts. District courts hold both civil and criminal trials. Juries listen to witnesses and decide guilt or innocence based on evidence.

Federal Districts

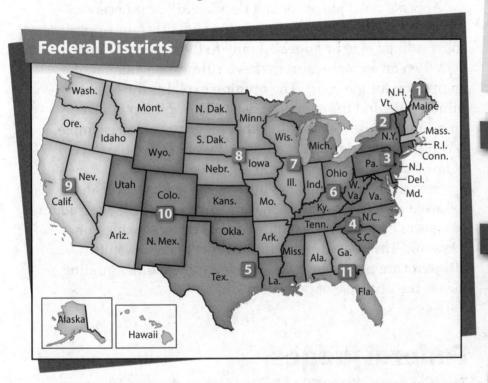

People who lose a case in district court may appeal it to a federal appeals court. This means they can ask a higher court to review and possibly change the result of the trial. The authority to review the fairness of a case appealed from a lower court is called **appellate jurisdiction.**

People appeal cases for different reasons. Usually a lawyer thinks that a district court judge has made a mistake. Other times new evidence becomes available that may change the outcome of the trial.

There are 12 federal appeals courts. Each court has jurisdiction over an area called a circuit. Thus these courts are also called circuit courts of appeals. There is also a thirteenth appeals court. It is called the Court of Appeals for the Federal Circuit. It has nationwide jurisdiction to hear special cases. These cases include patent law, international trade, and other civil cases of the U.S. government.

Think Critically

1. **Contrast** How does jurisdiction differ between district courts and courts of appeals?

_____

_____

_____

_____

_____

_____

Mark the Text

2. Circle the number of federal district courts.

Show Your Skill

3. **Make Inferences** Why do you think there are fewer federal appeals courts than federal district courts?

_____

_____

_____

_____

_____

_____

Show Your Skill

4. Classify Information
What kinds of rulings do appeals courts make?

_____

_____

_____

_____

_____

_____

Think Critically

5. Explain In your own words, explain why a precedent is important.

_____

_____

_____

_____

Take the Challenge

6. Research the names of the federal judges for the district court closest to where you live.

Appeals courts do not have trials. Judges make the decisions. Those decisions are called **rulings.** Three or more judges review each case. They listen to the lawyers' arguments. Then they meet and vote on how to rule. They can choose to do the following:

- uphold, or keep the original decision made by the district court,
- reverse the district court's decision, or
- remand the case.

To remand the case means to send the case back to the lower court to be tried again.

Appeals court judges do not decide guilt or innocence. Rather, they rule only on whether the trial was fair. Appeals court rulings may be appealed only to the Supreme Court.

When an appeals court makes a ruling, one judge writes an opinion for the court. The **opinion** explains the legal thinking behind the court's decision. The opinion is also an example to be followed by other judges. Such an example is called a **precedent.** A precedent does not have the force of law, but it is a powerful legal argument.

Since early in the nation's history, the federal courts have followed certain guiding ideas, or principles. One is that judges or justices cannot decide a question of law by seeking out a lawsuit. They have to wait for litigants to file lawsuits. **Litigants** are people involved in a lawsuit. Another guiding idea is the principle of precedent.

Federal Judges

There are more than 650 federal judges in the district courts. Each district court has at least two judges. Some districts with large populations have more. Each appeals court may have between 6 and 28 judges. The United States Supreme Court has nine judges. Supreme Court judges are called justices.

Federal Court	Number of Judges
Supreme Court	Nine justices
Federal District Court	At least two per district court
Federal Appeals Court	Between six and 28 per appeals court

The Constitution gives the president the power to appoint federal judges. However, the Senate must consent to, or approve, all appointments. This limits the president's power. When presidents appoint judges to district courts, they follow a practice called senatorial courtesy. This means they tell the senators from the nominee's home state about their choice before making the choice public. If the senators do not like the nominee, the president will usually choose a different person. This courtesy does not apply to the appointment of appeals court judges or Supreme Court justices.

Federal judges have their jobs for their life. They can be removed only through a process called impeachment. This kind of job security is called **tenure.** Judges who have tenure cannot be fired. This keeps them from being pressured when they have to make difficult decisions.

District courts also have magistrate judges who help judges with the workload. They do much of the routine work of the judge. They issue search and arrest warrants. They hear preliminary, or introductory, evidence to decide whether a case should be tried. They may also try minor cases.

Each district court has a United States attorney. These lawyers prosecute people accused of breaking federal laws. They also represent the United States in civil cases. They are appointed by the president and approved by the Senate.

Each district also has a United States marshal. Marshals keep order in the court. They make arrests and take convicted people to prison. They also serve, or deliver, subpoenas. A **subpoena** is a court order requiring someone to appear in court.

NGSSS Check List the three levels of federal courts and briefly describe what each level does. SS.7.C.3.11

_____

_____

_____

_____

_____

_____

_____

7. Explain How does a person become a federal judge?

_____

_____

_____

_____

8. Infer Why do you think the Senate must give consent to presidential appointments?

_____

_____

_____

_____

Mark the Text

9. Underline the titles of federal officials who work in judicial districts.

Think Critically

10. Analyze What are the duties of a magistrate judge? Why are they important?

_____

_____

_____

_____

_____

3 THE SUPREME COURT

NGSSS

SS.7.C.3.3 Illustrate the structure and function (three branches of government established in Articles I, II, and III with corresponding powers) of government in the United States as established in the Constitution.

SS.7.C.3.8 Analyze the structure, functions, and processes of the legislative, executive, and judicial branches.

SS.7.C.3.11 Diagram the levels, functions, and powers of courts at the state and federal levels.

Essential Question

How can governments ensure citizens are treated fairly?

Guiding Questions

1. What is the jurisdiction of the Supreme Court?
2. What powers are given to the Supreme Court?

Terms to Know

judicial review
the power to review any federal, state, or local law or action to see if it is constitutional

constitutional
allowed by the U.S. Constitution

nullify
to cancel

It Matters Because

The Supreme Court decides what the Constitution means and thus what rights Americans have.

The Supreme Court makes decisions that touch all our lives and cannot be appealed. What qualifications do you think would be important for a Supreme Court justice to have?

_____

_____

_____

What Do You Know?

Directions: In the first column, decide if you think the statement is true or false based on what you know before you read the lesson. After this lesson, complete the last column.

Before the lesson			After the lesson	
True	False	The Supreme Court only hears appeals from lower courts.	True	False
True	False	Justices to the Supreme Court serve eight-year terms.	True	False
True	False	If the Supreme Court refuses to hear a case, the lower court ruling stands.	True	False
True	False	Once a law is passed and signed by the president, it stays a law forever.	True	False
True	False	The Supreme Court determines if a law is popular with the voters.	True	False

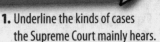 Read Chapter 9 Lesson 3 in your textbook or online.

Jurisdiction and Duties

The United States Supreme Court is the highest court in America. All other courts must follow the decisions made by the Supreme Court. The Supreme Court has eight justices and one chief justice. The justices' main job is to decide whether laws are allowed under the U.S. Constitution. The Supreme Court is also the final authority in all cases involving the Constitution, acts of Congress, and treaties with other countries.

The Supreme Court has original jurisdiction in only two kinds of cases. It can hear cases that involve diplomats from other countries. It can also hear cases that involve disputes between states. In all other cases, the Supreme Court hears appeals from lower courts.

Each year thousands of cases are appealed to the Supreme Court. The justices choose the ones they will hear. After deciding a case, the Court issues a written opinion. When the Court refuses to hear a case the decision of the lower court stands.

The Constitution does not list any specific requirements for becoming a Supreme Court justice. Before joining the Court, many justices worked as lawyers, law professors, or lower court judges. Once they are approved, Supreme Court justices have their jobs for life.

The Justices of the United States Supreme Court are shown here. Chief Justice Roberts is seated in the center.

Mark the Text ✎

1. Underline the kinds of cases the Supreme Court mainly hears.

Take the Challenge

2. There are no definite requirements for becoming a Supreme Court justice. Do you think that is a good thing or not? Defend your answer to someone with the opposite opinion.

Show Your Skill

3. **Identify Cause and Effect**
   What is the effect of the Supreme Court refusing to hear a case?

   _____

   _____

4. **Identify Cause and Effect**
   What branch of government organized the federal courts?

   _____

   _____

Take the Challenge

5. Research the names of the Supreme Court justices. Choose two of them and find a couple of interesting facts about their backgrounds.

Think Critically

6. Explain What is the power of judicial review?

_____

_____

_____

_____

_____

_____

7. Infer What does it mean to say that a law is unconstitutional?

_____

_____

_____

_____

_____

_____

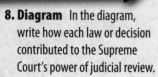

Mark the Text

8. Diagram In the diagram, write how each law or decision contributed to the Supreme Court's power of judicial review.

Powers and Limits

The Constitution gave Congress the power to decide how the Supreme Court should be organized and what its powers should be. Congress set the number of justices at nine.

A key power of the Supreme Court is the power of **judicial review.** This is the power to review any federal, state, or local law or action to see if it is constitutional. **Constitutional** means allowed by the Constitution. The Court may decide that a law or action is unconstitutional. That is, the law or action goes against what is written in the Constitution. In that case the Court has the power to **nullify,** or cancel, that law or action.

The Constitution did not give the Supreme Court the power of judicial review. That power came from the Judiciary Act of 1789, which gave the Supreme Court the power of judicial review over the acts of state governments. Later, the case of _Marbury v. Madison_ in 1803 established the Court's power of judicial review over laws passed by Congress. This power gives the court a check on the other two branches of government.

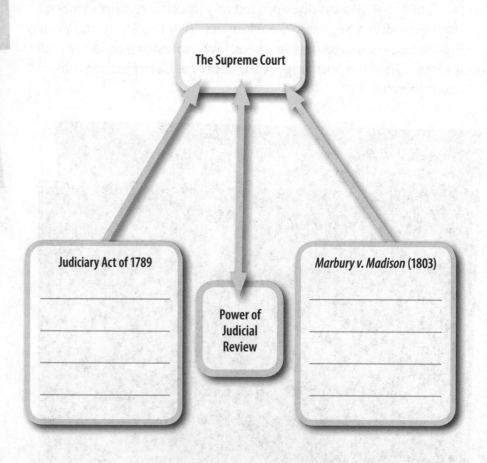

The other branches also check the Supreme Court's power. Congress can get around a Supreme Court ruling by passing a new law. It can change a law that has been ruled unconstitutional. Congress and the states can also try to undo Court rulings by amending the Constitution.

The Supreme Court's power is limited in other ways as well. The Court can only hear and rule on cases that come to it through the courts. A person cannot simply ask the Supreme Court to decide if a law is constitutional. The Court will only rule on a law that has been challenged, or objected to, on appeal. It can only take cases that concern a federal question.

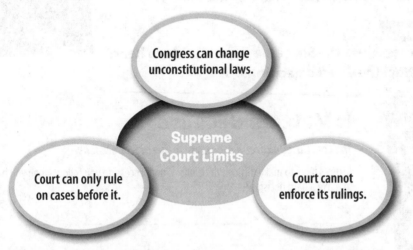

The Supreme Court does not have the power to enforce its rulings. It relies on the executive branch and on the states to do this. The executive branch usually enforces Supreme Court rulings, but not always. In 1832, the Supreme Court ruled in *Worcester v. Georgia* that the state of Georgia had to stop ignoring federal land treaties with the Cherokee Nation. President Andrew Jackson refused to enforce the ruling. Most people agreed with the president. As a result, he felt no pressure to take action.

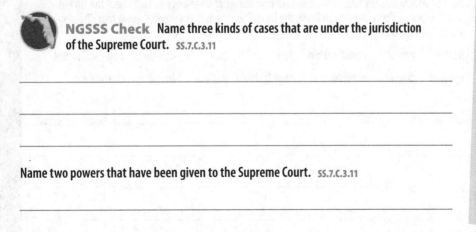

NGSSS Check Name three kinds of cases that are under the jurisdiction of the Supreme Court. SS.7.C.3.11

_____

_____

_____

Name two powers that have been given to the Supreme Court. SS.7.C.3.11

_____

_____

9. Explain What can Congress do if the Supreme Court rules that a law is unconstitutional?

_____

_____

_____

_____

Mark the Text

10. Underline the name of the president who refused to enforce a Supreme Court ruling.

Think Critically

11. Infer How does the Supreme Court depend on the executive branch?

_____

_____

_____

_____

Show Your Skill

12. Identify the Main Idea How is judicial review a part of our federal system of government?

_____

_____

_____

_____

_____

LESSON

4 SUPREME COURT PROCEDURES AND DECISIONS

NGSSS

SS.7.C.3.12 Analyze the significance and outcomes of landmark Supreme Court cases including, but not limited to, Marbury v. Madison, Plessy v. Ferguson, Brown v. Board of Education, Gideon v. Wainwright, Miranda v. Arizona, in re Gault, Tinker v. Des Moines, Hazelwood v. Kuhlmier, United States v. Nixon, and Bush v. Gore.

Essential Question

How can governments ensure citizens are treated fairly?

Guiding Questions

1. What kinds of cases does the Supreme Court decide to hear?
2. What factors affect the Court's decisions?

Terms to Know

writ of certiorari
an order from a higher court to see the records from a lower court case

docket
a court's calendar

caseload
the number of cases handled in a court term

brief
a written document explaining one side of a case

concurring opinion
a statement written by a justice who votes with the majority but for different reasons

dissenting opinion
a statement written by a justice who disagrees with the majority opinion

unanimous opinion
a ruling on which all the justices agree

stare decisis
the practice of using earlier rulings as a basis for deciding cases

It Matters Because

The Court uses a careful process to arrive at its decisions.

Justices have to make difficult decisions. What process do you follow when you have to make a hard decision?

_____

_____

_____

_____

What Do You Know?

Directions: Choose any four of the words below and write a sentence or two about the United States Supreme Court. When you finish the lesson, write another sentence using four different words from the list.

justice	equal	Constitution	fair	law	decide	appeal	final
opinion	power	president	legislative	judicial	highest	change	

_____

_____

_____

_____

Court Procedures

The Supreme Court meets each year for about nine months. Each term begins the first Monday in October and ends in the summer. So, the 2012 term began in October 2012. Sometimes special sessions are called to handle a serious matter.

The Supreme Court carefully chooses the cases it will hear. The justices look for cases that raise constitutional questions. These are questions about issues such as freedom of speech, equal protection of the laws, and the right to a fair trial. The justices also look for cases that deal with real people and events. They look for cases that affect the whole country, rather than just one person or group.

Almost all of its cases reach the Supreme Court on appeal from a lower court. Most appeals come to the Court as a petition, or request, for a writ of certiorari. A **writ of certiorari** (suhr•sheeuh•REHR•ee) orders a lower court to send its case records to the Supreme Court for review.

The justices receive about 10,000 petitions, or requests, for writ of certiorari each term. Of these, the Court accepts about 75 to 80 cases. The Court accepts a case when four of the nine justices agree to do so. The accepted cases go on the Court **docket,** or calendar of cases to be heard. The number of cases handled in a period of time is called the **caseload.**

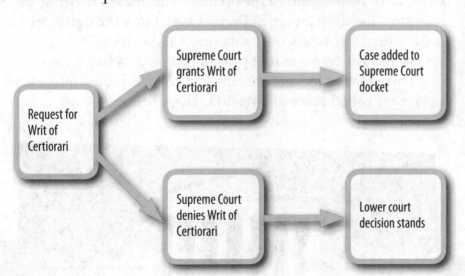

How the Court's Rulings Are Made

How are cases presented to the Supreme Court? First, the lawyers for each side in a case write a brief. A **brief** is a written document that explains one side's position, or point of view,

---

Mark the Text

1. Underline three factors that influence the Court when it is deciding what cases to choose.

Think Critically

2. **Explain** What is a *writ of certiorari*?

_____

_____

_____

_____

Show Your Skill

3. **Identify Cause and Effect** What is the outcome when a request for a writ of certiorari is denied and the court refuses to hear the case?

_____

_____

_____

_____

PHOTO: Hisham F. Ibrahim/Getty Images

Think Critically

4. Summarize How do the justices decide the merits of a case?

_____

_____

_____

_____

_____

5. Compare Explain what each type of opinion expresses.

majority opinion

_____

_____

dissenting opinion

_____

_____

concurring opinion

_____

_____

unanimous opinion

_____

_____

on the case. The two parties study each other's briefs and then give a second brief to the Court. The second brief is shorter and answers the arguments made in the first brief by the other side.

The justices study the briefs and ask questions. Next, the lawyers are given 30 minutes to present oral arguments before the Court. Each side lays out its case. The justices meet to make decisions about the cases they are studying. The meetings are secret. No official records are kept. At least six justices must be present to vote on a ruling. A majority vote decides a case.

When the Court has reached a decision, one justice writes the opinion for the majority. The opinion states the facts of the case and gives the ruling. It explains the reasoning that led to the decision. The Court's written opinion sets a precedent for the lower courts to follow.

Sometimes a justice agrees with the majority decision but for different reasons. He or she writes a **concurring opinion.** Justices might also disagree with the majority decision. They write **dissenting opinions.** Sometimes all the justices vote the same way. Then the Court issues a **unanimous opinion.** These decisions have special force.

After the opinions are drafted, or written in their first form, the justices who agreed with the decision look at each opinion. They comment on the draft and the justice who wrote the opinion takes their comments into account. If the justice who wrote the opinion does not do this, another judge might take away his or her support of the opinion. This makes revising, or rewriting, the draft a very important task. Once the drafts are in their final form the Court announces its decision.

The justices consider many factors when deciding a case. One important factor is precedent. Justices are guided by a principle called **stare decisis** (STEHR•ee•dih•SY•suhs).

The United States Supreme Court hears cases in this building in Washington, D.C., and court sessions are open to the public.

In Latin this means "let the decision stand." In other words, follow precedent.

However, the law must also be able to change with the times. The Supreme Court is the highest court in the land. It has the power to overturn outdated precedents. For example, in *Brown* v. *Board of Education*, the Court overturned an earlier decision that supported segregation laws. In that case, the Supreme Court changed its interpretation of the law to reflect changes in society.

Landmark Supreme Court Decisions
Marbury v. *Madison* (1803) established the Supreme Court's power of judicial review.
Plessy v. *Ferguson* (1896) upheld the "separate but equal" doctrine of public segregation.
Brown v. *Board of Education* (1954) overturned *Plessy* v. *Ferguson* and started public school integration.
Gideon v. *Wainwright* (1963) said that a person accused of a major crime had the right to a lawyer.
Miranda v. *Arizona* (1966) ruled that suspects must be informed of their rights before questioning.
Tinker v. *Des Moines* (1969) ruled that freedom of speech applies to students in public schools.
United States v. *Nixon* (1974) ruled that the president cannot use executive privilege as an excuse to withhold evidence.
Hazelwood v. *Kuhlmeier* (1988) said that public school officials may impose some limits on student newspapers.
Bush v. *Gore* (2000) ruled that Florida's recount of presidential votes violated the Fourteenth Amendment.

NGSSS Check List two Supreme Court cases and tell why the decisions made by the court were important. **SS.7.C.3.12**

_____

_____

_____

_____

Think Critically

6. Evaluate In your own words, why is *stare decisis* important?

_____

_____

_____

_____

_____

_____

Mark the Text

7. Which two cases had to do with the First Amendment rights of public school students? Circle your answers.

Take the Challenge

8. What importance do you think changing social conditions should play in Court rulings? Draft an email to a justice to explain your opinion.

ESSENTIAL QUESTION *How can governments ensure citizens are treated fairly?*

Reflect on What It Means . . .

The United States Constitution guarantees equality for all people. The first, great truth in the Declaration of Independence is equality:

"We hold these truths to be self-evident, that all men are created equal. . . ."

To the World

If you took a trip to a country you had never visited before, how could you tell if people were treated equally? What would equality or inequality look like?

To the Community

How have people in your community worked towards equality?

To Me

What can you do to stand for equality and fairness in your daily actions?

TAKE THE CHALLENGE

John Adams thought that the United States should have a "government of laws and not of men." How would this type of government help ensure citizens are treated fairly? Create a newspaper editorial or blog with a partner to respond to this question.

POLITICAL PARTIES

NGSSS

SS.7.C.2.8 Identify America's current political parties and illustrate their ideas about government.

ESSENTIAL QUESTION *How do citizens, both individually and collectively, influence government policy?*

George Washington published his Farewell Address toward the end of his second term as president of the United States. In it he included a warning to his fellow citizens:

" The alternate domination of one **faction** over another, sharpened by the spirit of revenge . . . is itself a frightful **despotism**. "

GEORGE WASHINGTON

faction

What is a "faction"?

_____

_____

despotism

A despot is a tyrant who rules with complete power. What is "despotism"?

_____

_____

DBQ BREAKING IT DOWN

Washington was worried about fighting within the government. What words does he use to describe that fighting?

_____

_____

_____

What effect does fighting among political groups have today?

_____

_____

_____

McGraw-Hill
networks™
There's More Online!

HISTORY OF POLITICAL PARTIES

NGSSS

SS.7.C.2.8 Identify America's current political parties and illustrate their ideas about government.

Essential Question

How do citizens, both individually and collectively, influence government policy?

Guiding Questions

1. Why did political parties develop in the United States?
2. What is the importance of third parties in American politics?
3. How do America's major modern political parties differ?

Terms to Know

political party
a group of people with similar ideas about government

two-party system
a practice by which two major political parties compete for power

third party
a term used for a minor political party

platform
the party's beliefs, principles, and positions on many issues

It Matters Because

Political parties are one of the major ways citizens participate in the political process and influence the direction of government.

Political parties are formed around some core beliefs about government. Rank these beliefs according to which are most important to you. Your most important belief should be ranked number one.

____ **Government should help people.**

____ **Government should protect people.**

____ **Government should spend less money.**

____ **Government should provide good schools.**

____ **Government should protect the environment.**

____ **Government should keep taxes low.**

What Do You Know?

Directions: In the first column, answer the questions based on what you know "Now." After this lesson, complete the "Later" column.

Now		Later
	Why do we need political parties?	
	How are the political parties different?	

Growth of American Parties

A **political party** is a group of people with general shared interests about government. They work together to help the candidates they support try to win elections. They also try to help shape government policy. The United States has a **two-party system.** The names and makeup of the two main parties have changed over the years. Today's major parties are the Democratic and the Republican parties.

The Constitution did not mention political parties. Still, political parties have been around for a long time. Not all of the Founders wanted them, however. They were afraid that political parties would divide and weaken the new nation. Despite this, by the late 1790s, political parties formed because people had different ideas about what the government should do.

The First Political Parties

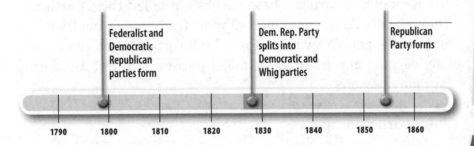

Federalist and Democratic Republican parties form				Dem. Rep. Party splits into Democratic and Whig parties			Republican Party forms	
1790	1800	1810	1820	1830	1840	1850	1860	

The first political parties formed in the late 1790s. Alexander Hamilton was the secretary of the treasury. He thought that the national government should have most of the power. He believed that the national government needed to be strong to protect people's rights. People who agreed with Hamilton's ideas formed the Federalist Party.

Thomas Jefferson was the secretary of state at that same time. He thought that state governments should have most of the power. The people who agreed with Jefferson's ideas formed the Democratic-Republican Party. Over the next several years, Jefferson's party grew stronger and Hamilton's party grew weaker. Soon, the Federalist Party was gone.

Show Your Skill

1. Identify the Main Idea What are the major goals of a political party?

_____

_____

_____

Mark the Text

2. Underline the names of the two major parties in the United States today.

Show Your Skill

3. Use Time Lines Use the time line to help you see how America's early political parties developed. As you read this lesson, place the correct dates next to the events shown on the time line.

Think Critically

4. Summarize How did Federalists view the power of the national government?

_____

_____

_____

_____

_____

Show Your Skill

5. Make Inferences What would a third party need to do to win national elections?

_____

_____

_____

_____

_____

Think Critically

6. Hypothesize Do you think a single-issue party could be widely accepted in the United States? Why?

_____

_____

_____

_____

_____

In 1828 the Democratic-Republicans split into two parties. People who supported Andrew Jackson for president called themselves the Democratic Party. They used that name because they wanted to stress their connection to the common people. Those who opposed Jackson were called the National Republicans. The National Republican Party did not last long.

The Whig Party was the main competition of the Democratic Party. The Whigs and the Democrats were the two major parties in the United States until the 1850s. Both parties tried to avoid the issue of slavery. The Whig Party broke up when slavery became a major political issue.

In 1854 people who were against slavery formed a new party. They named it the Republican Party. Some Republicans believed slavery should be abolished in Southern states. Others did not agree, but they did believe that slavery should not spread to the territories controlled by the U.S. government.

Third Parties

Sometimes small parties form to compete with the Democratic and Republican parties. These parties are called **third parties.** They usually do not get much support from voters, but they often make people aware of special issues. Some of those issues later become important to the major parties. Third parties form for many reasons.

Third parties form:

- to promote ideas that are new or unpopular with the major parties.
- to support a single issue.
- to promote their beliefs about government.
- to support an independent candidate.

Ralph Nader ran for president as a candidate for the Green Party in 1996 and 2000.

The following chart explains the roles third parties have played in American history.

Name of Party	Presidential Candidate, Election Year	Reason	Influence on America
Populist Party	James B. Weaver, 1892	promote ideas	Organized by farmers and laborers who wanted the direct election of senators and an eight-hour working day
Communist Party USA (1919–present)		beliefs	Wants more government and worker ownership of all resources and businesses
Prohibitionist Party	Aaron W. Watkins, 1920	single issue	Wanted to outlaw the sale of alcohol
Progressive Party	Vincent Hallinan, 1952	promote ideas	Wanted a direct primary election in order to give people more power in selecting candidates to run in the general election
Green Party	Ralph Nader, 2000	single issue	Wants more attention put on the environment
Tea Party (2008–present)		beliefs	Does not want any government control over business or people's personal lives

Take the Challenge

7. Make a poster for a single-issue political party that you think would be popular with your classmates.

Show Your Skill

8. **Draw Conclusions** Why is it difficult for third parties to win elections in the United States?

_____

_____

_____

_____

_____

Third parties usually lose major elections. There are many reasons for this. Candidates from the major parties get their names put on the general election ballot automatically. Third-party candidates have to get on the ballot by petition. A petition is a long process of collecting a large number of signatures from registered voters. Third parties also have difficulty raising enough money to compete with the major parties. Also, they may not have strong networks. Networks are groups of people who work together. The major parties have strong local, state, and national networks. These networks help candidates in many ways.

Most countries have political parties, but not two-party systems. Many democracies have multiparty systems. Countries with multiparty systems might have three or more major parties competing for power. Canada has three major parties. Germany has five major parties. Israel has more than 20 major parties. The People's Republic of China only has one political party.

These Florida delegates to the Republican National Convention in 2008 helped nominate John McCain as the party's candidate for president.

PHOTO: Paul J. Richards/AFP/Getty Images

Mark the Text

9. Underline the text that describes a platform.

Think Critically

10. Infer Why might political parties write platforms before presidential elections?

_____

_____

_____

_____

_____

_____

Party Differences

The Democrats and the Republicans both want to win as many elections as they can. They avoid taking extreme positions on most issues because most Americans are political moderates and generally agree on many social and political issues. As a result, the parties often also take moderate positions. A moderate is usually opposed to major social changes or making changes too quickly. One major difference between the two parties is over how much the government should be involved in people's lives. Democrats think that government should be more involved in helping to fix society's problems. Generally Republicans think that government should not get as involved in fixing those problems. Both parties think that economic growth will give poor people a better chance to find jobs.

One way to find out what each party believes about an issue is to read the party **platform.** The platform gives the party's positions on important issues. It also states the party's basic beliefs. The platform is written for each party's national convention. The convention is held every four years. Each party also chooses its candidates for president and vice president at the convention.

NGSSS Check Name two differences in the beliefs of the Democratic and the Republican parties today. SS.7.C.2.8

1. _____

_____

2. _____

_____

LESSON

2 POLITICAL PARTIES TODAY

NGSSS

SS.7.C.2.8 Identify America's current political parties and illustrate their ideas about government.

Essential Question

How do citizens, both individually and collectively, influence government policy?

Guiding Questions

1. How are political parties organized?
2. How do political parties nominate candidates?
3. What other roles do political parties play?

Terms to Know

national committee
group that organizes the party's national convention

caucus
meeting of state and local party members

precinct
the smallest election unit

political machine
powerful local political organization

direct primary
election in which voters choose candidates to run in the general election

closed primary
only people who choose a party can vote

open primary
people do not have to choose a party to vote

plurality
winning less than half the vote

majority
more than half the vote

It Matters Because

Understanding how political parties work helps citizens as they follow campaigns and decide on the candidates they wish to support.

You do not have to be of voting age to be involved in politics. Circle the method of getting involved that you think might work best for someone who is not yet old enough to vote.

Watch the news.

Go to a political rally.

Write a letter to someone in government.

Send an email to a politician.

What Do You Know?

Directions: In the first column, mark the statement true or false based on what you know before you read the lesson. After this lesson, complete the last column.

Now		Later	
True False	The governors of each state choose delegates to a political party's national convention.	True False	
True False	People who are in the same voting precinct might belong to different political parties.	True False	
True False	The political party that loses an election can be a watchdog for the people.	True False	
True False	Only the members of a political party can run for election.	True False	
True False	The country would be better off without political parties.	True False	

Show Your Skill

1. Identify the Main Idea Who makes up a national committee? What is the priority of the national committee?

_____

_____

_____

_____

Think Critically

2. Interpret How do higher-level party leaders depend on precinct leaders?

_____

_____

_____

_____

_____

_____

_____

Organization of Political Parties

Political parties have local, state, and national organizations. A **national committee** is in charge of each party. This committee includes people from every state. These people are called representatives, or delegates. The committee's most important job is to organize the national convention. The convention happens once every four years. Delegates at the convention choose the party's candidates for president and vice president. The delegates to the convention are chosen through presidential primary elections or by **caucuses** (KAW•kuhs•uhz). Caucuses are special meetings of state and local party organizations. The convention is an important time to build party unity. It also launches, or starts, the election campaign.

The major parties also have campaign committees for the candidates running for Congress. The committees help raise money for the candidates and give them advice and support.

Each party also has state and local organizations. They choose and help candidates run for state and local offices. They also support their party's candidates for president and vice president. Cities and counties are divided into small districts, or areas, called **precincts** (PREE•sinkts). Precincts are areas that have a certain number of voters. Therefore, a precinct might be a whole town or a group of adjacent neighborhoods in a larger city. Everyone in a precinct votes at the same place. County committees are the largest political units within the state. They are headed by a county chairperson. This person usually has a great deal of political power.

New members are welcomed to the Florida Legislature. They represent the voters in their home districts.

Precincts appoint a captain. Captains build support for the party at the local level. Captains also organize volunteers and register voters. Local leaders also make sure party members vote on Election Day.

Sometimes a local party organization becomes very strong and wins almost every election. Then it is called a **political machine.** One example of a political machine was Tammany Hall in New York City. In the late 1800s and early 1900s, Tammany Hall was led by William "Boss" Tweed. At that time, political machines gave immigrants and poor people food and fuel and helped them find jobs. Those people usually voted for the candidates that Tammany Hall supported. Unfortunately, some members of the political machine hurt the city. They cheated the city by taking bribes (illegal money payments) from people doing business with the city.

Selecting Party Candidates

Political parties are important in the government. Political parties are active all the time, but their busiest time is during an election. They nominate, or choose, the candidates who run for public office. Parties generally use **direct primaries** to nominate candidates for office.

This chart describes the different ways that candidates get on the ballot for the general election.

In most places, the candidate who wins the primary is the one who gets a **plurality,** or the most votes. A candidate with the most votes wins even if his or her share is less than 50 percent of the total votes.

Closed Primary
Voters have to choose a party to vote for that party's nominees.

Open Primary
Voters do not need to choose a party to vote for the party's nominees.

Petition
Candidates who are not members of either major party make a petition. They must have a certain number of voter signatures to have their name put on the general election ballot.

General Election Ballot

◯ John Diaz

◯ Janet Jones

◯ _____
 (Write-In Candidate)

Think Critically

8. Conclude Why do you think it is important for political parties to act as watchdogs?

_____

_____

_____

_____

_____

_____

Show Your Skill

9. Generalize How do political parties help the American people practice self-government?

_____

_____

_____

_____

_____

In a few states, the winner must have a **majority.** This means the winner must get more than 50 percent of the total votes. Sometimes no candidate gets a majority of the votes. Then the party holds another primary called a *runoff.* The winner of the runoff becomes the party's candidate in the general election.

Most offices have only one officeholder; for example, there is only one mayor in a city. Sometimes more than one type of position is vacant, or empty, in the same election. For example, a city might have many council members. In this case, the party can nominate more than one candidate. The party chooses the top vote-getters in the primary.

Other Political Party Functions

Political parties do more than just get candidates elected. They help citizens practice self-government. This means that they help people communicate with the government. Political parties also make sure that government listens to the people.

Political parties also:

- support candidates. After they nominate the candidates they help raise money for the campaigns. They also register citizens to vote and make sure supporters get to the polls on Election Day.

- communicate with citizens. Parties help citizens and candidates talk with each other.

- run different parts of the government. Congress and most state legislatures are organized by party. Leaders make sure that all the lawmakers in the party support the party position when making laws.

- link different parts of the government. Political parties make it easier for different levels of government to work together. Senators, governors, and others who are members of a major party usually know each other. This makes it easier for them to work together to solve problems.

- act as a watchdog for citizens between elections when their party is out of power. The party out of power is often called the opposition party. The opposition party gives voice to people who disagree with the party in power. This makes certain the party in power listens to all views.

 NGSSS Check Name a role other than nominating candidates that political parties play. SS.7.C.2.8

_____

_____

CHAPTER 10

MY REFLECTIONS

ESSENTIAL QUESTION ***How do citizens, both individually and collectively, influence government policy?***

Reflect on What It Means . . .

Do you ever wish you had the power to change the world? Political parties have a major effect on the world today. Suppose you could form a political party. What would its core values, or beliefs, be? How would you use it to improve your life, help your community, and change the world? Reflect on these things as you complete the graphic organizer.

My political party would affect my life:

____

____

____

____

Core Values

____

____

____

My political party could affect my community by:

____

____

____

____

My political party could affect the world through:

____

____

____

____

Keep Going!

TAKE THE CHALLENGE

To help get the word out about your new political party, you will create a bumper sticker. Think carefully about the colors, symbols, and words you will use. Remember that many people will be viewing this from moving cars. Keep it short, bold, and clear!

Colors

_____

Why I chose these colors

Symbols

_____

Why I chose these symbols

Words

_____

Why I chose these words

VOTING AND ELECTIONS

NGSSS

SS7.C.2.3 Experience the responsibilities of citizens at the local, state, or federal levels.

SS7.C.2.7 Conduct a mock election to demonstrate the voting process and its impact on a school, community, or local level.

SS7.C.2.9 Evaluate candidates for political office by analyzing their qualification, experience, issue-based platforms, debates, and political ads.

ESSENTIAL QUESTION *What are the rights and responsibilities of citizens?*

Like the young woman shown voting here, Joanna Fisher also remembers voting for the first time. Read her reflections on that experience.

PHOTO: Jim West/Alamy

Copyright © by The McGraw-Hill Companies, Inc.

"I always knew I would **register** to vote as soon as there was an election I was old enough to vote in. I guess I was raised in a family where you care about politics and you care about what's going on around you."

JOANNA FISHER

register

What does it mean to "register" to vote?

_____

_____

DBQ BREAKING IT DOWN

How would voting show that a person cares about the world around them?

_____

_____

_____

What are some ways to find out "what's going on around you"?

_____

_____

_____

McGraw-Hill
networks™
There's More Online!

WHO CAN VOTE?

NGSSS

SS.7.C.2.3 Experience the responsibilities of citizens at the local, state, or federal levels.

SS.7.C.3.7 Analyze the impact of the 13th, 14th, 15th, 19th, 24th, and 26th amendments on participation of minority groups in the American political process.

Essential Question
What are the rights and responsibilities of citizens?

Guiding Questions
1. What are the requirements to vote?
2. What steps must you follow to vote?
3. Why is it important to vote?

Terms to Know

suffrage
the right to vote

register
to sign up to vote

polling place
location where a person goes to vote

ballot
a list of candidates who are running for each office

voter turnout rate
the measure of how many people turn out to vote

apathy
a lack of interest

It Matters Because

The right to vote spread slowly to more and more people.

Voting is both a right and a responsibility. When you have voted in elections at school, how is it determined who can vote and how many times each person could vote? What might happen if there were no rules about voting?

_____

_____

_____

_____

What Do You Know?

In the first column, answer the questions based on what you know before you study. After this lesson, complete the last column.

Before the Lesson		After the Lesson
	What allows a person to vote?	
	How does a voter vote?	
	Why does voting matter?	

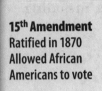
Qualifying to Vote

For most of history, countries were ruled by kings and queens. People did not have a say in how they were governed. Even in the United States, **suffrage,** or the right to vote, was limited to white men who owned land. The principle, or basic belief, that "all men are created equal" had not yet been achieved. Individuals and the government worked for many years to give more people the right to vote. Over time, all American citizens over the age of 18 were granted the right to vote. Most voting rights in the United States were granted through amendments to the Constitution.

15ᵗʰ Amendment
Ratified in 1870
Allowed African Americans to vote

→

19ᵗʰ Amendment
Ratified in 1920
Allowed women to vote

→

26ᵗʰ Amendment
Ratified in 1971
Lowered voting age to 18

Even after the Fifteenth Amendment passed, some states did not let African Americans vote. This lasted for another hundred years. Later, women fought for the vote. They were called suffragists. Famous suffragists included Alice Paul and Susan B. Anthony.

Millions of people are eligible, or allowed, to vote in the nation today. To be eligible to vote, a citizen must be at least 18 years old and be a U.S. citizen.

Some people are not eligible to vote. People who have committed serious crimes are not able to vote while in prison. Also, people who suffer from certain mental illnesses may lose their eligibility to vote. Most citizens over 18 in the United States can vote. Each time you vote, you are helping to run your government.

Suffrage parades were one way women showed that they wanted to have the right to vote. The ratification of the 19th Amendment in 1920 gave them that right.

Show Your Skill

1. Classify Information Which amendment to the Constitution removed gender as a qualification for voting?

_____

_____

Think Critically

2. Explain What does it mean to be *eligible* to vote?

_____

_____

_____

_____

Mark the Text

3. Underline two requirements for a person to vote.

Mark the Text

4. Underline the documents you might take with you when you register to vote.

Think Critically

5. **Explain** What is a polling place?

_____

_____

6. **Summarize** Summarize the three steps in the voting process.

_____

_____

Take the Challenge

7. Where is the polling place for your address? What type of location is it? How can you find out this information?

Steps in the Voting Process

Voting requires three steps:

1. Registering

2. Preparing

3. Casting your vote.

To **register** means to sign up. Most states require voters to register 25 days before the election. Some let you register on Election Day. Registering to vote is easy. You just fill out a form with your name, address, and age. You might also list your political party. You will need to show your driver's license, birth certificate, or another valid form of identification to prove your age and citizenship.

There are many ways you can register to vote, including

- using the mail,
- using the Web,
- visiting the library,
- visiting government offices, and
- visiting agencies that serve people with disabilities.

In addition, the National Voter Registration Act says that people are allowed to register to vote when they renew their driver's licenses. Some people call this the "Motor Voter" law.

After you register, you then prepare to vote. You should be informed about current issues because your vote will affect the lives of many people. You also need to find out about the candidates before you can decide for whom you want to vote.

Watching the news, reading the newspaper, using the Internet, listening to the radio, and reading books and magazines help you become an informed voter. You must be careful to separate facts from opinions as you gather information. Some people use bias in their materials. They try to tell you only their opinion instead of fact.

The third step is casting your vote. This is done at a **polling place.** Polling places are usually set up in schools, fire stations, or other public buildings. There is one polling place in each precinct, or voting district. Many states allow early voting. This means that citizens can vote before Election Day. This can be done by mail in some states and at certain locations in others.

When you get to your polling place, you will be asked to show identification. You will then enter a voting booth. The booth may have a curtain or other way to make certain your vote is secret.

A **ballot** is a list of candidates who are running for each office. The table below shows the different types of ballots used today.

Types of Ballots Used Today	
Paper ballot	Vote is marked using a special pen.
Absentee ballot	Vote is mailed in by people who know they cannot get to the polls on Election Day.
Touch-screen ballot	Vote is marked by touching a computer screen.

In the 2000 presidential election, ballots became a source of major conflict. Some of the ballots, especially some in Florida, were not marked clearly. This made it hard for election officials to read them properly. In the end, the U.S. Supreme Court had to make a decision. In the U.S. Supreme Court case *Bush* v. *Gore*, the Court said that the votes should not be recounted. The decision meant that George W. Bush won the election.

Some people cannot get to the polls on Election Day. They may be traveling. They may be serving in the military. These voters can send in an absentee ballot. You must get an absentee ballot before Election Day.

Why Your Vote Counts

Have you ever heard the phrase "every vote counts"? It is true. The United States is committed to the ideal of equality. When you vote, your vote will be counted exactly the same way, and be given the same value, as everyone else's vote.

Election officials in Florida had to carefully examine some of the ballots in Florida to determine how to count the votes in the 2000 election.

Show Your Skill

8. **Make Inference** How can a person vote who is in the military overseas?

_____

_____

Think Critically

9. **Summarize** What happened in the 2000 presidential election that brought a lot of attention to voting in Florida?

_____

_____

_____

_____

10. **Hypothesize** Why might voter turnout be higher in some elections than in others?

_____

_____

_____

_____

_____

Polling places might be in schools, recreation centers, libraries, or other places in the community.

PHOTO: Robert Sullivan/Getty Images

11. Identify the Main Idea
What does the saying "every vote counts" mean?

_____

_____

_____

Voting is a right. It is also a responsibility. There are many good reasons to vote.

- You can help choose government leaders.
- You can vote to keep leaders that you like.
- You can vote to remove leaders whose work you dislike.
- You will have a say in how your community, state, and nation are run.

The people who vote each Election Day know that every vote counts. They also feel that they have no right to complain about things if they have not voted. They believe in the democratic process.

But many people do not vote. **Voter turnout rate** is the measure of how many people come out to vote. In the United States this number is often under 50 percent. There are many reasons for this. Some people say they are too busy to vote. Others suffer from voter apathy. **Apathy** is a lack of interest. Still others forget to register to vote. Some others do not know that moving requires them to register again. If they wait too long to do this, they will not meet the deadline.

 NGSSS Check List two reasons why a voter should vote in every election. SS.7.C.2.3

_____

_____

_____

NGSSS

SS.7.C.2.7 Conduct a mock election
to demonstrate the voting process
and its impact on a school,
community, or local level.

SS.7.C.2.9 Evaluate candidates
for political office by analyzing
their qualification, experience,
issue-based platforms, debates,
and political ads.

LESSON

2 ELECTIONS AND CAMPAIGNS

Essential Question
Why do people create, structure, and change governments?

Guiding Questions
1. Why are there different types of elections in the American political system?
2. How are presidents elected?
3. How do candidates run for political office?

Terms to Know

issue
matter of public concern

initiative
process that lets voters propose new laws or amendments to state constitutions

referendum
process that allows voters to accept or reject a law passed by the state legislature

recall
election in which voters can remove a person from office

Electoral College
group of electors that chooses the president

popular vote
the votes cast by the people in the general election

winner-take-all system
Electoral College system in which the winner of a state's popular vote gets all of that state's electoral votes

canvass
to go from door to door to gather support for a candidate

political action committee (PAC)
organization set up by interest groups to raise money for candidates

It Matters Because

Elections are a key way that citizens express their will.

We elect people who have the power to make our towns, states, and nation better or worse.

Would you ever want to be a politician? Why or why not?

What Do You Know?

Directions: In the first column, decide if you think the statement is true or false based on what you know before you read the lesson. After this lesson, complete the last column.

Before the Lesson			After the Lesson	
True	False	The candidate for president with the most votes is always the winner.	True	False
True	False	The Electoral College trains new candidates for office.	True	False
True	False	A referendum gives people a chance to vote on an issue.	True	False
True	False	A recall election is held every four years.	True	False
True	False	The primary election comes before a general election.	True	False

1. Conclude Why do you think only one-third of senators are up for election every two years?

_____

_____

_____

_____

_____

2. Compare What is the difference between a primary election and a general election?

_____

_____

_____

_____

_____

Mark the Text

3. Underline what voters can do in some states if they want to change the state constitution.

netw⊕rks Read Chapter 11 Lesson 2 in your textbook or online.

Types of Elections

There are more than a half million elected officials in the United States today. All of these people had to run for office. To do so they had to understand the election process. The basic steps of that process are fairly simple.

The first step in most states is to win the primary election. A primary is usually held in the spring or summer. The purpose of the primary is to pick candidates for the general election in November.

There are times when none of the candidates wins a majority of votes in the primary. In this case, a runoff primary is held. The winner of the runoff goes on to run in the general election.

The general election is held on the same day across the country. This day is always the first Tuesday after the first Monday in November. National elections are held in even-numbered years. Elections for the entire House of Representatives and one-third of the Senate are held every two years. Elections for president are held every four years. State and local officials are usually elected at the same time.

During an election, people are often also asked to vote on issues. An **issue** is a matter of public interest. For example, if a city council wants to raise money to build a new school, the council may put the issue on a ballot. The voters decide if the money gets raised for the school or not.

There are two ways that voters can have a direct voice in government. The chart below explains these methods.

Initiative	process that lets voters propose new laws or amendments to state constitutions
Referendum	process that allows voters to accept or reject a law passed by the state legislature

In an initiative, a certain number of voters must sign a petition. The petition asks for a new law. If enough people sign the petition, the proposal is put on the ballot.

Some states also allow **recall** elections. These are special elections in which voters can remove a person from office. A recall begins with a petition. If enough people sign the petition, a recall vote is held. If the people vote to remove the official, another special election is held to find a replacement. Special elections may also be held to fill an office if an elected official has died or resigned.

Presidential Elections

The election of the president is different from other elections. The president is not elected directly by the people. When people vote for president, they are really voting for electors. These electors make up the **Electoral College.** The Electoral College actually chooses the president and vice president. The diagram will help you understand how this works.

1. The general election for president takes place in **November**. In most states, the candidate who wins the most popular votes in the general election wins all of that state's electoral votes.

2. In **December** the electors meet and cast their ballots. They send the results to the Senate.

3. In **January** the House and Senate meet in joint session to officially count the votes.

4. The candidate who wins a majority of the electoral votes (at least 270 of 538) wins the election.

Each state has the same number of electors in the Electoral College as it has members of Congress. The District of Columbia also has three electors. There are 538 in all. The purpose of the popular vote is to choose these electors. The **popular vote** is the vote cast by the people in the general election. The winning electors then choose the president. Because of this system, candidates for president spend most of their time and money in high-population states that have large numbers of electors.

Some people do not like the Electoral College system. They especially dislike that it is a **winner-take-all system.** The winner of the popular vote in each state gets all of that state's electoral votes. This is true even if the candidate wins by only a few votes.

It is possible for a person who wins the popular vote in a presidential election to not get enough electoral votes to become president. This has happened four times. It also means that it is hard for third-party candidates to win electoral votes even though they may have won millions of popular votes.

The Electoral College system was set up by the Constitution. The Framers settled on this system as a compromise. Some thought the people should have direct control of the

Mark the Text

4. Underline the sentence that tells who elects the president of the United States.

Think Critically

5. **Sequence** What happens between the general election and a candidate actually winning the election?

_____

_____

_____

_____

_____

Show Your Skill

6. **Identify Cause and Effect** How could a candidate for president win the popular vote but lose the election?

_____

_____

_____

_____

_____

_____

_____

Take the Challenge

7. Do you think the Electoral College is a good way to elect the president? Make a colorful poster that expresses your opinion. Include your reasons for your opinion.

Think Critically

8. Infer What is the purpose of a party's national convention?

_____

_____

_____

_____

government. Others thought that giving the people direct control might be dangerous. They were afraid that people would make bad decisions based on emotions. The Electoral College was their answer.

Today some people think that the voters should elect the president directly. Others think that a state's electoral votes should be divided among the candidates according to how many popular votes they get. Any change to the Electoral College system would require an amendment to the Constitution.

Running for Office

When a person tries to win an election, his or her efforts are called a *campaign*. A campaign begins when someone decides to run for office. The person must first make certain they meet the requirements for the office. Most offices require a person to be a certain age and a U. S. citizen. If someone wants to run for president, the candidate will form an exploratory committee. The committee's job is to find out how many people support the candidate.

If there is enough support, the candidate announces that he or she is running for office. Usually several people from each party decide to run for president. The party picks one of these people as their candidate at the national convention. The conventions are big events that get a lot of attention from the media.

No matter what office candidates are running for, they must make many public appearances before the election. They give speeches and interviews. They hold debates. They try to appeal to as many voters as possible.

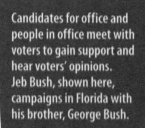

Candidates for office and people in office meet with voters to gain support and hear voters' opinions. Jeb Bush, shown here, campaigns in Florida with his brother, George Bush.

PHOTO: Brooks Kraft/Sygma/Corbis

The Federal Election Commission regulates how candidates spend campaign money. As seen here, commission members meet to review regulations and address issues.

Candidates usually have staff to help them. Volunteers help candidates pursue voters in many ways. Volunteers **canvass** neighborhoods. This means they go from door to door to gather support. They also make telephone calls and send e-mails to tell people about their candidate.

People running for office also try to get endorsements, or support, from important people or groups. They hope that voters who like these people or groups will vote for them. Some examples of this kind of support are celebrities, politicians, newspapers, and unions. Candidates also spend a great deal of money on ads in newspapers, on the radio, and on TV.

Campaigns cost a lot of money. The race for president costs each candidate hundreds of millions of dollars. Most of this money comes from donations. Donations are made by individuals, businesses, unions, and political action committees. **Political action committees (PACs)** are set up by interest groups to raise money for candidates.

The Federal Election Commission (FEC) makes rules about how much money candidates can spend and to keep elections fair. Many Americans still worry that campaigns cost too much. They also worry that elected officials will try to please big donors rather than being fair to everyone.

Think Critically

9. Explain What is the job of the FEC?

_____

_____

_____

_____

Show Your Skill

10. Make Decisions Do you think you would be influenced to vote for or against a candidate because of an endorsement? Explain.

_____

_____

_____

 NGSSS Check What are several ways voters learn more about a candidate running for office? SS.7.C.2.9

_____

_____

ESSENTIAL QUESTION *What are the rights and responsibilities of citizens?*

Reflect on What It Means . . .

Soon, you will be old enough to register and then vote. In the United States, voting is a privilege and a responsibility. In some countries around the world, people do not get to select their leaders. Here in the U.S., every vote counts.

To My Community

Voting is such a moving experience that most people remember the first time they cast a ballot. With your teacher's guidance, find one or more appropriate adults in your community to interview about the first time they voted.

To the World

In how many countries can people vote for their leaders? Conduct Internet research to find out. Express your findings in percentage form. What can you conclude from this number?

To Me

Write a journal entry that describes how you think it might feel to cast a ballot for the first time.

TAKE THE CHALLENGE

For some elections, fewer than half of the eligible voters cast their vote. Work with a small group to create a "get out and vote" commercial. Create a video of the commercial and perhaps have your teacher send it to your local television station.

CHAPTER 12

PUBLIC OPINION AND GOVERNMENT

NGSSS

SS.7.C.2.10 Examine the impact of media, individuals, and interest groups on monitoring and influencing government.

SS.7.C.2.11 Analyze media and political communications (bias, symbolism, propaganda)

SS.7.C.2.13 Examine multiple perspectives on public and current issues.

ESSENTIAL QUESTION *How do citizens, both individually and collectively, influence government policy?*

Study the political cartoon. What is the cartoonist trying to say?

Who or what does the giant man represent?

Who are the people being held?

NOW THIS IS A COMPLEX LOVE STORY...

CONGRESS

SPECIAL INTERESTS

Copyright © by The McGraw-Hill Companies, Inc.

DBQ BREAKING IT DOWN

Write a sentence that summarizes the message of this cartoon.

Do you think that political cartoons influence public opinion? Explain your answer.

PHOTO: By permission of Steve Breen and Creators Syndicate, Inc.

Public Opinion and Government Chapter 12 **175**

FORMING PUBLIC OPINION

NGSSS

SS.7.C.2.10 Examine the impact of media, individuals, and interest groups on monitoring and influencing government.

Essential Question

How do citizens, both individually and collectively, influence government policy?

Guiding Questions

1. What is public opinion?
2. How is public opinion measured?

Terms to Know

public opinion
the ideas and views of the people

mass media
media that reach large numbers of people

interest group
group of people who share the same opinion about an issue and unite to promote their beliefs

public opinion poll
a survey in which individuals are asked to answer questions about a particular issue or person

pollster
a person who conducts polls

It Matters Because

Public opinion affects leaders' actions, but leaders also try to shape public opinion.

What is public policy, and how can you influence it? How do government leaders try to influence public opinion? In the chart below, write a *P* for the influence of the public on public policy and *G* for the influence of government leaders on public opinion.

Showing an advertisement about a bill that legislators support	
Answering questions about the condition of the economy	
Joining a group to support an issue	
Answering questions at a town hall meeting about issues	

What Do You Know?

Directions: In the first column, answer the questions based on what you know before you study. After this lesson, complete the last column.

	Now	Later
What do you think public opinion includes?		
Can public opinion be measured?		

Public Opinion

Government leaders often talk about "the public." Who do they mean? Did you know that you are part of "the public"? The public is all of the people in our nation.

Many people want to know what the public thinks. Businesses and government leaders are especially interested in **public opinion.** Public opinion means the ideas and views of the people about an issue or a person. Public opinion is important in a democracy. Officials need to understand what the people they represent want them to do. Presidents often try to judge public opinion. This tells them when the public is ready for a new idea. It also helps them propose programs that people will support.

Americans often have different opinions about things. Those opinions are shaped by their experiences. Many things affect the kinds of experiences people have. One is a person's gender. Gender means whether a person is male or female.

People need information to form their opinions. A major factor shaping public opinion is the mass media. The **mass media** are all the types of communication that can reach a large number of people. These media include television, radio, Web sites, newspapers, books, recordings, and movies.

Think Critically

1. Explain What is meant by the term *public opinion*?

_____

_____

_____

Mark the Text

2. Circle the type of mass media that you use most often.

Show Your Skill

3. Identify Cause and Effect What factors influence public opinion?

_____

_____

_____

_____

_____

The mass media can affect public opinion about a government leader. A man in Coral Gables reads an article in *The Miami Herald* about the U.S. government bailout.

5. Evaluate What is a good sample for a poll?

6. Underline the definition of a pollster. Then give an example of a time when you or someone you know was approached by a pollster. Include the topic of the poll and the location.

Interest groups also try to shape public opinion. An interest group is a group of people who share the same opinion about an issue. They come together to support their beliefs. They try to persuade others to agree with them. This includes people in government as well as other citizens. Interest groups can put political pressure on government leaders to act a certain way, such as passing a law. Because of this, interest groups are sometimes called pressure groups.

Public opinion has three features:

- direction
- intensity
- stability

Direction tells whether the public's opinion agrees or disagrees with an issue or a person. Do people agree or disagree with a tax cut? In most cases, the direction is mixed, but one side can be stronger than the other. *Intensity* shows the strength of a person's or group's opinion. When people feel strongly about an issue, they may take action. Actions include voting, joining an interest group, or working on a campaign. *Stability* tells how firmly people hold their opinions. In other words, are they likely to change their minds? Opinions based on a strong belief are generally very stable. For example, most people's opinions about civil rights are more stable than their views about candidates.

Public Opinion Polls

Public opinion can be measured. One way is by looking at election results. Election results give only a general idea of public opinion, however. This is because people choose candidates for many reasons. They may not support all of the candidate's views.

A better way to measure public opinion is to ask many people what they think about a specific issue or person. This is called a survey, or **public opinion poll.** Such polls put many people's answers together to measure public opinion.

Hundreds of groups conduct public opinion polls. Political leaders use polls to help them keep in touch with public opinion on a more regular basis than waiting for election results. They also use polls to help them create programs or make laws that fit the people's needs. They also look at polls to try to win elections.

A person who conducts polls is called a **pollster.** Pollsters have different ways of selecting groups of people to answer their questions. One way they do this is at random, or

When polls are published, they can influence public opinion and public policy. This young woman is taking a poll at a local fair. The published results may or may not affect how citizens think about an issue.

by chance. A good sample is a smaller version of the whole population of the country. It reflects the opinions of people all over the United States.

Pollsters are very careful about how they word their questions. The way a question is asked can change the way a person answers it. A good poll is unbiased. Responsible pollsters do not want to influence the person taking the poll. Polls that are written to try to influence, or shape, the answers are called push polls. Citizens should ask themselves if the questions in a poll are fair and unbiased. The questions asked in push polls are not.

Polls can be both good and bad. Some people think polls tell leaders what people think about an issue. Others think that polls distract leaders or unfairly affect election results. They also say that polls can make people decide not to vote. If a poll shows that a candidate is far behind, people may think he or she has already lost and not bother to vote.

Public opinion affects the government's plan of action. But other factors are also at work. You will look at these other factors in the next lesson.

NGSSS Check List two reasons why public opinion is important in a democracy. SS.7.C.2.10

_____

_____

_____

_____

Think Critically

7. Analyze How can you recognize a push poll?

_____

_____

_____

Show Your Skill

8. Draw Conclusions Besides elections, what is another way to measure public opinion?

_____

_____

Take the Challenge

9. Conduct a public opinion poll about an issue that is important in your school or classroom. Collect the data and create the poll on poster board. Show the results, and ask your class how seeing the results affected their opinion.

THE MASS MEDIA

NGSSS

SS.7.C.2.10 Examine the impact of media, individuals, and interest groups on monitoring and influencing government.

SS.7.C.2.11 Analyze media and political communications (bias, symbolism, propaganda).

SS.7.C.2.13 Examine multiple perspectives on public and current issues.

Essential Question

How do citizens, both individually and collectively, influence government policy?

Guiding Questions

1. How do the media influence public opinion and government?
2. What are the restrictions on freedom of the press?

Terms to Know

public agenda
the set of issues the government focuses on

leak
to give information to the press secretly

watchdog
the role played by the media when they try to uncover government waste or corruption

prior restraint
restricting information before it is published or spoken

shield law
a law allowing the press to keep sources secret

libel
written false information that harms a person's reputation

malice
evil intent

It Matters Because

The mass media can be an important source of information about government and public issues.

Do you think that the mass media should have the freedom to say or print anything it wants to? Explain your answer.

_____

_____

_____

What Do You Know?

Directions: In the first column, circle *True* if you think the statement is true or *False* based on what you know before you read the lesson. After the lesson, complete the last column.

Now			Later	
True	False	The mass media can affect who runs for office.	True	False
True	False	Government officials pass information onto the press.	True	False
True	False	The government can stop the publication of something if it does not like the information to be published.	True	False

The Influence of the Media

The mass media can affect politics and government. They also link people and their elected leaders. The two broad types of mass media, print and electronic, are shown in the chart below.

Print Media	Electronic Media
• newspapers • magazines • books	• the Internet • television • radio

The government deals with many problems and issues. Those that receive the most time, money, and effort from government leaders make up what is often called the **public agenda.** An agenda is a set of items that a person or group wants to address.

The media have an effect on what problems officials see as important. When the media focus on a problem, people begin to worry about it. Then they expect the government to deal with it.

The mass media can affect who runs for office. Usually candidates are experienced politicians. They spend years working in their political parties. Some candidates, though, are people who were famous for their success in another field. For instance, actor Arnold Schwarzenegger was elected governor of California in 2003. When candidates are already well known, the media cover their campaigns with interest. In this way, the candidate takes advantage of the media's desire to cover a story.

Reporters and politicians have a complex relationship. They need each other. Reporters need information to write stories. Political leaders need media coverage to get their message out. At the same time, the two groups often clash. As one presidential assistant explained, "Politicians live— and sometimes die—by the press. The press lives by politicians."

Actor Arnold Schwarzenegger easily won the race for governor of California in 2003. Here, Schwarzenegger is being sworn in as governor.

Think Critically

1. Explain Why do politicians and reporters need each other?

_____

_____

_____

_____

2. Compare How does the media's role as a watchdog help both the public and the media?

_____

_____

_____

_____

_____

3. Sequence What must the government do first before classifying information?

_____

_____

_____

_____

4. Interpret Information
Describe a picture you might draw to illustrate the idea of a shield law.

_____

_____

_____

_____

_____

_____

_____

5. Take the role of a media watchdog. With a partner, write an editorial or script for a news broadcast dealing with an actual or imagined corrupt government activity.

Officials try to use the media to their advantage. They may **leak,** or secretly pass, information to reporters. They may do this to test the public's response to a proposal before they openly acknowledge, or admit, that they are considering it. If the public reacts well, officials might act on the idea. If the public reacts negatively, officials can drop it. Politicians also use leaks to shape public opinion on an issue, or to gain favor with a reporter.

At the same time, reporters can present stories in ways that show an official in a bad light. They can ask officials tough questions about the positions that the officials take. Politicians may try to avoid this difficulty by refusing to answer their questions. That practice, though, can result in criticism from the media.

The mass media also play a crucial **watchdog** role. That means it keeps a close eye on government activities. Journalists write stories that expose waste and corruption at all levels of government. These kinds of stories attract a large audience. Throughout our history the media have played this role, serving the interests of both the media and the public by exposing wrongdoing by officials.

Americans need to stay informed. At the same time, the government must keep some secrets for national security reasons. The government can classify, or label, some information as secret. That information is then off-limits to reporters.

The government can use other methods to try to shape the news. During the first part of the war in Iraq, some journalists went with American troops going into battle. They reported on battles and on the daily life of the troops. Some critics said that this practice allowed the government to control news reporting.

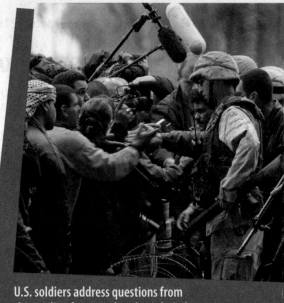

U.S. soldiers address questions from the media after a car bomb exploded in Baghdad, killing dozens of civilians.

PHOTO: Mario Tama/Getty Images

Protecting the Press

The founders of our nation knew that democracy needs information and ideas to be shared freely. This is why freedom of the press is one of the first freedoms in the Bill of Rights. The press refers to TV, radio, and the Internet as well as print media.

The Supreme Court has ruled that freedom of the press means that government cannot use **prior restraint.** Prior restraint is when the government censors material before it is published. To censor means to edit or stop a publication. In general, writers and editors are free to choose what they will write or say even if it is unpopular.

Sometimes people give information to the media even when doing so could cause them harm. For example, some people could lose their jobs if they share information about their business that the boss does not want the press to know about. Because of this, many states have laws to allow the press to keep their sources secret. These are called **shield laws.**

There are some limits on freedom of the press. The media cannot publish false written information that harms someone's reputation. This is called **libel.**

It is hard for public officials to prove libel. They must show that the publisher knew the information was false and published it anyway. This is called **malice.** Malice is evil intent.

The government controls some aspects of radio and TV. There are only so many airwaves available to broadcast on. The government decides who may use them. In addition, the Federal Communications Commission (FCC) makes rules about what can be seen or said on TV and radio shows. The FCC is a regulatory, or managing agency. It can punish broadcasters who break its rules.

Freedom of the press is an important right. Complete the chart below with information you have learned.

I. Freedom of the Press
A. Protections
1. _____
2. _____
B. Limits
1. _____
2. _____
3. _____

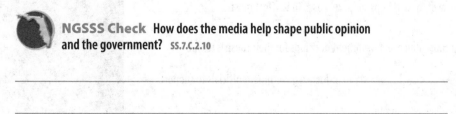

NGSSS Check How does the media help shape public opinion and the government? SS.7.C.2.10

_____

_____

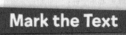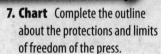

Take the Challenge

6. Identify the Main Idea
What are two ways the federal government can manage broadcast media?

_____

_____

_____

_____

_____

Mark the Text

7. Chart Complete the outline about the protections and limits of freedom of the press.

NGSSS

SS.7.C.2.10 Examine the impact of media, individuals, and interest groups on monitoring and influencing government.

SS.7.C.2.11 Analyze media and political communications (bias, symbolism, propaganda).

SS.7.C.2.13 Examine multiple perspectives on public and current issues.

Essential Question

How do citizens, both individually and collectively, influence government policy?

Guiding Questions

1. How do special-interest groups influence public policy?
2. How does the government regulate interest groups?

Terms to Know

public-interest group
a group that supports causes that affect most Americans

nonpartisan
not related to either political party

lobbyist
a person who works for an interest group

It Matters Because

Interest groups are one vehicle people use to make their views known and to work for causes they believe in.

List 1–2 issues or causes that are important to you.

Would you join an interest group for one of the causes you listed? Why or why not?

What Do You Know?

Directions: Use what you know to complete the paragraph below.

_____ groups are advocates for issues or causes. They work to influence the

_____. Some of these groups support causes that affect most _____.

One way that these groups influence government decisions for their cause is to hire

_____. The _____ try to influence government officials to support

the ideas of the _____ group.

Interest Groups

There are many ways to contact elected officials. Many have social media sites, Web sites, and e-mail. They are interested in what you have to say. You have the right to contact them, and you also have the right to join together with other people to make your voice heard. This right to assemble is guaranteed, or promised, in the First Amendment. When people join together on issues, they have a stronger voice. Interest groups are one way to join with others to influence the government.

There are many interest groups, and they can be broken down into types. One type represents particular kinds of businesses. These groups try to get the government to act in a way that benefits their business. The National Automobile Dealers Association is one such group. It works on behalf of companies that sell cars and trucks.

Some interest groups are based on shared economic goals. For example, the U.S. Chamber of Commerce works for businesses. Another type of interest group focuses its efforts on workers. These groups are concerned with issues such as wages and working conditions. The American Federation of Labor and Congress of Industrial Organizations (AFL-CIO) is the largest of these groups. It is a partnership of labor unions.

Another type of interest group works for people who share similar characteristics. One works for the rights of African Americans. It is called the National Association for the Advancement of Colored People (NAACP). Still other interest groups promote the rights of women and of older Americans. Other interest groups work for special causes, for example, the Sierra Club works to protect nature.

Think Critically

1. Summarize List six types of interest groups.

_____

_____

_____

_____

_____

_____

Show Your Skill

2. Recognize Point of View
Do you think that special interest groups have too much influence? Why or why not? Explain your answer.

_____

_____

_____

_____

In Miami, the president of the South Florida chapter of the AFL-CIO speaks with members at a rally to support workers of airport food services.

3. **Explain** What tools do interest groups use to influence government and public opinion?

_____

_____

Show Your Skill

4. **Explain** Why must former government officials wait before becoming lobbyists?

_____

_____

_____

5. **Draw Conclusions** How is lobbying used effectively?

_____

_____

_____

_____

_____

Take the Challenge

6. Think of a public-interest group or special-interest group active in Florida that you would like to join. Write about why you would like to join that group. Or, think of an idea for a new group and write about what the group's focus will be.

Yet another type of group is called a **public-interest group.** A public-interest group supports causes that affect most Americans. One example is the League of Women Voters. This **nonpartisan** group does not work for any political party. It supplies information about candidates and issues. Other groups work for disabled people.

Interest groups play an important role in the United States. Their main role is to shape government policy and do this by working in four areas: (1) on elections, (2) through the courts, (3) with lawmakers, and (4) trying to shape public opinion. Interest groups focus on elections and want to get people elected who support their ideas. Many interest groups have formed political action committees (PACs). A political action committee raises money from its members and then uses the money to help candidates who agree with their views get elected. Interest groups affect public policy by bringing cases to court. For instance, an interest group for women might help a woman worker sue a company if it feels she was paid unfairly. A group may also argue that a law or policy is unconstitutional.

One of the most important ways interest groups try to shape policy is by lobbying. Interest groups hire **lobbyists** to contact lawmakers directly on their behalf. They try to convince officials at all levels of government to support their ideas. This is called _lobbying_. Good lobbyists help government leaders by giving them information about issues and suggesting solutions to problems. They may also write drafts of bills and testify at hearings. Lawmakers appreciate this help but also know that lobbyists can be biased. This means the information they supply might not be neutral.

Interest groups want to sway public opinion and to get new members. Many use direct mail, e-mail, or advertising. They also try to get media attention by holding protests or public events. They even use propaganda to present information to make people believe in an idea. There are many ways of spreading propaganda.

Special-interest groups and public-interest groups can support similar causes. A national group called Stay Alive.... Just Drive! is working to ban the use of cell phones while driving.

Propaganda Techniques	
Technique	**Example**
Bandwagon	Join us, we're sure to win!
Name-calling	Candidate A is a dangerous extremist.
Endorsement	Movie star says, "I'm voting for Candidate A. You should, too!"
Stacked cards	Our candidate has the best record on the environment.
Glittering generalities	Our candidate will bring peace and prosperity.
Just plain folks	I'm running for office. My parents were plain, hardworking folks, and they taught me those values.
Transfer	Surround the candidate with patriotic symbols such as flags.

Mark the Text

7. Chart Number the propaganda techniques from 1 to 7, with 1 being the most effective.

8. Underline the sentence that explains why some people dislike interest groups.

Think Critically

9. Summarize Name two ways that the government regulates interest groups.

_____

_____

_____

_____

_____

_____

_____

_____

_____

_____

_____

Regulating Interest Groups

The Constitution protects the right of people to belong to interest groups. But laws do put some controls on interest groups. They limit how much money PACs can give candidates. Lobbyists must register, or sign up, with the government. They must report who they contact and how much money they spend. Former government officials must wait for a period of time after leaving office before they can become lobbyists. The delay is meant to stop them from using friendships and inside knowledge to help special-interest groups. This kind of law has not been very successful.

Some people criticize interest groups. They think these groups have too much influence. Others believe that interest groups make the government address people's concerns. They think that interest groups are one way that people can take part in government.

 NGSSS Check List four ways that interest groups influence public policy. **SS.7.C.2.10**

_____

_____

Reflect on What It Means . . .

Interest groups work and support many different causes. One of their goals is to influence the public and government policy. Search newspapers, magazines, or news Web sites for stories that relate to what you have learned about interest groups.

To My Community

Find a headline about an interest group operating in your community or in Florida's state capital, Tallahassee. The headline should relate to an interest group trying to influence government decisions. Copy the headline below, or cut it out of a newspaper or magazine and paste or tape it below. You may use another piece of paper if needed.

To the World

Find a headline about an interest group in a different country. Write it below, or cut it out of a newspaper or magazine and paste or tape it below.

To Me

Now, write a headline about your own life. It should take the following form: "(YOUR NAME) JOINS (NAME OF INTEREST GROUP)." The interest group can be real or fictional. Below the headline, write a sentence that tells why you joined the interest group.

TAKE THE CHALLENGE

The First Amendment to the Constitution reads:
"Congress shall make no law (1) respecting an establishment of religion, or (2) prohibiting the free exercise thereof; or (3) abridging the freedom of speech, or (4) of the press; or (5) the right of the people peaceably to assemble, and (6) to petition the Government for a redress of grievances."
Look at each numbered part. Write a sentence for each numbered detail that tells how you think it relates to interest groups in the United States today.

CHAPTER 13

STATE GOVERNMENT

NGSSS

SS.7.C.3.4 Identify the relationship and division of powers between the federal government and state governments.

SS.7.C.3.13 Compare the constitutions of the United States and Florida.

ESSENTIAL QUESTION *Why and how do people create, structure, and change governments?*

The Florida state government is powerful. It has the power to pass laws, collect taxes, and spend vast amounts of money. It has the power to set up local governments and conduct elections. Where does the State of Florida get all of this power?

> **We**, the people of the State of Florida, being grateful to Almighty God for our constitutional liberty, in order to secure its benefits, perfect our government, insure domestic tranquility, maintain public order, and guarantee equal civil and political rights to all, do ordain and establish this constitution. **"**

PREAMBLE TO THE FLORIDA CONSTITUTION

We

Who is included in *We, the people*?

_____

DBQ BREAKING IT DOWN

Parts of this passage are similar to the Preamble to the U.S. Constitution. Why do you think that is so?

_____

_____

_____

_____

Why does Florida need a constitution?

_____

_____

_____

_____

PHOTO: The Florida Senate

THE FEDERAL SYSTEM

NGSSS

SS.7.C.3.4 Identify the relationship and division of powers between the federal government and state governments.

SS.7.C.3.13 Compare the constitutions of the United States and Florida.

SS.7.C.3.14 Differentiate between local, state, and federal governments' obligations and services.

Essential Question
Why and how do people create, structure, and change governments?

Guiding Questions
1. How does the federal system allow the national government and state governments to share power?
2. What characteristics do all state governments share?
3. How does the Florida constitution compare to the U.S. Constitution?

Terms to Know

federal system
the sharing of power between the central and state governments

reserved powers
powers that the U. S. Constitution gives only to the states

concurrent powers
powers that states and the federal government share

supremacy clause
clause in the U.S. Constitution that says federal laws are above state laws

grants-in-aid
money given to the states by the federal government

It Matters Because

Both state and federal governments provide services to people.

What do you think are the three most important services that governments provide?

Explain your choices.

What Do You Know?

Directions: Work with a partner to list jobs you think are done by the state and federal governments. When you complete the lesson, you may be able to add more jobs to the chart.

State	Federal

Federal and State Powers

Earlier you learned that the Constitution gives certain powers only to the federal government. It leaves other powers to the states. Some powers are shared by both. This is our **federal system** of government. In a federal system, the national and the state governments share and divide powers. Both build highways. That is just one example of how these two levels of government do similar jobs.

In writing the Constitution, the Framers created a stronger central government than the one that existed under the Articles of Confederation. However, they also thought that states were important, too. As a result, the Framers created a federal system that divides powers between state and national governments. The Constitution limits the powers of states, but it also protects the states.

Constitutional Protections of States		
Article and Section of Constitution	Protection	Example
Article IV, Section 1	Says each state must respect legal actions taken by other states	One state accepts driver's license given by another.
Article IV, Section 2	Promises each state will treat the people of other states equally	One state cannot give people from another state tougher punishments for a crime than they would get in their own state.
Article IV, Section 3	Guarantees each state's area	Land cannot be taken from any state to make a new state without that state's approval.
Article IV, Section 4	Promises each state a republican form of government and vows to protect that government against enemy attack or revolt	Each state has control over its National Guard. In times of war, the federal government can call the National Guard into action to take part in federal missions.

Under the Constitution, the federal government has three kinds of powers:

- *Expressed* powers are listed in the Constitution. The power to coin money is an example.

- *Implied* powers are based on statements in the Constitution. For example, the Constitution says the president is commander in chief of the armed forces. This implies that the president has the power to send troops to respond to a crisis.

Copyright © by The McGraw-Hill Companies, Inc.

Think Critically

1. Explain What is a federal system?

_____

_____

_____

_____

2. Synthesize Think of another example for Article IV, Section 2.

_____

_____

_____

_____

_____

_____

_____

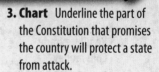

Mark the Text

3. Chart Underline the part of the Constitution that promises the country will protect a state from attack.

Think Critically

4. Categorize List three concurrent powers.

_____

_____

_____

Mark the Text

5. Graphic Organizer Circle powers held by both the national and state governments.

◆ _Inherent_ powers are the kind of powers a government has simply because it is a government. Buying land from another country is an example.

The Framers knew that state governments were important. So they kept certain powers only for the states. These are called **reserved powers.** Reserved powers come from the Tenth Amendment. An example of a reserved power is that states have the power to set up local governments. They also have the power to conduct elections.

Other powers are held by both the national and state governments. These are called **concurrent powers.** They include the power to tax, to borrow money, and to pass laws. They also include the power to spend money for the general good of the people. For example, both federal and state governments build highways. The diagram below shows how federalism divides powers between the national and state governments.

The Constitution also sets specific limits on the states. A state may not declare war. It may not enter into a treaty with another country. It cannot issue its own money. It cannot tax imports from other states or countries.

Division of Powers

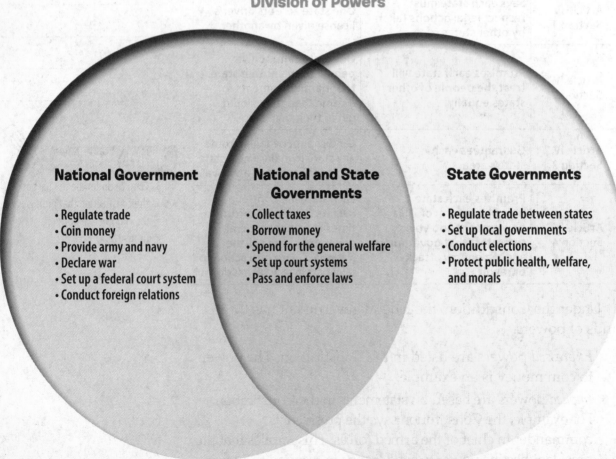

National Government

- Regulate trade
- Coin money
- Provide army and navy
- Declare war
- Set up a federal court system
- Conduct foreign relations

National and State Governments

- Collect taxes
- Borrow money
- Spend for the general welfare
- Set up court systems
- Pass and enforce laws

State Governments

- Regulate trade between states
- Set up local governments
- Conduct elections
- Protect public health, welfare, and morals

States must abide by the Bill of Rights. This is because the Fourteenth Amendment says that states must give all citizens "equal protection of the laws." States cannot take away the rights of its citizens "without due process of law."

State power is also limited by the **supremacy clause** in the Constitution. This clause puts the Constitution and federal law above state law. If a state law conflicts with the Constitution or a federal law, the state law is thrown out.

In our system, the federal and state governments work together. Each year the federal government gives large sums of money to the states. These sums are called **grants-in-aid.** The grants are to be used to meet goals that Congress has set. For example, grants might be used for health care or education.

State governments also work together. For example, several states are working as a group to design an energy policy. States often help each other with law enforcement.

The states and Congress do not always agree. Sometimes a federal law tells the states to meet certain goals, but does not give them the money to do so. Such laws are known as unfunded mandates. State officials complain that these laws violate, or go against, the rights of states. States may also disagree with what Congress wants them to do. For example, many states have protested the Real ID Act passed in 2005. The law set tough new standards for drivers licenses.

The State Constitutions

Every state has a constitution. These constitutions are similar to the federal constitution. For example, like the federal government, Florida's government is split into three branches—the legislative, the executive, and the judicial. It also spells out the powers of the three branches. State constitutions also list the rights guaranteed to each citizen. Florida's list is called the Declaration of Rights.

State constitutions are different from one another in some ways. For example, Massachusetts has the oldest constitution still in use. Its framework was written in 1780. Florida has had six constitutions; the most recent was approved in 1969.

Unlike the U.S. Constitution, state constitutions are often very specific. As a result, some of them are quite long. For example, Florida's constitution has a long passage that defines the state's boundaries. Florida's constitution is about 57,000 words long. It is not the longest state constitution.

Alabama has added the most amendments—more than 800. Florida has over 100 amendments, which is many more than the U.S. Constitution has.

Show Your Skill

6. Draw Conclusions How does the supremacy clause limit state power?

_____

_____

_____

Think Critically

7. Infer Why might a state argue that an unfunded mandate violates its rights?

_____

_____

_____

Show Your Skill

8. Draw Conclusions Why do you think both the federal and state governments were given the power to collect taxes?

_____

_____

9. Interpret Charts What are three of the specific provisions in Florida's constitution?

_____

_____

_____

Think Critically

10. Explain Why has Florida's constitution changed more often than the United States Constitution?

_____

_____

_____

_____

_____

Comparing Constitutions	
U.S. Constitution	**Florida Constitution**
1st constitution of nation	6th constitution in state's history
7 articles	12 articles
Bill of rights added as first 10 amendments	Begins with a declaration of rights
Establishes executive, legislative, and judiciary at the national level	Establishes executive, legislative, and judiciary at the state level
Is a broad framework of government	Contains many specific provisions, such as provisions regarding a state lottery, conservation, transportation, and smoking in the workplace
Establishes state government	Establishes local government
Does not establish public education	Establishes public education
Allows for amendments but does not require regular reviews	Requires a commission to review the constitution every 20 years for proposing changes

The Constitution of Florida

In 1821 the United States acquired Florida from Spain. It was a U.S. territory for about 17 years. Then, the people of Florida began to prepare to become a state. In 1838 they elected representatives to write a constitution.

Early forms of Florida's constitution included laws that made it clear that Florida was a slave territory.

Some of these laws

- gave voting rights only to free white men,
- banned lawmakers from passing "laws for the emancipation of slaves", and
- gave lawmakers the power to stop free blacks from entering the state.

In 1861 Florida joined the Confederacy. After the Civil War, Florida adopted a new constitution that outlawed slavery and gave voting rights to all male citizens age 21 and over. However in 1885 a new constitution allowed the state to limit voting using a tax on voting, or a poll tax. The 1885 constitution lasted more than 80 years but was amended 149 times as Florida changed. In 1968 a new constitution that reflected modern Florida was adopted.

Important Articles in Florida's Constitution Today

Article	Purpose
Article I	Says that all people are equal under the law. This article has many of the same rights as the U.S. Bill of Rights, such as the right to free speech.
Article II, General Provisions	Defines state boundaries and the location of state government. Protects the natural resources and scenic beauty of the state.
Articles III, IV, and V	Establishes the three branches of state government.
Article VI	Describes voting and election rules. Addresses campaign funding and spending limits.
Article VII	Gives tax rules for state and local governments.
Article VIII	Defines local governments.
Article IX	Creates Florida's public schools and state university system.
Article X	Includes 27 sections that cover a range of topics, such as minimum wage and animal cruelty.
Article XI	Explains how to amend Florida's constitution. Requires a constitutional review every 20 years to see if it still meets the state's needs.

NGSSS Check List three differences between the U.S. Constitution and Florida's state constitution. **SS.7.C.3.13**

_____

_____

_____

_____

_____

_____

What happens every 20 years to Florida's Constitution? **SS.7.C.3.13**

_____

_____

Think Critically

11. Evaluate Review the articles from Florida's constitution in the chart. Which article do you think is most important for the citizens of Florida? Explain.

_____

_____

_____

12. Evaluate Which article do you think is most important for the state government? Explain.

_____

_____

_____

_____

_____

_____

_____

Take the Challenge

13. Do you think it is a good idea for Florida to review its constitution every 20 years? Debate the issue with someone who has the opposite opinion.

NGSSS

SS.7.C.3.9 Illustrate the law making process at the local, state, and federal levels.

SS.7.E.2.1 Explain how federal, state, and local taxes support the economy as a function of the United States government.

Essential Question

Why and how do people create, structure, and change governments?

Guiding Questions

1. What are the functions of state legislatures?
2. What economic challenges do state legislatures face?

It Matters Because

State legislatures make laws that affect many aspects of your life such as the quality of schools, roads, and parks.

What state service do you appreciate the most? Explain.

Terms to Know

unicameral
having one house in the legislature

redistricting
to redraw the boundaries of a legislative district

malapportionment
an unequal representation in a state legislature

session
a meeting of a legislature to conduct business

special session
a legislative meeting called for a specific purpose

legislative referendum
a vote called by a legislature to seek voter approval of a law

popular referendum
a question placed on a ballot by a citizen petition to decide if a law should be repealed

What Do You Know?

Directions: You already know some facts about state government. In the space below, list words you already know that relate to the work of the state legislature. When you finish the lesson, add more words that you have learned.

How Legislatures Function

In all but one state, the legislative branch is bicameral. Bicameral means that the legislature has two houses, like the U.S. Congress. Nebraska is the only state with a **unicameral,** or a one-house, legislature. In every state, the upper house is called the senate. In most states, the lower house is usually called the house of representatives.

bicameral   unicameral

How old does a person have to be to serve in a state legislature? The minimum age varies from state to state. To serve in the lower house, a person has to be at least 18 years old in some states, and 21 in other states. State senators have to be at least 25 in many states. However, in some states an 18-year-old can serve in the senate.

In most states, state senators serve four-year terms. House members usually serve for two years. All states pay their lawmakers. However, the pay varies from state to state.

Each house of a legislature has a leader. In the lower house, this person is called the speaker. The speaker is chosen by the members of the house. The lieutenant governor of a state usually heads the senate. The members of each party in each house also choose a leader. They are the majority leader and the minority leader. They help set the schedule for legislation and planning when bills will be discussed.

Every member of a legislature represents a district. All the districts in a state are supposed to be about equal in population. Every ten years, the federal government takes a census, or count, of all Americans. The results are used to draw the borders of the districts. The task of drawing new borders every ten years is called **redistricting.**

In the past, states did not always draw new borders, even though district populations had changed. This meant that people were not being represented equally. Having unfair district sizes like these is called **malapportionment.** The U.S. Supreme Court ended this practice. In the 1962 *Baker* v. *Carr* case, the Court ruled that state legislative districts must be very close in terms of population size. This rule helps make sure that each citizen in a state has an equal voice in government.

Think Critically

1. Compare In what ways are most state legislatures like the U.S. Congress?

_____

_____

_____

_____

_____

2. Explain How does the federal government make certain that citizens are equally represented in state legislatures?

_____

_____

_____

_____

_____

_____

Show Your Skill

3. Draw Conclusions Why do district borders need to be redrawn every ten years?

_____

_____

_____

_____

_____

Mark the Text

4. Underline a state legislator's most important job.

Think Critically

5. **Explain** What can citizens in some states do if they do not like a state law?

_____

_____

_____

_____

_____

Mark the Text

6. **Chart** Circle the step that involves the governor of the state.

Lawmakers meet and work together during a legislative **session.** A session usually lasts a few months. Sometimes a legislature will call a **special session.** This is a meeting held for a particular purpose, such as dealing with a disaster.

State legislators do many jobs. They vote to approve a governor's choices for state offices. They help the citizens in their district. Their main job is to make laws.

To make a law, a lawmaker first suggests a bill. It goes to a committee for review. If this group approves the bill, it goes to the full house. If the house approves the bill, it goes to the other house. Bills follow the same process and steps before they become laws. Look at the diagram below to see the steps. Once both houses approve a bill, it goes to the governor. If the governor signs it, the bill becomes law.

Steps in How a Bill Becomes a Law

1. Legislator introduces a bill.
2. Committee reviews and votes on bill.
3. Full house reviews and votes on bill.
4. Bill goes to the other house.
5. Committee reviews and votes on bill.
6. Full house reviews and votes on bill.
7. Bill goes to governor for signature.

Sometimes voters are asked to approve a new state law. This type of vote is called a **legislative referendum.** In many states, citizens can also petition, or ask, for a **popular referendum** if they do not like a law. This is a vote to decide whether to repeal, or cancel, a law that people do not like.

Citizens, like these who are urging immigration reform, have a right and a responsibility to make their opinions known to lawmakers.

From public preschools to public universities, education is one of the largest areas of the budget for state and local governments.

PHOTO: Ilene MacDonald/Alamy

State Economic Issues

States face hard choices about what to spend money on. Almost all of them have laws that say the state budget must be balanced. This means the states cannot spend more money than they take in.

States rely on taxes for most of their income. Sales taxes and income taxes are the two main types. People pay sales taxes on goods that they buy. People pay income tax on the money they earn from work or other sources. States also make money by charging fees for licenses to drive, fish, and marry.

States spend most of their money on services. They aid local governments. They pay benefits to the poor and the disabled. They pay the salaries of state workers. They pay for health care, schools, police, roads, and parks.

When times are hard, paying for all this is a challenge. Starting in 2007, the American economy began to decline. Many businesses had to lay off workers. People had less income and so they spent less money. The states could not collect enough taxes to meet expenses. At the same time, states faced growing demands. People needed help from the government. The federal government stepped in to give states extra money.

 NGSSS Check List three things that state governments spend money on. SS.7.E.2.1

_____

_____

Think Critically

7. Explain What are the main sources of income for state governments?

_____

Show Your Skill

8. Draw Conclusions Why are hard economic times especially challenging for state governments?

_____

_____

_____

_____

_____

Take the Challenge

9. Gather contact information for your local state senator and representative. Write a letter to that person about an issue that matters to you.

STATE EXECUTIVE BRANCH

NGSSS

SS.7.C.3.4 Identify the relationship and division of powers between the federal government and state governments.

SS.7.C.3.9 Illustrate the law making process at the local, state, and federal levels.

SS.7.C.3.13 Compare the constitutions of the United States and Florida.

SS.7.C.3.14 Differentiate between local, state, and federal governments' obligations and services.

Essential Question

Why and how do people create, structure, and change governments?

Guiding Questions

1. What are the powers and duties of a governor?
2. What is the role of the executives who head a state's administrative departments?

Terms to Know

line-item veto
to veto only a specific part of a bill

commute
to decrease a criminal's sentence

parole
to give a prisoner an early release from prison, with certain limits

It Matters Because

The executive branch carries out the laws of the state.

The governor works for the people of the state. What do you think should be the governor's number one priority?

What Do You Know?

Directions: Use no more than three words to tell what you know about each of these terms. After you finish the lesson, adjust any of your descriptions if needed.

governor _____

term _____

lieutenant governor _____

executive officials _____

attorney general _____

The Governor

What does it take to become the governor of a state? In most states, a person has to be at least 30 years old and live in the state. In some states, the minimum age is 18. In a few states, the governor is not required to live there.

In most states, a governor's term lasts four years. The number of terms a governor may serve is different from state to state. Most states limit a governor to two terms. If a governor dies or leaves office, the person who fills the governor's position is the lieutenant governor.

Governors have many roles. Some of these roles are based on tradition, or custom, not law. For example, their ceremonial role and position as party leader are not in the state constitution.

Under the state constitution, a governor's main job is to head the executive branch. In this role, a governor is much like the president. The governor makes sure that state laws are carried out. He or she is head of the state's National Guard. The governor often has the power to name people to fill state offices. Usually the state senate has to confirm the governor's choices. The U.S. Constitution gives state governors an added power. Governors can choose someone to fill a seat in the U.S. Senate if it becomes vacant.

In most states the governor also writes the budget. Usually the legislature has to approve it before it goes into effect.

Governors have a role in passing laws. They can send bills to the legislature. They also have the power to veto a bill. For all but six governors, they can also use a **line-item veto.** This means they can veto specific parts of a bill instead of the whole law. Lawmakers can override both kinds of vetoes by voting to pass the bill again.

Governors also have some judicial powers. They appoint judges. They can pardon criminals and **commute,** or decrease, a criminal's sentence. Governors can also grant prisoners an early release from jail. That early release is called **parole.**

Governor's Roles

Think Critically

1. Infer What are some ceremonial tasks of a governor that are not required by law?

_____

_____

_____

_____

2. Compare How is a governor like the president?

_____

_____

_____

_____

_____

_____

Mark the Text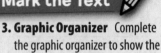

3. Graphic Organizer Complete the graphic organizer to show the roles of the governor.

Show Your Skill

4. Draw Conclusions What kind of check does a governor have on a state legislature?

_____

Rick Scott became Florida's governor on January 4, 2011.

State Executive Departments

In the federal government, departments are run by people that the president chooses and the Senate approves. In state governments, elected officials run many departments. The governor has no role in deciding who gets these jobs. Since the governor does not choose these officials, they may not want to take direction from the governor.

It is not uncommon for a state government to have dozens of agencies, boards, and commissions. In most states, five chief executive officials carry out important tasks.

- The secretary of state oversees elections and records state laws. He or she heads the department that keeps official records. In most states, voters elect this official.

- The attorney general is the state's chief lawyer. This department represents the state in legal matters. These include legal arguments with the federal government. In most states, voters elect the attorney general.

- The state treasurer handles and keeps track of the money that the state collects and spends. In most states, voters elect the state treasurer.

- The state auditor reviews the behavior of state departments and offices. He or she makes sure work is done honestly and that tax dollars are not misused. About half the states elect auditors. In other states, the legislature or the governor chooses auditors.

- The commissioner or superintendent of education oversees the state's public school system. More often than not, this official is appointed, not elected.

In most states, the cabinet is made up of the heads of executive departments. The cabinet meets with the governor to give advice and share information. These officials from different departments each bring special knowledge when talking about issues.

 NGSSS Check List three of the duties that are part of a governor's job.
SS.7.C.3.14

_____

_____

_____

_____

_____

PHOTO: Joe Raedle/Getty Images

Think Critically

5. Infer Why might a top state official not be willing to take direction from a governor?

_____

_____

_____

_____

6. Describe What is the job of the attorney general?

_____

_____

_____

Take the Challenge

7. Research the names and hometowns of Florida's elected executive officials. Mark their hometowns on a map of Florida drawn from memory.

STATE JUDICIAL BRANCH

NGSSS

SS.7.C.3.11 Diagram the levels, functions, and powers of courts at the state and federal levels.

Essential Question

Why and how do people create, structure, and change governments?

Guiding Questions

1. How is the state's judicial system organized?
2. What are the usual methods for selecting judges?

It Matters Because

State courts decide many issues affecting people's lives.

What makes a decision fair or unfair? Write to explain your answer.

Terms to Know

trial court
a court in which a judge or jury listens to evidence and reaches a verdict in favor of one party or another in the case

misdemeanor
the least serious type of crime

civil case
court case in which one party in a dispute claims to have been harmed by the other

plaintiff
the person in a civil case who claims to have been harmed

defendant
the person in a civil case who is said to have caused the harm

appellate court
type of court in which a party who lost a case in a lower court asks judges to review that decision and reverse it

felony
a type of crime more serious than a misdemeanor

What Do You Know?

Directions: In the first column, answer the questions based on what you know before you study. After this lesson, complete the last column.

Before the Lesson		After the Lesson
	What happens if someone has to appear in court?	
	How are judges chosen?	

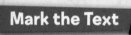

Show Your Skill

1. Draw Conclusions Why do you think state judicial systems have two levels of courts?

_____

_____

_____

_____

_____

Think Critically

2. Explain What part do the plaintiff and the defendant each play in a civil case?

_____

_____

_____

_____

_____

Mark the Text

3. Underline examples of felonies.

---

networks Read Chapter 13 Lesson 4 in your textbook or online.

The Structure of State Courts

Each state has its own court system. These systems are all organized in a similar way. Each state has lower courts and higher courts. The cases heard in the higher courts are more serious and complex than the cases heard at the lower level.

The lower courts are **trial courts.** In a trial court, a judge or jury listens to evidence and reaches a verdict, or decision. Lower courts have different names. They may be called justice courts, district courts, or municipal courts.

Lower courts handle both criminal and civil cases. In a criminal case, a person is accused of a crime. A trial is held to decide if the person is innocent or guilty. The crimes at this level are simple ones. They may be traffic violations or **misdemeanors.** Misdemeanors are the least serious of crimes. Punishment is usually a fine or a short stay in a local jail rather than in prison. A judge instead of a jury often decides these cases.

In a **civil case,** one party claims to have been harmed by another party. The person who claims to have been harmed is the **plaintiff.** The person said to have caused the harm is the **defendant.** Civil cases in the lower courts usually involve small amounts of money.

The higher state courts can be either trial courts or **appellate courts.** An appellate court is one in which appeals are heard. To appeal means to ask a judge to review and reverse, or undo, an earlier court decision.

Higher-level trial courts handle crimes that are more serious. Such crimes are called **felonies**. They include robbery and murder. These courts also handle more serious civil cases. The cases often have to do with a lot of money. Either a jury or a judge may decide civil or criminal cases.

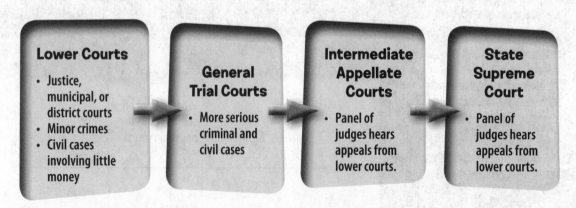

Lower Courts
- Justice, municipal, or district courts
- Minor crimes
- Civil cases involving little money

General Trial Courts
- More serious criminal and civil cases

Intermediate Appellate Courts
- Panel of judges hears appeals from lower courts.

State Supreme Court
- Panel of judges hears appeals from lower courts.

Most states have two levels of appellate courts. The first level is the intermediate appellate court. Some states with small populations do not have intermediate appellate courts. This court is often called the court of appeals. Here, a group of judges reviews each case and agrees on a decision. They may decide to accept or throw out the earlier court decision.

The top appellate court is the state supreme court. Every state has one. This court hears appeals from the intermediate appellate courts. Like the U.S. Supreme Court, state supreme courts put out written explanations of their rulings. These explanations guide state judges in future cases. State supreme court rulings are final. However, a state supreme court ruling may be appealed to the U.S. Supreme Court if a person thinks the decision goes against his or her rights under the U.S. Constitution.

Staffing the Courts

What qualities should a judge have? Judges must know the law. They should be free of **bias** so they can judge a case fairly. Bias is good or bad feelings about a person or group that affect judgment. Judges should also be independent—so they will not be swayed by political pressure. U.S. judges serve in a representative democracy. This means that people usually vote on who holds an office. However, the way states choose judges is different from state to state.

Think Critically

4. Explain What is the role of state supreme courts?

_____

_____

_____

_____

Show Your Skill

5. Draw Conclusions Why is it important for judges to be free from bias?

_____

_____

_____

_____

_____

There are seven members on Florida's Supreme Court. The justices are appointed to 6-year terms by the governor. The terms are staggered so there is no point at which all of the justices are new.

Think Critically

6. Summarize What are the most common ways to select appellate judges?

____

____

____

____

Mark the Text

7. Underline the role of a state supreme court in a situation in which a judge has been charged with doing something wrong.

Take the Challenge

8. Work with a small group of classmates. Take the role of a newspaper editorial board trying to decide which person to endorse for judge in an upcoming election. What questions will you ask the candidates and what qualities are you looking for when making your choice? Write your questions on a separate piece of paper.

Trial court judges are chosen in many different ways. Trial court judges may be chosen by the governor, the legislature, the state supreme court, or by city officials. Other judges are elected by the voters. In other states, judges are appointed for one term and then run for election after that. Some states use a mixture of ways to staff their courts. The length of a term for judges varies from four to ten years.

Election systems differ, too. Some states have nonpartisan elections. This means that candidates are not linked to any political party. Other states allow judges to run as members of political parties.

Choosing judges for the appellate courts is simpler. About half of the states elect them. In the other half, the governor chooses them. In some states, judges who are chosen must be accepted by the legislature or another body.

The length of time an appellate judge serves is different from state to state. In most states, once a term is done, a judge has to be approved again for the next term. In 41 states this is done by popular vote. In the other states, either the governor or the legislature makes the decision.

Judges can be removed from office by impeachment, but this takes a long time. Most states have a board that looks into complaints about judges. If the board finds that the judge's actions were wrong it can make a recommendation, or suggestion, to the state supreme court. The court has the power to suspend or remove the judge.

NGSSS Check **List the two levels of state courts. Give a brief description of each.** SS.7.C.3.11

____

____

____

List three ways states choose trial judges. SS.7.C.3.11

____

____

____

____

____

ESSENTIAL QUESTION *Why and how do people create, structure, and change governments?*

Reflect on What It Means...

Think about what you have learned about the state government in Florida and about its purpose, powers, and branches. Think about departments in the executive branch. Then, identify ways the state government of Florida might affect people. Explain at least two ways for each.

How the state government could affect ME ...

How the state government could affect MY COMMUNITY ...

Keep Going!

How the state government could affect
PEOPLE IN ANOTHER COUNTRY . . .

TAKE THE CHALLENGE

Work with others to make a bulletin board of Florida's state government. Use photos, headlines, and drawings to show what the parts of state government do and how they work together.

LOCAL GOVERNMENT

NGSSS

SS.7.C.3.9 Illustrate the law making process at the local, state, and federal levels.

SS.7.C.3.14 Differentiate between local, state, and federal governments' obligations and services.

ESSENTIAL QUESTION *Why do people create, structure, and change governments?*

The city of Orlando is a city on a mission. Read what that mission is:

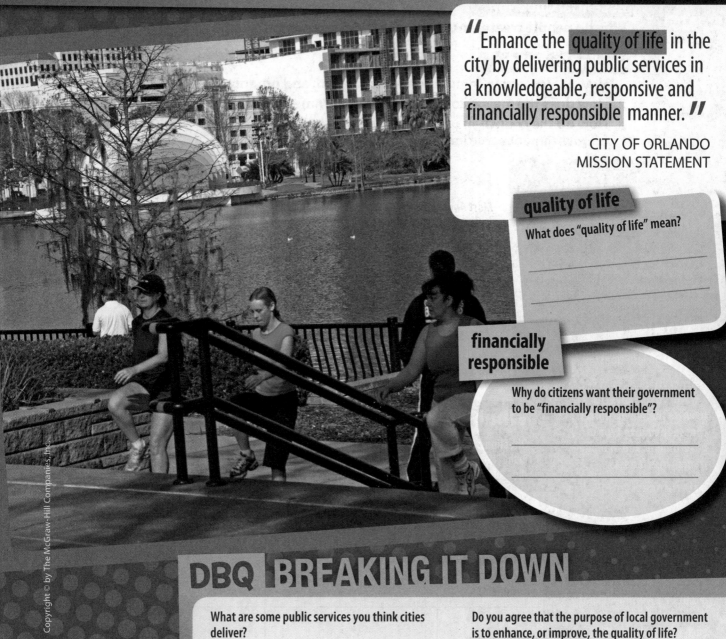

*"*Enhance the quality of life in the city by delivering public services in a knowledgeable, responsive and financially responsible manner.*"*

CITY OF ORLANDO
MISSION STATEMENT

quality of life

What does "quality of life" mean?

_____

_____

_____

financially responsible

Why do citizens want their government to be "financially responsible"?

_____

_____

DBQ BREAKING IT DOWN

What are some public services you think cities deliver?

_____

_____

_____

Do you agree that the purpose of local government is to enhance, or improve, the quality of life? Why or why not?

_____

_____

_____

McGraw-Hill
networks™
There's More Online!

PHOTO: M. Timothy O'Keefe/Alamy; TEXT: City of Orlando

1 CITY GOVERNMENTS

SS.7.C.3.9 Illustrate the law making process at the local, state, and federal levels.

SS.7.C.3.14 Differentiate between local, state, and federal governments' obligations and services.

Essential Question
Why do people create, structure, and change governments?

Guiding Questions
1. How are local governments created, funded, and organized?
2. How does the mayor-council form of government operate?
3. How do the council-manager and commission forms of government serve local communities?

Terms to Know

incorporate
to apply for and receive a state charter to set up a local government

city charter
a document granting power to a local government

home rule
a status that allows cities to write their own charters, choose their own type of government, and manage their own affairs

ordinance
a city law

at-large election
an election for a city or other area as a whole

special district
a unit of government that deals with a single service, such as education, water supply or transportation

metropolitan area
a large city and its suburbs

suburb
a community near or around a city

It Matters Because

Most Americans live in cities and towns. Their local government has a direct influence on their daily lives.

The local government for your community provides many services to help you. Circle the jobs that you think your city or town government handles.

pass federal laws · · · · · · · · · · · pass state laws

police protection · · · · · street repairs

· · · · · collect garbage · · · · fire protection

What Do You Know?

Directions: Use the table below to answer the questions based on what you know now in the "Now" column. After the lesson, complete the table by writing your answers in the "Later" column.

	Now	Later
How are local governments similar to the federal government?		
Who heads your local government?		
How do local governments help their community?		

Copyright © by The McGraw-Hill Companies, Inc.

210 Chapter 14 Local Government

How City Governments Are Created

About three out of four Americans live in cities or urban areas. City governments play a big role in people's daily lives. They provide local services, such as police and fire protection, water and sewer service, schools, public transportation, and libraries. Local governments are not independent, though. Their powers and duties come from their state constitutions.

New cities are created when communities **incorporate.** That term describes a local area with an organized government that gives services to the people who live there. An area incorporates when the people ask the state for a **city charter.** A city charter is a plan for city government. The charter gives power to a local government. Communities must meet certain conditions to get a city charter. Sometimes a certain number of people have to live there. Like a constitution, a city charter describes the city's type of government, how it will be set up, and its powers. An incorporated city is also known as a municipality.

Sometimes a state legislature gives a city **home rule.** This lets cities write their own charters. These cities choose their own form of government. They run their own affairs. However, they still have to follow state laws.

How do local governments pay for the services they provide? Much of the money comes from federal and state grants. Money also comes from taxes. The rest comes from fees and fines for things like dog licenses and traffic tickets.

| A community meets the requirements and applies to the state legislature for a city charter. | The state legislature grants the charter. The charter describes the form of government the city must have. | The community incorporates. It forms a city government based on its charter. |

Think Critically

1. **Summarize** How do local governments pay for the services they provide?

_____

_____

_____

_____

_____

Show Your Skill

2. **Interpret Charts** How are city governments created?

_____

_____

_____

_____

_____

_____

Take the Challenge

3. In a small group, think of an original city name, and then write a city charter for it.

Mark the Text

4. Underline the term that serves as the basis for the mayor-council form of city government.

Think Critically

5. Analyze Use the term *reluctant* in a sentence using the same context as the text.

_____

_____

_____

_____

_____

Show Your Skill

6. Draw Conclusions Why would successful government be less likely under a weak-mayor plan?

_____

_____

_____

The Mayor-Council Form

Most American towns and cities use one of three forms of government. They are:

- the mayor-council form
- the council-manager form
- the commission form.

The mayor-council form is the oldest type of city government. Most of the nation's biggest cities use it. This form is based on a separation of powers. The mayor is the chief executive. He or she oversees city departments such as police and fire. The mayor often appoints people to head the departments. The council has legislative power. It passes city laws called **ordinances.** It approves the city's budget.

The voters elect the mayor and members of the council. In some cities, each voting district elects a representative to the city council. Other cities hold **at-large elections** for council members. This means they are elected by the whole city, not individual districts.

There are two types of mayor-council government. One is the strong-mayor system. This system gives the mayor strong powers. The mayor can veto, or cancel, laws passed by city council, appoint department heads, and write the budget. Strong mayors tend to dominate, or control, a city government.

Under the weak-mayor system, the mayor's power is limited. The council appoints department heads and makes the key decisions. Under this plan, many people share responsibility. The mayor usually directs council meetings but will only vote if there is a tie. Success in this system depends on how well the mayor and the council work together. The weak-mayor system dates back to colonial days when people were reluctant to give any official too much power.

In Broward County, the elected commission chooses a mayor. Here, mayor Kristin Jacobs speaks to reporters about Hurricane Katrina in 2005.

Council-Manager and Commission Governments

The council-manager form of government began in the early 1900s. It was seen as a way to make city government more honest and well organized. Under this plan, an elected city council hires a city manager. The manager oversees city departments and suggests a budget. The city council can fire the manager by a majority vote. Most city managers have special training in areas like managing money and planning.

The commission form of government also began in the 1900s. It does not separate legislative and executive powers. Instead, the government is divided into departments, such as fire, police, and health. The heads of these departments are called commissioners. The people elect them. As department heads, they have executive power, or they run the day-to-day activities of the departments they lead. The commissioners meet regularly as a body called a commission, and one of the commissioners serves as mayor. The commission meets to pass city laws.

This system has some problems. No one person is in charge of a commission. Without clear leadership, a commission has trouble setting and meeting goals. Commissioners will usually focus on their own individual departments. They may compete for resources like money. So, they don't think about what is best for the city as a whole. Only a few cities still use this form of government.

Think Critically

7. Explain Why has the council-manager form of city government replaced the mayor-council form in many cities?

_____

_____

_____

8. Infer What is the main drawback to a commission form of government?

_____

_____

_____

_____

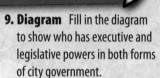

Mark the Text

9. Diagram Fill in the diagram to show who has executive and legislative powers in both forms of city government.

Council-Manager Government

Executive
_____

Legislative
_____

Commission Government

Executive
_____

Legislative
_____

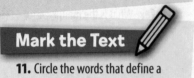

Think Critically

10. Analyze Why do you think that special districts are created?

_____

_____

_____

_____

Mark the Text

11. Circle the words that define a metropolitan area.

Two other types of local government are the special district and the metropolitan area. A **special district** is a unit of government formed to handle one task. This might be water supply, education, or transportation. A special district is run by a board or a commission. Its members may be elected or appointed. Local school districts are the most common example of a special district.

A **metropolitan area** is a city and the **suburbs** around it. A suburb is a community near or around a city. A metropolitan area can also include the small towns outside the suburbs. Suburbs have grown since the 1950s. As a result, more people live in some suburbs than the cities they surround. More people and more businesses can create additional problems. Some metropolitan areas are challenged in the areas of transportation, pollution, and land use and have formed councils to work on these issues.

Tourism is an important part of Ft. Lauderdale's economy. The issues that the local government faces are related to the economic activity of the area.

NGSSS Check Name the three forms of government used by cities and towns. Then list the duties performed by mayors in the strong-mayor form of government. **SS.7.C.3.14**

_____

_____

_____

_____

_____

NGSSS

SS.7.C.3.9 Illustrate the law making process at the local, state, and federal levels.

SS.7.C.3.14 Differentiate between local, state, and federal governments' obligations and services.

Essential Question

Why do people create, structure, and change governments?

Guiding Questions

1. How is county government organized?
2. What functions do county governments perform?

It Matters Because

Like city governments, county governments affect people's everyday lives.

However, county governments provide different services and meet different needs.

What county do you live in?

How many communities do you think are in your county?

Terms to Know

county
a land and political subdivision of a state

county seat
the town where a county courthouse is located

What Do You Know?

Directions: Choose any four of the words below and write a sentence or two about what services county governments provide or how they are organized. When you finish the lesson, write another sentence using four different words from the list.

		members
police protection	public	fire protection
commissioners	board	supervisors
transportation	elected	road repair
laws		

_____

_____

_____

netw🕸rks Read Chapter 14 Lesson 2 in your textbook or online.

Think Critically

1. Compare In what way is a county seat like a capital?

_____

_____

_____

_____

Show Your Skill

2. Draw Conclusions What geographic factors influenced the location of county seats?

_____

_____

_____

_____

_____

_____

How County Governments Are Organized

Most states are divided into smaller units of land called **counties.** There are more than 3,000 counties or county-like divisions in the nation. County government is another type of local government.

Each county is very different. One county might have millions of residents. Another county might have only a few dozen. Counties also range in size. Some counties in the West are bigger than whole states in the East. Two states do even not use the term *county*. In Alaska, counties are called boroughs. In Louisiana, they are known as parishes.

In the 1800s, the county courthouse was the center of county government. The town where the county courthouse was located became known as the **county seat.** Officials at that time wanted to be sure that all citizens could get to a county courthouse. It was where trials were held and legal records were kept. In the Midwest and South they thought most people should be able to get to the county seat and back home by horse and buggy in one day. This is why states in those areas have relatively small counties.

Each county in Florida has a courthouse. This is Florida's Supreme Court building in Tallahassee.

The Functions of County Government

Counties today play a different role than they once did. As cities have grown, many have taken over the services that counties once handled. However, in some places counties are more important than ever. Many have taken on the duties of city governments. These duties include sewer and water service, police and fire protection, road repairs, and public transportation.

Most counties are governed by a board of three to five elected members called commissioners or supervisors. The board acts as a legislature. It passes ordinances, or laws. It sets a yearly budget for the county, levies taxes, and oversees law enforcement.

The most common form of county government is the strong commission form. Two other forms are the commission-manager and commission-elected executive.

In the strong commission form, the county board has both legislative and executive powers. It passes and carries out the laws. It works with other county officials to do some executive work, and oversees people it has placed in charge of other offices. People on county boards do not always have a lot of experience in government. Some states have started training programs for their board members.

As public needs have grown, many counties have changed the function of the county board. In these counties, the board only has legislative power. Executive power goes to either the commission-manager or commission-elected executive. In the commission-manager form, the board names a county manager. This person is a lot like a city manager. In the commission-elected executive form, counties create a new office and the voters elect the executive.

In both of these forms, the county manager or the executive manages the county government and carries out its laws. The county board works with this leader.

Commission-Manager

Commission-Elected Executive

Strong Commission

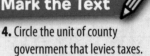

Show Your Skill

3. Identify the Main Idea Name three ways that county government can be organized.

_____

_____

_____

_____

Mark the Text

4. Circle the unit of county government that levies taxes.

Think Critically

5. Infer Why might a county executive be more independent of the board than a county manager?

_____

_____

_____

_____

Mark the Text

6. Diagram In each box, write one or two sentences describing how that form of government is organized.

7. Explain How are county sheriffs and district attorneys chosen?

_____

_____

8. Summarize Use the term _estimate_ in a sentence about county government.

_____

_____

_____

_____

_____

_____

Take the Challenge

9. Draw a county map of your county or for the state of Florida. Use references to help you. Label your town or city on the map.

A Manatee County sheriff patrol car makes a stop in Bradenton to check out an alleged crime.

Some important county officials are elected on their own to do very specific jobs. One of these is the county sheriff. He or she is in charge of law enforcement. The sheriff's department enforces court orders and runs the county jail.

Another is the district attorney (DA). The DA is the county's prosecutor. He or she looks into crimes and brings charges against people suspected of breaking the law. He or she tries to prove in court that they are guilty.

Other county officials may be appointed or elected:

- The county assessor decides how much land and buildings are worth. The county's property tax is based on his or her estimate, or general idea.
- The county treasurer is in charge of the county's money. The treasurer collects taxes and pays the bills.
- The auditor makes sure the county follows state and local laws when spending its money.
- A county clerk keeps official records for the government.
- A county coroner works with the police department. He or she tries to figure out the cause of death in unusual cases.

 NGSSS Check What services does county government provide for citizens? SS.7.C.3.14

_____

_____

_____

TOWNS, TOWNSHIPS, AND VILLAGES

NGSSS

SS.7.C.3.9 Illustrate the law making process at the local, state, and federal levels.

SS.7.C.3.14 Differentiate between local, state, and federal governments' obligations and services.

Essential Question
Why do people create, structure, and change governments?

Guiding Questions
1. How and why did town governments and meetings develop?
2. How are township and village governments organized?

Terms to Know

town
a political unit that is smaller than a city and larger than a village

township
a subdivision of a county that has its own government

town meeting
a gathering of local citizens to discuss and vote on important issues

village
the smallest unit of local government

It Matters Because

American democracy began in towns. The town meetings held in the New England colonies allowed community members to take part in their government. Town meetings are still held today.

Have you ever attended a town hall meeting or know someone who has? What items were on the agenda? Do you think it is important for a community to get people involved in the local government?

_____

_____

_____

What Do You Know?

Directions: What would you like to know about town hall and village governments? Write two questions you have about what they do. After you have finished the lesson, come back and see if you can answer the questions.

_____

_____

_____

_____

Think Critically

1. Summarize Why have some New England towns given up the town meeting form of government?

_____

_____

_____

_____

_____

Show Your Skill

2. Identify the Main Idea What is the purpose of town meetings, and how often are they held?

_____

_____

_____

_____

_____

Take the Challenge

3. Work with a small group to design a Web page to advertise a town meeting.

Mark the Text

4. Circle three things that citizens may be asked to vote on in a town meeting.

Towns and Town Meetings

Counties are often divided into smaller political units. In the New England states, units that are smaller than cities and larger than villages are called **towns.** In other states, especially in the Midwest, they are called **townships.** These governments get their powers from the state, just as county and city governments do.

In New England, town governments take care of the needs of most small communities. Elsewhere, townships and counties share powers. In the South and West, where there may be no townships, county governments are usually more important.

Many New England towns have a **town meeting** form of government. This kind of government began in the 1600s. In a town meeting, the people of a town gather once a year. They discuss local and world issues and vote on town rules, taxes, and budgets. Citizens, not elected representatives, make the decisions. This is direct democracy, one of the oldest forms of government in the country.

This town hall meeting in Palm City was set up in order to discuss immigration reforms.

Yearly town meetings are good for making broad decisions, but not for day-to-day governing. So towns also elect people to take care of the daily work of government. These officials are called "selectmen." This is an old title and is used today for both men and women.

As towns grew, the duties of government became more complex. Direct democracy did not always work well. As a result, some New England towns have changed to representative town meetings. Other towns no longer hold town meetings. Instead, they elect a town council to run the local government.

Townships and Villages

In New York, New Jersey, Pennsylvania, and some other states, counties are divided into townships. Township governments are similar, or alike, to town governments.

The Midwestern states also have townships. They were made when the nation was growing to the west. Congress divided new land into square blocks. Each block was six miles wide and six miles long. The early settlers set up local governments also called townships.

Most townships elect a group of officials. They pass ordinances and deal with government business. The group may be called a township committee, board of supervisors, or board of trustees. This group has the power to make laws. It will usually hold regular meetings so citizens have a voice in their government. Sometimes township and county governments work together to provide local services.

PHOTO: Universal Images Group Limited/Alamy

Copyright © by The McGraw-Hill Companies, Inc.

Like many states in the Midwest and in the Northeast, Pennsylvania is divided into numerous counties, shown here. The counties are further divided into townships.

Show Your Skill

5. Draw Conclusions Why do you think many Midwestern townships today look perfectly square on a map?

_____

_____

_____

Think Critically

6. Explain How are most townships governed?

_____

_____

_____

_____

_____

PHOTO: Creatas/PunchStock

Think Critically

7. Compare How is setting up a village government like setting up a city government?

_____

_____

_____

_____

_____

Show Your Skill

8. Make Inferences Why might people not want to pay higher taxes to have a village government?

_____

_____

_____

_____

_____

_____

_____

_____

_____

The smallest unit of local government is the **village.** Villages are usually inside a township or county. In some communities, people grow unhappy with the county's services. For example, they may want to set up their own school system. When that happens, the people may ask the state for permission to set up a village government.

Most villages elect a board of trustees to run their government. Some villages also elect an executive, who may be called a mayor, chief burgess, or president of the board. A large village might hire a city manager. The village board has the power to collect taxes. It may spend this money on projects that help the community, such as water systems and taking care of the streets.

The people in a village usually have better services than they had before. This can attract visitors, new residents, and businesses. But becoming a village has a downside: Taxes may be higher to support the added layer of government. However, many people think that the higher taxes are worth the other benefits of living in a village.

Village boards can make decisions that affect schools, such as this one in Florida.

 NGSSS Check How can village governments be organized? SS.7.C.3.9

_____

_____

ESSENTIAL QUESTION *Why do people create, structure, and change governments?*

Reflect on What It Means . . .

At every level, local government works to improve the lives of its citizens.

KEEP . . .

. . . a log of how your local government affects you. For one weekend,
jot down a note every time you or your community are affected by a
local public service.

Keep Going!

SUPPOSE...

... you were starting a new town. What services would your
government provide to its residents? What type of government
would you set up?

POST...

... a message on an appropriate Web site to find out what people
your age around the world are learning about their local
governments. Your teacher will help guide you.

TAKE THE CHALLENGE

How many local governments are there in the United States? Think about all of
the towns and cities and counties in the country. Each has its own government.
What do you think the total is? Take a guess and write it down. Then conduct
research to see if you were close!

CITIZENS AND THE LAW

NGSSS

SS.7.C.3.10 Identify sources and types (civil, criminal, constitutional, military) of law.

ESSENTIAL QUESTION *How do laws protect individual rights?*

The members of the police department in Palm Beach, Florida, share a vision:

" We, the members of the Palm Beach Police Department, are committed to achieving the highest possible quality of life for the community, of which we are an integral part, and are resolved to providing the highest levels of protection and service through community partnerships based on honesty, trust, fairness, compassion, respect, cooperation and shared vision. "

MISSION STATEMENT, PALM BEACH POLICE DEPARTMENT

TEXT: Palm Beach Police Department

Copyright © by The McGraw-Hill Companies, Inc.

TREAT YOUR POLICE OFFICERS FAIRLY

we are an integral part

What does it mean to be *integral* to something?

_____

_____

resolved

What is another word for *resolved*?

_____

_____

DBQ BREAKING IT DOWN

What is the tone, or feeling, of this passage?

_____

_____

How would you feel, promising to follow this vision? Explain.

_____

_____

McGraw-Hill
networks™
There's More Online!

PHOTO: Joe Raedle/Getty Images

1 SOURCES AND TYPES OF LAW

NGSSS

SS.7.C.3.10 Identify sources and types (civil, criminal, constitutional, military) of law.

Essential Question
How do laws protect individual rights?

Guiding Questions
1. What is the purpose of laws?
2. What early legal systems influenced the laws we live by today?
3. What types of laws exist in the American legal system?

Terms to Know

common law
law that grew from court decisions over many years

precedent
earlier ruling on which decisions in later cases are based

statute
law made by a legislature

lawsuit
a civil case brought before a court to collect damages for some harm that has been done

constitutional law
branch of the law dealing with forming and interpreting constitutions

case law
branch of law based on judge's decisions

administrative law
branch of law that includes all the rules the executive branch makes as it does its job

It Matters Because

Laws protect public safety and keep order in society.

What is an important law that affects your life? Write a sentence about the law. After you have read the lesson, write another sentence about it based on what you have learned.

What Do You Know?

Directions: In the first column, decide if you think the statement is true or false based on what you know in the "Now" column. Circle your answers. After the lesson, circle your answers in the "Later" column.

Now		Later
True False	Most of our laws come from Hammurabi, a Babylonian king.	True False
True False	The most important source of U.S. laws is English common law.	True False
True False	Roman law is a blend of English and French laws.	True False

networks Read Chapter 15 Lesson 1 in your textbook or online.

Why We Have Laws

Laws are sets of rules. They allow people to live together in peace and help prevent violence. Laws explain which actions are allowed in a society and which will be punished. If you break the law, you can expect to be punished. Punishments are used to discourage potential, or possible, criminals from breaking the law.

Some laws are better than others. The table below shows the four main qualities of good laws.

Fair	Reasonable	Understandable	Enforceable
A fair law treats people equally. Fair laws do not make different rules for different groups of people.	To be reasonable, a law must not be too harsh. Cutting off someone's hand for stealing a loaf of bread would not be reasonable.	They must be easy to understand. Otherwise people might break them without realizing it.	Laws that are hard for police and other officials to enforce are not good laws.

Development of the Legal System

Scholars think that there were laws even in the earliest societies. It is thought that prehistoric people had rules about behavior. The earliest laws were not written, they were spoken. Over time, people began to write them down.

In about 1760 B.C. King Hammurabi (HA•muh•RAH•bee) of the Middle Eastern empire in Babylonia created the oldest written law. It is called the Code of Hammurabi. A code is an organized collection, or set, of laws. The Code of Hammurabi was written in a wedge shaped script called cuneiform. The code included laws related to the family, such as marriage and slavery, as well as business practices. It also set prices for goods and services.

The Israelites were a people who lived near the eastern Mediterranean coast. They also followed a set of written laws. These laws outlawed such acts as murder and theft. Many of these acts are still considered crimes today.

The ancient Romans developed a set of laws that were the most important in the Western world. The first Roman laws were published in 450 B.C. As their empire grew the laws spread

Show Your Skill

1. Interpret Charts What are the four qualities of a good law?

_____

_____

_____

2. Make a Connection How do laws help people live together peacefully?

_____

_____

_____

_____

_____

_____

_____

Take the Challenge

3. Research some examples of Roman laws. Then choose one Roman law and illustrate it or cut out pictures to show its meaning and/or consequence if it is broken.

Justinian I developed the Justinian Code.

Napoleon Bonaparte (Napoleon I) created the Napoleonic Codes.

PHOTO: (l) Pixtal/age Fotostock; (r) Fototeca Storica Nazionale / Photodisc / Getty Images

Think Critically

4. Summarize What contribution did the French emperor Napoleon make to the body of written law?

_____

_____

_____

_____

5. Contrast What is the difference between a precedent and a statute?

_____

_____

_____

_____

_____

_____

to parts of Europe, Asia, and Africa. In A.D. 533 the ruler of the Eastern Roman Empire, also called the Byzantine (BIH•zehn•TEEN) Empire, simplified the Roman laws into a body of rules. It was called the Justinian Code. Roman law also became part of the laws of the Roman Catholic Church. This part of church law is called canon law.

The Justinian Code was updated in 1804 by the French emperor Napoleon Bonaparte. He called it the Napoleonic Code. Napoleon spread his code to all the lands he conquered. The Louisiana Territory had been under French control before the United States bought it in 1803. As a result, Louisiana still has laws that were based on the Napoleonic Code.

The most important source for American laws is English **common law.** Common law is law based on court decisions and customs. It began after the Normans of France took control of England in 1066. Judges were sent into the countryside to hear cases. These judges based their rulings on **precedents,** or the rulings given earlier in similar cases. This practice of following precedent became part of the common law. Common law is considered judge-made law.

The English blended Roman law and canon law into common law. Common law included the basic principles of individual rights, such as the idea that a person is innocent until proven guilty. Over time the English added to the common law by allowing Parliament to make laws. Laws made by a legislature like Parliament are called **statutes.** When English settlers came to North America in the 1600s and 1700s, they brought their traditions of common law and individual rights with them. They are a key part of the United States judicial system today.

Early Legal Systems	
Code of Hammurabi	Earliest example of a written code.
Israelites	Followed a written set of laws that outlawed acts such as theft and murder.
Ancient Roman law	Most important laws in the western world. Partly written by judges and adopted by the senate.
Justinian Code	Simplified Roman law into an orderly body of rules.
English common law after 1066	Law based on court decisions, not a legal code. Considered judge-made law.
U.S. laws developed 1600s–1700s	Principles of English common law and individual rights became key parts of the basic laws of the new nation.
Napoleonic Code 1804	Updated the Justinian Code to a new body of laws.

Types of Laws

There are three basic types of laws—criminal, civil, and public. Earlier you learned about public laws.

Criminal laws seek to protect public safety. These crimes are divided into two types:

1. **Felonies** These are serious crimes such as murder and robbery. They have serious penalties.

2. **Misdemeanors** These are less serious crimes such as vandalism. They usually involve a fine or jail time of less than one year.

Crimes against property are the most common type of crime. They can be either misdemeanors or felonies. They do not involve force or the threat of force toward other people. Examples include shoplifting, identity theft, and vandalism.

Civil laws handle arguments between people and groups. They often involve broken contracts. For example, if you order something from a store, but do not receive the item, the seller has broken a contract with you. You could sue them in court.

A civil case brought before a court is called a **lawsuit.** A lawsuit is legal action to collect damages, or money, for some harm that has been done. Individuals who think they have been wronged must file a lawsuit themselves. The government cannot bring such a case.

6. **Interpret Charts** How are Roman law, the Justinian Code, and the Napoleonic Code related?

_____

_____

_____

_____

_____

_____

_____

Mark the Text

7. Underline which crime is more serious, felonies or misdemeanors.

Think Critically

8. **Analyze** Why would someone want to file a lawsuit in a felony?

_____

_____

_____

_____

_____

9. Interpret Information
If you were to visualize the sources of law as a pyramid, which source would be at the bottom?

_____

_____

Think Critically

10. Evaluate What is the most important source of law in the United States?

_____

_____

Take the Challenge

11. Make a diagram to show the different kinds of laws and give examples of each.

Military law is a set of statutes that people serving in the U.S. armed forces have to follow. Civilians who work for the military also have to follow those laws. However, people serving in the military do have to follow civil laws. Military laws cover crimes such as disobeying a superior officer and desertion. If the crime is serious a person can end up at a court-martial. That is the court that tries people accused of breaking military laws.

Criminal and civil laws come from several main sources. These include:

- the United States Constitution
- state constitutions
- statutes
- case law
- administrative agencies.

The Constitution is the highest law in the nation. If there is a conflict between it and one of the other sources of law, the Constitution is always followed.

Constitutional law deals with the structure and meaning of constitutions. It handles questions about the limits of government power. It also deals with individual rights.

A statute is a law written by a legislature. The United States Congress, state legislatures, and local lawmakers write thousands of statutes. Statutes control our behavior in many ways. For example, they set speed limits and minimum wages. Statutes are also the source of many rights. One example is the right to a free public education.

Case law is law that is based on judge's decisions. Some cases brought to court cannot be decided based on existing statutes. In these cases judges look to precedent to make their rulings. These rulings have the same weight as laws.

Administrative law involves all the rules the executive branch makes as it does its job. The federal and state constitutions give legislatures the power to create administrative agencies. For example, Congress created the Federal Aviation Administration. Any orders this agency hands down to airlines have the same weight as other laws.

NGSSS Check How did English law affect our laws today? SS.7.C.3.10

_____

_____

_____

_____

NGSSS

SS.7.C.3.10 Identify sources and types (civil, criminal, constitutional, military) of law.

Essential Question
How do laws protect individual rights?

Guiding Questions
1. What basic legal rights are provided to all Americans?
2. What legal protections does the U.S. Constitution offer a citizen who is accused of a crime?

Terms to Know

writ of habeas corpus
court order that says officials cannot put a person in prison without explaining why he or she is being held

bill of attainder
a law that punishes a person without a trial

ex post facto law
a law that punishes a person for an action that was not illegal when it was done

due process
principle that says the government must act fairly and follow the law

search warrant
court order allowing a search

exclusionary rule
rule that says that evidence obtained by police illegally may not be used in court

Miranda Warning
list of rights that must be read to a suspect before questioning

double jeopardy
being tried twice for the same crime

bail
money that a person waiting for a trial may give the court in order to be set free from jail until the trial

It Matters Because

Under the American system of justice, the U.S. Constitution protects the rights of individuals.

Individual rights that are protected by the Constitution include which of the following? Place a check mark next to all that apply. If you do not understand the meaning of one of these rights, circle it and come back to it after you have read the lesson.

habeas corpus

due process

right to counsel

right to know the accusations

right to a speedy public trial

right to confront witnesses

right to be tried by an impartial jury

no cruel and unusual punishments

no excessive bail

no self-incrimination

no double jeopardy

In your opinion, which of these is the most important? Why?

_____

What Do You Know?

Directions: Use the table below to answer the questions based on what you know in the "Now" column. After the lesson, write your answers in the "Later" column.

	Now	Later
What are your basic legal rights?		
How does the Constitution protect your rights?		

Mark the Text

1. Circle the main idea in the first paragraph.

Show Your Skill

2. **Compare and Contrast** What is the difference between the due process guarantees in the Fifth and Fourteenth amendments?

_____

_____

_____

_____

_____

_____

Think Critically

3. **Explain** How does the Constitution protect you from unlawful imprisonment?

_____

_____

_____

_____

_____

_____

Basic Legal Rights

The U.S. Constitution includes many important protections for citizens. These protections prevent the government from using the law unfairly. One of the most important protections is found in Article I. It says that someone who is arrested has the right to ask for a **writ of habeas corpus** (HAY•bee•uhs KAWR•puhs). A writ is a court order. A writ of habeas corpus makes officials explain to a judge why they are holding someone in jail. The judge decides if their reason for holding the person is legal or not. This rule stops officials from putting people in jail unlawfully.

Article I also stops the government from delivering bills of attainder and ex post facto laws. A **bill of attainder** is a law that punishes a person without a trial. An **ex post facto law** punishes a person for doing something that was not illegal at the time it was done. *Ex post facto* means "after the fact."

The Constitution guarantees individual rights as it carries out the law. After the Civil War, the Fourteenth Amendment gave civil rights to formerly enslaved people. This amendment says the states must treat all people equally under the law. It bans unequal treatment based on factors such as gender, race, and religion. It has been used to win rights for minorities and women.

The Fourteenth Amendment strengthened the Fifth Amendment right of **due process.** This right says that the government cannot take away our lives, liberty, or property without following the law. For example, a person has the right to a trial by jury.

The Rights of the Accused

The Constitution makes sure that people accused of crimes are treated fairly. It also makes sure they have a chance to defend themselves. These rights are based on the presumption of innocence. This means a person is believed to be innocent until proven guilty in court.

One right of the accused is found in the Fourth Amendment. It protects us against "unreasonable searches and seizures." That means a law officer cannot search your home or take your property without a sound reason. It says that police must get a **search warrant** before searching a person's home or property. A search warrant is a court document that says a search is allowed. To get a search warrant, police must tell a judge exactly what they are looking for. They must prove that they have a good reason, or probable cause, for the search.

If police find evidence without a warrant, that evidence cannot be used in court. This is true in both federal and state cases. It is known as the **exclusionary rule.**

The Fifth Amendment protects the rights of the accused. Those rights are listed in the graphic organizer below.

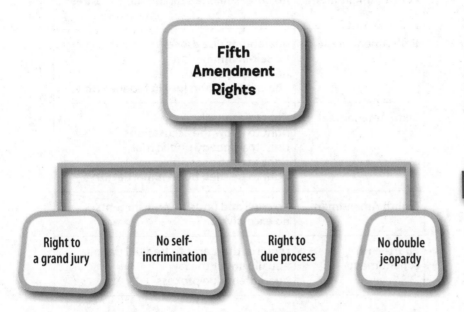

No self-incrimination means that a person has the right to remain silent. That means a person does not have to answer questions that might show they took part in a crime. This was decided in 1966 in the case *Miranda v. Arizona.* That year the Supreme Court said that police must issue the **Miranda Warning** to suspects.

It tells suspects that

- they have the right to remain silent.
- anything they say may be used against them.
- they have the right to an attorney; if they cannot afford one, the court will provide one.

Double jeopardy means to be tried twice for the same crime. The Fifth Amendment does not allow this. A person who was tried once and found not guilty cannot be tried again for the same crime.

The Fifth Amendment protects the right of an accused person to have his or her case brought before a grand jury. This is mainly used for federal crimes. A grand jury is a group of people who decides whether the government has enough evidence to hold a trial. If the grand jury believes there is enough evidence, it indicts the suspect. This means the suspect is formally charged with a crime.

Think Critically

4. **Summarize** How does the Fifth Amendment's guarantee of due process work?

_____

_____

_____

_____

_____

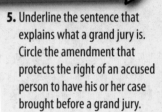

Mark the Text

5. Underline the sentence that explains what a grand jury is. Circle the amendment that protects the right of an accused person to have his or her case brought before a grand jury.

Mark the Text

6. **Chart** Circle the amendment that guarantees the right to trial by jury.

Show Your Skill

7. **Interpret Information**
What is meant by the Eighth Amendment's guarantee that punishments should not be "cruel and unusual"?

_____

_____

_____

_____

_____

_____

Think Critically

8. **Identify the Main Idea**
Explain why illegally obtained evidence cannot be used in court.

_____

_____

_____

_____

_____

Constitutional Rights of the Accused	
Source	**Rights**
Article I	habeas corpus no bills of attainder no ex post facto laws
Fourth Amendment	no unreasonable searches and seizures
Fifth Amendment	guarantees due process no self-incrimination no double jeopardy guarantees grand jury in federal crimes
Sixth Amendment	right to counsel right to know the accusations right to a speedy public trial right to confront witnesses right to be tried by an impartial jury
Eighth Amendment	no cruel and unusual punishments no excessive bail
Fourteenth Amendment	requires the states to treat all people equally under the law guarantees due process

Some rights of the accused are also found in the Sixth Amendment. It says that the defendant is entitled to representation by a lawyer. The Sixth Amendment also promises that accused people

- have a right to know the charges against them.
- can question their accusers.
- have the right to be tried by an impartial jury.

An impartial jury is a jury made up of people who know no one in the case and have no opinion about it.

The Sixth Amendment also guarantees a speedy public trial. This protects people from being held in jail too long. It also means that trials should be open to the public or the media.

Other rights of the accused are found in the Eighth Amendment. This amendment prohibits, or does not allow, "cruel and unusual" punishments. A punishment may not be out of proportion to the crime. This means that a punishment must fit the crime. For example, a life sentence in jail for shoplifting would be too severe. Some people believe that the death penalty is cruel and unusual punishment. In 1972 the Supreme Court ruled on this matter. The Court did not agree that it was cruel, but it did find that it was not applied equally to all persons. It targeted African Americans and poorer populations. The Court said that the death penalty was being used in a way that was not constitutional. State death penalty laws and Supreme Court guidelines were changed after this ruling.

The Eighth Amendment also says that a judge cannot set bail too high. **Bail** is money that a person may give the court in order to be set free from jail until the trial. It is like a security deposit. When the person shows up at the trial the money is returned. When determining bail, the judge looks at how serious the crime is and the criminal record of the accused.

Judge Krista Marx sits on the Florida 15th Judicial Circuit. One of the roles of a criminal judge is to set bail during hearings.

Think Critically

9. Analyze Why does the Eighth Amendment say that a judge cannot set bail too high?

_____

_____

_____

_____

_____

Take the Challenge

10. Write an editorial explaining which right of the accused is the most important. Defend your choice.

NGSSS Check List five basic legal rights that the Constitution guarantees to all American citizens. SS.7.C.3.10

_____

_____

_____

_____

_____

CHAPTER 15

MY REFLECTIONS

ESSENTIAL QUESTION *How do laws protect individual rights?*

Reflect on What It Means . . .

Many individual rights are protected by the U.S. Constitution. These rights are protected in the United States as well as other countries around the world.

Choose a topic that relates to an individual right protected by the U.S. Constitution. You will show through visuals and words how that right protects you and people in your community. Do research to find out if that right is protected in another country. Use the Internet or print resources to find photos and other images that relate to your topic. Print out the pictures or make photocopies, and then use them to create a collage. You may also use words or phrases in your collage. Jot down phrases below that you would like to use in your collage.

My Community

___

___

The World

___

___

To Me

___

___

TAKE THE CHALLENGE

Under the Constitution, anyone accused of a crime has the right to a "speedy" trial. In your opinion, how soon must a trial take place after someone is accused for it to be considered "speedy"? A week? A month? A year? Some other period of time? Explain your answer.

CIVIL AND CRIMINAL LAW

NGSSS

SS.7.C.3.10 Identify sources and types (civil, criminal, constitutional, military) of law.

SS.7.C.3.11 Diagram the levels, functions, and powers of courts at the state and federal levels.

SS.7.C.3.12 Analyze the significance and outcomes of landmark Supreme Court cases including, but not limited to, Marbury v. Madison, Plessy v. Ferguson, Brown v. Board of Education, Gideon v. Wainwright, Miranda v. Arizona, in re Gault, Tinker v. Des Moines, Hazelwood v. Kuhlmier, United States v. Nixon, and Bush v. Gore.

ESSENTIAL QUESTION *Why does conflict develop?*

In 1963 the U.S. Supreme Court ruled that the government must provide an attorney for anyone accused of a crime. In the past, only people who could afford attorneys had them. In the case, Supreme Court Justice Hugo Black delivered the unanimous decision:

PHOTO: Stan Stearns/Bettmann/Corbis

Copyright © by The McGraw-Hill Companies, Inc.

" [A]ny person hauled [forced] into court, who is too poor to hire a lawyer, cannot be assured a fair trial unless counsel is provided for him . . . . lawyers in criminal courts are necessities, not luxuries. "

GIDEON V. WAINWRIGHT (1963)

assured

What is a synonym for *assured*?

_____

_____

counsel

Who serves as counsel?

_____

DBQ BREAKING IT DOWN

What might "lawyers in criminal courts are necessities, not luxuries" mean?

_____

_____

_____

Do you think taxpayers should have to pay for an attorney for a defendant who cannot afford to pay for one? Why or why not?

_____

_____

_____

McGraw-Hill
networks™
There's More Online!

CIVIL LAW

NGSSS

SS.7.C.3.10 Identify sources and types (civil, criminal, constitutional, military) of law.

SS.7.C.3.11 Diagram the levels, functions, and powers of courts at the state and federal levels.

Essential Question

Why does conflict develop?

Guiding Questions

1. What is civil law?
2. What legal procedures are followed in civil lawsuits?

Terms to Know

contract
an agreement between two or more parties to exchange something of value

tort
a wrongful act for which a person has the right to sue

negligence
a lack of proper care and attention

plaintiff
the party in a lawsuit who claims to have been harmed

defendant
the party in a lawsuit said to have done the harm

complaint
a formal notice that a lawsuit is being brought

damages
a sum of money ordered by a court to pay for injuries or losses suffered

summons
a notice directing a person to appear in court to answer a complaint

discovery
a process by which lawyers check facts and gather evidence before a trial

It Matters Because

Civil law makes it possible for people to settle disputes in an orderly way.

Think of a time when you have had an argument with a friend. How did you resolve the argument? Did one of you compromise? Write about what happened.

_____

_____

_____

_____

_____

What Do You Know?

Directions: Use the table below to answer the questions based on what you know now in the "Now" column. After the lesson, complete the table by writing your answers in the "Later" column.

	Now	Later
Why might you sue someone?		
What happens when you file a lawsuit?		

Types of Civil Law

Civil law is the branch of the law that has to do with disputes between people, companies, or the government. Such disputes come up when people think they have been harmed by someone else's actions.

In civil law, court cases are called lawsuits. Most lawsuits involve one of four types of civil law.

One type of civil law involves contracts. A **contract** is an agreement between two or more parties to exchange something of value. A written contract is written out and signed by both parties. A contract is broken when one party fails to keep his or her promise. If that happens, the second party can sue. In that lawsuit, the second party claims to have been injured in some way by the failure of the other party to follow the contract.

Not all contracts have to be written. Some everyday actions are contracts though no papers are signed. For example, when a restaurant takes your order for food, a contract is made. The restaurant has promised food. You have promised to pay for the food. That is an example of an oral, or spoken, contract.

Branches of Civil Law

Property law includes rules about the buying, selling, and use of land or a building. For example, suppose someone rents a house. The law says that the renter must take care of the house while living in it. The owner must keep the house in good shape for the renter's use. Arguments may arise over who should pay to repair, or fix, something that is broken. For example, if the roof leaks, it is the owner's duty to make the repair. But, what if the renter does not tell the owner the roof is leaking until there is major damage? Who should pay for the repairs? If the owner and renter cannot agree, one might take the other to court.

Copyright © by The McGraw-Hill Companies, Inc.

Mark the Text

1. Underline the meaning of a contract, and circle the text that describes why contracts are important.

Think Critically

2. **Categorize** Which branch of civil law would apply in a case in which one sister sues another over the possessions or property given to them after a family member dies?

_____

_____

Show Your Skill

3. **Interpret Diagrams** Fill in the diagram with the four main branches of civil law.

4. Analyze What types of issues are dealt with by family law?

_____

_____

_____

_____

_____

5. Summarize If a court ordered you to pay damages, what would you have to do?

_____

_____

_____

_____

_____

Take the Challenge

6. With a small group, role-play a civil lawsuit. Make sure that you show one of the four types of civil law.

Family law has to do with rules applied to family relationships. For example, suppose a married couple is getting a divorce. The way they split their property is a matter of civil law. So is the question of how to divide who will take care of any children they have. A court often decides disputes over such issues. Deaths in a family can also lead to property disputes. For example, people sometimes disagree on who should be given possessions or property when a family member dies.

Personal injury is another branch of civil law. These cases are also called **torts.** A tort is a wrongful act that causes injury to another person or damage to his or her property. For example, a person throws a ball and breaks a window. The flying glass cuts someone nearby. The injured person can sue the person who threw the ball to make them pay for the injury.

A tort may be intentional. This would be the case if the person threw the ball at the window on purpose. But suppose the thrower simply was not paying attention. Then the tort would be a result of **negligence** (NEH•glih•juhnts). Negligence is acting in a careless or reckless way. It happens when someone does something a reasonable person would not have done.

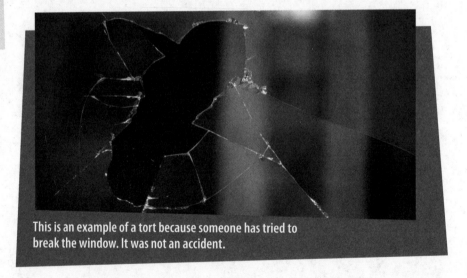

This is an example of a tort because someone has tried to break the window. It was not an accident.

The Legal Process in Civil Cases

Every lawsuit begins with a plaintiff. The **plaintiff** is the person who brings the lawsuit. The **defendant** is the person being sued.

First, the plaintiff's lawyer files a complaint with the court. The **complaint** describes the wrong and the harm that was done. It usually asks the court to order the defendant to pay the plaintiff a sum of money, called **damages,** to repay the plaintiff for the loss. It may ask the court to order the plaintiff to take a certain action, such as honoring a contract.

In a courtroom, the jury (top) hears the case that is presented. Here, the plaintiff (seated on the stand) is being questioned by the defendant's lawyer.

Next, the court sends the defendant a **summons.** It tells the defendant that he or she is being sued. It tells the defendant when and where to appear in court.

The defendant's lawyer may respond to, or answer, the complaint by filing an answer to the charges. Then both lawyers gather evidence about the dispute. This step is called **discovery.**

At this point, if one side seems likely to win, the other side may offer to come to a settlement, or an agreement. If both sides can agree on the terms, then a settlement is reached. This can be done at any time, even during the trial. But because trials are so costly, people usually reach settlements before trials start. Many civil cases never even get to trial.

If the two sides do not settle, the suit goes to trial. First the plaintiff presents evidence. Then the defendant presents evidence. Each side sums up its case. Then the judge or a jury reaches a verdict, or decision, in favor of one party.

If the defendant wins, the plaintiff gets nothing. In fact, the plaintiff may even have to pay the defendant's court costs.

If the plaintiff wins and damages are involved, the judge or jury sets the amount of damages. Sometimes a judge or jury will also order the defendant to pay punitive damages. This type of damages is meant to punish. Sometimes the judge does not award damages. The judge may order the defendant to take a certain action. The defendant can appeal the verdict to a higher court. He or she may ask to have the verdict overturned or to have the damages reduced.

NGSSS Check Explain the difference between a complaint and a summons. SS.7.C.3.10

_____

_____

_____

_____

Show Your Skill

7. Predict Outcomes What might happen if the discovery step does not result in one side seeming more likely than the other to win?

_____

_____

_____

Think Critically

8. Make Generalizations Suppose a judge or jury rules in favor of the plaintiff. What happens next?

_____

_____

_____

_____

_____

_____

_____

NGSSS

SS.7.C.2.6 Simulate the trial process and the role of juries in the administration of justice.

SS.7.C.3.11 Diagram the levels, functions, and powers of courts at the state and federal levels.

Essential Question

Why does conflict develop?

How can governments ensure citizens are treated fairly?

Guiding Questions

1. What does criminal law involve?
2. What are the legal procedures in a criminal law case?

Terms to Know

crime
an act that breaks the law and harms people or society

penal code
the body of law that describes crimes and punishments

misdemeanor
minor crime for which a person can be fined a small sum of money or jailed for up to a year

felony
more serious crime such as murder, rape, kidnapping, or robbery

sentence
punishment for committing a crime

prosecution
the party who starts the legal process against a person for breaking the law

plea bargaining
a process in which a defendant agrees to plead guilty to a less serious crime in order to avoid a trial

cross-examination
the questioning of a witness at a trial to check or discredit the witness's testimony

It Matters Because

When you are an adult, you will probably be called at some time to serve on a jury. When that time comes, knowing about criminal law will make you a better juror.

Write about a time when you were asked to make a decision about an important matter. How did you make the decision? Did you look at the facts? Did you listen to what other people said about it?

_____

_____

_____

_____

What Do You Know?

Directions: Circle the crimes that you think are misdemeanors. Underline the crimes that you think are felonies. When you are finished with the lesson, review your answers and make any necessary changes.

kidnapping a person

bank robbery without weapon

breaking into a car

robbing a person with a weapon

stealing a loaf of bread

causing harm to a person

Crime and Punishment

A **crime** is any act that breaks the law and harms people or society. The type of law that deals with crime is called criminal law. Criminal laws are rules for behavior. They outlaw things like stealing, damaging property, or attacking someone. All these actions are crimes.

Each state has a list of laws called a **penal** (PEE•nuhl) **code.** It describes every crime and the punishment that goes with it. The federal government also has a penal code. Examples of federal crimes are robbing a bank or committing an act of terrorism. Most crimes break state laws. So, most cases are tried in state courts and most inmates are in state prisons. In general, more serious crimes receive harsher punishments.

Crimes are classified in different ways. There are two broad categories of crimes based on how serious they are. A crime can be a misdemeanor (MIHS•dih•MEE•nuhr) or a felony. A **misdemeanor** is a less serious crime. A person can be fined a small amount of money or spend up to one year in jail. For example, stealing a $40 shirt from a store is a misdemeanor. A **felony** is a more serious crime. A person who commits a felony is punished by spending at least one year in prison. Robbing a store at gunpoint is a felony.

Crimes can be grouped as being against people or property. Crimes against people include things like assault and kidnapping. Crimes against people are considered more serious than crimes against property because they cause harm to a person. Almost all crimes against people are felonies.

Crimes against property include things like theft and vandalism. An illustration, or example, of vandalism is if someone were to purposely throw a bucket of paint onto a neighbor's new car. If the value of what is stolen or damaged is less than $100, the crime is a misdemeanor. Otherwise it is a felony. It is also a felony if it involves the threat or use of force against a person.

Crimes against property, such as this one, can be felonies or misdemeanors.

Show Your Skill

1. Compare and Contrast How are crime and penal code related?

_____

_____

_____

Think Critically

2. Analyze Suppose someone uses a weapon to steal $20 from a person. Is this crime a misdemeanor or a felony? Why?

_____

_____

_____

_____

Mark the Text

3. Photograph Circle the crime in the image. Then write on the line below whether you think it is a felony or a misdemeanor.

_____

Most penal codes set minimum and maximum penalties for each crime. Within those limits, a judge decides what **sentence,** or punishment, a person will serve.

Some prisoners are able to get paroled, or released early, after serving part of their sentence. Prisoners who are granted parole must report to a parole officer for the remainder of their sentence.

A prison sentence has a number of purposes. One is simply to punish, while another is to protect society by keeping dangerous people locked up. A third is to serve as a warning to others not to commit crime. A sentence can also be used to change a person's behavior. Many prisons have programs to educate and train prisoners for jobs. Learning new skills prepares criminals to become responsible citizens when they are released.

Criminal Case Procedure

In a criminal case, the government is always the plaintiff. That is, the government is the party that brings charges against a defendant. It is called the **prosecution.** This means that it starts the legal process against the defendant for breaking the law. During this process, the defendant's rights are protected by the Bill of Rights. The government must follow the rules of due process to treat a suspect fairly.

A criminal case begins when the police believe a crime has been committed. An arrest is made based on evidence. Police have to collect evidence to convince a judge to arrest someone for the crime. When they do, a judge issues an arrest warrant; the warrant lists the suspect's name and the crime. When the police arrest someone, they have to advise the suspect of the right to remain silent and the right to an attorney.

The suspect is then taken to a police station. The police make a record of the arrest. This is called a booking. The police will usually take a picture of the suspect and take fingerprints.

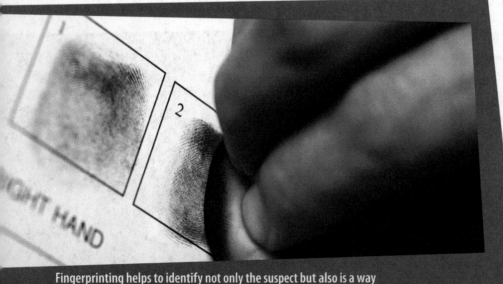

Fingerprinting helps to identify not only the suspect but also is a way that the police can check to see if the suspect has a record or prior arrests.

PHOTO: Jack Star/PhotoLink/Getty Images

Copyright © by The McGraw-Hill Companies, Inc.

Next, the suspect appears before a judge for a preliminary hearing. The judge explains the charges. The prosecution has to prove to the judge that there is probable cause—a good reason—for believing the accused is guilty of the crime. If the suspect does not have the money for a lawyer, the judge appoints one. If the crime is a misdemeanor, the suspect pleads either guilty or not guilty. If the plea is guilty, the judge sentences the suspect. If the plea is not guilty, the judge sets a date for a trial.

If the crime is a felony, no plea is made. Instead, the judge sets a date for a hearing to learn more about the case. The judge also decides whether to hold or release the suspect. A judge may have a suspect post bail, an amount of money left with the court until the trial. Suspects can also be released on their own recognizance, or control. When that happens, the suspect promises in writing to return to appear in court.

The next step is to indict, or charge, the accused with the crime. Many states have a grand jury do this; others allow the judge to decide. If there is not enough evidence against the suspect, the case is dismissed.

If the case is not dismissed, the next step is the arraignment. For a felony, the suspect is formally charged and enters a plea of guilty or not guilty. The prosecution and defense lawyers begin **plea bargaining.** This is a form of compromise. The prosecution agrees to a less serious charge. The defendant agrees to plead guilty. Plea bargains save the government the time and cost of a trial. Many criminal cases end with a plea bargain and never go to trial.

Defendants in a felony case can choose to be tried by a jury or a judge. In a jury trial, the lawyers choose a jury from a large group of citizens who have been called to serve.

Think Critically

7. Summarize What happens at a preliminary hearing? A cross-examination?

_____

_____

_____

_____

_____

_____

Mark the Text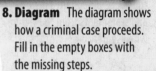

8. Diagram The diagram shows how a criminal case proceeds. Fill in the empty boxes with the missing steps.

Take the Challenge

9. Write down an example of a misdemeanor and a felony on two separate blank index cards. In small groups, shuffle the cards that each team member made and have other team members guess what they illustrate.

Steps in Criminal Procedure

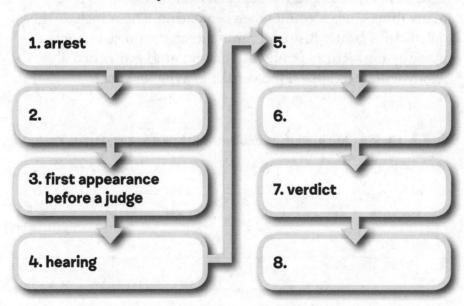

1. arrest
2.
3. first appearance before a judge
4. hearing
5.
6.
7. verdict
8.

As a juror, you review a case with other jurors and try to come to a unanimous decision.

PHOTO: David Young-Wolff/Riser/Getty Images

Think Critically

10. Infer Why do you think judges consider a defendant's history and statements from the victim when sentencing?

_____

_____

_____

_____

_____

_____

11. Explain Why are most criminal cases settled without going to trial?

_____

_____

_____

_____

The trial begins with an opening statement from each side. Then each side presents its case. The prosecution goes first. Each side offers evidence and presents witnesses. Witnesses swear to tell the truth. Each side can question the other side's witnesses. This is called **cross-examination.** After both sides have presented their case, each makes a closing statement.

If a jury is present, the judge explains to the jury how the law applies in the case. Then the jurors go into a room to review the case. Their discussions are secret. To find a defendant guilty, the jurors must be convinced beyond a reasonable doubt. In other words, they must decide that there is no other reasonable explanation except that the accused committed the crime. In almost all states, the verdict, or vote, must be unanimous. This means all the jurors must agree. If a jury cannot agree on a verdict, the judge will declare a mistrial. The prosecution may or may not retry the case.

A defendant who is found not guilty is set free. A guilty defendant is sentenced in court at a later date. Judges take many things into account when sentencing. These include the defendant's family history, criminal record, and statements made by the victim's family. A person found guilty of a felony will often appeal the verdict to a higher court.

 NGSSS Check What two conditions must be met for a jury to reach a guilty verdict? SS.7.C.2.6

_____

_____

_____

_____

LESSON
3

NGSSS

SS.7.C.3.10 Identify sources and types (civil, criminal, constitutional, military) of law.

SS.7.C.3.11 Diagram the levels, functions, and powers of courts at the state and federal levels.

THE JUVENILE JUSTICE SYSTEM

Essential Question

How can governments ensure citizens are treated fairly?

Guiding Questions

1. How has treatment of young criminal offenders changed?
2. What procedures are followed when a young person breaks the law?

Terms to Know

rehabilitate
to correct a person's behavior

juvenile delinquent
a child or teenager who commits a crime or repeatedly breaks the law

delinquent offender
a youth charged with breaking a criminal law

status offender
a youth charged with being out of the control of his or her parents or guardian

custody
taking charge, or control, of someone in an official way

detention hearing
the procedure by which a judge decides whether to charge a juvenile with an offense; like a preliminary hearing in an adult trial

adjudication hearing
the procedure used to determine the facts in a juvenile case; like a trial in criminal law

disposition hearing
the sentencing in a juvenile case

It Matters Because

The juvenile justice system is structured differently from the adult system.

This system handles cases of crimes committed by juveniles and also neglect of juveniles.

Why do you think the justice system is structured differently for young people and adults?

What Do You Know?

Directions: In the "Now" column, circle "True" if you think the statement is true or "False" if the statement is false based on what you know before you read the lesson. After you have read the lesson, complete the "Later" column.

Now		Later
True False	It is less serious when a youth breaks a law than when an adult breaks one.	True False
True False	When a youth breaks the law, he or she could be charged as an adult.	True False
True False	Most juvenile delinquents serve from one to three years.	True False
True False	Every state has a juvenile court system.	True False

Think Critically

1. Summarize How did the treatment of children who committed crimes begin to change in the 1800s?

_____

_____

_____

_____

Mark the Text

2. Circle the juvenile system's two main approaches for dealing with children who break the law.

Show Your Skill

3. Compare and Contrast What is the difference between a delinquent offender and a status offender?

_____

_____

_____

_____

_____

_____

_____

Juvenile Justice

At one time, children in this country who committed crimes were tried and punished like adults. They were sent to adult jails. They often served long prison terms.

This began to change in the 1800s. People began to believe that juveniles committed crimes because their families did not teach them proper values. Reformers wanted a special court that would do the parent's jobs. Instead of punishing these children as adults, the court would **rehabilitate** (REE•uh•BIH•luh•TAYT), or correct, their behavior and teach them right from wrong.

The first juvenile court was set up in Chicago, Illinois, in 1899. Today, every state has a juvenile court system. The Supreme Court has ruled that children charged with crimes have the same legal rights as adults. They have the right to be told the charges against them; to an attorney; to cross-examine, or question, witnesses against them; and to remain silent when questioned.

People continue to argue whether the goal of the juvenile system should be punishment or rehabilitation. In the 1990s, public opinion began to change. The emphasis, or weight, shifted back to punishment. Juvenile crime rates had quickly risen. The public wanted law and order. The legislatures took action by changing the laws. Now, in many states, it is easier to try young offenders in adult courts. Also, in most states, a juvenile charged with a felony can be tried as an adult. Most states consider anyone under age 18 to be a juvenile. In some states the age is 16.

A **juvenile delinquent** (JOO•vuh•NEYE•uhl dee•LIHN•kwuhnt) is a young person who commits a crime. There are two types of juvenile delinquents. **Delinquent offenders** are youths who have committed acts that would be crimes if done by an adult, like stealing a car. **Status offenders** have committed minor, or comparatively less

Reformer Jane Addams, who founded Hull House in Chicago, worked to establish the first juvenile court in 1899.

Social services are available to help juveniles. Here, a counselor talks to a young person at a correctional youth facility.

important, acts that would *not* be crimes if done by an adult. Examples include skipping school or running away from home. Status offenders do not listen to their parents or other adults; they cannot be controlled by them. For this reason, the court supervises, or takes control of, status offenders.

The Juvenile Court System

Juvenile courts handle two kinds of cases: neglect cases and delinquency cases. Neglect cases concern young people who are abused or not taken care of by their parents or guardians. A juvenile court can remove these children from their homes. The court places them with other families.

Delinquency cases concern young people who break the law. The legal process begins when the police take a young person into custody. **Custody** is to take charge, or control, of someone in an official way. If the offense is not serious, the police may give the youth a warning and release them to a caregiver. They may also pass the case on to a social service agency.

If the offense is serious or the youth has a prior, or past, record, the police may turn him or her over to the juvenile court. A social worker reviews the case and decides how it should be handled. This review is called intake. Some cases are dismissed during intake. Others are sent to adult court. Some young people receive services such as counseling or drug treatment and do not have to go to court. This is called diversion.

Youths who are still in the system after intake face up to three hearings. The first is a **detention hearing.** This is like a preliminary, or first, hearing in an adult trial. The state must show that there is good reason to charge the youth with the crime.

Think Critically

4. Explain What adult rights has the Supreme Court extended to juvenile offenders?

_____

_____

_____

_____

_____

_____

Mark the Text

5. Underline the meaning of custody.

Take the Challenge

6. With a partner, make a list of solutions that a counselor working with a juvenile delinquent could share to help that young person.

Mark the Text ✏️

7. Chart Fill in the chart to show what happens in a juvenile court case.

Think Critically

8. Compare What steps in the juvenile court system are similar to a trial and a sentencing hearing in the adult court system?

_____

_____

_____

_____

Show Your Skill

9. Interpret Information Why do you think a social worker reviews the case?

_____

_____

_____

If the youth is charged, the next step is an **adjudication** (uh•joo•dih•KAY•shuhn) **hearing.** This is like a trial in an adult case. Each side has an attorney. Evidence is presented and witnesses are questioned and cross-examined. A judge's finding that the juvenile is delinquent is like a guilty verdict.

A **disposition hearing** is next. This is like a sentencing hearing for an adult. Some youths receive probation. They are allowed to stay free as long as they meet the conditions of the court for a set period of time. Examples of those conditions are doing community service or completing a drug treatment program. For youths who finish the conditions of probation without getting into more trouble, the charges are dropped and taken off their record.

For serious crimes, a youth may be sent to an institution for young offenders. Most delinquents serve from one to three years. In some states they can be held until age 18 or 21.

Juvenile Case Procedure	
Step	**What Happens**
1.	Police bring a young offender into confinement.
2.	A social worker reviews the case.
3. detention hearing	
4.	Evidence is presented; witnesses are questioned; the judge reaches a finding.
5. disposition hearing	

 NGSSS Check What two kinds of cases does the juvenile court system see? **SS.7.C.3.11**

_____

_____

ESSENTIAL QUESTION *Why does conflict develop?*

Reflect on What It Means . . .

The civil and criminal justice systems are in place to help resolve conflict, to protect individuals and communities, and to hand out consequences for crimes. Read the news on the Internet or in a newspaper. Find three stories that describe either a civil or criminal law being broken. Then complete the graphic organizer below.

News Story:	News Story:	News Story:
Type of Crime (civil or criminal):	Type of Crime (civil or criminal):	Type of Crime (civil or criminal):
Location:	Location:	Location:
Details:	Details:	Details:

Keep Going! ⇥

Choose one of the three examples from the graphic organizer on the previous page. Draw another graphic organizer below to show the effects of a particular type of crime that you read about in this chapter.

TAKE THE CHALLENGE

Read a news story about a crime in your community. Try to determine how many people were directly or indirectly affected by the criminal's actions.

INTRODUCTION TO ECONOMICS

NGSSS

SS.7.E.1.1 Explain how the principles of a market and mixed economy helped to develop the United States into a democratic nation.

SS.7.E.1.3 Review the concepts of supply and demand, choice, scarcity, and opportunity cost as they relate to the development of the mixed market economy in the United States.

ESSENTIAL QUESTIONS *Why and how do people make economic choices? How do economic systems influence societies?*

The imaginary world of Harry Potter includes many encounters that reflect real-life economics. For instance, students of Hogwarts need to buy books for school, a broom for Quidditch, or a wand at Ollivander's Wand Shop. A replica of Mr. Ollivander's shop is part of a theme park in Orlando.

PHOTO: AP Photo/John Raoux, FIL

Copyright © by The McGraw-Hill Companies, Inc.

"**Scarcity exists in the magic world just as much as in the Muggle world. There are a limited number of tickets to the Quidditch world cup, magical creatures shed only so many feathers or hairs to go into wands, and not everyone has an invisibility cloak.**"

—FROM *THE GUARDIAN*

limited number

What might limit the number of tickets available for an event?

_____

_____

_____

DBQ BREAKING IT DOWN

Why is the phrase "not everyone" appropriate for the idea of scarcity?

_____

_____

_____

What is an example of scarcity in your own life?

_____

_____

_____

TEXT: Long, Heather. "Even in Potter's World, you can't just wave a magic wand." The Guardian, Monday 18 July 2005. http://www.guardian.co.uk/business/2005/jul/18/harrypotter.books.

LESSON 1

WHAT IS ECONOMICS?

NGSSS

SS.7.E.1.1 Explain how the principles of a market and mixed economy helped to develop the United States into a democratic nation.

SS.7.E.1.3 Review the concepts of supply and demand, choice, scarcity, and opportunity cost as they relate to the development of the mixed market economy in the United States.

Essential Questions

Why and how do people make economic choices?
How do economic systems influence societies?

Guiding Questions

1. What is scarcity and how does it affect economic choices?
2. What determines how societies make economic choices?

Terms to Know

wants
things people would like to have

resource
anything that can be used to make goods or services

economics
the study of how people use limited resources to satisfy unlimited wants

scarcity
not having enough resources to satisfy all one's needs and wants

economic system
a nation's way of producing the things its people want and need

traditional economy
an economic system in which major economic decisions are based on custom or habit

market economy
an economic system in which people and businesses own all resources and make economic decisions on the basis of price

command economy
an economic system in which the government makes the major economic decisions

mixed market economy
an economy in which businesses and individuals make the major economic decisions but in which the government also plays a role

It Matters Because

As someone who uses goods and services and will some day be a worker, you are part of the American economic system.

You want to make freshly squeezed orange juice. You go to the store to buy oranges, but the store has no oranges available. List reasons that could explain why there are no oranges.

What Do You Know?

Directions: Use the table below to answer the questions based on what you know now in the "Now" column. After the lesson, complete the table by writing your answers in the "Later" column.

	Now	Later
1. How do people fill their wants and needs when there are not enough resources?		
2. What are economic choices? List some examples.		

Our Wants and Resources

When people shop, they sometimes want to buy more than they can afford. For example, suppose a girl named Jayna is shopping for a new dress. She finds a dress she likes, but she also sees a sweater she wants. She does not have enough money to buy both. What should she do?

Jayna has a problem we all face at one time or another. She must decide how best to use her money to satisfy her wants. **Wants** are desires that people have that can be met by getting a product or a service. Most people want many things. In fact, our wants are almost without limit.

Wants can be either goods or services. Goods are things we can touch or hold. Dresses and sweaters are examples of goods. A service is work done for someone else. For example, the store clerk who rings up Jayna's purchase is performing a service.

Jayna must use her money to pay for her new dress. Money is a resource. **Resources** include everything that can be used to make or get goods and services. Economists talk about three kinds of resources, shown in the diagram below.

```
                    ┌──────────────┐
                    │  Resources   │
                    └──────────────┘
```

Natural Resources
- Land
- Things from the land that can be used to make goods and services

Labor
- Workers
- Workers' abilities
- More workers = more goods and services

Capital
- Money
- Buildings, tools
- Used to make or move goods or services

Resources are limited but wants are not. This means we must make choices. **Economics** is the study of how people use limited resources to satisfy unlimited wants and needs.

It is not only individuals who have many wants. City, state, and national governments have wants, too. Sometimes there are not enough resources to satisfy, or meet, wants and needs. This is known as **scarcity.** In fact, no country has all of the resources it needs. Both individuals and governments are affected by scarcity. This makes scarcity the basic economic problem in the world. Economics looks at how people and governments deal with the problem of scarcity.

Show Your Skill

1. Interpret Information What resources would the owner of a pizza parlor need? Write an example of each kind of the three types of resources.

natural resources

_____

_____

labor

_____

_____

capital

_____

_____

Think Critically

2. Compare How are economics and scarcity related?

_____

_____

_____

_____

Mark the Text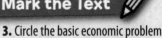

3. Circle the basic economic problem that people and nations face.

Take the Challenge

4. With a partner, draw an illustration to show how the three types of resources are used to produce a good or service.

Think Critically

5. Analyze What must a society consider when deciding what goods and services to produce?

Show Your Skill

6. Make Inferences In Country X a government planner has decided that half the nation's factories will make televisions. What type of economic system does Country X have?

7. Interpret Information What determines the kind of economy a nation has?

Societies and Economic Choices

Individuals, or people, make economic choices all the time. So do countries. Nations must decide how to use their limited resources in the best way to care for and protect their citizens. For example, a government must decide whether it will spend more money on health care or defense, education or the environment. The scarcity of resources forces societies to make these types of choices. These choices can be summed up by three basic questions:

1. What goods and services will be produced?
2. How will the goods and services be produced?
3. Who will consume, or use, goods and services?

What goods and services will be produced? For example, should a piece of land be used for farming or to build an airport? It cannot be used for both. Should a government improve roads or build schools? To decide questions like these societies must think about their resources. A nation with good soil and a long growing season might use much of its land to grow crops.

How will goods and services be produced? For example, should food be produced on big factory farms or small family farms?

Who will get the goods and services? Societies must decide who gets goods and how much people can have. They have different ways of distributing goods. Should new cars go to public officials or to the highest bidder? Should new housing units be reserved for low-income people or should they be available to anyone?

Societies answer these questions in different ways. Every country has its own **economic system,** or way of producing the things people want and need.

There are three basic types of economic systems, shown in the chart below.

The Three Types of Economic Systems	
Traditional Economy	**Individuals own resources. Economic decisions are made based on custom and habit.**
Market Economy	**Individuals and businesses own resources. They make economic decisions based on prices.**
Command Economy	**The government owns resources. Government planners make economic decisions.**

The first type is the **traditional economy.** People in a traditional economy base their economic choices on custom or habit. A person whose parents and grandparents were farmers would also be a farmer. This type of economy is not very productive. It also does not change much over time. New ways to produce goods are not usually tried.

PHOTO: (t) Christine Osborne Pictures/Alamy ; (b) Stuart Westmorland/Encyclopedia/CORBIS

Copyright © by The McGraw-Hill Companies, Inc.

In Tunisia, which is in northern Africa, a man tries to plough his field with help from a camel.

Another type of economy is the **market economy.** In this system, people and businesses own the resources. They use them to produce goods and services. They answer the three economic questions based on price.

At this major toy store in the United States, goods are often abundant, unless demand is higher than supply.

Show Your Skill

8. Compare and Contrast
What is the difference between a traditional economy and a market economy?

_____

_____

_____

_____

_____

_____

_____

Take the Challenge

9. With a partner or small group, research a country that once had a traditional economy and now has a market economy. Make a poster with charts or graphs to show how the change in economic system has affected the country's economy.

Show Your Skill

10. Compare and Contrast How is a command economy different from the other economic systems?

_____

_____

_____

_____

_____

_____

_____

_____

Think Critically

11. Analyze Do you think that the United States has always had a mixed market economy, or has it evolved over time? Explain.

_____

_____

_____

_____

_____

_____

_____

_____

The third type of economic system is the **command economy.** In this system, the government makes the economic decisions. Planners and officials decide what goods to produce. They also decide how much to produce and who is allowed to buy them.

Zimbabwe, a country in Africa, has a command economy, which can sometimes result in empty shelves in stores like this deli.

The United States has a **mixed market economy.** In this system, businesses compete for profit, but the government also plays a role. People and businesses choose what to produce and how to produce it. Who receives the goods and services is decided on the basis of price. At the same time, the government makes rules for how workers should be treated. It oversees markets to make sure businesses are honest. It provides some services, such as schools and defense.

 NGSSS Check How is scarcity related to economic choices in the development of the mixed market economy in the United States? **SS.7.E.1.3**

_____

_____

_____

_____

_____

NGSSS

SS.7.E.1.1 Explain how the principles of a market and mixed economy helped to develop the United States into a democratic nation.

SS.7.E.1.3 Review the concepts of supply and demand, choice, scarcity, and opportunity cost as they relate to the development of the mixed market economy in the United States.

LESSON

2

ECONOMIC DECISIONS

Essential Questions

Why and how do people make economic choices?

How do economic systems influence societies?

Guiding Questions

1. **Why are trade-offs important in making economic decisions?**
2. **How do costs and revenues influence economic decision making?**

Terms to Know

trade-off
giving up one option in order to get something else

opportunity cost
the loss of the next-best option when choosing to do one thing or another

revenue
the money a business gets from selling a good or service

fixed cost
an expense that does not change no matter how much a business produces

variable cost
an expense that changes depending on how much a business produces

total cost
the sum of all fixed and variable costs

marginal cost
the additional expense of producing one more unit of something

marginal revenue
the additional income received from selling one more unit of something

benefit-cost analysis
a comparison of the marginal costs and marginal benefits of a decision

It Matters Because

You make economic decisions every day, and you will do so all your life.

Suppose you went to the store to buy a video game with the money that you earned. At the store, you run into a friend who asks you to go to the movies. You do not have enough money to buy the video game and go to the movies. What choice will you make? What will you have to give up for your choice?

_____

_____

_____

_____

What Do You Know?

Directions: In the example above, there was a trade-off and an opportunity cost. Complete the sentences below. After reading the lesson, review your answers and make any necessary changes.

The trade-off was _____

_____ .

The opportunity cost was _____

_____ .

Trade-Offs

When you make a choice between two things you want to buy, you are making an economic decision. To make a good decision, you must think about the benefits and costs of each choice.

Once you choose you give up one option in favor of a better one. This is called a **trade-off.** Suppose you turn down a night out with friends in order to study for a test. You decide studying is a better use of your time. You have made a trade-off with your time.

Businesses and governments also make trade-offs. A town might have to choose between building a new school or a new road, for example. Trade-offs are necessary when money, time, and other resources are limited.

In making a trade-off, a person chooses one option over all others. In economics, the loss of the second-best use of your money or time is the **opportunity cost.** For example, when you chose to study you gave up the chance to visit friends. The opportunity cost of your choice is the fun you would have had with your friends.

Choices made by businesses and governments also have opportunity costs. A city might decide to spend money to improve a park rather than to fix sidewalks. The opportunity cost is the sidewalks that do not get fixed.

Opportunity costs are not always measured in money or things. One example for a business is the work time that is lost while employees are trained in a new computer program. If the training will improve employees' future work, then the opportunity cost is worthwhile.

Measuring Costs and Revenues

Business people have to make economic decisions every day. In order to better understand how those decisions are made, let us look at an example. Joe owns a restaurant called Joe's Seafood Depot. It is open from four o'clock in the afternoon to ten o'clock at night. Joe wonders if his restaurant would make more money if he kept it open longer every day.

In order to find out if it will be profitable to stay open longer, Joe has to figure out his **fixed costs** and his **variable costs.** His fixed costs, like rent and insurance, will not increase if he stays open a few more hours. But his variable costs will **vary,** or change. His variable costs include the money he pays his workers, his electric and gas bills, and the supplies he uses

to produce his product. His **total costs** for running the business are the sum of his fixed costs and his variable costs.

Before deciding how many hours longer he wants to stay open, Joe will figure out his **marginal costs.** Economists define marginal cost as the increase in expense caused by producing one more unit of something. In Joe's case this additional unit is staying open for one more hour.

Once Joe knows his costs for staying open later he has to decide if he can make enough **revenue** to pay the costs and still make a profit. Revenue is the money Joe's customers pay him when they eat in his restaurant. The chart below shows both the marginal cost and the **marginal revenue** Joe expects to make for each added hour he keeps his restaurant open.

Marginal Cost and Revenue for Joe's Seafood Depot		
Added Hours	**Marginal Cost**	**Marginal Revenue**
1	$30	$70
2	$30	$60
3	$30	$50
4	$30	$40
5	$30	$30
6	$30	$20

Sometimes business people, like Joe, want to grow their business, serve more customers, and make more money. When trying to decide between different options, they will likely use a benefit-cost analysis. In Joe's case, he might be trying to

Think Critically

5. Interpret Why would the cost of labor and supplies go up if Joe's stays open longer?

_____

_____

_____

_____

_____

_____

Show Your Skill

6. Interpret Charts At how many additional hours does the marginal cost equal the marginal revenue?

_____

7. Summarize What are two things that are compared in a marginal analysis? Explain your answer.

_____

_____

_____

_____

_____

_____

8. Write down an example of marginal analysis that is not described in the lesson. Think of what the benefits and costs are. Trade examples with a partner, and see if your partner can guess what the benefits and costs are.

decide if he should build an addition onto the Seafood Depot or perhaps open a second Seafood Depot in a neighboring town.

Benefit-cost analysis compares the size of the benefit with the size of the cost by dividing the two. This type of analysis helps businesses choose among two or more options. For example it will help a business choose between options A and B. If option A creates revenue of $100 at a cost of $80, the benefit-cost ratio is 1.25. We get the number 1.25 by dividing $100 by $80. If option B creates revenue of $150 and costs $90, the benefit-cost ratio is 1.67. In order to be profitable, businesses will choose the option with the higher benefit-cost number.

Business people also use another type of analysis to compare two options. It is called marginal analysis. Marginal analysis compares the additional benefit of doing something with its additional cost. If the additional benefit is greater than the additional cost, the choice is a good one.

Joe could use marginal analysis to help him decide how many more hours to stay open. Look at the Marginal Costs and Revenues Chart For Joe's Seafood Depot on the previous page. The chart shows that the marginal revenue of staying open one more hour is $70 and the marginal cost is $30. Because the benefit is greater than the cost, Joe will likely stay open at least one more hour and perhaps longer.

When looking at marginal analysis, the rule is to continue doing something until the marginal cost is equal to the marginal revenue. For Joe, they are equal at five hours. Costs and benefits both equal $30. Then benefits go down.

Marginal analysis even works for decisions that are not about money. It can apply to a decision about how long a nap should be! The benefits of the nap are highest during the first hour. After that they gradually decline.

The cost of taking a nap would be the opportunity cost of what you were not doing while you napped. The ideal length of your nap is the point at which the declining benefits equal the rising costs.

NGSSS Check How are trade-offs and opportunity costs related? SS.7.E.1.3

_____

_____

_____

_____

NGSSS

SS.7.E.1.1 Explain how the principles of a market and mixed economy helped to develop the United States into a democratic nation.

SS.7.E.1.3 Review the concepts of supply and demand, choice, scarcity, and opportunity cost as they relate to the development of the mixed market economy in the United States.

Essential Questions

Why and how do people make economic choices?
How do economic systems influence societies?

Guiding Questions

1. **How do demand and supply affect prices?**
2. **How do prices help consumers and businesses make economic decisions?**

Terms to Know

producer
a person or business who provides a good or a service

consumer
a person or business who buys a good or service

demand
the amount of a good or service that consumers are willing and able to buy at a particular price

supply
the amount of a good or service that producers are willing and able to sell at a particular price

market
a place where buyers and sellers come together

competition
struggle among sellers to attract buyers

equilibrium price
the price set for a good or service in the marketplace at which demand and supply are balanced

surplus
a situation in which supply is greater than demand

shortage
a situation in which demand is greater than supply

It Matters Because

Demand and supply work together to set the prices of the goods and services you buy and use.

Suppose you have saved your money to buy a pair of shoes that you really like. They cost more than you want to pay, but you think they are worth it. But, you find out that every store is sold out of the shoes. When you go back to the store a week later, the shoes are in stock but their price has increased. Write to explain what happened.

_____

_____

_____

_____

What Do You Know?

Directions: Draw a simple illustration or create a chart to show the relationship between the price of a good or service and demand for the good or service. When you are finished with the lesson, check your work and make any necessary changes.

Show Your Skill

1. Identify the Main Idea
What two forces determine prices in a market economy?

_____

_____

Think Critically

2. Compare What is the relationship between price and supply?

_____

_____

_____

_____

Show Your Skill

3. Interpret Charts What happens to demand as the price per barrel of crude oil increases?

_____

_____

_____

Demand and Supply

What makes prices go up and down? Are prices important? You will soon see that they are. In a command economy, government officials set most prices. In a mixed market economy like the United States, prices are set by the interaction of demand and supply. **Producers** are the people and businesses that provide goods and services. **Consumers** are the people who buy goods and services. Producers create supply and consumers create demand.

In economics, **demand** is the amount of a good or service that people are willing and able to buy at a particular price. This definition has four key parts:

1. Amount Demand measures how much of something consumers will buy. This amount changes as prices change.

2. Willing to buy Consumers must want to buy the good or service or there is no demand.

3. Able to buy Consumers also must be able to buy. Wanting an item without having the money to pay for it does not count as demand.

4. Price Demand is tied to price. How much of an item people are willing and able to buy is related to the item's price.

Supply is the amount of a good or service that producers are willing and able to sell at various prices during a set time period. As the price of a product goes up, producers are willing to supply more. As the price goes down, they supply less.

The amount of a good or service that is supplied and demanded at each price can be shown in a schedule. The schedules below show how much oil consumers demanded and producers supplied at certain prices.

Demand Schedule for Crude Oil		Supply Schedule for Crude Oil	
Price per Barrel	Quantity Demanded	Price per Barrel	Quantity Supplied
$10	50	$10	10
$20	40	$20	20
$30	30	$30	30
$40	20	$40	40
$50	10	$50	50

Economists use graphs to show how much of a good is supplied and demanded at each price. The data from schedules can be plotted on a graph. These graphs are called a demand curve and a supply curve. The graph below shows the demand and supply curves for oil.

As you can see, the demand curve slopes down to the right. The supply curve slopes up to the right. They go in opposite directions. That is because as the price goes up, producers supply more, but consumers demand less. When prices are low, people demand more.

Demand and supply curves together show a **market.** A market is anywhere buyers and sellers of the same good or service come together. In order to work well, markets need many buyers and sellers. This **competition** keeps prices down. Competition is the sellers' struggle to attract buyers. If the market does not have enough sellers, prices may go too high. That is why U.S. laws ban most monopolies.

Show Your Skill

4. Interpret Graphs What is the equilibrium price of oil according to the graph?

_____

5. Identify Cause and Effect How do prices help determine for whom goods will be produced in a market economy?

_____

_____

_____

_____

Think Critically

6. Analyze Are prices more changeable in a market economy or in a command economy? Why?

_____

_____

_____

_____

_____

_____

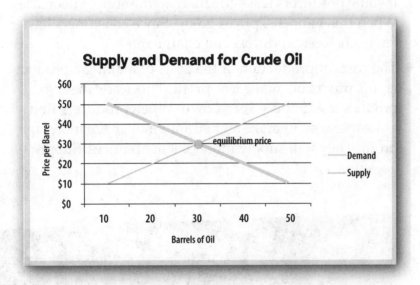

Supply and Demand for Crude Oil

Markets are important in many ways. One major way is that they set prices. Look again at the graph above. Note that the lines on the graph cross at one point. This point is the price set by the market. At this price demand and supply balance. This is the **equilibrium** (EE•kwuh•LIH•bree•uhm) **price.** At this price, consumers want to buy just as much oil as producers want to sell.

If the price of oil rises higher than the equilibrium price, producers will supply more. However, consumers will not buy more. This will result in a surplus of oil. A **surplus** occurs when supply is greater than demand. A surplus makes prices fall.

If the price of oil falls below the equilibrium price, the opposite will happen. There will be a shortage. A **shortage** occurs when there is not enough supply to meet demand. A shortage makes prices rise.

7. Compare and Contrast
What is the difference between a surplus and a shortage?

_____

_____

_____

_____

_____

_____

Take the Challenge

8. Create an idea for a product that is similar to a product that already exists and that interests you. Find out what the price of the competitive product is, and then determine how you will price your product.

Price is not the only thing that affects demand. Other factors that change the demand for a good or service are

- The number of consumers: More consumers mean more demand. Fewer consumers mean less demand.

- Consumer income: If people have more money to spend, they buy more. Demand goes up. If people have less money to spend, they buy less. The equilibrium price decreases.

- Consumer preferences: If people decide they like a product, demand for it goes up. Demand goes down if consumers do not like it.

Supply is also affected by factors other than price. Key factors are

- The number of suppliers: When more suppliers enter the market for a product, the supply increases.

- If some producers leave the market, the supply decreases. When this happens, prices go up. Since consumers have fewer choices, producers can charge more.

- The costs of production: If the costs of making a product go up, producers make less profit. This leads them to produce less. Supply goes down. When producers find a cheaper way to make something, they make more profit. They will supply more of it at all prices. Supply goes up.

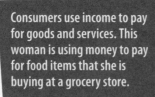

Consumers use income to pay for goods and services. This woman is using money to pay for food items that she is buying at a grocery store.

The Economic Role of Prices

Prices play a key role in a market economy. First they help answer the three basic economic questions. These questions are *what* to produce, *how* to produce, and *for whom* to produce.

Businesses decide what to produce based on consumer demand. If a business cannot sell a product, the price falls. When the price falls, producers stop making the product. So prices determine what gets produced.

In the same way, prices determine how things are produced. Cars provide one example. Cars built by hand would cost too much. For this reason automakers use mass production to keep prices down. All businesses try to keep production costs down. This allows them to sell at prices consumers will pay.

Prices also answer the last question: *for whom* are goods produced? They are produced for those who have the money and desire to buy them at a given price.

In a market economy, prices also have other uses. They measure value. They send signals to producers and consumers about the value of a product or service. For producers the signals help them decide where to set prices. If consumers will not buy an item at a certain price, producers realize they should lower that price. For consumers, prices signal what an item is worth. If no producer offers an item at the low price consumers want, then consumers must adapt. This means they must change their expectations about what they will have to pay.

Prices do not play the same role in a command economy. In this case government officials answer the three basic economic questions. Prices are not set by supply and demand. Instead, officials set prices based on their idea of the value of goods and services.

NGSSS Check How do prices help businesses decide what items to produce? S.7.E.1.3

9. Identify the Main Idea In a market economy, what questions do businesses ask?

_____

_____

_____

10. Infer When do consumers need to change their expectations?

_____

_____

_____

_____

_____

_____

Cars are often put together on an assembly line like this one in Flint, Michigan, because they are cheaper to mass-produce than to produce by hand.

MY REFLECTIONS

ESSENTIAL QUESTIONS *Why and how do people make economic choices? How do economic systems influence societies?*

Reflect on What It Means . . .

Micro means "small." *Macro* means "big." Can you guess what *microeconomics* is? What about *macroeconomics*? How do these relate to economic choices?

Microeconomics is the study of smaller economic decisions—those made by individuals and businesses. *Macroeconomics* is the study of larger economic decisions—those made by entire countries. Write an example of economics in action for each level.

Macroeconomic

My World

My Community

Myself

Microeconomic

TAKE THE CHALLENGE

President Franklin Roosevelt believed that people have freedom when they have economic security. What do you think he meant by that? Do you agree?

THE AMERICAN ECONOMY

NGSSS

SS.7.E.1.1 Explain how the principles of a market and mixed economy helped to develop the United States into a democratic nation.

SS.7.E.1.2 Discuss the importance of borrowing and lending in the United States, the government's role in controlling financial institutions, and list the advantages and disadvantages of using credit.

SS.7.E.1.3 Review the concepts of supply and demand, choice, scarcity, and opportunity cost as they relate to the development of the mixed market economy in the United States.

SS.7.E.1.4 Discuss the function of financial institutions in the development of a market economy.

ESSENTIAL QUESTION *Why and how do people make economic choices?*

These men are installing solar panels. Their work is the result of new ideas in building construction. In his State of the Union address, President Obama spoke of the relationship between new ideas, the American dream, and the economy:

> " From the earliest days of our founding, America has been the story of ordinary people who dare to dream. That's how we win the future. We're a nation that says, 'I might not have a lot of money, but I have this great idea for a new company.' "
>
> PRESIDENT BARACK OBAMA

win the future

What do you think "winning the future" means?

_____

_____

How might someone find the money to start a company?

_____

_____

DBQ BREAKING IT DOWN

What is the tone or feeling of the last sentence of the excerpt?

_____

_____

_____

Do you agree with President Obama's description of America as "the story of ordinary people who dare to dream"? Explain.

_____

_____

_____

McGraw-Hill
netw⊚rks™
There's More Online!

PHOTO: Juan Silva/The Image Bank/Getty Images

1 GROSS DOMESTIC PRODUCT

NGSSS

SS.7.E.1.1 Explain how the principles of a market and mixed economy helped to develop the United States into a democratic nation.

SS.7.E.1.3 Review the concepts of supply and demand, choice, scarcity, and opportunity cost as they relate to the development of the mixed market economy in the United States.

Essential Question

Why and how do people make economic choices?

Guiding Questions

1. Why is Gross Domestic Product important to a nation?
2. Why is GDP difficult to measure?

Copyright © by The McGraw-Hill Companies, Inc.

Terms to Know

product
item produced in an economy

Gross Domestic Product (GDP)
the total market value of all final goods and services produced in one year

entrepreneur
a person who starts a new business

GDP per capita
the total amount of final goods and services produced in a year divided by the population

standard of living
quality of life based on how well people are able to meet their needs and wants

It Matters Because

The success of the U.S. economy affects the quality of life for everyone who lives here.

Have you ever wanted to start your own business? Would you make a product or provide a service? Draw a sketch of the good or service you would provide.

What Do You Know?

Directions: Use the table below to answer the questions based on what you know now in the "Now" column. After the lesson, complete the table by writing your answers in the "Later" column.

	Now	Later
What do you think Gross Domestic Product (GDP) is?		
What factors does society have to think about when deciding how to use money?		

Why GDP Is Important

The United States economy has many parts. For example, farmers grow crops, factories make many kinds of goods, and people buy goods. These are all part of the economy. An item produced, or made, in an economy is called a **product.** A product may be a good such as a video game, or a service such as a haircut. Goods are things that you can use. Bicycles, cell phones, books, boxes of cereal, pens, cars, clothes are all goods. Services are jobs done for someone else for pay. Repairing a car and babysitting a child are examples of services.

The making of goods or providing of services are the activities that make up the **Gross Domestic Product (GDP).** GDP is the total market value of all the final products made in a country in one year. The United States has the world's largest economy. In 2010 the output, or amount of products produced, in the United States was about 15 trillion dollars ($15,000,000,000,000). That is about 20 percent or one-fifth of the output of the entire world.

To find GDP you must know the price of final goods and services and how many were sold. Multiply these two numbers, then add your answers. The table below shows an example of how to calculate GDP. This is a simple version of the kind of math economists use to figure out the GDP of a nation.

Calculating Gross Domestic Product (GDP)			
Final Goods and Services	Price X	Number Sold =	Total
Game downloads	$5	20	$100
Books	$10	12	+ $120
Haircuts	$12	5	+ $60
		GDP	$280

Making goods and providing services creates income for people. When people get paid for their work, they earn income. GDP is a way to measure the income of the nation. GDP includes purchases made by consumers, businesses, and the government.

It takes many people to create a product. When a bicycle is made, the people who mine for the metal, create the frame of the bicycle, make the tires, and paint it are all paid. Then the people who fix parts of bicycles that break after they have been used are paid for their work.

Think Critically

1. Explain What is an example of a service that you might use?

_____

_____

_____

_____

2. Analyze Why does GDP represent income for all factors of production?

_____

_____

_____

_____

_____

_____

_____

Mark the Text

3. Chart Circle the number that shows the GDP.

People called entrepreneurs are very important to the economy. An **entrepreneur** (AHN•truh•pruh•NUHR) is a person who takes a risk and starts a new business. The new business may or may not succeed. The risk is rewarded if the business earns money.

An entrepreneur is a factor of production. Businesses bring together the other three factors of production. They are: natural resources (land, soil, forests, and mineral deposits); labor (factory workers, miners, and store owners); and capital (tools, buildings, and money). The diagram below shows which factors of production are used to make a bicycle.

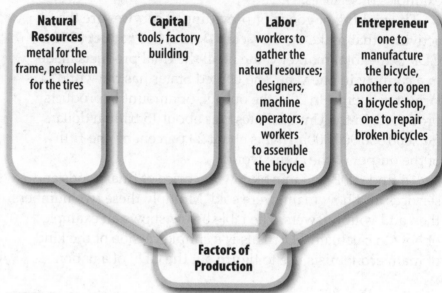

Natural Resources
metal for the frame, petroleum for the tires

Capital
tools, factory building

Labor
workers to gather the natural resources; designers, machine operators, workers to assemble the bicycle

Entrepreneur
one to manufacture the bicycle, another to open a bicycle shop, one to repair broken bicycles

Factors of Production

Measuring GDP

Think about how many goods and services are offered in your own community. How difficult do you think that may be to measure? Now try to imagine how many goods and services are provided in the whole country!

Suppose a country only produced a small number of goods and services. The GDP would be much easier to calculate. Measuring the GDP of the United States is very hard because the total number of goods and services is huge. However, before we can really understand how the GDP is figured out, there are other things we need to know.

GDP does not include all goods and services. It only includes final goods and services sold in the market. A final good or service is something that is sold directly to the user. A book is a final good. The ink and paper used to make the book are not final goods. They are not part of the GDP. Intermediate goods are ones that go into making a final product. The parts used to make a bicycle are intermediate goods. Used goods do not count, either. They were already counted when they were first sold. Transferring them, or re-selling them, does not involve new production.

GDP tells how large a country's economy is. When we compare countries, it is better to measure **GDP per capita.** The phrase "per capita" means *per person.* It is best to compare countries using GDP per capita because countries have different populations and different size economies. This calculation gives the share of GDP each person would get if it were divided equally. To find the GDP per capita, you take the country's total GDP and divide it by the total population.

The **standard of living** is the quality of life for the people in a country. It is based on how well people are able to meet their needs and wants. The GDP does not measure the standard of living. If the GDP of a nation is high, it does not mean that the standard of living for all citizens is good. In general, the higher the GDP per capita, the better the standard of living. Environmental conditions are also looked at when measuring the standard of living. Pollution lowers the standard of living. The United States has many laws to control pollution, but some other countries, such as China, do not.

Sarasota, Florida, was voted among the top metropolitan areas in the United States with a high standard of living.

 NGSSS Check What does GDP measure? What does a high GDP reveal about a country? SS.7.E.1.1

_____

_____

_____

_____

Show Your Skill

7. Compare and Contrast How would the standard of living of a country with a high GDP per capita compare to that of one with a low GDP per capita?

_____

_____

_____

_____

_____

_____

Take the Challenge

8. With a partner, do research to find out which countries have a high standard of living. Find at least the top three. Then find the GDP for these countries. Were they low or high? Make a chart or graph to show the data you have collected. Share your findings with the class.

2 ECONOMIC FLOW AND ECONOMIC GROWTH

NGSSS

SS.7.E.1.2 Discuss the importance of borrowing and lending in the United States, the government's role in controlling financial institutions, and list the advantages and disadvantages of using credit.

SS.7.E.1.3 Review the concepts of supply and demand, choice, scarcity, and opportunity cost as they relate to the development of the mixed market economy in the United States.

SS.7.E.1.4 Discuss the function of financial institutions in the development of a market economy.

Essential Question

Why and how do people make economic choices?

Guiding Questions

1. Why do resources, goods, and services flow in a circular pattern in a market system?
2. How can nations create and promote economic growth?

Terms to Know

circular flow model
the circular flow of resources, goods, services, and money through the economy

factor market
where factors of production are bought and sold

product market
where businesses sell goods and services to buyers

economic growth
an increase in the output of goods and services over time

productivity
a measure of how efficiently resources are used to create products

specialization
when businesses and people focus their work on one product or service

division of labor
breaking down a large job into smaller tasks, each of which is done by a different worker

human capital
the knowledge, skills, and experience of workers

It Matters Because

People of all ages and from every part of the country contribute to the U.S. economy.

Complete the sentences below.

A product that I bought recently was _____.

A service that I paid for recently was _____.

A job that I have done is _____.

When I grow up I would like to work as a _____.

What Do You Know?

Directions: A circular flow model shows how resources, goods, services, and money flow through the economy. Draw a circular flow model based on this description. When you are finished with the lesson, check your model and make any necessary changes.

The Circular Flow Model

It can be hard to understand what happens in a country's economy. Economists use models to help understand the economy. A model can be a graph or a diagram. The **circular flow model** is used in this lesson. It shows how resources, goods and services, and money flow between businesses and consumers in a circular path.

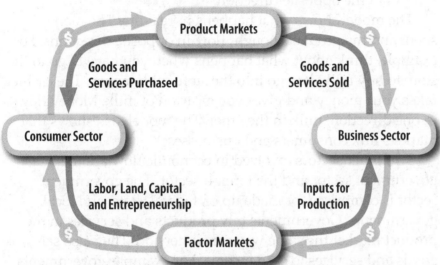

Circular Flow of Economic Activity

The model has four main parts. Two parts are markets where buying and selling take place. The other two parts are sectors, or categories. These show the two main groups of participants in markets, or the people and businesses active in the economy.

Find the boxes on the diagram that show the two markets. They are the **factor market** and the **product market.** The factor market is where factors of production are bought and sold. When people go to work they are selling their labor in the factor market. Machines, tools, and natural resources such as oil are also part of the factor market. The product market is where businesses sell goods and services. An easy way to remember the product market is to think of it as one store where all goods and services are sold.

The consumer sector is made up of all the people in the economy who get paid and who buy goods and services. Consumers, or buyers, take part in both the factor and product markets. Workers are paid for their time and skill. They sell their labor in the factor market. Then they use that money to buy goods and services in the product market.

Think Critically

1. **Synthesize** List all of the factors of production and give an example of each.

_____

_____

_____

_____

Show Your Skill

2. **Interpret Information** A student works part time in a video game store. Which part of the circular flow model does this represent?

Take the Challenge

3. Prepare and deliver a short speech to the class in which you explain how you have participated in the product market.

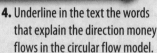
The business sector includes all the companies that produce goods and services. Businesses sell goods and services in the product market. Businesses use the money they make to buy land, labor, and capital in the factor market.

Look at the circular flow diagram on the previous page. You can see that money always flows in a clockwise direction. First, look at the loop that shows where the money goes. The money starts in the consumer sector then moves through the product market to the business sector. The money then flows through the factor market back to the consumer. Next, look at the loop that shows the goods, services, and factors of production. It flows in the opposite direction.

The model shows what happens in real life. The money spent and the products bought flow in opposite directions. For example, think about what happens when you have to go to the store to buy milk. You go into the store with money. The cashier takes your money and gives you a carton of milk. Money flows in one direction, milk in the other. The model also shows that markets link consumers and businesses.

Two other sectors involved in economic flow are the government sector and the foreign sector. The government sector is comprised, or made up of, federal, state, and local governments. Governments buy products and services in the product market the same way consumers do. They also sell goods and services to earn income. For example, governments charge park entry fees, state universities charge tuition, and local bus systems charge fares. Governments also collect taxes.

The foreign sector is made up of the people and businesses from other countries that buy and sell goods in the United States. Americans buy more from other countries than we sell to them.

Consumers spend money at a local market in North Miami, which contributes to the circular flow model.

Promoting Economic Growth

Economic growth is an increase in the output of goods and services over time. Economists track economic growth in many ways. One way is by watching the changes in the GDP. When the GDP is higher than the previous year, the economy has grown. Government and business leaders try to promote economic growth. This growth raises our standard of living.

As you remember, the four factors of production are used to make goods and provide services. A country's natural and human resources are very important for economic growth. Natural resources are often in limited supply. For instance, there is a limited amount of land. Also, we could use up all the oil in the world or use wood faster than it can grow back.

For the economy to grow, the population also needs to grow or to become more productive. **Productivity** is a measure of how efficiently resources are used. Say a factory that has made 1,000 computers a week begins to make 1,200 a week without adding any new workers. This means productivity has increased. Productivity usually improves when businesses and people focus on one product or service. This is called **specialization.** Specialization allows businesses and people to become experts at what they do.

Specialization leads to **division of labor.** Division of labor breaks down a large job into smaller tasks. A different worker does each task. Each worker can focus on his or her task and find ways to do it faster and better. This is one way that specialization increases productivity.

Businesses often try to increase productivity. They do this by focusing on their **human capital,** or workers. As workers gain training, education, and experience, their work improves. The productivity of the business increases. This leads to economic growth and a higher standard of living.

NGSSS Check List three things that businesses do to promote economic growth. SS.7.E.1.3

_____

_____

_____

6. Compare and Contrast What is the difference between GDP and productivity?

_____

_____

_____

_____

_____

7. Identify the Main Idea What must governments and businesses do to create economic growth?

_____

_____

Think Critically

8. Infer How do people benefit from economic growth?

_____

_____

With specialization and the division of labor, people and businesses can often be more productive.

NGSSS

SS.7.E.1.1 Explain how the principles of a market and mixed economy helped to develop the United States into a democratic nation.

SS.7.E.1.2 Discuss the importance of borrowing and lending in the United States, the government's role in controlling financial institutions, and list the advantages and disadvantages of using credit.

SS.7.E.1.3 Review the concepts of supply and demand, choice, scarcity, and opportunity cost as they relate to the development of the mixed market economy in the United States.

SS.7.E.1.4 Discuss the function of financial institutions in the development of a market economy.

Essential Question
Why and how do people make economic choices?

Guiding Questions
1. What makes capitalism a successful economic system?
2. How is the history of capitalism associated with the Founders?

Terms to Know

capitalism
economic system in which private citizens own the factors of production and decide how to use them to make money

free enterprise
economic system in which individuals and businesses are allowed to compete for profit with little government intrusion

voluntary exchange
when buyers and sellers choose to take part in an exchange

profit
the money left over from the sale of goods or services after all costs have been paid

profit motive
the desire to earn money by creating and selling goods and services

competition
when businesses try to sell the best products at the lowest prices to the most consumers

private property rights
the right to own, use, and sell property

laissez-faire economics
economic system in which the government's role is small

It Matters Because

Each of us enjoys the freedom to choose a job and decide how to use our money under the economic system called capitalism.

Write about a time when you made a profit for selling a good or service. For example, you could have earned money mowing someone's lawn or washing someone's car. Did you have any expenses to do the job?

_____

_____

_____

_____

What Do You Know?

Directions: Circle the terms below that relate to the American economy. Check your answers after you complete the lesson.

free enterprise	**command economy**
communism	**laissez-faire economics**
capitalism	**socialism**

Write a sentence that uses two of the terms that you circled.

_____

_____

Capitalism in the United States

The U.S. market economy is huge. One reason why it is so large is that citizens, not the government, make most of the economic decisions. Another word for this type of system is **capitalism.** Under capitalism, private citizens own the factors of production. They decide how to use them to make money. Our economy is also called a **free enterprise** system. In this type of system, businesses can compete with one another without the government getting in the way. Free enterprise has helped the U.S. economy grow to become the wealthiest in the world.

Six features of a free enterprise system help make the U.S. economy work. The chart below shows what each factor is and explains how it works in the U.S. economy.

The first is economic freedom. The American people are free to buy and sell the factors of production. They can choose how they will earn and spend their money. This freedom allows the economy to be more organized and productive.

Mark the Text

1. Underline the name for the economic system in which businesses are allowed to compete without government intrusion.

2. **Table** Complete the table by writing in the missing features of the U.S. economy and the explanations for how the different features work.

Feature of U.S. Economy	How It Works
Economic Freedom	Americans choose how they will earn and spend their money.
	The place where buyers and sellers interact. Supply and demand drive the markets.
Voluntary Exchange	
Competition	
	People have the right to use or sell their property as they see fit. People get to keep the profits they make off their property. Therefore they are more likely to take care of or invest in their property.

3. Summarize List the six main factors of capitalism that contribute to its success.

_____

_____

_____

_____

Show Your Skill

4. Draw Conclusions Why do people risk their money to start businesses?

_____

_____

_____

5. Analyze What factor of capitalism encourages the upkeep of property? Why?

_____

_____

_____

_____

The second feature is the market. The market is the place where buyers and sellers interact. Supply and demand drive the U.S. markets. Consumers like you demand products and services. Businesses supply them. In our economy buyers and sellers decide what those goods and services will be and who will use them. Though there can be problems in markets, over time they have proven to be the best way to bring buyers and sellers together. Markets encourage competition and set prices.

The third factor of capitalism is **voluntary exchange.** This happens when buyers and sellers choose to take part in an exchange. Buyers give up their money to gain a product. Sellers give up their products to gain money. Buyers and sellers both benefit.

The fourth factor is the profit motive. A desire to make money encourages a person to offer a product to buyers. The potential for **profit** leads entrepreneurs to take risks. Profit is the money left over from the sale of goods or services after all the costs of making it have been paid. The **profit motive** is the main reason capitalism succeeds. Profit motive is the desire to earn money by creating and selling goods and services. It also pushes people to invent new goods and services. The profit motive drives the economy.

Competition is the fifth factor of capitalism. Competition is when businesses try to sell similar products at the best prices. Businesses that have lower prices usually win the most buyers. But if a business can offer a higher quality product than the competition, it may win the buyers over.

The final factor is **private property rights.** People in this country have the right to own and use their own property. They can also choose to dispose of, or get rid of, their property. A person cannot use property in a way that violates the rights of others, however. Private property rights give people the incentive to work because they are able to keep any profits they might earn. Incentive is the desire or drive to do something. These rights also motivate people to save, invest, and to take care of their property.

This woman is checking out the price of limes at a local food store. She may check another store to see if it offers a competitive price so that she can buy the limes for less.

Everyday **Low Price**

38¢ ea

The Origins of U.S. Capitalism

In 1776 Adam Smith published a book called *The Wealth of Nations.* Smith was a Scottish philosopher and economist. He believed that self-interest, or well-being, makes people work. It also causes them to use resources wisely. He supported the idea that the market works best on its own, without government involvement.

Smith believed in **laissez-faire economics.** *Laissez-faire* (leh•say•FEHR) is a French term. It means "to leave alone." In economics it means that the government should keep its hands off of the marketplace. It should only make sure that competition is allowed.

Smith's ideas helped shape the ideas of many of the nation's Founders, including Alexander Hamilton, Thomas Jefferson, and James Madison.

Adam Smith supported laissez-faire economics, a term that most likely originated with the finance general for France's King Louis XIV. The king was told that business should be "left alone" to keep it going.

Mark the Text

6. Circle the name of the book that Adam Smith published in 1776.

Think Critically

7. Draw Conclusions How did the ideas of Adam Smith shape the history of the United States?

_____

_____

_____

_____

_____

_____

Take the Challenge

8. With a partner or small group, make a word web and write the term *laissez-faire* in the center oval. Add circles to describe its meaning, give examples, and include its effects in the marketplace.

 NGSSS Check What are two benefits of private property rights? SS.7.E.1.3

1. _____

2. _____

List the two ideas about government found in Adam Smith's laissez-faire economics. SS.7.E.1.2

3. _____

4. _____

ESSENTIAL QUESTION *Why and how do people make economic choices?*

Reflect on What It Means . . .

The profit motive is a main reason that capitalism succeeds. Profit motive is the desire to earn money by creating and selling goods and services. It also pushes people to invent new goods and services. The profit motive drives the economy.

Search online and in your library for examples that relate to how people have been motivated by the profit motive, such as through a business opportunity.

You Explain or give an example of how you are motivated by the profit motive.

_____

_____

_____

The Community Explain or give an example of how your community is motivated by the profit motive.

_____

_____

_____

_____

The World Explain or give an example of how people around the world are motivated by the profit motive.

_____

_____

_____

_____

TAKE THE CHALLENGE

A business plan is a written plan of the goals of a business and steps to meet those goals. Write a business plan for a business you would like to open, either now or when you are in the workforce.

PERSONAL FINANCE

NGSSS

SS.7.E.1.2 Discuss the importance of borrowing and lending in the United States, the government's role in controlling financial institutions, and list the advantages and disadvantages of using credit.

SS.7.E.1.6 Compare the national budget process to the personal budget process.

ESSENTIAL QUESTION *Why and how do people make economic choices?*

These high school students are receiving instructions before volunteering in their community of Little Haiti in Miami. Their hard work and volunteer hours will teach them a valuable lesson in earning and saving when they are in the workforce. President John Tyler spoke of wealth in a speech he gave in 1843. Yet, what he said more than 150 years ago is still true today:

"Wealth can only be accumulated by the earnings of Industry and the savings of frugality."

JOHN TYLER

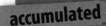

accumulated

What does it mean to *accumulate* wealth?

_____

_____

_____

Someone who is *industrious* works hard. To what do you think "earnings of industry" refers?

_____

_____

_____

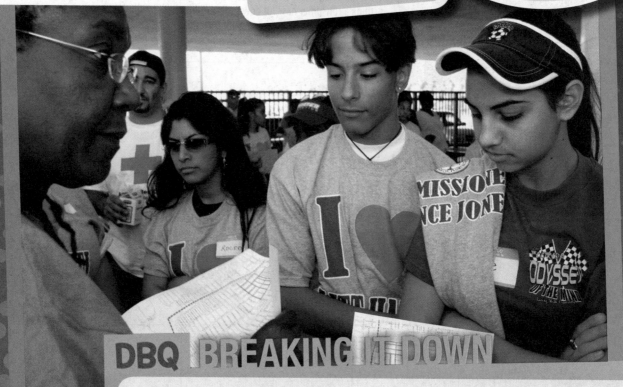

DBQ BREAKING IT DOWN

Someone who is frugal is careful with money. To what do you think the "savings of frugality" refers?

_____

_____

Benjamin Franklin said, "A penny saved is a penny earned." Was he referring to the "earnings of industry" or the "savings of frugality"?

_____

_____

McGraw-Hill
networks™
There's More Online!

PHOTO: Jeff Greenberg/Alamy

CONSUMERISM

NGSSS

SS.7.E.1.2 Discuss the importance of borrowing and lending in the United States, the government's role in controlling financial institutions, and list the advantages and disadvantages of using credit.

SS.7.E.2.3 Identify and describe U.S. laws and regulations adopted to promote economic competition.

Essential Question
Why and how do people make economic choices?

Guiding Questions
1. What rights do you have as a consumer?
2. What responsibilities do you have as a consumer?
3. What steps can you take to be a successful consumer?

Terms to Know

consumerism
a movement to educate and protect buyers

redress
to receive some type of payment or have the problem corrected for false claims or harmful products

comparison shopping
comparing prices of products at different stores

generic good
a good that does not have a brand name but is similar to a more expensive, well-known product

warranty
the promise of the person who made or sold the product to fix or replace it

disposable income
the portion of income remaining after paying taxes

discretionary income
the portion of income remaining after buying the things you need to survive, which you can spend any way you choose

impulse buying
unplanned purchasing

It Matters Because

The decisions we make as consumers affect our well-being and our financial goals.

Do you know that you are a consumer and that you have rights? What rights do you think a consumer has? Jot down some rights that you think consumers should have when they buy a product or pay for a service.

_____

_____

_____

_____

What Do You Know?

Directions: Use the table below to answer the questions based on what you know in the "Now" column. After the lesson, write your answers in the "Later" column.

	Now	Later
What is a consumer?		
How do you make smart decisions about what you buy?		

networks™ Read Chapter 19 Lesson 1 in your textbook or online.

Consumer Rights

Have you ever seen a commercial for a new product on television? Should you believe everything it says about the product? You have certain rights as a consumer. These rights have been won partly through **consumerism,** a movement to teach buyers about what they buy. The movement also insists that manufacturers make better and safer products.

The government started to protect consumers back in the late 1800s. In 1906 it created the Food and Drug Administration (FDA). The FDA guarantees the safety of food, drugs, and medicine sold in the United States. Eight years later Congress created the Federal Trade Commission (FTC). The FTC protects consumers from businesses that are dishonest and act in an unfair way such as selling a product that does not work.

In 1962 President John F. Kennedy proposed a consumer bill of rights. He did so because he believed that the average person could not be sure that products were safe. The chart below shows the rights given to consumers in the consumer bill of rights.

The Consumer Bill of Rights

Consumers have the right to . . .	This means . . .
safety	products should not be harmful
information	consumers should have the facts they need to make good choices about products; they should be protected from dishonest information
choice	a variety of goods and services should be available to consumers and offered at competitive prices
a voice	consumers' interests should be considered when laws are being made
redress	consumers have the right to have problems fixed and should receive payment for false claims, poor service, or harmful products
environmental health	consumers should not have to suffer harmful air, water, or soil conditions because of economic activity; consumers have the right to work in healthy and safe environments
service	consumers should be treated respectfully, have their questions and concerns answered, and have the right to refuse service
consumer education	consumers have the right to receive information and training that helps them understand the rights listed above

Show Your Skill

1. Interpret Charts If a consumer is the victim of a false claim, what does the Consumer Bill of Rights say they are entitled to?

Think Critically

2. Defend What consumer rights do you think are the most important? Defend your choices.

Take the Challenge

3. Choose a right from the Consumer Bill of Rights and make a poster to illustrate it. Use words and pictures. You can even cut out pictures from magazines and newspapers to show how that right is protected.

Copyright © by The McGraw-Hill Companies, Inc.

Consumer Responsibilities

Think Critically

4. Infer Before buying a new digital audio player, you check prices at three different stores and two online retailers. What is this called?

_____

_____

 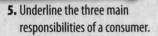
Think Critically

6. Explain What are some ways to be an informed consumer?

_____

_____

_____

Consumers have rights. They also have responsibilities. One responsibility is to make smart decisions about what you buy. Look for information about the products you want to buy. You can use consumer magazines and Web sites to learn about a product. These sources tell you what other buyers thought about the product.

Advertising gives buyers brief information about the goods and services being sold. However, ads may try to make you buy a product you do not need. Be aware that advertisers only give you the information that will make you want to buy their product. They may not tell you if a product they are selling breaks easily.

After you learn about a product, you must decide where to buy it. Look at the prices at different stores. This is called **comparison shopping.** Check newspapers, store flyers, and Web sites. Visit different stores and look at both name-brand and generic goods. A **generic good** is an item that does not have a brand name but is similar to a more expensive and well-known product.

Another responsibility is to report any problems with a product. If you buy a product or service that does not work correctly, report the problem right away. Do not try to fix a broken product yourself. This may not be safe and it could cancel the **warranty.** A warranty is the promise of the person who made or sold the product to fix or replace it if it breaks within a set time. If the product breaks, return it to the store. You can also contact the manufacturer of the product. They may fix it or give you a new one. Keep a record of your attempts to get a product fixed. If the seller or manufacturer will not fix the problem, contact your state's consumer protection agency.

Consumers have the right to expect that producers and sellers will be honest. That means that consumers also have a responsibility to be honest with producers and sellers. A consumer should not try to return a product to the store if he or she broke it.

This consumer is checking two products that are similar. In comparison shopping, she may consider the price and quality of a product before making her purchase.

Making Purchasing Decisions

Can you think of a time you spent your money on something you wanted instead of something you needed? Were you happy with that decision? Making smart buying decisions first involves distinguishing between wants and needs. To distinguish means "to see the differences." A need is something you must have to survive. A want is something extra that you would like to have.

You also must find out how much money you have to spend. The money you have left after paying taxes is your **disposable income.** Disposable income is used to pay for needs like food, clothing, and housing. **Discretionary income** is the money you have left after you have paid for the things you need to live. With discretionary income, you choose how you want to spend it.

Disposable Income	Discretionary Income

 Have you ever seen something in a store window and thought, "I have to have that!"? How many times have you gone in to buy it? When deciding how to spend your money it is important to avoid **impulse buying.** Buying that is unplanned is often based on emotion.

There are many ways to avoid impulse buying. Before you shop, make a list of what you need. Buy only what is on the list. Think before you buy. Be careful with online buying. It is quick and simple, which makes it easy to overspend. Set up a budget and stick to it.

When deciding how to spend your money, you have to think about opportunity costs. Remember that opportunity cost is the value of the choice you did not make. For example, if you want to buy new shoes, what will you give up to spend money on the shoes? What opportunities will be lost? Are the shoes worth it?

NGSSS Check What steps can you take to help you make smart buying decisions? SS.7.E.1.6

_____

_____

_____

_____

Mark the Text

7. Donovan lives in an apartment in town. Underline in the text the name for the income that he uses to pay his rent.

8. Table Fill in the table by listing three examples of what a person would buy with each type of income. Remember, sometimes a need could also be a want.

Show Your Skill

9. Draw Conclusions Why does waiting awhile before buying something you do not need help avoid impulse spending?

_____

_____

_____

_____

_____

2 BUDGETING YOUR MONEY

NGSSS

SS.7.E.1.2 Discuss the importance of borrowing and lending in the United States, the government's role in controlling financial institutions, and list the advantages and disadvantages of using credit.

SS.7.E.1.6 Compare the national budget process to the personal budget process.

Essential Question
Why and how do people make economic choices?

Guiding Questions
1. How can making a personal budget lead to financial responsibility?
2. Why is it important to use credit responsibly?

Terms to Know

budget
a record of all the money a person earns and spends

expense
ways in which a person spends money

balance
the money that is left after subtracting expenses from income

deficit
a negative balance; more expenses than income

credit
money borrowed to pay for something

interest
the fee charged for borrowing money

loan
money lent for interest

borrower
person taking out a loan

annual percentage rate (APR)
annual cost of credit; a percentage of the amount borrowed

It Matters Because

Making and following a budget can help you organize your finances.

If someone asked you to write down how much money you spent this month, would you know the amount? Write to explain what would happen if you spent more money than you had.

_____

_____

_____

_____

_____

What Do You Know?

Directions: What information would you need to include when making a budget? Circle all of the words below that you would consider when keeping a budget.

expenses	balance
credit	income
debit	work

Using a Personal Budget

Making a **budget** can help you make sure you have enough money to do the things you want to do. A budget keeps track of all the money you earn and spend. It is a useful tool to help you make sure you do not spend more money than you should.

The process of budgeting money is the same for a student or the president of a huge company. The money you earn or other money you receive is your income. The ways you spend your money are called your **expenses.** The **balance** is the money that is left after you have paid your expenses. If you have more income than expenses you have a surplus. If you have more expenses than income you have a **deficit.** The goal is to keep a positive balance. Keeping a positive balance helps make sure you will have enough money to meet any emergency expenses or add to your savings.

It is not hard to make a budget. Just follow the steps listed below.

How to Create a Budget

1. Make a list of all the money you spend for two weeks. Include food, clothing, entertainment, savings, and everything else. If there are some items that do not fit into any category (group), list them under extra expenses. Include impulse buying.

2. Make a list of all the money you earn for the same two weeks. List the sources of that money. They might include an allowance, pay from a job, or gifts.

3. Analyze your data (information). Subtract the total of everything you spent from what you earned. Did you have a surplus, deficit, or balanced budget? A balanced budget is one in which income equals expenses.

4. If you have a deficit at the end of the two-week period, you should look for ways to cut your spending or earn more money. If you have a surplus, you can increase spending or you can save the extra money.

Using Credit

Almost everyone needs to borrow money at some point. That includes businesses as well as people. The key tool for borrowing money is **credit.** Credit is money borrowed to pay for goods or services. Credit lets you buy now and pay later.

Show Your Skill

1. Identify the Main Idea Write a simple equation to show how to calculate your balance in a budget.

_____

_____

Think Critically

2. Summarize In your own words, write how to create a budget.

_____

_____

_____

_____

_____

_____

_____

_____

_____

_____

_____

Take the Challenge

3. Create a balanced budget for a month. Make sure you include income and expenses.

4. Identify Cause and Effect
How would borrowing money affect your budget?

_____

_____

_____

_____

_____

_____

5. Compare and Contrast What is the difference between a bank and a credit union?

_____

_____

_____

_____

There are many places where you can get credit. One such place is at stores that have their own store credit cards. The maximum credit amount will often be small, from $250–$1000. Once you use your credit card to make purchases you will have to pay at least a small amount back each month. That amount includes some of the money you borrowed and the **interest** you owe on that money.

When you are an adult and need to buy a car or a home, you will be able to get higher amounts of credit from banks, credit unions, and other types of financial companies. To be approved for credit you have to have a history of paying back the money you borrowed.

The table below lists several sources of credit.

Sources of Credit	
Banks	Banks provide many services. They accept deposits, offer checking accounts, and make loans.
Credit unions	A credit union is a bank formed by a group with a common bond. That bond may be an employer, for example.
Finance companies	These businesses specialize in loans to individuals. They do not accept deposits. They charge a higher rate of interest than banks.
Stores	Many stores that sell items such as clothing, electronics, or furniture offer credit cards. They usually have low credit limits. A credit limit is the maximum amount a customer can borrow.

Loans for large purchases, such as cars or homes, require a down payment from the **borrower.** A down payment is a payment for part of the purchase price. The rest of the price is the amount borrowed. The amount borrowed is divided into equal loan payments, with interest added.

In the Little Havana neighborhood in Miami, a banker helps her customers with a credit application.

Credit cards are the most common type of credit. They are issued by banks, credit card companies, and stores. Credit cards allow you to borrow money to pay for goods and services. Credit cards set a limit on the amount of money you can borrow.

To obtain a credit card, you must first apply for a card. The card issuer will check your credit rating and set a limit on the card based on what they think you can afford. Some companies will not charge you interest if you pay the full balance each month. If you make your payment late, you can be charged a fee, and your interest rate could increase. Even without these fees, credit card balances can add up quickly. This can ruin your finances. For example, if you have purchased a $2,000 item with a credit card that charges 18 percent interest, and you pay only the minimum payment each month, it will take you more than 10 years to repay the credit card loan for the item. By then you will have paid $1,142 in interest. The $2,000 item will have cost you a total of $3,142.

This diagram shows the good and bad sides of credit cards.

Benefits

- Person can buy now and pay later
- Making payments on time teaches discipline
- Requires analysis of finances, an important life skill

Drawbacks

- Can cause big financial trouble if a person borrows more than he or she is able to pay back
- Can make things cost more because of interest

A sudden job loss or serious medical problem can make it hard to keep up with payments. This hurts your credit rating and your ability to get loans.

To be a responsible borrower you have to make payments on time and not borrow more than you can afford. Also, before applying for credit ask the following important questions: What is the **annual percentage rate (APR)?** How much time will I have to make payments? What are the penalties for late payments? Are there extra fees?

NGSSS Check Name three sources of credit. What four questions should you ask before applying for credit? SS.7.E.1.2

NGSSS

SS.7.E.1.2 Discuss the importance of borrowing and lending in the United States, the government's role in controlling financial institutions, and list the advantages and disadvantages of using credit.

SS.7.E.1.6 Compare the national budget process to the personal budget process.

SAVING AND INVESTING

Essential Question

Why and how do people make economic choices?

Guiding Questions

1. Why is it important to save part of your income?
2. What types of savings plans exist?
3. How do investments in stocks and bonds promote long-term financial goals?

Terms to Know

principal
money deposited into a savings account

maturity
the time at which a CD is due for payment

penalty
fee for early withdrawal of funds

return
the profit earned by an investor

bond
interest-bearing certificate of agreement between a borrower and a lender

stock
a share of a company owned by an investor

dividend
a portion of a company's earnings paid to shareholders

mutual fund
an investment company that buys stocks and bonds for its investors

It Matters Because

Saving part of your income is the key to meeting many of your short-term and long-term financial goals.

If you earned $10 and put it in a savings account, what would happen to the money? If you invested it, might you earn more money? What risks are involved with investing?

What Do You Know?

Directions: Write the choices that you can make when investing money. Use the words below to help you.

invest	stock	bond	mutual fund

Saving Money

Saving means setting aside some of your income so you can use it later. Saving lets you plan for long-term goals. Your long-term goal may be to buy a car or go on a vacation. You might also choose to plan ahead and save money for college.

Saving also allows you to be ready for an emergency. If your car breaks down, you will have the money to get it fixed. One way to save money is to open a savings account at a bank. Banks pay you interest, which makes your savings grow. Interest is the payment people are given when they let the bank use their money. The interest you earn is added to your **principal.** Principal is the money that you deposit into your account.

Saving money is also good for the economy. The banks loan your money to other customers. This money finds its way into your local community and helps it grow.

Checking accounts are used for money that you need to have access to easily to pay bills and buy things. Checking accounts pay little or no interest. There are several ways to access the money in your checking account. They are shown in the chart below.

Accessing Checking Account Funds	
Checks • Can be used to pay bills or make purchases.	**Example:** You write a check to buy a shirt. The store sends your check to your bank. The bank then sends the money to the store from the funds in your account.
Debit card • Issued by your bank. Works like a credit card.	**Example:** When you buy something using a debit card, the money comes out of your checking account.
Electronic banking • Pay bills online.	**Example:** You use your online account to direct the bank to make a payment, which is automatically deducted from your account.

The biggest difference between a checkbook and a debit card is what happens if someone steals your card or checkbook. If someone writes a check for $500 without your approval, your loss is limited to $50 by law. The other $450 is a loss to the bank. If someone uses your debit card to charge $500 without your approval, your loss can be as high as $500. That is because the bank is not responsible for the misuse of your card. Banks have been encouraging customers to use debit cards instead of checks. One reason is the lower liability they face for debit card misuse.

Show Your Skill

1. Compare and Contrast What is the difference between interest and principal?

_____

2. Compare and Contrast How is a savings account different from a checking account?

_____

Mark the Text

3. Chart Circle the method of payment that you think is the best option. Then write to explain your choice.

_____

Think Critically

4. Analyze For what sorts of emergencies might a person need savings?

_____

_____

_____

_____

Mark the Text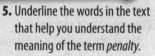

5. Underline the words in the text that help you understand the meaning of the term *penalty*.

Think Critically

6. Explain Why do longer-term CDs usually pay a higher interest rate?

_____

_____

_____

_____

_____

Show Your Skill

7. Make Inferences Which type of account is more flexible, a checking account or a CD?

_____

Savings Plans

No matter how much you decide to save, it is always a good idea to have some kind of savings plan. There are many ways to save money. Opening a savings account is one way. One good thing about savings accounts is easy access to the money. No fees are charged for taking money out of the account.

Another way to save is through a money market account. A money market account is like a savings account, but you usually have to deposit a larger amount of money than in a savings account. Another difference between a savings account and a money market account is the type of access you have to your money. In a money market account, access to your funds is limited. You can only make a set amount of transactions each month. A good thing about a money market account is that it often pays more interest than a regular savings account.

A third way to save is to put your money into certificates of deposit (CDs). With a CD you agree to deposit money with a financial institution for a set length of time. This set time is usually several months or years. In return you get a fixed rate of interest. That means that it will not change during the set length of time you have your CD. The interest is usually higher than you would earn if your money were in a regular savings account. The interest will be added to your principal when the CD reaches **maturity,** or comes due. If you break your agreement and take out your money early, you must pay a **penalty.** CDs with longer terms, or lengths of time, generally pay a higher rate of interest than those with shorter terms.

This banker is helping a customer with her savings plans options. Finding out what the interest rates are for each option and the penalties are important factors before making a decision.

Stocks and Bonds

Savings accounts, money market accounts, and CDs are all useful ways to save money. However, the **return** they offer is usually low. *Return* is another word for the profit earned by an investor. Other investments have higher returns but at a higher risk.

Bonds are money a person lends to a company or the government. When you buy a bond you are lending money for a set length of time, usually 5, 10, or 20 years. Companies sell bonds to raise money. They use the money to buy new equipment, land, or to pay expenses. In return for borrowing your money, the company will pay you a fixed rate of interest for a set number of years. Buying bonds is also a risk, but they are thought to be safe investments. If the company does not do well, it may not be able to pay the loan back. The U.S. government also issues bonds.

When people buy **stock,** they are buying part of a company. Stock is sold in pieces called shares. A person who owns stock is called a shareholder. The value of shares can go up or down. Share values usually go up when a company is making money and down when a company is not. You can sell your shares of stock at any time. The goal is to sell when the price is higher than what you paid for them. Then you will make a profit.

Some companies pay **dividends.** A dividend is a portion of the company's profit. Shareholders get an equal dividend payment for each share they own.

A final type of investment is a **mutual** (MYOO•chuh•wuhl) **fund.** Mutual funds combine money from many people. The money is invested in a group of stocks chosen and managed by experts. The risk is lower because so many different stocks are owned. Stocks that go up in value can balance stocks that go down.

The government and individuals keep track of stocks, bonds, and mutual funds. This is done using a measuring system called an index. The Dow Jones Industrial Average (DJIA) and the Standard & Poor's 500 (S&P 500) are the two most common.

NGSSS Check Why is it important to save part of your income, and what are three ways that you can save money? **SS.7.E.1.6**

_____

_____

_____

_____

Mark the Text

8. Compete these statements.

Safer investments = _____ risk

Higher returns = _____ risk

Think Critically

9. Explain How does a mutual fund help reduce risk?

_____

_____

_____

Take the Challenge

10. With a partner, research a Florida company that sells stocks. Find out if it pays dividends. Write about your findings below.

_____

_____

_____

_____

_____

Reflect on What It Means . . .

A budget is a record of all the money earned and money spent. Individuals, families, businesses, communities, and even states and nations have budgets. Since none of these has an unlimited amount of money, they have to make tough choices.

Read the following budget choices for an individual, a community, and the world. Which one is the best choice? Circle it, and then explain the reason for your choice.

An Individual

buy a new computer

buy a used computer and use the savings for college

save all the money for college

pay to get your old computer upgraded and buy a printer

A Community

build a new community swimming pool

hire more police officers

pay down the community's debt

improve the roads

The World

expand the military

provide better public health care

fund preschool education for all young children

buy endangered forest land

TAKE THE CHALLENGE

Do research to learn how the federal government spends money. What are the three largest categories in its budget? Draw a circle graph to show how money is spent.

BUSINESS IN AMERICA

NGSSS

SS.7.E.1.5 Assess how profits, incentives, and competition motivate individuals, households, and businesses in a free market economy.

SS.7.E.2.4 Identify entrepreneurs from various gender, social, and ethnic backgrounds who started a business seeking to make a profit.

SS.7.E.2.5 Explain how economic institutions impact the national economy.

SS.7.E.2.3 Identify and describe United States laws and regulations adopted to promote economic competition.

ESSENTIAL QUESTION • *Why and how do people make economic choices?* • *How do economic systems influence societies?*

Like individuals, businesses have responsibilities. They have responsibilities to their communities, consumers, and their employees. Fulfilling these responsibilities can reward businesses:

Copyright © by The McGraw-Hill Companies, Inc.   PHOTO: Tim Kitchen/Digital Vision/Getty Images

"A large and growing number of employers recognize the imperative of adjusting to the new face of the American workforce. The new reality requires breaking away from traditional modes of how work gets done, and how careers progress. Employers that get this will win the loyalty of talented working mothers, and all employees who desire vibrant work and personal lives."

"WHAT MOMS THINK: THE WORKING MOTHER REPORT", BY *WORKING MOTHER* MAGAZINE

imperative

What is another word for *imperative*?

_____

_____

_____

DBQ BREAKING IT DOWN

According to this quote, what should employers "get" or understand?

_____

_____

Suppose you own a business. Would you be willing to change a worker's schedule so a parent could pick up a child after school? Why or Why not?

_____

_____

McGraw-Hill
netw⚙rks™
There's More Online!

TEXT: "What Moms Think: The Working Mother Report", by Working Mother Magazine. 2010

HOW BUSINESSES ARE ORGANIZED

NGSSS

SS.7.E.1.5 Assess how profits, incentives, and competition motivate individuals, households, and businesses in a free market economy.

SS.7.E.2.4 Identify entrepreneurs from various gender, social, and ethnic backgrounds who started a business seeking to make a profit.

SS.7.E.2.5 Explain how economic institutions impact the national economy. *Remarks/Examples*: Examples are the stock market, banks, credit unions.

Essential Question

Why and how do people make economic choices?

Guiding Questions

1. What are the advantages and disadvantages of a sole proprietorship?
2. What are the advantages and disadvantages of a partnership?
3. How is a corporation structured, and what are its advantages and disadvantages?

Terms to Know

sole proprietorship
a business owned by one person

financial capital
the money needed to run or expand a business

liability
legal responsibility

partnership
a business owned by two or more people

corporation
a business owned by many people that has the legal status of a person

charter
a government document permitting a corporation to organize

board of directors
a group of people elected by the shareholders of a corporation to act on their behalf

franchise
permission to sell a company's goods or services in a specific location in exchange for a sum of money

nonprofit organization
a business that does not intend to make a profit from the goods and services it provides

It Matters Because

The three main types of businesses—proprietorships, partnerships, and corporations—play an important part in the nation's economy and in the daily life of nearly every American.

You might have a great idea for a business, but an idea isn't enough. There are many things to consider. Can you do all the work yourself? Would you enjoy working with a partner? Would the people who work with you share the risk and the rewards? If you started a business, how would you answer these questions?

_____

_____

_____

_____

What Do You Know?

Directions: In the first column, answer the questions based on what you know before you study. After this lesson, complete the last column.

Now	Questions	Later
	What is a sole proprietorship?	
	What is a partnership?	

Sole Proprietorships

If you have ever made money doing yard work or babysitting, then you have had your own business. If you worked by yourself, you were a sole proprietor. A **sole proprietorship** is a business owned by one person. It is also the most common form of business. It is often a small business serving a local community. For example, a local auto repair shop, ice cream shop, or dentist's office is likely to be a sole proprietorship.

Sole proprietors are their own bosses. They decide what products or services to sell. They make their own hours. They keep all profits. They do not have to consult, or ask, anyone when making decisions. These are advantages of a sole proprietorship.

There are also disadvantages. Sole proprietors often have trouble raising **financial capital.** This is money that is needed for a business to run and grow. Sole proprietors also have unlimited **liability** for their business. Liability is legal responsibility. That means the owner has to pay all the business debts. It also means that if someone brings a lawsuit against the business and wins, the owner has to pay. Sometimes the owner's house or other personal property may be taken and sold to pay the debts.

Partnerships

What if your business started to take up all of your free time and you wanted some of that time back? You could ask a friend to help you. In return you could give your friend a share of your business. This form of business is called a **partnership.** A partnership is a business that two or more people own and operate.

To form a partnership, two or more people sign a legal agreement called articles of partnership. This agreement explains what each partner will do in the business. It clarifies, or explains, how much money each will put in and how much of the profits each will get.

There are two kinds of partnerships, general and limited. In a general partnership, all the partners own the business. Every partner is responsible for managing the business and paying its debts. They are all called general partners.

A limited partnership has both general partners and limited partners. Limited partners own a part of the business. They provide the money needed for the business, but they do not help run it. They also share in the profits and have less liability than general partners. They are liable only for the amount of money they invested in the business.

Think Critically

1. Infer How does knowing the meaning of *sole* help you remember what a sole proprietorship is?

_____

_____

_____

2. Evaluate Why is unlimited liability a disadvantage for a business owner?

_____

_____

_____

_____

_____

Show Your Skill

3. Draw Conclusions What are advantages of a sole proprietorship?

_____

_____

_____

Mark the Text

4. Underline the definition of a partnership.

5. Contrast In what ways are a partnership and a sole proprietorship different?

_____

_____

_____

_____

_____

_____

6. Compare What disadvantage do general partners and sole proprietors share?

_____

_____

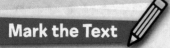

The main advantage of a partnership is that the business can raise more money to grow. New partners can be added to bring in money. Each partner brings different strengths to the business. That gives it a better chance of success.

The main disadvantage for general partners is that each one has unlimited liability. For example, if a business has two general partners, each partner gets one-half of the profits. Then suppose the business falls into debt. One of the partners has no money. The other partner is responsible for the whole debt.

Corporations

The third form of business is the **corporation.** Under the law, a corporation is a legal body separate from its owners. It has the rights and responsibilities of an individual. It can own property. It can make contracts, sue, and be sued. It also pays taxes.

To form a corporation, a person or group applies to a state government for a **charter.** The charter describes the business and tells how much stock the corporation can sell. The chart below shows how corporations are organized.

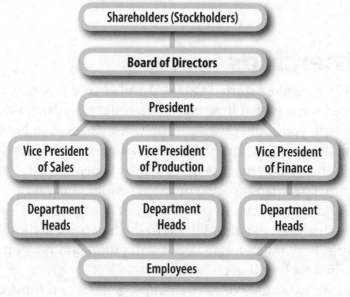

How a Corporation is Organized

There are advantages to a corporation. It is easier to raise money, because corporations can issue and sell stock, and it is easy to transfer ownership. Stockholders can sell their stock to other investors. Also, when a stockholder dies, the stock is passed down like other property. As a result, corporations have a long life. They also have limited liability. This means that if the business owes money, it is responsible for its debts, not the owners. The personal property of the owners cannot be sold to pay those debts.

Corporations also have disadvantages. They can be difficult and expensive to set up. They must follow more government rules than other businesses. They must also hold stockholder meetings once a year. All of those rules mean the actions of the company are watched more closely than other forms of business.

Form of Business	Advantages	Disadvantages
Sole proprietorship	• Do not have to consult others before making decisions • Owner keeps all profits	• Difficult to raise money • Difficult to borrow money • Unlimited liability
Partnership	• Partners can raise more money • Partners have different strengths	• General partners have unlimited liability • Partners share profits
Corporation	• Easier to raise money • Have a long life • Owners have limited liability	• More government regulation • Difficult and expensive to create • Stockholders have little say in running the business

Another way to set up a business is as a **franchise** (FRAN•chyz). The owner of a franchise pays a fee and part of the profits to a supplier. In return the owner of the franchise has the right to sell a certain product in a certain area. Many national fast-food restaurants and hotel chains are set up this way.

Owning a franchise has advantages. There is no competition from nearby sellers of the same product. Suppliers help franchise owners advertise and run the business. The main disadvantage is that a franchise owner does not have total control over his or her business. In all these forms of business, the goal is to make a profit.

During events like this one in Miami, small business owners receive support and advice.

Show Your Skill

8. Formulate Questions After learning about these three types of business organizations, what question might you want to ask a business owner?

_____

_____

_____

Think Critically

9. Describe In your own words, how does a franchise work?

_____

_____

_____

10. Evaluate What is the main disadvantage of owning a franchise? Why might someone choose to open one anyway?

_____

_____

_____

_____

_____

_____

_____

_____

PHOTO: Ian Dagnall/Alamy

11. Contrast In what way is a nonprofit organization different from other forms of business?

_____

_____

Show Your Skill

12. Predict Outcomes What might make a cooperative unsuccessful as a business?

_____

_____

_____

_____

_____

Take the Challenge

13. Interview two business owners. Write your questions before you visit with them. Create a visual diagram to share what you learn about how their businesses are organized.

A **nonprofit organization** is a different form of business. It provides goods or services without trying to make a profit. Often the goals of these organizations are to provide charity for those in need or perhaps educational or cultural experiences for the community. For example, the American Red Cross is a nonprofit organization.

One type of nonprofit is a **cooperative.** This is a group formed to carry on economic activity for the benefit of its members. There are many kinds of cooperatives. For example, a consumer cooperative buys goods in large amounts to keep costs down for its members. A farmers' cooperative helps its members sell their crops and livestock to large central markets where they can get better prices.

The Salvador Dali Museum in St. Petersburg is an example of a nonprofit organization that is supported by the community.

NGSSS Check List the three basic forms of business organization and give one advantage of each. SS.7.E.1.5

_____

_____

_____

_____

_____

NGSSS

SS.7.E.1.5 Assess how profits, incentives, and competition motivate individuals, households, and businesses in a free market economy.

Essential Question
Why and how do people make economic choices?

Guiding Questions
1. What is the role of organized labor in the U.S. economy?
2. How do labor and management work out agreements?

Terms to Know

labor union
a group of workers formed to improve wages and working conditions for its members

right-to-work laws
state laws that forbid employers from requiring workers to join unions

collective bargaining
a process by which unions and employers negotiate the conditions of employment

strike
a refusal to work, meant to force an employer to give in to demands

picketing
a union method in which striking workers demonstrate with signs outside the workplace

lockout
the closing of a workplace to prevent union members from working

injunction
a court order to stop an action

mediation
a process in which union and company officials bring in a third party to help them reach an agreement

arbitration
a process in which union and company officials submit to a third party for a final decision

It Matters Because

The relationship between labor and management affects the nation's economic and political life.

Workers have many needs that they hope will be provided by management.

Fair wages	Chance for advancement	Safe workplace
Interesting and meaningful work		Reasonable work hours

Which of these would be most important to you as a worker? Explain your choice.

What Do You Know?

Directions: In the first column, answer the questions based on what you know before you study. After this lesson, complete the last column.

Before the Lesson	Questions	After the Lesson
	What do labor unions do?	
	How do management and labor work out their differences?	

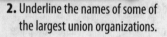

Show Your Skill

1. Interpret Graphs Use the details in the text and the graph to explain the changing trends of labor unions in recent years.

_____

_____

_____

_____

_____

_____

_____

Mark the Text

2. Underline the names of some of the largest union organizations.

Think Critically

3. Contrast How does a trade union differ from an industrial union?

_____

_____

_____

_____

_____

_____

netw⊙rks   Read Chapter 20 Lesson 2 in your textbook or online.

Organized Labor

An important part of any economy is its labor force. In the past 40 years, America's labor force has doubled in size. However, fewer workers are joining **labor unions.** A labor union is an organized group of workers that helps to make wages and working conditions better for its members.

One reason that fewer people are joining unions is that there are now fewer manufacturing jobs and more service jobs available. Fewer workers in service jobs join unions. More employers are also keeping unions out of their businesses.

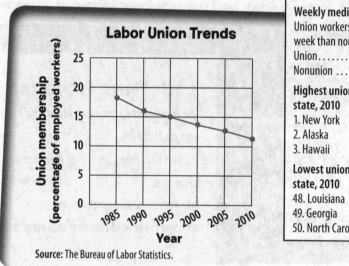

Labor Union Trends

Weekly median earnings, 2010
Union workers earn more money a week than nonunion workers.
Union................$917
Nonunion $717

Highest union membership by state, 2010

1. New York	24.2%
2. Alaska	22.9
3. Hawaii	21.8

Lowest union membership by state, 2010

48. Louisiana	4.3%
49. Georgia	4.0
50. North Carolina	3.2

Source: The Bureau of Labor Statistics.

Today, there are more government workers than factory workers who belong to unions. The largest union is the American Federation of State, County, and Municipal Employees (AFSCME). Members of this union hold many different jobs. A few examples of these jobs are garbage collectors, school nurses, and prison guards.

There are two types of unions. In a trade union the members all work at the same craft or trade. For example, printers and bakers have trade unions. In an industrial union members do different types of work in the same industry. The United Auto Workers (UAW) is an industrial union. Its members work in the car industry.

Unions are organized. The basic unit of a union is the local. The workers in one factory or location form a local union. All of a union's locals form the national union. Most national unions belong to the AFL-CIO. This stands for the American Federation of Labor-Congress of Industrial Organizations. It is the country's largest labor group.

Workers in a workplace must vote to join a union. A federal agency watches these votes to make sure they are fair. That agency is the National Labor Relations Board.

One way that unions organize in the workplace is as a union shop. In a union shop the employer can hire anyone for a job. Shortly after starting the job, however, that person must join the union.

Many companies do not like union shops. In some states companies have convinced state governments to make them illegal. As a result, 23 states have **right-to-work laws** that ban, or outlaw, union shops.

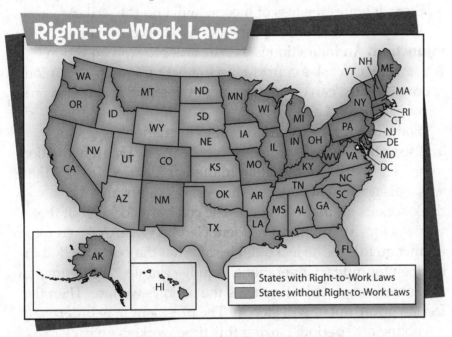

Right-to-Work Laws

States with Right-to-Work Laws
States without Right-to-Work Laws

There are other circumstances, or situations, in which a worker does not have to join a union. Some states have a modified union shop. This means that workers can choose whether or not they want to join a union. Workers who join the union have to remain members as long as they keep their jobs. Other workplaces have an agency shop. Workers in agency shops who do not join a union must still pay a fee to the union for representing them.

Labor Negotiations

The goal of a union is to get an employer to agree to what the workers want or need. This is usually done through **collective bargaining.** In this process union leaders and employers meet to work out the employees' contract. The contract states the workers' wages, hours, benefits, and conditions of work. Sometimes the union and the employer cannot agree. The unions and the employers have several tools to use to help them get what they want.

Think Critically

4. Infer How do you think right-to-work laws might affect union membership?

_____

_____

_____

_____

_____

_____

_____

_____

_____

_____

Show Your Skill

5. Formulate Questions Write one question a worker might want to ask when deciding whether or not to join a union.

_____

_____

_____

_____

_____

_____

Think Critically

6. Explain What is collective bargaining?

_____

_____

_____

_____

_____

A union may call a **strike.** In a strike all union members refuse to work. The idea is that one company–or all the companies in the industry–cannot survive without workers and will be forced to give in to the union's demands. Strikers often stand outside the workplace with "on strike" signs. This is called **picketing.** It is meant to embarrass the company and stop other workers from going in to work. Picketing also helps the workers get support from the public.

Employers have tools to put pressure on the unions. A company may order a **lockout.** This keeps union workers from entering the building. Then the company hires replacement workers. It hopes the loss of income will end the strike.

Companies and unions can both ask the courts for an **injunction.** An injunction is a court order to stop an action. A company can ask a court for an injunction to stop the union's actions. A court can order a union not to strike. It can also order a company to end a lockout.

Some industries are important to the nation's economy and security. The federal government can ask for an injunction to prevent a strike or a lockout in these industries. In 2002 there was a disagreement between the port operators and the dockworkers on the west coast. The company locked out the workers for five months. President George W. Bush asked for an injunction to end the lockout. He said that the ports needed to be open for military operations. A judge granted the injunction.

Sometimes a strike threatens the nation's welfare. Then the federal government will step in. The president may order a "cooling off" period. During this time workers go back to work. The union and employer try again to reach an agreement. In a crisis the government may even take over an industry while the two sides work to reach an agreement.

There are other options available to unions and employers to reach an agreement. They may try **mediation.** This brings in a third party to help reach a compromise. They may also try **arbitration.** In arbitration a third party decides on a solution. Both the employer and union agree in advance to accept its decision.

 NGSSS Check Complete the chart showing the different tools used to reach a contract. SS.7.E.1.5

Management tactics	Negotiation	Labor tactics
lockouts	collective bargaining	strikes
_____	_____	_____
	_____	_____

NGSSS

SS.7.E.2.3 Identify and describe United States laws and regulations adopted to promote economic competition.

Essential Question

How do economic systems influence societies?
Why and how do people make economic choices?

Guiding Questions

1. In what ways do businesses help their communities?
2. How do businesses carry out their responsibilities to their consumers, owners, and employees?

Terms to Know

social responsibility
the duty that businesses have to pursue goals that benefit others as well as themselves

foundation
an organization created by a person or a business to provide money for charity or research

transparency
the process of making business dealings visible, or understandable, to everyone

It Matters Because

All of society benefits when business provides safe, good-quality products to consumers and gives fair treatment to employees.

Have you ever bought something that didn't work as you expected or broke quickly?

Describe that experience and tell what the business would need to do to keep you

as a customer.

What Do You Know?

Directions: Choose any four of the words below and write a sentence or two about business in the United States. When you finish the lesson, write another sentence using four different words from the list.

charity	honesty	regulations	fairness
responsible	stockholder	report	safety
donation	hiring	insurance	free	helpful

Show Your Skill

1. Draw Conclusions Why do many businesses donate to causes? Give some examples of how businesses donate.

_____

_____

_____

_____

_____

Think Critically

2. Explain What is a foundation?

_____

_____

_____

_____

Show Your Skill

3. Interpret Charts Compare the amount given by foundations to the amount given by corporations. Why might that be the case?

_____

_____

_____

_____

_____

_____

The Social Responsibility of Business

Does your school ever get help from a business? Take a look around to answer that question. Have you ever seen a car wash for your school being held on a business's property? Are your sports teams sponsored by local businesses? Are there business advertisements in the back pages of your school's theater programs or your yearbook? If you can answer "yes" to any of these questions, then a business has helped your school.

Businesses have many important roles in society. As producers they supply the food, clothing, and shelter that meet our basic needs. They also supply many of the things that make life enjoyable. Businesses also have a **social responsibility.** This is the duty to work toward goals that help others as well as themselves.

Each year U.S. corporations give away about $14 billion. Some give away free goods and services. For example, some drug companies give medicines to people who cannot afford to pay for them. Other companies donate money to causes they support.

Wealthy business owners often set up **foundations.** A foundation is an organization set up by a person or a company to give money for a specific purpose. Foundations often support a charity or research. Bill Gates, the founder of Microsoft Corporation, started a foundation. It has given away about $23 billion. The money aids health and education programs in the United States and around the world.

Corporations also set up foundations to support causes. The Wal-Mart Foundation plans to give away over $2 billion by the year 2015 to help stop hunger in the United States.

Business giving does not just come from big corporations. About 75% of small companies also give money to help others. Some lawyers and accountants give free services to the poor or to nonprofit groups. These are just a few of the ways that businesses give to their communities. The charts below show the amounts of money donated to different kinds of charities in 2009.

2009 Contributions By Source	
Individuals	$227.4 billion
Foundations	$38.4 billion
Bequests	$23.8 billion
Corporations	$14.1 billion

SOURCE: Giving USA 2010

Other Business Responsibilities

Businesses have a responsibility to many groups. Consumers are one group. Businesses are required to sell products that are safe. Their products must work as promised. Advertising must be truthful. Businesses must treat customers fairly.

Businesses are also responsible to their owners. This responsibility is crucial, or important, for corporations because the owners do not manage the company. Stockholders own a corporation. Managers run it. These are two separate groups of people.

The law says that corporations must send out reports about their finances regularly. These reports reveal, or make public, the amount of money a company makes and spends. This is called **transparency.** Investors use these reports to make decisions about buying and selling stock in a company. It is illegal for corporations to give false information.

Businesses are responsible to their employees. Businesses have to provide a safe workplace. They also have to treat all workers fairly. They may not treat employees differently because of race, religion, color, gender, age, or disability. Doing so is against the law.

Many companies provide benefits to their workers, such as paying for education or childcare. In 2010 Congress passed a health care reform law. It requires most businesses to provide health insurance to employees. These types of benefits help the company as well as the worker. Healthy, better-educated workers can be more productive.

Responsibilities of Business			
To consumers	To employees	To stockholders	To communities

 NGSSS Check Give two examples of how government is involved in regulating businesses. SS.7.E.2.3

_____

_____

_____

Show Your Skill

4. Draw Conclusions Why is it important for a business to maintain transparency?

_____

_____

_____

_____

_____

_____

_____

_____

Mark the Text

5. Graphic Organizer Complete the graphic organizer. Identify the responsibilities of business in each category.

Take the Challenge

6. Identify a company that provides some financial support of a cause you think is important. Write a thank-you letter to the company.

MY REFLECTIONS

ESSENTIAL QUESTION · *Why and how do people make economic choices?* · *How do economic systems influence societies?*

Reflect on What It Means . . .

Businesses come in all shapes and sizes. Some businesses may be run by people you know. Think about businesses that you know.

In the space below, write down businesses that fit in each category. You can write down types of businesses, the names of actual businesses, or possible businesses.

My Businesses

Describe a business that you could run right now.

My Community's Businesses

Describe two businesses that are located in your community that serve only members of your community.

Worldwide Businesses

Describe three businesses that operate in many different countries.

TAKE THE CHALLENGE

With your teacher's help, find a local business owner to interview. Possible questions: How is your business organized? What do you like best about owning a business? What does it take to be successful in business? Share what you learn with the class.

GOVERNMENT'S ROLE IN THE ECONOMY

NGSSS

SS.7.E.2.3 Identify and describe United States laws and regulations adopted to promote economic competition.

ESSENTIAL QUESTION *How does government influence the economy and economic institutions?*

You probably know that the more education you get the better off you will be. Did you know that the more education everyone gets the better off the economy will be? Here is what the governor of Ohio, Bob Taft, said about that in 2003:

> "A dynamic economy begins with a good education."
>
> BOB TAFT

dynamic economy

A dynamic person is energetic, a go-getter. What is a dynamic economy?

_____

_____

good education

How does education help the economy?

_____

_____

DBQ BREAKING IT DOWN

Why is it in the interest of government officials to encourage people to get an education?

_____

_____

_____

Why is it in your interest to get an education?

_____

_____

_____

McGraw-Hill
networks™
There's More Online!

LESSON 1
GOVERNMENT INVOLVEMENT IN THE ECONOMY

NGSSS

SS.7.E.1.5 Assess how profits, incentives, and competition motivate individuals, households, and businesses in a free market economy.

SS.7.E.2.1 Explain how federal, state, and local taxes support the economy as a function of the United States government.

SS.7.E.2.3 Identify and describe United States laws and regulations adopted to promote economic competition.

Essential Question
How does government influence the economy and economic institutions?

Guiding Questions
1. What goods does government provide?
2. How does government encourage or increase competition among businesses?
3. How does government regulate business?

Terms to Know

private good
a good that must be paid for in order to be used and that can be used by only one person

public good
a good provided by government that is used by everyone, such as highways

externality
a side effect

monopoly
when only one supplier controls a market

antitrust law
law that prevents new monopolies from forming

merger
when two or more companies combine to form one business

natural monopoly
allowing a single company to produce a product so that costs to the consumer are kept low

recall
removal of an unsafe product from store shelves

It Matters Because

Consumers benefit when the government promotes competition and responsible actions by businesses.

There are all sorts of competitions. You might compete in spelling bees, sports, science fairs, or playing a video game. What are some of the benefits of competition?

What Do You Know?

Directions: In the first column, answer the questions based on what you know before you study. After this lesson, complete the last column.

Before the Lesson	Questions	After the Lesson
	What are goods and services?	
	What helps businesses succeed?	

Providing Public Goods

Most goods produced by businesses are private goods. **Private goods** have two features:

1. Private goods are items that people cannot have unless they pay for them.

2. Private goods can be used by only one person. If you buy a shirt, no one else can buy that exact shirt, for example. Food, clothing, books, and cars are examples of private goods.

Public goods are different from private goods. People do not pay for public goods. More than one person can use public goods. Sidewalks are an example. If one person walks on a sidewalk, this does not stop others from walking on that same sidewalk. Public goods include many services that benefit people in their communities. Included are police and fire protection, public parks, and public libraries. Similarly, the entire nation is made safer by the armed forces.

Businesses do not often provide public goods. This is because it is hard to charge everyone who uses them. For example, how much should you be charged for using the sidewalk? How much for police protection? Instead, government takes on the responsibility for providing public goods. It pays for them with taxes and fees.

At times economic activities and the use of public goods cause side effects called **externalities.** Externalities are positive or negative side effects of an action that affect, or impact someone else.

Good highways are an example of a positive externality. Good roads make it cheaper for companies to transport goods. The goods can then be sold for lower prices. Lower prices benefit all consumers.

Externalities can also be negative. Pollution from cars is a negative externality. Even people who do not have a car can suffer from air pollution's negative effects, like having trouble breathing. One role of the government is to try to prevent negative externalities. This is why the government regulates auto exhaust.

Show Your Skill

1. **Classify Information** Give an example of a public good other than those given in the text.

_____

_____

_____

_____

_____

Think Critically

2. **Synthesize** When one person takes a radio to the beach and plays music so loudly that it disturbs others, what is this an example of?

_____

_____

3. **Explaining** How does government pay for public goods?

_____

_____

The Metromover in Miami is operated by Miami-Dade Transit. It transports workers and tourists around the downtown area. It is largely funded by government money.

_____

_____

_____

_____

_____

_____

Think Critically

5. Infer Why does the government sometimes allow monopolies?

_____

_____

_____

_____

6. Summarize Why does the government promote competition?

_____

_____

_____

_____

_____

Maintaining Competition

One goal of the government is to make certain there is competition in the marketplace. Markets are places where goods and services are sold. Markets work best when there are large numbers of buyers and sellers. If there is no competition, then only one supplier controls the market. This is called a **monopoly.** With no competition a monopoly can charge any price it wants. Customers are forced to pay because they cannot get the product or service anywhere else.

To prevent monopolies, the government has passed **antitrust laws.** A trust is several businesses banded together that threaten competition. Antitrust laws prevent trusts and work to keep competition in the marketplace.

In 1890 the government passed the Sherman Antitrust Act. It bans monopolies and other forms of business that prevent competition. In 1911 this law was used to break up the Standard Oil Company's monopoly on oil. In the 1980s, it was used to break up American Telephone and Telegraph's (AT&T) monopoly on telephone service.

In 1914 Congress passed the Clayton Antitrust Act. It banned specific business practices that limit competition. For example, the law no longer allowed one person to be on the board of directors of two competing companies. The law also gave the government power over some mergers.

When two or more companies combine to form one business, this is called a **merger.** Mergers can threaten competition and lead to higher prices for consumers. If a merger goes against antitrust laws and threatens competition, the government can step in and stop it. This is the job of the Federal Trade Commission (FTC).

In addition to encouraging competition, the government also regulates other business activities. These include natural monopolies, product advertising, and product safety.

When a good or service is expensive to produce, it can actually be cheaper to have one company produce it. This is called a **natural monopoly.** Many public services are delivered by natural monopolies. Natural gas and electricity are examples.

The government sometimes allows these natural monopolies because they serve the best interest of the public. However, the company with the monopoly must agree to government regulation. Regulation might include setting prices or quality standards.

In recent years, governments moved to end natural monopolies to bring back, or restore, competition. This is called deregulating.

Protecting Consumer Health and Safety

The government also plays a key role in protecting the public's health and safety. Federal agencies such as the Food and Drug Administration (FDA) oversee the safety of food, medical equipment, and many other things. The chart below shows some important federal agencies and their jobs.

Selected U.S. Government Regulatory Agencies	
Department or Agency	**Purpose**
Consumer Product Safety Commission (CPSC)	**Protects the public from risks of serious injury or death from consumer products**
Environmental Protection Agency (EPA)	**Protects human health and the natural environment (air, water, and land)**
Food and Drug Administration (FDA)	**Makes sure food, drugs, and cosmetics are truthfully labeled and safe for consumers**
Federal Trade Commission (FTC)	**Promotes and protects consumer interests and competition in the marketplace**
Occupational Safety and Health Administration (OSHA)	**Makes sure workers have a safe and healthful workplace**

The Consumer Product Safety Commission (CPSC) aims to protect consumers from injury. If the CPSC decides a product is unsafe, it issues a **recall.** This means the product must be removed from store shelves. The manufacturer must make the product safe. It can also offer a substitute product or refund the customer's money.

NGSSS Check What major laws have been passed to prevent monopolies and trusts? What is the overriding goal of these laws? SS.7.E.2.3

_____

_____

_____

Why has the U.S. government set up agencies such as the FDA and OSHA? SS.7.E.2.3

_____

_____

_____

Copyright © by The McGraw-Hill Companies, Inc.

Think Critically

7. **Explain** Why would the government regulate a meatpacking plant?

_____

_____

_____

_____

Show Your Skill

8. **Interpret Charts** Choose one agency from the chart and state one way that agency touches your life.

_____

_____

_____

_____

Take the Challenge

9. Interview three adults and ask them what government services they feel are doing the best jobs of serving the public.

MEASURING THE ECONOMY

 NGSSS

SS.7.E.1.5 Assess how profits, incentives, and competition motivate individuals, households, and businesses in a free market economy.

SS.7.E.2.5 Explain how economic institutions impact the national economy.

SS.7.E.2.3 Identify and describe United States laws and regulations adopted to promote economic competition.

Essential Question

How does government influence the economy and economic institutions?

Guiding Questions

1. Why is it important to measure an economy's performance?
2. What are other signs of an economy's health?
3. How is the stock market a measure of the economy's performance?

Terms to Know

real GDP
Gross Domestic Product after adjustments for inflation

business cycle
alternating periods of economic growth and decline

recession
a time of declining economic activity lasting six months or longer

depression
state of the economy with high unemployment, severely depressed real GDP, and general economic hardship

unemployment rate
the percentage of people in the civilian labor force who are not working but are looking for jobs

fixed income
income that does not rise even though prices are going up

inflation
long-term increase in the general level of prices

bear market
a time when stock prices fall for a substantial period

bull market
a time when stock prices rise steadily

It Matters Because

Tracking the growth of the economy helps the government craft appropriate economic policies.

The government needs to manage the money in the national economy. How do you keep track of the money you have? How do you plan for future purchases?

_____

_____

_____

_____

What Do You Know?

Directions: What would you like to know about the nation's economy? Write two questions you have about our economy. After you have finished the lesson, come back and see if you can answer the questions.

_____

_____

_____

_____

_____

Economic Performance

Many people and groups want to know how the economy is doing. Prices are the signals that help people, businesses, and the government make economic decisions. Prices are a key part of a market economy, but they can show information about the Gross Domestic Product (GDP) that may be misleading.

For example, if a country has a bigger GDP in one year than it had the year before, we may think that the economy has grown. But that may not be true. A country's GDP grows only if the increase is due to a higher rate of output, or production, and not because prices of products have gone up. Simply put, a GDP grows only if the nation produces more, not if products cost more. For this reason, economists cannot depend on the GDP alone. Instead, they use a measurement called the real GDP.

Real GDP is the GDP after the changes caused by price increases have been removed. It is basically the same thing as GDP in an economy where prices do not change. It is a better measure of an economy over time than GDP.

Having a measure like real GDP is important. Government leaders want to know if their policies are working. Investors want to know where to put their money. Consumers want to plan future purchases. Growth in real GDP indicates, or signals, a healthy economy. In a healthy economy, jobs are produced and people have opportunities.

The U.S. economy does not grow at a steady rate. Instead it goes through ups and downs. This series of ups and downs is called the **business cycle.** Business cycles have two parts.

1. The cycle starts at a peak and continues until the next peak. The peak is the point where real GDP stops going up and starts to go down.

2. Real GDP will eventually stop going down and start to rise again. The economy recovers. The point where GDP stops going down is called a trough. The trough is the lowest part of the business cycle.

Think Critically

1. **Synthesize** What image can you think of to illustrate the ups and downs of the business cycle?

_____

_____

_____

_____

Show Your Skill

2. **Interpret Graphs** What does a peak on a business cycle graph mean?

_____

_____

_____

_____

Take the Challenge

3. Interview five people and ask them to point to where in the cycle they think the American economy is now. Record their reasons.

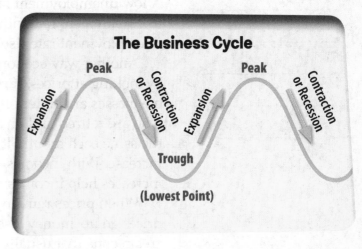

The Business Cycle

Peak — Expansion — Contraction or Recession — Peak — Expansion — Contraction or Recession — Trough (Lowest Point)

If real GDP stays down for six months or more, the economy is in a **recession.** Recessions tend to last less than a year. An exception is the recession of December 2007 to June 2008. This was the longest recession since the 1930s.

Periods of expansion tend to be longer than declines. Most recent expansions have lasted from 6 to 10 years. The new peak can be even higher than the one before.

A **depression** is a period of severe economic decline. A recession may turn into a depression if real GDP continues to go down rather than turning back up. The U.S. economy has had one major depression. It was called the Great Depression, and it started with the stock market crash of 1929. The fall in real GDP was enormous. Between 1929 and 1933, prices fell by about one-third. One in four Americans was out of work. Many banks closed, and many stocks became worthless.

As a result of the Great Depression, many new government programs were put in place to protect people financially. Because of these safeguards, many economists believe a depression of this size will never happen again.

Other Measures of Performance

In addition to real GDP, economists have other ways to tell how the economy is doing. One way is by tracking the number of people who have or do not have jobs. Economists are mostly interested in the civilian labor force. *Civilian* means people outside the military. The civilian labor force is made up of all of the people 16 and older who are either working or are looking for work.

The **unemployment rate** is the number of people in the civilian labor force who are out of work and looking for jobs. A low unemployment rate indicates a healthy economy. A high unemployment rate indicates a troubled economy. The unemployment rate rises sharply during recessions.

Another way economists tell how the economy is doing is by looking at prices. If prices stay level, consumers and businesses are better off. This is especially important for people who are retired and on a **fixed income.** A fixed income stays the same each month. It does not have the possibility to increase. With incomes that are not fixed, raises or other increases help incomes rise as prices rise.

When prices remain stable, money keeps its value. When prices go up, money loses value. For example, suppose an ice cream cone that usually costs a dollar doubles in price. Now you need twice as many dollars to buy the same ice cream cone. The higher price means that your dollar buys less.

A long-term increase in prices is called **inflation.** The government tracks inflation by checking the prices of about 400 products commonly used by consumers. The prices of these products make up the consumer price index (CPI). The CPI shows the rate of inflation.

How Inflation Affects the Economy

Inflation → Reduces buying power → Changes people's economic decisions

Economic Indicators

We have already looked at several ways to measure the health of the economy. They include real GDP, the unemployment rate, and prices. Another economic indicator is the stock market.

The price of a company's stock is set by supply and demand. Supply is the number of stocks available. Demand is the number of stocks investors want to buy. Changes in a company's profits or the release of a new product can change the demand for a stock. If the demand for stock changes, its price changes, too. But economists do not look at the price of just one company's stock. They look at overall changes in stock prices.

To find out how all stock prices are changing over time, we use stock indexes. The Dow Jones Industrial Average (DJIA) and Standard and Poor's (S&P) 500 are the most common indexes. The DJIA tracks prices of 30 representative stocks. They include companies such as Coca-Cola™, McDonald's™, and Wal-Mart™. The S&P 500 index tracks 500 stocks by their total market values rather than by their prices. The total market value is the price of a company's stock times the number of stocks or shares that are out there.

Indexes like the DJIA and the S&P 500 reveal investors' attitudes about the future. A **"bear market"** is when stock indexes are going down. It can sometimes signal a coming recession. A rising stock market is called a **"bull market."** Bull markets are a sign that the economy is doing well.

Another way to measure economic growth is the Leading Economic Index. This index combines data from ten sources. It uses the S&P, the number of hours worked in manufacturing, the number of building permits issued in the previous month,

7. Predict Outcomes How might inflation change people's buying habits?

_____

_____

_____

_____

Think Critically

8. Explain What does inflation do to purchasing power? Why?

_____

_____

_____

_____

_____

9. Contrast Fill in the blanks:

The DJIA tracks _____ , while the S&P 500 tracks

_____ .

10. Draw Conclusions Which type of market is more likely when unemployment is low? Why?

_____

_____

_____

_____

Think Critically

11. Explain Why is the Leading Economic Index considered to be more accurate?

_____

_____

_____

_____

and other data. No one indicator works all of the time. This combined average is more accurate.

The index is called "leading" because real GDP generally follows it. If the leading index goes down, real GDP usually goes down a few months later. If the leading index goes up, real GDP usually goes up. The Leading Economic Index is seen as a good tool for predicting the future of the economy.

Employment is one of the indicators of the health of the economy. People seeking jobs often attend job fairs like this one in Miami.

NGSSS Check Give examples of two groups that want to know how the economy is doing and why they need this information. SS.7.E.2.3

_____

_____

_____

_____

Describe how stock prices can indicate the overall health of the economy.

_____

_____

_____

_____

3 THE GOVERNMENT AND INCOME INEQUALITY

NGSSS

SS.7.E.1.3 Review the concepts of supply and demand, choice, scarcity, and opportunity cost as they relate to the development of the mixed market economy in the United States.

SS.7.E.2.3 Identify and describe United States laws and regulations adopted to promote economic competition.

SS.7.E.2.5 Explain how economic institutions impact the national economy.

Essential Question
How does government influence the economy and economic institutions?

Guiding Questions
1. What factors influence income?
2. In what ways does government help those in poverty?

Terms to Know

welfare
money or necessities given to the poor

Temporary Assistance for Needy Families (TANF)
welfare program paid for by the federal government and run by the states

workfare
aid programs that require people who are receiving welfare to do some work for their benefits

compensation
temporary payment to unemployed or injured workers to replace lost wages

It Matters Because

Income inequality hurts individuals and the economy as a whole.

People make different amounts of money for doing different types of work. What type of work do you think should pay the highest? Explain your thinking.

_____

_____

_____

_____

_____

What Do You Know?

Directions: In the first column, answer the questions based on what you know before you study. After this lesson, complete the last column.

Before the Lesson	Questions	After the Lesson
	What can you do to make sure you have a job that pays well in the future?	
	How do your community leaders help people in need?	

networks™ Read Chapter 21 Lesson 3 in your textbook or online.

Think Critically

1. Explain What are three factors that affect income?

_____

_____

_____

Show Your Skill

2. Predict Outcomes What are the likely economic consequences of dropping out of high school?

_____

_____

_____

_____

Think Critically

3. Describe How does the government encourage people to go to college?

_____

_____

_____

Income Inequality

The United States is a wealthy nation. Not all Americans are wealthy though. Some have high incomes, and others are quite poor. People's incomes are different for many reasons. Education level, family wealth, and discrimination each play a role.

Education is a key to income. That is why the government encourages Americans to graduate from high school and go on to college. A person with a college degree can earn quite a bit more income than a person with a high school diploma.

When teens drop out of high school they harm the nation's economy. Having a poorly educated workforce hurts our country's ability to compete with other nations. The level of education a person attains, or achieves, influences his or her income. The more education a person has, the greater his or her potential, or possible, income. People without high school diplomas normally earn lower wages and have higher rates of unemployment.

The government tries to encourage people to go to college. Some programs help students from low-income families and students with disabilities prepare for college. The government also offers low-cost loans and grants to help pay for college.

Family wealth is also a factor that affects income. People born into wealthy families often have better educational opportunities than those who do not. They also may be able to join an established family business. Many inherit wealth from their parents.

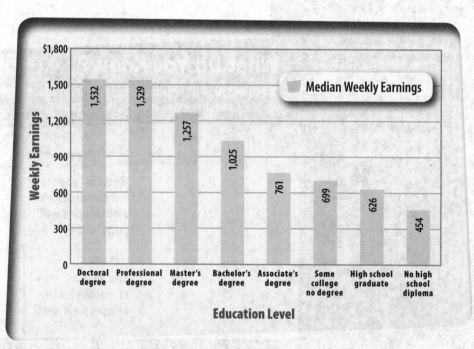

Median Weekly Earnings

- Doctoral degree: 1,532
- Professional degree: 1,529
- Master's degree: 1,257
- Bachelor's degree: 1,025
- Associate's degree: 761
- Some college no degree: 699
- High school graduate: 626
- No high school diploma: 454

Weekly Earnings / Education Level

Discrimination also affects income. Women and minorities may face discrimination that keeps them from getting jobs they are qualified for. They may also have trouble getting promotions and earning higher salaries.

Congress has passed laws to help protect people from discrimination. People can use the courts to enforce these laws.

Law	Year Passed	Content
Equal Pay Act	1963	Requires men and women to be given equal pay for equal work.
Civil Rights Act	1964	Bans discrimination on the basis of gender, race, color, religion, and national origin.
Equal Employment Opportunity Act	1972	Strengthens the government's ability to enforce the Civil Rights Act.
Americans with Disabilities Act	1990	Gives job protection to those with physical and mental disabilities.
Lilly Ledbetter Equal Pay Act	2009	Allows workers who face gender discrimination to sue employers.

Poverty

In a recent year, more than 40 million people lived in poverty. This means they did not earn enough income to pay for basic needs such as food, clothing, and shelter. Nearly 44 million people in this country fell into this category in 2009. Millions found themselves there as a result of the recession that began in 2007.

Both federal and state governments give welfare to struggling families. **Welfare** is money or necessities given to the poor. Welfare programs began in the United States during the Great Depression in the 1930s.

The government uses income guidelines to decide if an individual or a family can receive this help. The guidelines are based on how much it costs to buy enough food, clothing, and shelter to survive.

Food stamps help those in need purchase groceries.

Think Critically

4. **Synthesize** Choose one of the laws in the chart. Explain what might happen if the law did not exist.

_____

_____

_____

_____

_____

Take the Challenge

5. The government is not the only help available for families in need in your community. Learn about two other agencies that provide assistance.

6. Explain Who does the TANF program target for help?

_____

_____

_____

7. Draw Conclusions What is a benefit of unemployment insurance?

_____

_____

_____

_____

_____

_____

8. Chart Complete the chart to show what each program does.

A short-term form of help is **Temporary Assistance for Needy Families (TANF).** TANF is paid for by the federal government, but is run by the states. The program began in 1996. It replaced another welfare program that had begun in the 1930s. The new program has stricter rules. These rules are intended to encourage participants to find jobs quickly.

In many states TANF programs require people to work in order to get help. These programs are called **workfare.** The work often involves community service. Those getting the aid may also be required to go to job training or education programs.

Unemployment insurance provides **compensation** for workers who lose their jobs. This compensation is temporary payment to make up for lost wages. Workers who have been hurt on the job can receive workers' compensation. It includes wages and medical expenses.

Program	What it Does
Welfare	
Workfare	
Unemployment Insurance	
Workers' compensation	

NGSSS Check Describe ways in which the government tries to improve economic opportunities for individuals. SS.7.E.2.3

_____

_____

_____

_____

How does the government try to help those in poverty? SS.7.E.2.5

_____

_____

_____

_____

MY REFLECTIONS

ESSENTIAL QUESTION *How does government influence the economy and economic institutions?*

Reflect on What It Means . . .

Government affects your life, the lives of people in our community, state, and nation, and the lives of people around the world. Sometimes individuals, communities, and other nations need and welcome the help and involvement of our government. Sometimes each group would rather the government be less involved.

In each speech bubble, write reasons why individuals, communities, or other nations might want more or less government involvement.

"Help me out!"

"Leave me alone!"

Individual

"Help me out!"

"Leave me alone!"

Community

Keep Going! ⏵⏵

"Help me out!"

Nation

"Leave me alone!"

TAKE THE CHALLENGE

In general, do you think the government should play a larger or a smaller role in the economy? Why? Choose a side and think of three compelling reasons for your choice. Be prepared to defend your choice to someone with the opposite opinion in a group discussion.

THE GOVERNMENT AND BANKING

NGSSS

SS.7.E.1.4 Discuss the function of financial institutions in the development of a market economy.

SS.7.E.2.2 Describe the banking system in the United States and its impact on the money supply. Remarks/Examples: Examples are the Federal Reserve System and privately owned banks.

ESSENTIAL QUESTION *How does government influence the economy and economic institutions?*

Most countries have their own money. There are nearly 200 different money systems in the world today. The American dollar is just one of them. Someone once said, "Money makes the world go round." Aphra Behn, an English author from the 1600s, had this to say:

> "Money speaks sense in a language all nations understand."

speaks sense

What does *speaks sense* mean?

_____

_____

Besides American dollars, what are some other types of money?

_____

_____

DBQ BREAKING IT DOWN

Why is it that "all nations" understand money?

_____

_____

How could our economy function without money?

_____

_____

McGraw-Hill
networks™
There's More Online!

PHOTO: Danita Delimont/Gallo Images/Getty Images

MONEY

 NGSSS

SS.7.E.1.4 Discuss the function of financial institutions in the development of a market economy.

SS.7.E.2.2 Describe the banking system in the United States and its impact on the money supply. Remarks/Examples: Examples are the Federal Reserve System and privately owned banks.

Terms to Know

barter
to trade a good or a service for another good or service

coin
piece of metal used as money, such as a penny

currency
another name for coins and paper bills

electronic money
money that exists as a computer entry at a financial institution

deposit
the money that customers put into a financial institution

commercial bank
financial institution that offers full banking services to both individuals and businesses

savings and loan association (S&L)
financial institution that once loaned money to people buying homes

credit union
nonprofit financial institution that offers banking services to members only

deposit insurance
government program that protects deposits up to a certain amount if a bank fails

Essential Question

How does government influence the economy and economic institutions?

Guiding Questions

1. What gives money value?
2. What do financial institutions do?

It Matters Because

Money is used to make economic transactions.

Think of all the ways a person could get an item that he or she wants. List them below and circle the three you use most often.

_____

_____

_____

_____

What Do You Know?

Directions: In the first column, answer the questions based on what you know before you read the lesson. After this lesson, complete the last column.

Before the Lesson		After the Lesson
	Where does the value of money come from?	
	What is a financial institution?	

All About Money

Money is anything that people use in exchange for goods. It can include objects such as stones, salt, shells, gold, or silver. Money has value because it performs three functions.

The Three Functions of Money

1. Money is a medium of exchange. A medium is a means or way to do something. Money is a way to exchange, or trade, goods and services. Without money, people barter. **Barter** means to trade goods or services directly. For example, if you wanted to buy an apple, you would have to have something to trade for an apple. You would then have to find someone else who both had an apple and wanted what you had in trade.

2. Money is a store of value. This means it is a way to hold wealth. You can hold money until you are ready to use it.

3. Money is a measure of value. You can get an idea of an item's value by knowing how much money it costs. For example, a ring that costs $100 has more value than one that costs $10.

The Four Characteristics of Money

An object must have four characteristics in order to work as money.

1. Portable It must be easy to carry around.

2. Divisible It must be easy to break down into smaller amounts. That way it can be used for both large and small purchases. Strings of beads worked for some societies because beads could be removed to make smaller payments.

3. Durable Money changes hands many times. Whatever is used must be able to last for a long time.

4. Limited supply If money were easy to make, everyone would make it. Then it would become worthless.

Money can take different forms. **Currency** is another name for the objects we use as money, such as coins and paper bills. **Electronic money** does not have a physical form. The money in a checking or savings account is an example of electronic money.

Think Critically

1. Synthesize Suppose a customer sees an advertisement from a car dealer offering one car that costs $15,000 and another that costs $30,000. What function is money performing in this situation? Explain.

_____

_____

_____

_____

_____

_____

_____

Show Your Skill

2. Classify Information What form of money is a person accessing when using online banking?

_____

Electronic money

Money

Paper money

Coins

Think Critically

3. **Explain** How and why are interest rates different for loans versus deposits?

_____

_____

_____

_____

_____

Show Your Skill

4. **Classify** What are the three main types of financial institutions?

_____

_____

_____

Take the Challenge

5. Find an advertisement for a financial institution. Identify what type of institution it is, and list three benefits the advertisement features to attract customers.

Financial Institutions

Many people and businesses store their money in a financial institution such as a commercial bank. Financial institutions are businesses that store money for and loan money to other businesses and individuals. The money that a person puts into a financial institution is called a **deposit.** A deposit can be made using paper money, coins, checks, or electronic money. Some workers have their pay automatically deposited into their bank accounts. The deposit decreases the funds, or money, in the employer's account and increases the money in the workers' accounts.

Banks take the deposits made by customers and lend that money to other people and businesses. Banks charge interest and other fees for these loans to make money. They also pay interest on deposits to attract customers. Banks charge high interest rates on loans and pay low interest rates on deposits. That way they make a profit and stay in business.

There are three main types of financial institutions. One kind is a **commercial bank.** A commercial bank provides full banking services to people and businesses. Some of these services include checking accounts, savings accounts, and loans. Commercial banks are the biggest and most important part of the financial system.

Another kind of financial institution is a **savings and loan association (S&L).** At one time S&Ls mainly loaned money for buying homes. Now they work like commercial banks. The biggest difference is that most S&L customers are people rather than businesses.

A third kind of financial institution is a **credit union.** A credit union is a nonprofit cooperative business. People who work in the same industry or company, or belong to the same labor union, come together, or cooperate, to form one. This kind of institution accepts deposits, makes loans, and offers other banking services. You must, however, be a member of the cooperative to use the services. Credit unions often charge lower interest rates.

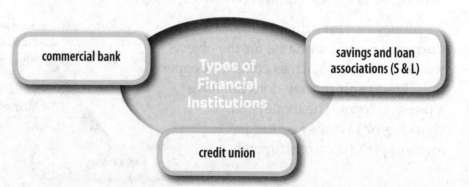

commercial bank

Types of Financial Institutions

savings and loan associations (S & L)

credit union

Unlike times past, few banks in Florida are based locally. Most banks are national banks. There are advantages and disadvantages to each type.

Money deposited in a financial institution is safe. This is because the government backs every bank with **deposit insurance.** This insurance protects customers' money if the bank goes out of business. The Federal Deposit Insurance Corporation (FDIC) insures the commercial banks and S&Ls.

The program for credit unions is the National Credit Union Share Insurance Fund (NCUSIF). Both programs cover deposits of up to $250,000.

The government began insuring deposits in 1933 as a result of the Great Depression. Depositors began to mistrust the banks and started pulling all their money out. So many people did this that the banks did not have enough money available. This caused banks to go out of business and their customers to lose money.

The government started the FDIC after these bank failures so that people would have more trust in the safety of banks. Today people feel secure about putting their money in banks. That trust allows the economy to grow.

Banks are also regulated, or watched over, by federal and state governments. A bank must have a government-issued charter to go into business. To get the charter, the bank needs a government agency to check its finances to make sure it has enough money. The government also makes sure the people who will run the bank have the knowledge and experience to do it well.

After the charter is issued, government officials continue to watch the bank. They make sure that it follows the law and is in good financial condition. These rules were put in place to protect the money that depositors put into banks.

 NGSSS Check List three functions that financial institutions perform. SS.7.E.2.2

_____

_____

_____

Think Critically

6. Describe What is the FDIC, and what does it do?

_____

_____

_____

_____

_____

Show Your Skill

7. Draw Conclusions What is the underlying reason for deposit insurance and government regulation of the banking industry?

_____

_____

_____

_____

NGSSS

SS.7.E.1.4 Discuss the function of financial institutions in the development of a market economy.

SS.7.E.2.2 Describe the banking system in the United States and its impact on the money supply. Remarks/Examples: Examples are the Federal Reserve System and privately owned banks.

Essential Question

How does government influence the economy and economic institutions?

Guiding Questions

1. What is the structure of the Federal Reserve System?
2. What are the functions of the Federal Reserve System?

Terms to Know

central bank
a bank from which other banks can borrow money

Federal Open Market Committee (FOMC)
part of the Federal Reserve System that is responsible for managing the money supply

monetary policy
changing the money supply to keep the economy growing and to keep prices stable

open market operations (OMO)
the FOMC's buying and selling of government bonds and Treasury bills to change the money supply

discount rate
amount of interest that the Fed charges banks

reserve requirement
the amount of money the Fed requires banks to keep on hand

It Matters Because

Your economic well-being is influenced by the Federal Reserve System.

What if everyone could print money? Write three outcomes of this imaginary situation.

What Do You Know?

Directions: In the first column, circle "True" if you think the statement is true and circle "False" if you think it is false based on what you know before you read the lesson. After this lesson, complete the last column.

Before the Lesson		After the Lesson	
True False	The government is involved with money at only the state and local levels.	True False	
True False	The government prints the money you use.	True False	
True False	The members of the Board of Governors for the Federal Reserve serve 14-year terms.	True False	
True False	The federal government makes rules that apply to local banks.	True False	

networks™ Read Chapter 22 Lesson 2 in your textbook or online.

The Fed's Structure

In the early 1900s, the United States had several recessions. A recession is a period of time when the economy does not grow. During these hard times, banks could not make new loans. Many people thought that a **central bank** would fix this problem. A central bank is a bank for banks. It can loan money to banks.

The government needed help creating a central bank. So it turned to the national banks. All banks with a national charter had to give money to create the new bank. The banks would have stock in the new bank. Stock is a share of the ownership of a business.

The new central bank was created in 1913. It was named the Federal Reserve System. This system is sometimes called "the Fed."

The Fed has many important functions. It manages our money and watches over commercial banks. It is the government's bank, and it helps keep the U.S. economy healthy. The chart shows how it is organized.

Think Critically

1. Explain Why was the Fed created?

Show Your Skill

2. Interpret Charts How do the District Advisory Committees assist the District Banks?

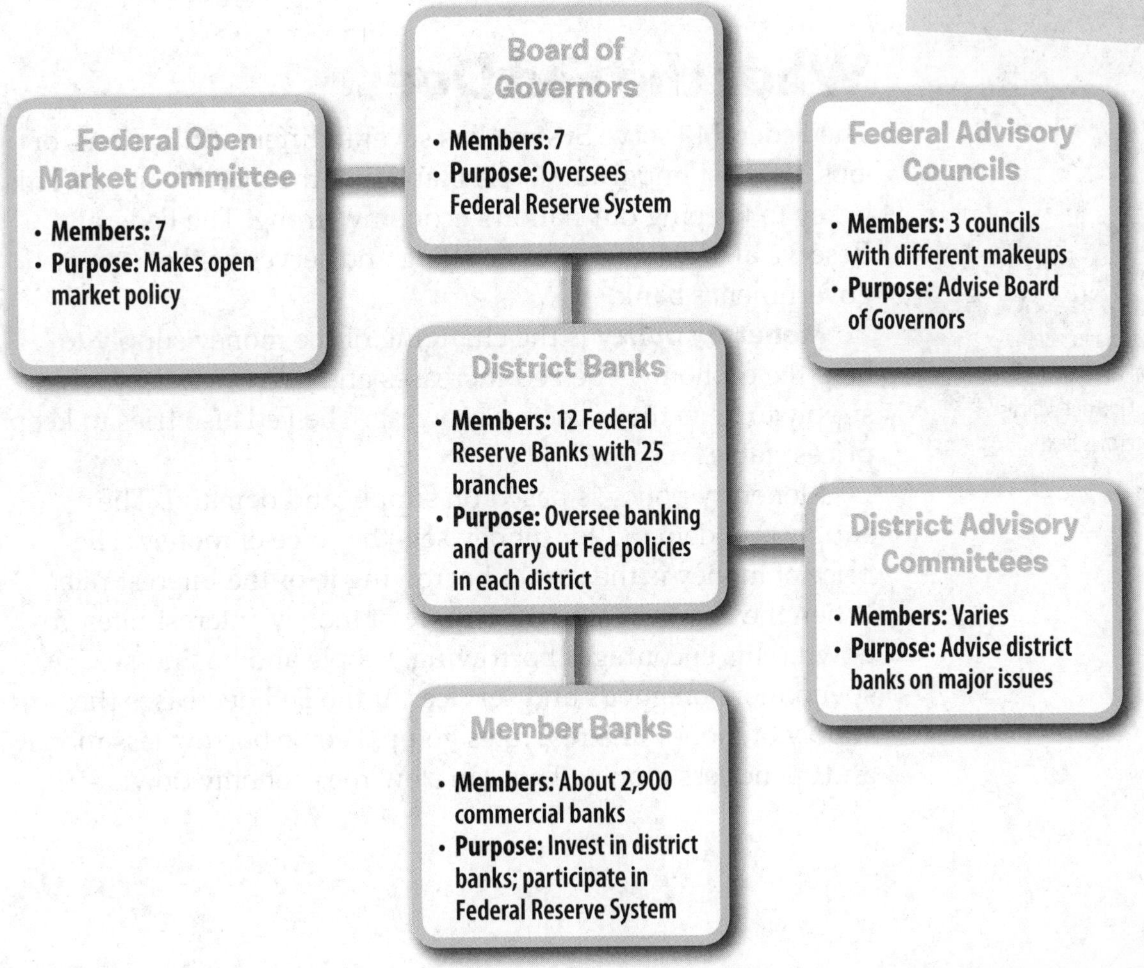

Board of Governors
• Members: 7
• Purpose: Oversees Federal Reserve System
Federal Open Market Committee
• Members: 7
• Purpose: Makes open market policy
Federal Advisory Councils
• Members: 3 councils with different makeups
• Purpose: Advise Board of Governors
District Banks
• Members: 12 Federal Reserve Banks with 25 branches
• Purpose: Oversee banking and carry out Fed policies in each district
District Advisory Committees
• Members: Varies
• Purpose: Advise district banks on major issues
Member Banks
• Members: About 2,900 commercial banks
• Purpose: Invest in district banks; participate in Federal Reserve System

Think Critically

3. Evaluate The members of the Board of Governors serve for 14 years. Do you think that is a good length for the term? Why or why not?

_____

_____

_____

_____

_____

Show Your Skill

4. Identify the Main Idea
What makes the FOMC powerful?

_____

_____

_____

_____

Take the Challenge

5. Research the names of the members of the Board of Governors. Find out which member's term is next to expire.

Organization of the Fed

Board of Governors The president and the Senate choose the board members. They serve for 14 years. This long term length makes sure board members are fairly free of influence from elected officials as they do their jobs.

District Banks There are 12 Federal Reserve districts in the United States. Each district has one main Federal Reserve Bank and several branch banks. These banks carry out the policies set by the Board of Governors. A nine-member board of directors runs each district.

Councils The Federal Reserve System also includes several councils. One of the most important is the **Federal Open Market Committee (FOMC).** This committee manages the country's money supply. The council manipulates, or makes changes to, the supply of money. This ability gives the council a lot of power over the economy.

Member Banks About one-third of all commercial banks belong to the Federal Reserve System. Remember, however, that they cannot vote on Fed policies.

What the Fed Does

The Federal Reserve System has several different functions, or jobs. Its most important job is managing the money supply. This is key to keeping our nation's economy strong. The Federal Reserve also watches over banking and serves as the government's bank.

Monetary policy is the changing of the money supply to help the economy. The Fed increases and decreases the money supply to keep the economy growing. The Fed also tries to keep prices stable.

Monetary policy is based on supply and demand. The supply and demand for money sets the price of money. The price of money is the cost of borrowing it, or the interest rate. When the Fed increases the supply of money, interest rates go down. This encourages borrowing. People and businesses spend more on goods and services. If the Fed decreases the supply of money, interest rates go up. People borrow less money and spend less money. This can slow the economy down.

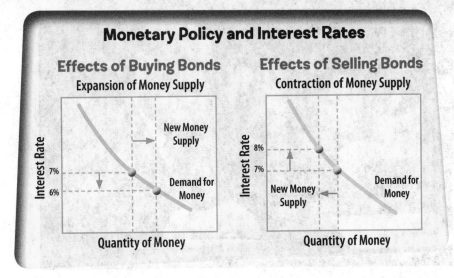

Monetary Policy and Interest Rates

Effects of Buying Bonds
Expansion of Money Supply

Interest Rate / Quantity of Money
7%
6%
New Money Supply
Demand for Money

Effects of Selling Bonds
Contraction of Money Supply

Interest Rate / Quantity of Money
8%
7%
New Money Supply
Demand for Money

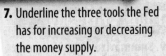

Show Your Skill

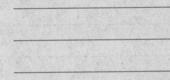

Show Your Skill

6. Interpret Charts How does increasing the money supply affect interest rates?

_____

_____

_____

_____

The Fed has three tools to control the money supply. The first is called **open market operations (OMO).** It includes the buying and selling of government bonds and Treasury bills. Bonds and bills are the way the government borrows money from the public.

The Fed's second tool is the discount rate. The **discount rate** is the interest rate banks pay to borrow money from the Fed. To grow the money supply, the Fed lowers the discount rate. This encourages banks to borrow money and lend it out. To shrink the money supply, the Fed raises the discount rate. This discourages borrowing.

Mark the Text

7. Underline the three tools the Fed has for increasing or decreasing the money supply.

Think Critically

8. Summarize Why does the Fed regulate monetary policy?

_____

_____

_____

_____

_____

_____

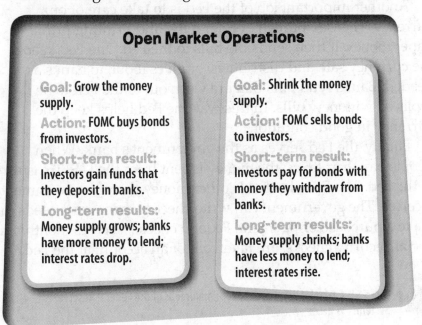

Open Market Operations

Goal: Grow the money supply.

Action: FOMC buys bonds from investors.

Short-term result: Investors gain funds that they deposit in banks.

Long-term results: Money supply grows; banks have more money to lend; interest rates drop.

Goal: Shrink the money supply.

Action: FOMC sells bonds to investors.

Short-term result: Investors pay for bonds with money they withdraw from banks.

Long-term results: Money supply shrinks; banks have less money to lend; interest rates rise.

The Fed's third tool is the reserve requirement. The **reserve requirement** is the amount of a deposit a bank must keep on hand. For example, if the reserve requirement is 40% and someone makes a $100 deposit, then the bank must keep $40 as a reserve. It can lend the remaining $60.

The chairman of the Federal Reserve is often asked to appear before Congress to answer questions or explain decisions. Here, Ben Bernanke speaks to members of Congress about financial issues in 2011.

Think Critically

9. Summarize What is the major job of the Bureau of Engraving and Printing? Why is this a government role?

_____

_____

_____

_____

_____

_____

When the Fed increases the reserve requirement, banks must keep more money on hand. As a result they have less money to lend. When the Fed decreases the reserve requirement, banks have more money to lend.

The Fed also regulates banks. It writes rules that lenders must follow and makes sure the rules lenders make are easy for their customers to understand. Regulations, or rules, cover many areas, including ways member banks have to report their reserve requirements. The Fed also has many other regulatory responsibilities.

Another important job of the Fed is to take care of our currency. The U.S. Bureau of Engraving and Printing prints paper money. It then sends the bills to the Fed. The Fed keeps the currency safe and distributes, or gives it out, to banks as needed. Banks send bills that are worn out to the Fed to be replaced with new bills. In this way the Fed helps keep the currency in good condition.

Finally, the Fed serves as the government's bank. When people pay their taxes, the money is sent from the U.S. Treasury to the Fed. The Fed also holds other money that the government receives. The government can write checks whenever it needs to make a purchase or payment. Federal checks, such as monthly Social Security checks, are taken out of an account at the Fed.

NGSSS Check What are the four major jobs of the Federal Reserve System? SS.7.E.2.2

_____

_____

_____

_____

PHOTO: James Berglie/ZUMA Press/Corbis

Copyright © by The McGraw-Hill Companies, Inc.

NGSSS

SS.7.E.1.4 Discuss the function of financial institutions in the development of a market economy.

SS.7.E.2.2 Describe the banking system in the United States and its impact on the money supply. Remarks/Examples: Examples are the Federal Reserve System and privately owned banks.

Essential Question

How does government influence the economy and economic institutions?

Guiding Questions

1. What purpose do banks serve in the economy?
2. How has banking become safer, faster, and more efficient over the years?

Terms to Know

savings account
a type of bank account that pays interest and allows withdrawals

certificate of deposit (CD)
a type of account that pays higher interest than a regular savings account but has a fixed term

money market account
type of account that pays interest and also allows check writing

checking account
type of account from which deposited funds can be withdrawn by check at any time and in any amount without penalty

It Matters Because

Banks are an important part of the nation's economy, and people entrust banks with their money.

List at least three ways you might use a bank now or in the future. Share your ideas with two other students and see if you can expand your list to five.

_____

_____

_____

_____

What Do You Know?

Directions: You may have visited a bank and have seen advertisements for banks. What happens in a bank? Who are the people involved? Why do we have banks? In the space below, list words you already know that relate to banks. When you finish the lesson, add more words that you learn.

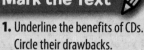
Think Critically

2. **Describe** What is a bank loan, and what do the loan terms include?

_____

_____

_____

_____

_____

_____

_____

3. **Contrast** How is a checking account used differently than a savings account?

_____

_____

_____

_____

Banks in the Economy

Banks offer many types of accounts. Some are used to save money. Others are used to pay bills and buy goods and services. Savings accounts and certificates of deposit are used for saving money. Most **savings accounts** pay interest and allow people to make withdrawals. The interest payments are meant to encourage people to keep their money in the bank and add to it.

A **certificate of deposit (CD)** pays more interest than regular savings accounts. However, it has a fixed term. This means that you must keep your money in the account for a set period, or length of time, if you want to get the higher rate of interest. You will get a lower interest rate as a penalty for taking your money out early.

A third type of account is a **money market account.** This account is like a checking and a savings account combined.

It pays interest, but also allows the customer to write checks. There are special restrictions. Some banks set the number of withdrawals that are allowed, and some demand a minimum balance for this type of account.

Money deposited in a **checking account** can be taken out at any time by writing a check, using a debit card, or making an electronic payment. People use checking accounts to pay bills and buy things. Some checking accounts pay interest, but it is usually lower than that offered by other types of accounts.

In addition to offering accounts, banks also make loans, or lend money. People and businesses sometimes need to borrow money from a bank. They do this by getting a loan. The loan process involves the borrower and the bank (the lender) agreeing to loan terms. This agreement includes the amount borrowed, the interest rate, and the time in which the loan needs to be repaid.

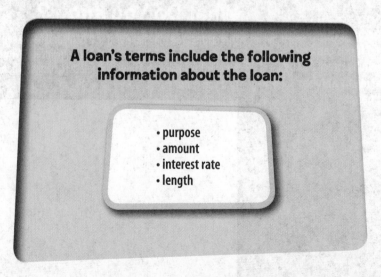

A loan's terms include the following information about the loan:

- purpose
- amount
- interest rate
- length

How Banking Has Changed

Banking has changed over the years. One of the first changes happened in 1791 with the First Bank of the United States. It was founded to collect money, make payments, and make loans for the national government. Some leaders feared that the Bank would become too powerful. They limited its charter to 20 years, then it went out of business.

During the War of 1812, it became clear that the government needed a bank from which it could borrow money. The Second Bank of the United States was created in 1816. At that time the country had hundreds of state banks. When the Civil War began in 1861, the banking industry was in chaos. About 1600 banks were operating across the nation. They used their own currencies. People did not know which banks to trust.

The federal government passed the National Bank Act in 1863. Under the new law, the national government began issuing charters to banks. The national banks were funded better and regulated. They all used the same currency backed by U.S. government bonds. These changes helped bring some order to the banking industry.

Despite these improvements, the banks still had problems. Congress created the Federal Reserve System in 1913 to try to fix the banking system. For the first time, banks were organized under one main power: the Federal Reserve. The country was divided into 12 districts. Each district has one main Federal Reserve bank and several branch banks. The problem was that the 12 districts did not work together. This lack of cooperation made it hard for the Federal Reserve to stop the Great Depression, which began in 1929.

Think Critically

4. Summarize Describe the U.S. banking system between the War of 1812 and the start of the Civil War.

_____

_____

_____

_____

_____

Banking Legislation from the Nation's Birth to the Depression

1791 First Bank of the United States → **1816** Second Bank of the United States → **1863** National Bank Act → **1913** Federal Reserve System → **1933** Bank Act

These people are in line to get their money out of the bank after the stock market crash in 1929. This situation is called a "panic."

Show Your Skill

5. Generalize How did the changes after the S&L crisis make the banking industry safer?

_____

_____

_____

_____

_____

Think Critically

6. Hypothesize What could be done to prevent a future panic related to banks?

_____

_____

_____

_____

Take the Challenge

7. Research editorial cartoons from the 2007 financial crisis. Select one and explain its meaning to the class.

As you read earlier, thousands of banks failed during the Great Depression. Many people began to panic. They then tried to take their money out of banks at the same time. The banks that did not have enough money failed and closed. These bank closures caused more people to panic and more banks to fail. Many people lost all their money.

To stop the panic, President Franklin D. Roosevelt closed all the banks for four days in 1933. He sent inspectors to see which banks had enough money and which were about to fail. Only healthy banks were allowed to reopen. Congress then passed the Banking Act of 1933. This law created deposit insurance and gave the Federal Reserve more power. A second law in 1935 made this power even greater. The changes gave the Board of Governors more power over the district banks. This central control helped the Fed to be more united.

These actions kept the banks running smoothly until the 1980s. Then a crisis hit savings and loan associations (S&Ls). Many had made risky loans that were never paid back. Hundreds of S&Ls failed. In 1989 Congress made the FDIC larger so it could cover S&Ls. The FDIC began to watch over them more closely.

Then in 2007 the economy went into a deep recession. Many banks had been making risky loans for years. So many banks were in danger of failing that the entire financial system was in crisis. In 2008 the Federal Reserve and the U.S. Treasury loaned trillions of dollars to banks to stop the crisis. The plan worked, but the recovery was slow.

 NGSSS Check What role do banks play in the economy? SS.7.E.2.2

_____

_____

ESSENTIAL QUESTION *How does government influence the economy and economic institutions?*

Reflect on What It Means...

Banks come in all sizes. There are neighborhood banks, national banks, and even a world bank. Whatever their size, banks are a vital part of the economy.

Write in the boxes to show how banks affect you and others.

What role do
banks play . . .

. . . in my life?

. . . in my community?

Keep Going!

What role do
banks play . . .

. . . in the world?

TAKE THE CHALLENGE

Visit the Web sites of several banks. What services are available for someone
your age? Report what you learn to the class.

CHAPTER 23 FINANCING THE GOVERNMENT

NGSSS

SS.7.E.1.2 Discuss the importance of borrowing and lending in the United States and the government's role in controlling financial institutions, and list the advantages and disadvantages of using credit.

SS.7.E.1.6 Compare the national budget process to the personal budget process.

Remarks/Examples: Prepare an individual budget which includes housing, food, leisure, communication, and miscellaneous categories and compare that to federal government budget allocations.

SS.7.E.2.1 Explain how federal, state, and local taxes support the economy as a function of the United States government.

ESSENTIAL QUESTION *How does government influence the economy and economic institutions?*

Each year, the president sends a budget message to Congress. It states how much money the president wants to spend on government programs. In his budget message for 2012, President Barack Obama stated:

> "My budget makes **investments** that can help America ... transform our economy, and it does so fully aware of the very difficult fiscal situation we face."
>
> THE BUDGET MESSAGE OF THE PRESIDENT

investments

How are *investments* different from expenditures?

_____

_____

_____

DBQ BREAKING IT DOWN

Reading in context, what do you think *fiscal* means?

_____

_____

What "difficult fiscal situation" might a president giving a budget message be referring to?

_____

_____

PHOTO: Kristoffer Tripplaar / Alamy

McGraw-Hill
networks™
There's More Online!

LESSON 1

THE FEDERAL BUDGET: REVENUES AND EXPENDITURES

NGSSS

SS.7.E.1.2 Discuss the importance of borrowing and lending in the United States and the government's role in controlling financial institutions, and list the advantages and disadvantages of using credit.

SS.7.E.1.6 Compare the national budget process to the personal budget process. Remarks/Examples: Prepare an individual budget which includes housing, food, leisure, communication, and miscellaneous categories and compare that to federal government budget allocations.

SS.7.E.2.1 Explain how federal, state, and local taxes support the economy as a function of the United States government.

Essential Question

How does government influence the economy and economic institutions?

Guiding Questions

1. How does the federal budget reflect choices?
2. How do state and local revenues and expenditures differ from those of the federal government?

Terms to Know

fiscal year
any 12-month period chosen for keeping accounts

mandatory spending
federal spending required by law that does not need approval from Congress each year

discretionary spending
federal spending that must be approved by Congress each year

appropriations bill
legislation that determines spending for specific programs for the coming year

intergovernmental revenue
money that one level of government receives from another level of government

sales tax
a tax paid by consumers when they buy a good or a service

subsidize
to aid or support with money

entitlement program
a government program that makes payments to certain people to help them meet their needs

property tax
a tax on the value of land and property owned by someone

It Matters Because

Government tax and spending policies affect you.

You go into the store with $10 in your pocket. You see something you want and the price tag reads $9.98. Do you have enough money for the purchase? Why or why not?

_____

_____

_____

What Do You Know?

Directions: In the first column, answer the questions based on what you know before you study this lesson. After this lesson, complete the last column.

Before the Lesson		After the Lesson
	What services does the federal government pay for?	
	What services do local governments pay for?	

Understanding the Federal Budget

A budget is a spending plan for the future. To make a personal budget, you figure out all of your income for a certain period. Then you figure out all of your expenses for the same period. If your expenses exceed, or are more than, your income you need to find ways to spend less or to make more money.

The federal government does basically the same thing. Each year it makes a budget for the coming **fiscal year.** A fiscal year is any 12-month period used for keeping accounts. The federal government's fiscal year begins on October 1 and ends on September 30. The budget is named for the calendar year in which it ends. For example, the budget for fiscal year (FY) 2015 covers the period from October 1, 2014, to September 30, 2015.

The president and Congress both work on the budget. The diagram shows how they do this. First, the president sends a budget message to Congress. It states how much money the president wants to spend on every federal program.

Step 1	Step 2	Step 3
The president sends Congress a budget message that: • estimates revenue and expenses; • indicates spending priorities; • states plans for taxes.	The House and Senate pass budget resolutions that outline spending and taxes for the next five years. Caps on spending are set for areas controlled by committees of Congress.	The House and Senate pass bills authorizing spending, which cannot exceed limits set in Step 2.

Next, Congress reviews the president's message. Then it writes a plan called a budget resolution. It sets limits on spending in areas such as defense. It says how much total revenue the government will collect. The budget resolution goes to the full House and Senate for approval.

The federal budget also has two different kinds of spending. **Mandatory spending** is spending that is set by law. It does not need to be approved each year. An example is Social Security. **Discretionary spending** is spending on budget choices that are made and approved each year. It can go up or down from year to year. An example is spending on defense.

Show Your Skill

1. Make Inferences What are the two basic budget choices people can make to bring spending in line with income?

_____

_____

Think Critically

2. Synthesize When does the federal government's fiscal year 2016 begin?

_____

3. Sequence What is the first step involved in creating the federal budget?

_____

_____

_____

4. Compare What is the difference between mandatory spending and discretionary spending?

_____

_____

_____

_____

_____

_____

Congress passes a number of **appropriations bills.** This is legislation that lists specific programs and how much the government will spend on each one. These bills start in the House, but must also be approved by the Senate. Spending cannot exceed the limits in the budget resolution.

After each bill is passed by the House and Senate, it is sent to the president. The president can sign it into law or veto it. If the bill is vetoed, Congress has two choices. It can either rewrite the bill or override the veto.

The finished federal budget has two parts—revenues and expenditures. Revenue is the money a government collects to use for its spending. The biggest source of revenue is personal income tax. People pay this tax on the money they earn.

The circle graphs below show the federal budget for FY 2011. Most revenue comes from personal income taxes and payroll taxes. Defense and Social Security are the two biggest expenses. Note the category called "interest on debt." This is the interest the government must pay on the money it has borrowed.

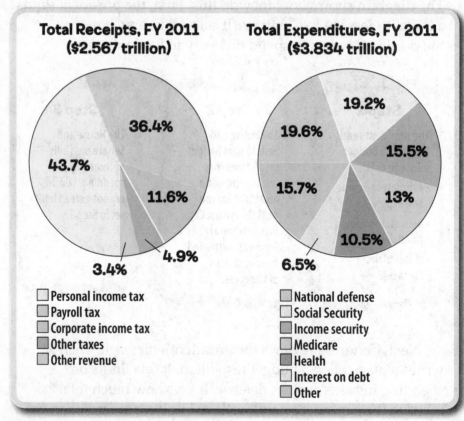

Total Receipts, FY 2011 ($2.567 trillion)

43.7% 36.4% 11.6% 3.4% 4.9%

- Personal income tax
- Payroll tax
- Corporate income tax
- Other taxes
- Other revenue

Total Expenditures, FY 2011 ($3.834 trillion)

19.2% 19.6% 15.5% 15.7% 13% 10.5% 6.5%

- National defense
- Social Security
- Income security
- Medicare
- Health
- Interest on debt
- Other

Budgeting for State and Local Governments

State and local governments also make budgets. In all the states except Vermont, the law says the government cannot spend more money than it takes in. Local governments also have to spend no more than they take in.

State governments get most of their money from **intergovernmental revenue.** This is money that one level of government gets from another. The states get money from the federal government.

Another large source of money for states is **sales taxes.** Consumers pay sales tax when they buy a product or service. Most states have sales taxes. Most also have a personal income tax.

Government leaders at every level, including these in Palm Beach County in Florida, have to make tough budget decisions.

For states, the greatest expenses are public welfare and education. Some state education money goes to help local governments. Some education money is used to subsidize college for young people. To **subsidize** means to help pay for.

States also spend on **entitlement programs.** These are called "entitlements" because the law sets the requirements, or rules, for the programs. An example is the Medicaid program. Medicaid helps people get health care.

Like state governments, local governments rely on intergovernmental revenue. Local governments get money from state governments. This money is their largest source of revenue. They also collect **property taxes** to raise money. These are taxes on the value of the land and buildings people own. Property taxes are a big source of income for local governments. Some local governments have sales or income taxes. Traffic fines and permit fees also bring in revenue for local governments.

Local governments provide many of the services people depend on. This is where most local spending goes. Education is the largest portion of local spending. Other services include police and fire protection, libraries, water service, sewage, trash collection, and street repair.

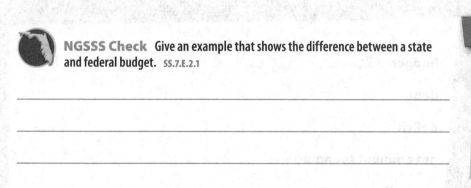

NGSSS Check Give an example that shows the difference between a state and federal budget. SS.7.E.2.1

_____

_____

_____

Think Critically

8. Explain What is intergovernmental revenue?

_____

_____

_____

_____

Show Your Skill

9. Formulate Questions Write a question for a member of the state legislature about a program that is subsidized by the state.

_____

_____

_____

Take the Challenge

10. Choose a part of Florida's state budget that you think should get more funding. Give three reasons to support your choice. Do the same with a part of the state's budget you think should receive less funding.

FISCAL POLICY

 NGSSS

SS.7.E.1.2 Discuss the importance of borrowing and lending in the United States and the government's role in controlling financial institutions, and list the advantages and disadvantages of using credit.

SS.7.E.1.6 Compare the national budget process to the personal budget process. Remarks/Examples: Prepare an individual budget which includes housing, food, leisure, communication, and miscellaneous categories and compare that to federal government budget allocations.

SS.7.E.2.1 Explain how federal, state, and local taxes support the economy as a function of the United States government.

Essential Question

How does government influence the economy and economic institutions?

Guiding Questions

1. What do governments do when the budget does not balance?
2. How does the government try to influence the economy?

Terms to Know

balanced budget
a budget in which expenditures and revenue are equal

budget surplus
a situation in which a government collects more revenues than it spends

budget deficit
a situation in which a government spends more than it collects in revenues

debt
money borrowed and not yet paid back

fiscal policy
the government's use of spending and taxes to help the economy grow

automatic stabilizer
a built-in effect of an economic slowdown that helps to compensate for loss of income

It Matters Because

Government spending is an important part of the economy, with lasting effects for all citizens.

What has the government done for you? With a partner, brainstorm and list ten ways your life is touched by money spent by the government.

What Do You Know?

Directions: Use no more than three words to tell what you know about each of these terms. After you finish the lesson, adjust any of your descriptions if needed.

budget _____

debt _____

deficit _____

government spending _____

expenditure _____

Surpluses and Deficits

Making a government budget is easier than following one. Budgets are made based on what officials predict is going to happen in the future. Unexpected events such as natural disasters can happen that cause spending to increase. Revenues can go down when the economy slows.

Governments try to balance their budgets. A **balanced budget** is one in which revenue and spending in a year equal each other. When a government collects more money than it spends, it has a **budget surplus.** Governments often save budget surpluses to use as a reserve. This reserve is spent to balance the budget in years when revenues are low. When a government spends more money than it collects, it has a **budget deficit.** In all states except Vermont, the law says that the state must have a balanced budget. If spending exceeds revenues, the state cannot borrow money to make up the difference. It has to cut spending, raise taxes—or both.

The federal government does not face the same limits. It can and often does have a budget deficit. To make up the difference between what the government spends and what it collects, the federal government borrows money. It does this by selling bonds. The government also sells Treasury bills.

Borrowing to cover budget deficits puts the government in **debt.** Debt is money that has been borrowed and not yet paid back. Being in debt means owing money. For each year the federal government has a deficit, its total debt goes up. The graph below shows that the federal government's debt has been growing for many years.

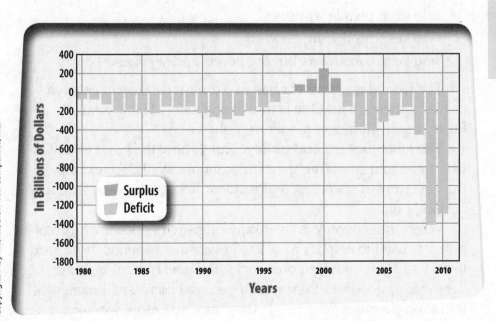

Think Critically

1. Explain What is a balanced budget?

_____

_____

_____

2. Contrast How is a budget surplus different from a budget deficit?

_____

_____

_____

_____

_____

_____

Show Your Skill

3. Identify Cause and Effect What causes the federal debt to grow?

_____

_____

_____

_____

_____

4. Identify Cause and Effect
What are some possible effects of the federal debt?

_____

_____

_____

_____

5. Summarize What are the federal government's goals for the economy?

_____

_____

_____

_____

_____

6. Explain What is fiscal policy?

_____

_____

_____

_____

The federal debt is expected to keep growing in the future. This growing debt has some negative effects:

- *The interest on the debt is costly.* Interest payments are a large part of the federal budget. As the debt grows, so does the interest.
- *Federal borrowing can slow down the economy.* Many Americans buy government bonds. Bonds are a way to save for the future. Buyers plan to get their money back with interest later on. But people who save for the future have less money to spend now. Less spending means slower business growth.
- *Federal borrowing can cause interest rates to rise.* When the government borrows money, it leaves less money for others to borrow. This can cause the price of borrowing to go up.
- *Long-term debt could cause investors to lose confidence in the government.* People might begin to see the federal government as a bad investment. They could force the government to pay higher interest rates.

Managing the Economy

For much of U.S. history, the federal government did not take an active role in the economy. That changed during the Great Depression in the 1930s.

Banks and businesses collapsed. Millions of people were out of work. President Roosevelt stepped in to help the economy recover. He started government programs to give people jobs and increase their income.

In the late 1940s, Congress set official goals for the economy. They were:

- to keep people working
- to keep producing goods
- to keep consumers buying goods and services.

The federal government has two tools it can use to achieve, or reach, these goals. One is monetary policy. The Federal Reserve is in charge of monetary policy.

The other tool is **fiscal policy.** This is how the government uses taxes and spending to reach economic goals. For example, the government spending by President Roosevelt is an example of fiscal policy.

When the economy is shrinking or growing too slowly, fiscal policy is used to help it grow. The government spends more and taxes less. By spending more money, the government increases demand for goods and services. If demand increases, businesses will produce more. As a result, they may hire more workers.

By cutting taxes, the government takes less of people's earnings. People keep more money. Economists think that if people have more money, they will spend it. This spending increases demand.

The government usually takes these steps when the economy slows down or enters a recession. A plan to spur the economy by spending more and taxing less is called an economic stimulus. For example, in 2009 Congress passed a stimulus plan to help the country during a deep recession.

Fiscal policy can be hard to put into practice. Many leaders do not agree with spending money when the government is already in debt. That makes it hard to agree on how much to spend and on what programs.

Fiscal policy is slow, and its effects can be hard to predict. It takes time for leaders to agree on a plan and put it into action. The economy is complex, and a program may not always be strong enough to have the desired effect.

For these reasons the federal government prefers to use programs called **automatic stabilizers.** These programs help the economy automatically, without other action from the government. The two most important automatic stabilizers are unemployment insurance and the progressive income tax system. Both are always in place. They begin to work as soon as the economy slows down.

For example, when people lose jobs in a recession, they start getting unemployment insurance payments. This program pays unemployed people income while they are looking for new jobs. They spend the income and help keep the economy from slowing further.

The federal income tax also works as a stabilizer. This is because it is a progressive tax. People with lower incomes pay a lower percentage in taxes than people with higher incomes. When people lose their jobs, their income goes down. They pay a lower percentage of their income in taxes, because their income is lower. This partly makes up for the loss of income. When they go back to work, their income grows. They are then taxed at a higher rate. This helps the government to lower the deficit caused by the recession.

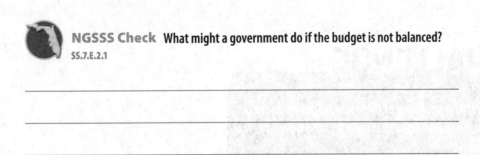 **NGSSS Check** **What might a government do if the budget is not balanced?**
SS.7.E.2.1

_____

_____

_____

Think Critically

7. Explain Why are unemployment insurance and the progressive income tax known as automatic stabilizers?

_____

_____

_____

_____

Show Your Skill

8. Identify Cause and Effect Under what conditions does the federal government use fiscal policy? Why?

_____

_____

_____

_____

_____

_____

Take the Challenge

9. Look online to find one of the national debt clocks. Check back three times and record the change.

MY REFLECTIONS

ESSENTIAL QUESTION *How does government influence the economy and economic institutions?*

Reflect on What It Means . . .

There are three levels of government in the United States: local, state, and national. Together, they spend trillions of dollars a year. How much is that per person? Find out.

My Community	Florida	The United States
Annual Local Government Expenditures	**Annual State Government Expenditures**	**Annual Federal Government Expenditures**
_____	_____	_____
÷	÷	÷
Community's Population	**State's Population**	**Country's Population**
_____	_____	_____
=	=	=
$ _____	$ _____	$ _____
Spending Per Person	**Spending Per Person**	**Spending Per Person**

TAKE THE CHALLENGE

Choose another country and research the spending of the national government of that country. What is the per-person spending in that country, and how does it compare to that of the United States?

INTERNATIONAL TRADE AND ECONOMIC SYSTEMS

NGSSS

SS.7.C.4.2 Recognize government and citizen participation in international organizations. (*Remarks/Examples*: Examples are United Nations, NATO, Peace Corps, World Health Organization, World Trade Organization, International Court of Justice.)

ESSENTIAL QUESTION • *Why do people trade?* • *Why and how do people make economic choices?*

The World Trade Organization (WTO) is a group that helps regulate international trade. The WTO is often invited to participate in meetings with leaders from many nations. What is the purpose of the WTO? According to its Web site:

"There are a number of ways of looking at the WTO. It's an organization for liberalizing trade. It's a forum for governments to negotiate trade agreements. It's a place for them to settle trade disputes. It operates a system of trade rules. (But it's not Superman, just in case anyone thought it could solve—or cause—all the world's problems!)"

THE WORLD TRADE ORGANIZATION

G20 SEOUL SUMMIT 2010

THE SEOUL SUMMIT 2010
Shared Growth Beyond Crisis

liberalizing

Liberalizing is the opposite of restricting. Why would the WTO want to liberalize trade?

_____

_____

DBQ BREAKING IT DOWN

What can you conclude from the fact that the WTO claims it does not cause all the world's problems?

_____

_____

_____

Only about half of the world's countries are members of the WTO. Why might this be the case?

_____

_____

_____

McGraw-Hill
networks™
There's More Online!

PHOTO: Stefan Rousseau/ POOL/epa/Corbis

NGSSS

SS.7.E.3.1 Explain how international trade requires a system for exchanging currency between and among nations.

Essential Question
Why do people trade?

Guiding Questions
1. Why do nations trade with one another?
2. How does a nation's trade balance affect its economy?

Terms to Know

import
to bring goods into a country from other countries

export
to sell goods to other nations

comparative advantage
ability of one country to produce an item at less cost than another country

protectionism
government strategy to protect industries at home by using trade barriers

tariff
a tax on imports

quota
a limit on how much of a certain item is allowed to enter a country

free trade
policy in which countries join with key trading partners to lower trade barriers with the intention of increasing trade

balance of trade
difference between the value of a nation's imports and the value of its exports

exchange rate
the value of a nation's money when compared to other nations

It Matters Because

National, state, and local economies depend in large part on international trade.

You may be wearing something right now that was made in another country. You may have eaten something for dinner last night that was grown outside of the United States. Find three items that are produced someplace outside of this country. List the items below and write the names of the countries that produced them.

What Do You Know?

Directions: Circle the problems you think the United States faces related to trade with other countries. When you finish the lesson, come back and circle using a different color.

Too many exports	Too many imports	Too few exports
Too few imports	Trade surplus	Trade deficit

netw⬤rks™ Read Chapter 24 Lesson 1 in your textbook or online.

Trade Between Nations

Nations do not always have the resources they need to make the things their people want. To solve this problem of scarcity, nations trade with one another. They trade food, goods, services, and natural resources. Nations **import,** or bring into the country, goods produced in other nations. They **export,** or sell to other nations, goods they produce. For example, the United States does not produce enough oil to meet its needs. To solve this problem, the U.S. imports oil from other countries.

The main reason countries trade is because of **comparative advantage.** Comparative advantage is the ability to produce something at a lower opportunity cost than another country can.

Suppose that Countries A and B can produce only two goods, bread and bicycles. The opportunity cost of making one bicycle is the bread each country cannot produce while its resources are being used to make a bicycle. Country A can produce one bicycle at an opportunity cost of 10 units of bread. Country B can produce one bicycle at an opportunity cost of 15 units of bread. Country A has a lower opportunity cost. It has the comparative advantage in producing bicycles.

A country's factors of production—natural resources, labor, capital, and entrepreneurs—usually decide its comparative advantage. China is a good example of this. China has a huge labor force. Many workers in China earn low wages. This means that labor in China costs less than labor in many other countries. As a result, China has a comparative advantage in making goods that need a lot of labor to produce. The United States and Brazil have a large amount of farm and ranch land. This gives them a comparative advantage in farm products. Brazil is the world's largest exporter of beef.

Some less advanced economies produce only one product for export. These economies are called single resource economies. The danger is that if the price for that product goes down, the nation's economy goes down, too.

Most people look for low prices when they shop. To give people the low prices they want, many U.S. stores sell goods made in countries like China. It costs less to make most goods in China than it costs to make them in the United States. Goods that cost less to make can be sold for lower prices. Lower prices are good for consumers, but not always for companies. When people buy cheaper products imported from other countries, U.S. manufacturers can lose money. This sometimes causes them to produce less, lay off workers, or even shut down.

Think Critically

1. Synthesize Give two examples of countries that have a comparative advantage in producing something. Name the country and the product.

_____

_____

_____

2. Summarize Why is the size of China's labor force a comparative advantage?

_____

_____

_____

_____

_____

_____

Mark the Text

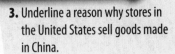

3. Underline a reason why stores in the United States sell goods made in China.

4. Explain How do tariffs affect the price of imported goods?

_____

_____

5. Compare and Contrast What is the relationship between trade barriers and free trade?

_____

_____

_____

_____

_____

_____

When trade hurts a nation, that nation may turn to protectionism. **Protectionism** means doing things to make goods made at home cheaper than imported goods.

The two most common kinds of trade barriers are tariffs and quotas. A **tariff** is a tax on imports. This tax raises the price of imported goods. This makes them more costly than they otherwise would have been. Tires are one example. Recently, many U.S. tire companies had to shut down because tires made in China cost less money. To help U.S. tire makers, President Obama placed a tariff on tires from China. This raised the price of Chinese tires.

A **quota** limits the amount of an item that is allowed to enter a country. The United States has placed quotas on sugar imports for years. Limiting sugar imports helps keep prices higher for sugar made at home.

A third way the government tries to help U.S. producers is with subsidies. A subsidy is a payment or benefit the government gives to help a domestic producer. The United States and many European nations pay subsidies to farmers. These payments help farmers keep their prices competitive. These methods to limit imports have a major drawback: In exchange for protecting jobs, the price of goods goes up.

Government Actions to Help U.S. Producers	
Action	**Explanation**
Tariff	
Quota	
Subsidy	

Many economists think trade barriers do more harm than good. Many countries try to have fewer or no trade barriers. This is called **free trade.** When countries try to increase trade, they join with trading partners and set up areas of free trade called free trade zones.

In 1994 the United States, Canada, and Mexico joined together to create the largest free trade zone in the world. In the North American Free Trade Agreement (NAFTA), the three countries agreed to remove most trade barriers. Since then, trade among the three nations has more than tripled. This increase in trade has brought lower prices and a greater variety of goods to consumers in all three countries. However, many companies hurt by these imports lost sales and had to close factories. As a result, thousands of jobs have been lost.

The benefits of free trade encouraged 27 European nations to integrate, or join, their economies. They formed the European Union (EU), one of the largest economies in the world. Most EU nations use the same currency, the euro. Using the euro makes trade easier. The EU also creates a large free trade zone. Goods, services, and workers can travel freely among the nations of the EU. Other free trade zones include the African Union (AU) and the Asia-Pacific Economic Cooperation (APEC).

The World Trade Organization (WTO) helps regulate international trade. The WTO has 153 member nations. It makes trade rules and settles disagreements between members. One of its goals is to help countries that are trying to build their economies.

Show Your Skill

7. Draw Conclusions Why might nations join together to remove trade barriers?

_____

_____

Think Critically

8. Explain What is NAFTA? What countries are involved?

_____

_____

_____

_____

_____

Take the Challenge

9. Research Florida's leading exports. Identify one export and locate countries on a world map that import that product from Florida.

The European Union is made up of 27 countries that together have a population of about half a billion people.

10. Contrast What is the difference between a trade deficit and a trade surplus?

_____

_____

_____

_____

_____

_____

_____

11. Explain What is the exchange rate?

_____

_____

_____

_____

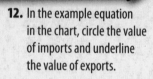

Mark the Text

12. In the example equation in the chart, circle the value of imports and underline the value of exports.

Balance of Trade

The difference between the value of a nation's imports and the value of its exports is its **balance of trade.** If the value of a nation's exports is greater than the value of its imports, it has a _trade surplus._ If the opposite is true, it has a _trade deficit._ The example below shows a country that has a trade surplus of $30 billion.

Balance of Trade
$100 billion   − $70 billion   = $30 billion
(value of exports) − (value of imports) = (positive balance of trade)

Trade deficits can slow down an economy. If a country imports more than it exports, production slows and jobs may be lost. It also leads to debt. When a country's exports are low, it must borrow money from other countries to pay for the goods it imports. A trade deficit can also make a country's currency, or money, go down in value.

The value of one currency when exchanged, or traded, for another is its **exchange rate.** The value of one currency to another is set by supply and demand.

Suppose the United States wants to import goods from China. China's currency is the yuan. The United States must sell dollars and buy yuan to buy Chinese goods. Selling dollars makes more dollars available in the currency markets. The larger supply of dollars drives down the value of dollars. This is how heavy importing can hurt a nation by lowering the value of its currency.

The lower currency value might not be completely bad. It should help the country to export more. Because its currency is worth less than before, its goods are cheaper for other countries to buy.

NGSSS Check What is a trade surplus, and why is it good for a nation's economy? SS.7.E.3.1

_____

_____

_____

_____

_____

NGSSS

SS.7.E.3.3 Compare and contrast a single resource economy with a diversified economy.

LESSON 2
ECONOMIC SYSTEMS AND DEVELOPMENT

Essential Question
Why and how do people make economic choices?

Guiding Questions
1. What characteristics do market economies share?
2. Who makes the basic economic decisions in a command economy?
3. Why do most countries have a mixed economy?
4. What kinds of challenges do developing countries face?

Terms to Know

privatization
the change from state-owned businesses, factories, and farms to ones owned by private citizens

mixed economy
an economy that combines parts of a market economy with parts of a command economy

developed country
a country with a high standard of living and many industries

developing country
a country with low per-capita income and a low standard of living that is struggling to develop a market economy

It Matters Because

The type of economic system determines the way in which a society organizes the production and consumption of goods and services.

What types of economic choices do you and your family make?

Why is it important to be able to make those choices?

What Do You Know?

Directions: In the first column, answer the questions based on what you know before you study. After this lesson, complete the last column.

Before the Lesson		After the Lesson
	What is a market economy?	
	Who makes the decisions in a command economy?	
	Why might a mixed economy work best for some countries?	

Think Critically

1. Explain What is the difference between the GDP and GDP per capita?

_____

_____

_____

_____

_____

Show Your Skill

2. Classify Information
List two positive and two negative characteristics of market economies.

_____

_____

_____

_____

_____

Market Economies

Market economies are one of several different kinds of economies in the world. All economies answer three basic questions: *what* to produce, *how* to produce, and *for whom* to produce. How a society answers these questions determines what kind of economy it has. In market economies, individuals decide what to produce, how to produce, and for whom to produce.

The people, not the government, own the factors of production in a market economy. The factors of production are natural resources, capital, labor, and entrepreneurship. Since the people are the owners, they also decide how the factors of production will be used. No central power runs the economy.

In a market economy, supply and demand combine to set prices, or how much goods and services cost. Supply is the amount of a good that is made. Demand is the amount of a good that consumers want. The way supply and demand interact is what drives a market economy.

Market economies give people a lot of freedom. People can own property and control their own labor. This freedom can give people a high level of satisfaction.

Most countries with high GDP per capita have market economies. GDP per capita is the total value of goods produced in a country, divided by the country's population. GDP per capita allows economists to compare economies of different sizes.

Market economies do have some drawbacks.

- They do not grow steadily. Sometimes the economy rises and sometimes it falls.

- They are profit driven—the main goal of most businesses is to make money, so the workers may not have good working conditions or fair pay.

Command Economies

The opposite of a market economy is a command economy. People in a command economy have little say in how the economy works. The government owns the factors of production. It decides what to produce, how to produce, and for whom to produce. This is also called central planning.

Sometimes central planning works. It helped the Soviet Union's economy rebuild quickly after World War II. But it can also mean that there is not enough food or goods. Command economies are inefficient and usually grow slowly. They have low GDP per capita.

These problems caused many countries with command economies to make the switch to market economies. Around 1990, Russia and many Eastern European countries began moving toward market economies. This was not easy. First, nations had to change from having state-owned businesses and farms to ones owned by private citizens. This is called **privatization.**

Newly private businesses had to learn to be more efficient, or organized. Some countries are still waiting for their economies to improve.

China started using some features of a market economy in the 1970s. China has been successful. Both its GDP and GDP per capita have grown. China's economy is now the second largest in the world.

Show Your Skill

3. Identify the Main Idea Who owns the factors of production in a command economy?

Mark the Text

4. Find and underline the phrases that identify consequences of China's economic reforms.

Think Critically

5. Explain What is privatization?

Advantages of a Command Economy
- works well in national emergencies
- can result in fast growth of some parts of the economy

Drawbacks of a Command Economy
- inefficient
- grows more slowly than market economies
- low GDP per capita

6. Interpret Information What two things are mixed in a mixed economy?

_____

_____

7. Explain What are signs that the United States does not have a pure market economy?

_____

_____

_____

_____

Mixed Economies

Mixed economies combine parts of a market economy with parts of a centrally planned economy. Most countries have mixed economies. Both the market and the government are important in this type of economy.

The United States has a mixed economy. Private citizens own the factors of production and make the economic choices. This means the economy is market-oriented, or directed by the market. At the same time, the government does play a role. It provides some goods and services, such as schooling and roads. It encourages competition, and it regulates, or watches over, businesses. For example, the government has passed laws that set minimum pay for workers and make sure products are safe.

Developed and Developing Countries

Countries that have a high standard of living and a lot of industry are called **developed countries.** Only about 35 countries are considered developed. Examples include the United States, Canada, Japan, and Germany.

Some countries have started taking steps to become developed countries. They are building export businesses to help their economies grow. They are called _newly industrialized countries._ China and India are examples.

Countries that are not very productive and have low GDP per capita are called **developing countries.** They are struggling to develop market economies.

Developing countries often have both extreme poverty and expanding wealth.

One thing that gets in the way of development is high population growth. Often, when a country's population is growing fast, the economy cannot keep up. Each person then gets a smaller and smaller share of what the economy is making. The country's GDP per capita goes down.

Some countries have too many trade barriers. The barriers sometimes protect industries that are not efficient.

A country's location can make it hard for its economy to grow. Landlocked countries cannot use ocean trade routes. They have difficulty getting their goods to other nations.

Wars are another obstacle. They ruin resources and destroy lives. Productivity goes down and people face a shortage of food, health care, and education. As a result, countries have more difficulty investing in their economies.

Many developing countries have large debts. These countries borrowed large amounts of money to help their economies grow. Their economies did not grow fast enough to pay the loans back. Now they have to use too much of their income to pay off their debt.

Finally, government corruption is a problem in some countries. Leaders have stolen money that was meant to help their nations' economies and their people.

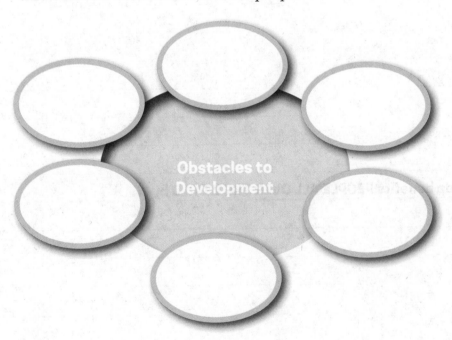

Obstacles to Development

NGSSS Check What is the major difference between a market economy and a command economy? SS.7.E.3.3

_____

_____

_____

Think Critically

8. Explain How can trade barriers hurt development?

_____

_____

_____

_____

Mark the Text

9. Graphic Organizer Complete the graphic organizer to show the obstacles to development.

Take the Challenge

10. Create a fictional country. You want your country to have a robust economy. Describe the country's economy, location, and resources. Compare your country to a partner's country. Decide which economy would be stronger and why.

ESSENTIAL QUESTIONS *Why do people trade? Why and how do people make economic choices?*

Reflect on What It Means . . .

The countries of the world trade *trillions* of dollars worth of goods every year. Why? The answer is simple: trade provides benefits. It makes more goods available to more people and more places. Think about how trade benefits people. Then complete the sentences below and use each as the topic sentence for a short paragraph.

1. **International trade benefits ME by . . .**

2. **International trade benefits PEOPLE IN MY COMMUNITY by . . .**

3. **International trade benefits PEOPLE ALL OVER THE WORLD by . . .**

TAKE THE CHALLENGE

Find out where several items in your home or in your classroom were made. Make a graph as a class to show the countries that produced the goods.

THE UNITED STATES AND FOREIGN AFFAIRS

NGSSS

SS.7.C.4.1 Differentiate concepts related to United States domestic and foreign policy.

SS.7.C.4.2 Recognize government and citizen participation in international organizations. *(Remarks/Examples:* Examples are United Nations, NATO, Peace Corps, World Health Organization, World Trade Organization, International Court of Justice.)

ESSENTIAL QUESTIONS *Why and how do nations interact with each other? Why does conflict develop?*

The Peace Corps is a unit of the federal government. It sends volunteers to poorer nations to improve living conditions there. President John F. Kennedy established the Peace Corps in 1961 to accomplish three simple goals:

1. Helping the people of interested countries in meeting their need for trained men and women.
2. Helping promote a better understanding of Americans on the part of the peoples served.
3. Helping promote a better understanding of other peoples on the part of Americans.

trained

What sort of training do you think this refers to?

_____

_____

_____

understanding of Americans

Why would this be a good goal?

_____

_____

DBQ BREAKING IT DOWN

Which of the goals do you think is the most important?

_____

_____

Would you be willing to volunteer for two years in a poor country to help farmers learn modern farming techniques? Why or why not?

_____

_____

McGraw-Hill
netw⊙rks™
There's More Online!

TEXT: Peace Corps Mission Statement. Peace Corps. http://www.peacecorps.gov/index.cfm?shell=about.mission
PHOTO: David Boyer/National Geographic/Getty Images

1 GLOBAL INTERDEPENDENCE AND ISSUES

 NGSSS

SS.7.C.4.1 Differentiate concepts related to United States domestic and foreign policy.

SS.7.E.2.5 Explain how economic institutions impact the national economy.

Essential Question
Why and how do nations interact with one another?

Guiding Questions
1. Why do nations depend upon one another?
2. What are some consequences of global interdependence?

Terms to Know

global interdependence
the reliance of people and nations around the world on one another for goods and services

trade war
economic conflict that occurs when one or more nations put up trade barriers to punish another nation for trade barriers it erected against them

deforestation
the mass removal of trees from large areas

ethnic group
a group of people who share the same race, language, or culture

terrorism
the use of or the threat of violence against civilians to attain a particular goal

refugee
a person who has unwillingly left his or her home to escape war, famine, or natural disaster

It Matters Because

Growing global interdependence offers both opportunities and challenges for the people of the world.

Explain the idea of global interdependence in your own words.

_____

_____

_____

_____

What Do You Know?

In the first column, answer the questions based on what you know before you study. After the lesson, complete the last column.

Before the Lesson		After the Lesson
	Why do nations trade?	
	What issues affect the whole world community?	

Global Interdependence

Nations depend on one another for goods and services. This is called **global interdependence.** Countries trade things they have for things they do not have. Rich nations buy raw materials and local products from poor nations. Poor nations buy technology, medicine, and other goods from developed countries.

Global trade works because nations have different resources. One country may have advanced technology but few natural resources. Another may have natural resources but little technology. Yet another country may have a large labor force but not enough food to feed its people. These differences encourage trade between nations.

The United States exports many goods. It sells wheat, aircraft, computer software, video games, and much more. The United States also imports many goods. One major import is oil.

Sometimes nations cooperate on trade issues. One example is the European Union. This group of 27 European nations has ended most trade barriers among its members. The North American Free Trade Agreement (NAFTA) is another example. It is an agreement among the United States, Canada, and Mexico. The goal of these agreements is to promote free trade.

Global Issues

Countries' dependence on one another has led to increased trade in many parts of the world. People usually have more choices when trade increases. Prices usually go down. Increased trade has costs as well as benefits, however.

Workers, for example, can lose jobs due to international trade. One reason is that some companies hire workers in other countries that have low labor costs.

Nations sometimes try to protect their industries from imports produced in countries with cheaper labor. They do this by putting up barriers to trade. A trade barrier is any government policy that limits trade among nations. One type of trade barrier is the tariff. A tariff is a tax on imports. Tariffs raise the price of imported goods. This makes goods produced at home more competitive with imported goods.

Other nations may respond with trade barriers of their own. Sometimes tariffs lead to trade wars. A **trade war** is an economic conflict that occurs when one or more nations put up trade barriers to punish another nation for its trade barriers against them. Trade wars raise prices and reduce choice for everyone.

1. Summarize What is global interdependence?

_____

_____

_____

_____

_____

2. Synthesize Why do nations trade with each other? Give examples of things nations trade with each other.

_____

_____

_____

_____

_____

_____

_____

_____

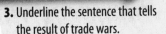

Mark the Text

3. Underline the sentence that tells the result of trade wars.

4. Contrast What is one difference between developed and developing countries?

_____

_____

5. Recognize Point of View Why do nations sometimes disagree?

_____

_____

_____

Economic inequality among nations is a major global challenge. Nations have grown at different rates, widening the wealth gap between rich and poor.

Nations with a high standard of living are called developed countries. Developed countries usually have economies and governments that are stable. This means they are unlikely to change very much. The United States and Germany are examples of developed countries.

Developing countries have low standards of living. They are trying to build modern economies. Many struggle with political unrest and conflict. Haiti is one example of a developing country. It is the poorest nation in the Western Hemisphere.

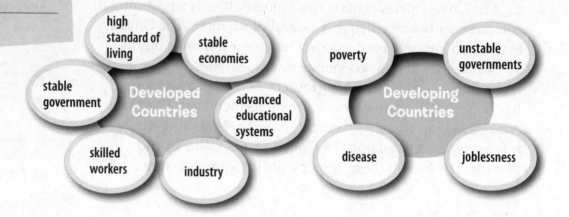

Sometimes nations disagree. Nations have different forms of government and different views about the world. The United States and Venezuela are one example. The two nations dislike each other's economic policies. They trade with each other in spite of this. Venezuela needs money from the United States. The United States needs oil from Venezuela. The two nations depend on each other.

The environment is another global concern. As nations have developed their industries they have hurt the environment. The removal of trees from large areas, known as **deforestation,** leads to flooding and mudslides. Since trees absorb carbon dioxide, their destruction has led to higher levels of it in the air. Many experts believe that burning oil, gas, and coal has helped cause climate change.

One way to help the environment is through conservation. Conservation means using resources carefully. It also means limiting bad effects of human activity. For example, conserving gasoline helps reduce air pollution.

The movement of people between countries is an example of global interaction. In the United States, illegal immigration is an issue over which people disagree.

People disagree about conservation. Supporters say it will help save the environment, prevent climate change, and help prevent health problems. Critics say that conservation drives up the costs of goods and services. Developing nations struggle to balance concern for the environment with the need for economic growth.

Today's world faces other challenges as well. Tension over immigration is one such problem. Immigrants are people who move willingly. People often move to a new country in search of better lives. When large groups move, they place added demands on resources in their new country. This can cause tension within nations. Differences among religious and **ethnic groups** can make such problems worse. An ethnic group is a group of people who share the same race, language, or culture.

Other global issues today are the threat of war and **terrorism.** Terrorism is the use of violence or the threat of violence against civilians to attain a goal.

When wars, natural disasters, or famine force people to leave their homes, they are called **refugees.** Millions of refugees need help from the nations of the world. In addition many people in the world do not have enough food, clean water, or health care. Nations must cooperate with one another in order to meet these challenges.

 NGSSS Check Why does global interdependence increase trade? SS.7.C.4.1

_____

_____

_____

Think Critically

6. **Defend** The United States has laws regulating immigration. Should the United States open its borders to all who want to enter? Defend your answer.

_____

_____

_____

_____

_____

Take the Challenge

7. What do you think is the most important issue facing the world today? Choose one issue and develop points to make a persuasive argument about why the issue is so important. Have a discussion with someone who thinks a different issue is more important.

THE UNITED STATES AND INTERNATIONAL ORGANIZATIONS

NGSSS

SS.7.C.4.2 Recognize government and citizen participation in international organizations. Remarks/Examples: Examples are United Nations, NATO, Peace Corps, World Health Organization, World Trade Organization, International Court of Justice.

Essential Question
Why and how do nations interact with each other?

Guiding Questions
1. What is the purpose of international organizations?
2. How do international organizations help people?

Terms to Know

diplomat
an official representative of a country

non-governmental organization
international organization that is not connected to any government

prisoner of war
person captured during a war

It Matters Because

International organizations help nations communicate and work together to solve global problems.

Why might actions of nations working together be more effective than one nation working alone?

How might trying to reach agreement among nations slow down progress on an issue?

What Do You Know?

Directions: Choose any four of the words below and write a sentence or two about international efforts. When you finish the lesson, write another sentence using four different words from the list.

disaster	Red Cross	United Nations	peace	famine
aid	plantation	international	court	discuss
war	help	meet	charity	

The Purpose of International Organizations

Nations join together for many reasons. One is to help a country in times of trouble. When a natural disaster strikes one nation, the world community tries to help. Nations send food, water, medical aid, and equipment. Nations also join together to deal with issues that affect the entire world. These include

- environmental problems,
- fights between countries, and
- trade and economic issues.

Nations try to solve problems by talking directly with one another through **diplomats.** Diplomats are officials who represent their countries. They often meet to discuss issues and find solutions.

Countries also form organizations to address international problems. These are called governmental organizations. Diplomats from each member country meet regularly to discuss problems. Sometimes they agree about what to do to solve a problem. Sometimes they disagree.

Each member nation provides part of the money needed to run a governmental organization. They agree to follow the rules of the organization and support its decisions.

Some governmental organizations have a single purpose. For example, the North Atlantic Treaty Organization (NATO) was formed to defend its members.

Other governmental organizations have many goals. The goals of the United Nations include promoting peace, building schools, and improving health care.

Governmental organizations can change the world. For example, the European Union (EU) set up a common unit of money for most of its members. The euro is now a standard currency, which makes it easier for nations to trade. At times, group efforts are less effective. Terrorism persists, although all international organizations condemn it.

Some international organizations are not connected to any government. These are called **non-governmental organizations (NGOs).** NGOs are founded by people who see a need or want to work for a cause such as fighting hunger or poverty. NGOs usually rely on volunteers and donations.

Sometimes governmental organizations and NGOs work together. After the earthquake in Haiti in 2010, many organizations worked together to help.

Think Critically

1. **Contrast** How do the finances of governmental and non-governmental organizations differ?

Show Your Skill

2. **Classify Information** List one success and one failure of governmental organizations in recent times.

Show Your Skill

4. **Classify Information** Which part of the UN is connected with settling disputes?

_____

_____

_____

_____

Think Critically

5. There are five permanent members to the Security Council. Do you think that is fair? Why or why not?

_____

_____

_____

_____

_____

Take the Challenge

6. Who is the current UN representative from the United States? Write a letter explaining an international issue you think is important and how you think the UN should respond.

NGOs can do things that governments cannot. For instance, they may be able to get aid into countries that would not accept help from groups connected with governments. The International Committee of the Red Cross (ICRC), for example, does not take sides in a war. It serves people in need on both sides.

International Organizations

There are many international organizations at work today. A few of the most important are discussed below.

The United Nations One of the most important international organizations is the United Nations (UN). It was formed at the end of World War II and has 192 member nations. The main goal of the UN is to keep peace among nations. It also works to fight poverty and protect human rights. The following chart shows some of the most important of the UN's many parts.

Organization of the United Nations		
Part of United Nations	**Membership**	**Purpose**
General Assembly	All 192 UN member nations	Main meeting of UN
Security Council	5 permanent: Britain, China, France, Russia, U.S.; 10 temporary: 2 years, rotates	World peace and security
International Court of Justice (World Court)	15 judges elected by General Assembly, Security Council	Settles disputes between nations
Other UN councils	Various nations	Economic issues, social justice, public health

North Atlantic Treaty Organization Another important international group is the North Atlantic Treaty Organization (NATO). NATO has 28 member nations in Europe and North America. They have pledged to work for peace and to defend one another in times of war. NATO has at times sent soldiers to crisis situations around the world. This happened in Afghanistan in 2001 and Iraq in 2003.

World Trade Organization The World Trade Organization (WTO) has over 150 member nations. Its goal is to arrange trade agreements and settle trade disputes. The WTO works to abolish, or get rid of, trade barriers. Its decisions are usually

The Red Cross provides important assistance during times of crisis, such as after an earthquake or flood, or during a war.

made by consensus. Consensus is general agreement. Some people believe that the WTO favors large developed nations. Other people think that it ignores concerns about the environment. WTO members disagree with these opinions.

World Health Organization The World Health Organization (WHO) is part of the United Nations. It fights disease around the world. It does this through improving health guidelines and studying public health issues. The efforts of this group have educated the public about many diseases, such as the HIV virus, and led to the decline of others, such as smallpox.

Peace Corps The Peace Corps is a volunteer organization run by the U.S. government. Its original goal was to help Americans and people from other nations understand each other. Nearly 8,000 American volunteers work in countries all over the world. Some work on public health projects such as providing clean water. Others teach or help with local business development.

International Committee of the Red Cross The International Committee of the Red Cross (ICRC) provides aid to victims of war. The ICRC works to protect those who are not part of the fighting. It also tries to make sure that prisoners of war are treated well. **Prisoners of war** are people captured during a war. The ICRC stays neutral. This means it does not take sides during a war. Most nations respect the efforts of the ICRC and allow it to do its work.

Many other international organizations, both governmental and non-governmental, exist throughout the world. They work on many issues of global importance.

NGSSS Check List three ways that nations work together in international organizations. SS.7.C.4.2

_____

_____

Think Critically

7. Predict In our world of global interdependence, which organization(s) discussed here might become even more important? Why?

_____

_____

_____

_____

8. Summarize What are some main goals of international organizations?

_____

_____

_____

_____

_____

_____

_____

THE UNITED STATES AND WORLD AFFAIRS

 NGSSS

SS.7.C.4.1 Recognize concepts related to United States domestic and foreign policy.

SS.7.C.4.2 Recognize government and citizen participation in international organizations. Remarks/Examples: Examples are United Nations, NATO, Peace Corps, World Health Organization, World Trade Organization, International Court of Justice.

SS.7.C.4.3 Describe examples of how the United States has dealt with international conflicts.

Essential Question

Why does conflict develop?

Guiding Questions

1. What are human rights?
2. Why does conflict among nations occur?
3. Why has the United States engaged in conflict in recent years?

Terms to Know

universal
worldwide, or applying to all

human right
a protection or a freedom that all people should have

repression
preventing people from expressing themselves or from freely engaging in normal life

genocide
the attempt to kill all members of an ethnic group

communism
a one-party system of government based on the idea of state ownership and control of property and industry

weapon of mass destruction (WMD)
a weapon that can kill or harm large numbers of people and destroy or damage a large area

It Matters Because

Recognizing potential causes of conflict helps us to understand and address challenges facing the world.

Give an example of a time when you have tried to solve a problem before it became a bigger problem.

What are some advantages of working to resolve international conflicts before they grow?

What Do You Know?

Directions: Write two questions you have about conflicts in the world. After you have finished the lesson, come back and see if you can answer the questions.

_____

_____

_____

_____

_____

networks™ Read Chapter 25 Lesson 3 in your textbook or online.

Human Rights

Many differences exist between people around the world. Governments, cultures, languages, and beliefs are all different. Culture means the ideas, skills, art, and customs of a people. Groups and individuals around the world have many things in common as well. For instance, everyone wants to be safe and to have enough to eat. Everyone wants a place to live. These ideas are **universal.** This means they apply to everyone.

Every person in the world has certain basic rights known as **human rights.** Human rights include the right to food, safety, shelter, protection under law, and freedom of thought. These ideas have inspired people around the world. They have shaped events such as the American Revolution. They continue to affect the world today.

The rights of millions of people were violated during World War II. After the war the United Nations took a stand for human rights. In 1948 it adopted the Universal Declaration of Human Rights. This declaration defined the rights that all people should have.

The Declaration has 30 articles. Article 1 says that all people are born free and have equal rights. Article 2 says that no one should be treated differently due to things such as race, sex, or religion. These two articles form the basis for the other rights. The chart below shows a partial list.

Universal Declaration of Human Rights

People should be . . .	People should have . . .
free from arrest without cause	equal protection under law
free from slavery and torture	the right to own property
free from forced marriages	the right to move about freely
	the right to take part in government
	equal pay for equal work
	the right to a decent standard of living
	the right to medical care

Unfortunately some governments do not protect their people's rights. Some rulers use **repression** to stay in power. Repression means preventing people from expressing themselves or from freely living a normal life. These rulers often deny their citizens basic human rights and protections.

Some nations do not uphold the right to freedom of ideas and the press. China, Iran, Saudi Arabia, and North Korea limit people's ability to get information. North Korea does not allow its people to criticize the government.

Think Critically

1. What are some basic human rights?

Show Your Skill

2. Make a Connection Which of these human rights listed in the Universal Declaration of Human Rights do you recognize from the U.S. Constitution?

3. Defend Do you think the international community has the right to try to influence what happens in a country that violates the human rights of its citizens? Explain.

_____

_____

_____

_____

_____

Mark the Text

4. Underline the organizations involved in working for human rights.

Show Your Skill

5. Classify Information What two types of governments opposed one another during the Cold War?

_____

_____

Conflict between ethnic groups sometimes leads to war and even genocide. **Genocide** is the attempt to kill all members of an ethnic group. It happened to Jews in World War II. It also happened in the 1990s. Millions of people were killed in East Africa due to ethnic conflict between Hutus and Tutsis in Rwanda and Burundi.

The U.S. government tries to promote human rights. It protests governments that take away people's freedoms. Sometimes it refuses to trade with such countries.

The UN Human Rights Council reports on human rights issues around the world and suggests possible actions to be taken. The UN Security Council can refer cases of human rights abuse by governments to the International Criminal Court for trial.

Many non-governmental organizations (NGOs) also work for human rights. Amnesty International and Human Rights Watch campaign around the world to end human rights abuses. They bring abuses to the world's attention. This puts pressure on governments that disobey international human rights laws.

Democracy, Liberty, and Conflict

How much a nation respects human rights depends on its type of government. Democratic nations usually protect human rights better than nondemocratic nations do. There were few democracies in the world in the early 1900s. Since then many nations have become democratic.

The United States has made the spread of democracy a goal of its foreign policy. Both World War I and World War II were fought to stop governments that were not democratic from overpowering other nations.

During World War II the United States, Great Britain, and the Soviet Union were the Allied Powers. After the war the Allies split into two camps. On one side were the United States and Western Europe. These nations were democracies with market-based economies. The Soviet Union and Eastern Europe were on the other side. They practiced communism. **Communism** is a system of government in which one party is in control, and the government owns the property and industry. People living under communist governments do not have many of the freedoms that people in democracies have.

The Soviet Union came to control most of Eastern Europe. The United States and its allies tried to keep communism from spreading further. A bitter struggle developed. This clash of ideas was known as the Cold War because not much actual fighting took place. At times, however, violence did occur.

In its fight against communism, the United States sometimes supported rulers who abused human rights. Chile, Cuba, and Iran were not democratic, but the United States supported them because they opposed communism.

The Cold War ended with the collapse of the Soviet Union in 1991. New democracies emerged, but progress has slowed. The struggle for human rights continues. Many people in the world are still not free. Governments in large parts of South America and Africa restrict human rights. North Korea, China, and Cuba still deny their citizens freedom of speech and of the press.

New threats to peace have emerged, such as terrorism. Groups such as al-Qaeda and the Taliban use terrorist attacks to try to impose their beliefs on others.

Recent Conflicts

On September 11, 2001, terrorists attacked the United States. Almost 3,000 people died. The United States responded in several ways.

The government set up the Department of Homeland Security. Its three main goals are to

- try to stop terrorist attacks on the United States,
- reduce the threat of terrorist attacks,
- help with recovery from attacks or other disasters.

Another response was the Patriot Act of 2001. This law gave the government new powers to fight terrorism. This included the power to search financial and phone records secretly. Some people disliked the law. They said it gave the government too much power and infringed on rights such as the right to privacy and freedom from unreasonable searches.

The United States also responded to the September 11th attacks with military force. In October 2001, the U.S. military attacked Afghanistan. Afghanistan's rulers, the Taliban, were supporting a terrorist group called al-Qaeda. Al-Qaeda was responsible for the September 11th attacks.

The United States quickly defeated the Taliban, but al-Qaeda's leader Osama bin Laden escaped. In the years following, little progress was made toward democracy. The Taliban returned again and again. President Obama sent more troops to Afghanistan in 2009 to stop the Taliban from taking control. In May 2011, U.S. forces located Bin Laden hiding out in Pakistan. Bin Laden was killed during a U.S. raid on his hiding place.

Think Critically

6. Conclude Did the United States' policies during the Cold War advance or hold back human rights?

_____

_____

_____

_____

_____

_____

_____

_____

_____

Mark the Text

7. Underline the goals of the Department of Homeland Security.

Think Critically

8. Evaluate Do you think individuals should give up rights to become secure from terrorism? Explain.

_____

_____

_____

_____

_____

_____

_____

U.S. troops worked to help establish Iraq's democratic government.

PHOTO: Credit AHMAD AL-RUBAYE/AFP/Getty Images

U.S. troops were also sent to Iraq. After the attacks of 2001, President George W. Bush feared that terrorist groups might get **weapons of mass destruction (WMDs).** A weapon of mass destruction is a weapon that can harm or kill large numbers of people. Leaders believed that Iraq's dictator Saddam Hussein might give WMDs to terrorist groups.

The United States attacked and defeated Iraq's army in 2003, removing Hussein from power. No WMDs were found. American troops stayed to help set up a democracy. This proved difficult. Rebel groups attacked U.S. troops and their allies. Violence between different ethnic and religious groups flared. In 2008, the addition of more U.S. troops helped calm the violence.

It was not until 2010 that President Obama took American combat troops out of Iraq. Some soldiers stayed behind to help the country continue to set up a democratic government.

The United States continued to face challenges in the world. Iran's efforts to build a nuclear weapon were a serious concern. Iran was also suspected of helping terrorist groups. Some groups in Pakistan were suspected of the same thing. Conflict continued between Israelis and Palestinians. Other nations around the world were torn by conflicts. Terrorism, the new weapon of global warfare, played a role in many of them.

Think Critically

9. Summarize What was the main reason given by President Bush for the attack on Iraq by the United States in 2003?

_____

_____

_____

_____

_____

Take the Challenge

10. Research how Florida is involved in fighting terrorism. Make a diagram that shows involvement in efforts at home and abroad.

NGSSS Check Why do nations and people continue to fight for human rights? SS.7.C.4.2

_____

_____

_____

_____

List two ways that differing political views led to conflict between nations during the Cold War. SS.7.C.4.3

_____

_____

MY REFLECTIONS

ESSENTIAL QUESTIONS *Why and how do nations interact with each other?*
Why does conflict develop?

Reflect on What It Means . . .

The world is a big place. It is home to hundreds of countries, thousands of cultures, millions of places, and billions of people. Yet it is also a small place. Transportation and communication have made it easier than ever before for people to come together. Some people say that these advances have "shrunk" the world and made the Earth "a global village."

How do you think transportation and communication advances will affect . . .

You as you get older?

The world during your lifetime?

Your community over the next ten years?

Keep Going!

Draw and label a picture of life 50 years from now. Show the changes in transportation and communication you predict will occur.

TAKE THE CHALLENGE

Tell a partner which of the following you would rather be, and why: an aid worker in a foreign country; a soldier serving overseas; a business person stationed abroad; a tourist who sees the world; a captain of a ship that crosses the Pacific; a diplomat stationed in a foreign city.

NGSSS Inventory Test

The state of Florida uses tests to measure your knowledge in different subject areas. An end-of-course test will be given in Civics. You will take that test online. Get ready for your end-of-course test by learning all you can during the school year. Keep these tips in mind, too:

✓ **Be Prepared**

To do your best on test days, you need to take care of yourself beforehand. Try to get plenty of sleep for several nights before the test. Make sure to eat a good breakfast and lunch on test day. Then, be ready to do your best!

✓ **What to Expect**

The questions on your end-of-course tests will be multiple choice. Each question will be followed by four answer choices. Your job is to decide which of the four is the best possible answer.

Sometimes you absolutely know the answer to a question and the right answer leaps out at you. Other times you have to analyze the options and eliminate ones you know are wrong in order to zero in on the right answer.

✓ **Pace Yourself**

When you take an end-of-course test, it is important to pace yourself. If you work too quickly, you will be more likely to make mistakes. Instead, read each question and all of the answer choices carefully. If there's a question you can't answer, skip it and answer the next question. When you are done with the test, you can go back and reread those questions you did not understand.

✓ **Read Every Word**

Pay extra attention to every word in the questions. Just a word or two can change the meaning of the question.

✓ **Make Your Best Guess**

Make sure you go back and answer every question before submitting your test. Any question left blank will be marked wrong, so it's better to make your best guess. Remember to use the process of elimination to narrow the possibilities. Then make your guess from the remaining choices.

✓ **Check Your Work**

After you finish the test, go back to the beginning and check your work.

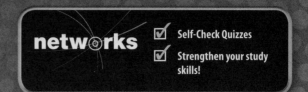

Directions: Circle the best answer.

1 The Florida Everglades are an example of a(n)

A wetland.

B highland.

C island.

D plateau.

 SS.7.G.2.2 Locate major physical landmarks that are emblematic of the United States.

2 The institution responsible for the safekeeping and distribution of newly printed money is

A Congress.

B the Federal Reserve.

C commercial banks.

D a savings and loan association.

 SS.7.E.2.2 Describe the banking system in the United States and its impact on the money supply.

3 If the value of the American dollar was lower than the value of the Chinese yuan

A American goods could be cheaper in China.

B China would refuse to import American goods.

C the Federal Reserve would release more money into the U.S. economy.

D the U.S. budget would have a surplus.

 SS.7.E.3.2 Assess how the changing value of currency affects trade of goods and services between nations.

4 The Supreme Court has final authority in all cases involving

A trade.

B state taxes.

C the Constitution.

D impeachment.

SS.7.C.1.7 Describe how the Constitution limits the powers of government through separation of powers and checks and balances.

5 Serving on a jury is considered a duty of citizenship rather than a responsibility of citizenship because

A serving on a jury is not something a responsible citizen would do.

B jury service is required by law.

C only adults 18 and over can serve on a jury.

D only citizens are chosen for jury duty.

 SS.7.C.2.2 Evaluate the obligations citizens have to obey laws, pay taxes, defend the nation, and serve on juries.

6 The form of government most closely associated with the idea of "majority rule" is

   F authoritarian.

   G totalitarian.

   H democracy.

   J monarchy.

 SS .7.C.3.1 Compare different forms of government (direct democracy, representative democracy, socialism, communism, monarchy, oligarchy, autocracy).

7 What idea expressed by the Magna Carta is a principle of the U.S. Constitution?

   A separation of powers

   B limited government

   C popular sovereignty

   D division of powers

 SS.7.C.1.2 Trace the impact that the Magna Carta, English Bill of Rights, Mayflower Compact, and Thomas Paine's "Common Sense" had on colonists' views of government.

8 The Stamp Act and the Townshend Acts

   F angered the colonists because the acts established taxes and duties.

   G frightened the colonists because the acts made them quarter soldiers.

   H annoyed the colonists because the acts made British tea more expensive.

   J angered the colonists because they restricted where colonists could live.

 SS.7.C.1.3 Describe how English policies and responses to colonial concerns led to the writing of the Declaration of Independence.

9 The first 10 amendments to the U.S. Constitution both safeguard and limit individual rights. What is another name for the first 10 amendments?

   A The Articles of Confederation

   B The Federalist Papers

   C The Bill of Rights

   D Declaration of Sentiments

 SS.7.C.2.5 Distinguish how the Constitution safeguards and limits individual rights.

10 Which pairing shows the correct function of one branch of government?

   F legislative branch: enforces laws

   G executive branch: interprets laws

   H executive branch: makes laws

   J judicial branch: interprets laws

 SS.7.C.3.3 Illustrate the structure and function (three branches of government established in Articles I, II, and III with corresponding powers) of government in the United States as established in the Constitution.

11 Politics in the United States is dominated by which two major political parties?

A Democratic and Republican

B Republican and Whig

C Progressive and Democratic

D Green and Republican

SS.7.C.2.8 Identify America's current political parties, and illustrate their ideas about government.

12 The 19th Amendment granted the right to vote to

A all male U.S. citizens older than 18.

B African-American men.

C women.

D all U.S. citizens aged 18 and older.

SS.7.C.3.7 Analyze the impact of the 13th, 14th, 15th, 19th, 24th, and 26th amendments on participation of minority groups in the American political process.

13 One outcome of *Bush v. Gore* was that

A Al Gore was elected president.

B George Bush resigned from office.

C Al Gore ceded the 2000 presidential election to George Bush.

D the U.S. Supreme Court declined to hear the case.

SS.7.C.3.12 Analyze the significance and outcomes of landmark Supreme Court cases including, but not limited to, Marbury v. Madison, Plessy v. Ferguson, Brown v. Board of Education, Gideon v. Wainwright, Miranda v. Arizona, in re Gault, Tinker v. Des Moines, Hazelwood v. Kuhlmeier, United States v. Nixon, and Bush v. Gore.

14 According to the Constitution, the power to declare war is given to

F the president.

G the legislative branch.

H the executive branch.

J the judicial branch.

SS.7.C.3.3 Illustrate the structure and function (three branches of government established in Articles I, II, and III with corresponding powers) of government in the United States as established in the Constitution.

15 Following the end of World War II, the United States joined with nations around the world to establish

A the International Red Cross.

B the League of Nations.

C the United Nations.

D Amnesty International.

SS.7.C.4.2 Recognize government and citizen participation in international organizations.

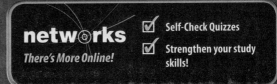
16 In the division of powers between the federal government and state governments, which powers are held only by the state governments?

F enumerated powers

G federal powers

H reserved powers

J concurrent powers

 SS.7.C.3.4 Identify the relationship and division of powers between the federal government and state governments.

17 What is the title of the state official who oversees state elections and records and publishes state laws?

A treasurer

B secretary of state

C auditor

D governor

 SS.7.C.3.14 Differentiate between local, state, and federal governments' obligations and services.

18 The loss of steel and automobile factories in the late 1900s led to what nickname for the Midwest?

A the Bread Basket

B Silicon Valley

C the Grain Belt

D the Rust Belt

 SS.7.G.2.4 Describe current major cultural regions of North America.

19 A person steals a bicycle. What type of law has been broken?

A civil

B administrative

C criminal

D constitutional

 SS.7.C.3.10 Identify sources and types (civil, criminal, constitutional, military) of law.

20 You have $20 and decide to spend it on music downloads rather than an e-book. What is the economic term that now describes the e-book?

F total cost

G fixed cost

H marginal cost

J opportunity cost

 SS.7.E.1.3 Review the concepts of supply and demand, choice, scarcity, and opportunity cost as they relate to the development of the mixed market economy in the United States.

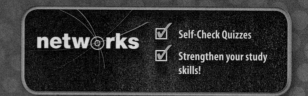

networks
- ☑ Self-Check Quizzes
- ☑ Strengthen your study skills!

21 A bank loans Miguel money. He uses the money to open a sandwich shop. Which of the following prompted both Miguel and the bank to take these actions?

A   the factor market

B   the standard of living

C   the profit motive

D   the division of labor

 SS.7.E.1.5 Assess how profits, incentives, and competition motivate individuals, households, and businesses in a free market economy.

22 One advantage of using credit is

F   a high annual percentage rate (APR)

G   the interest costs.

H   the delayed payments.

J   that it saves money.

 SS.7.E.1.2 Discuss the importance of borrowing and lending in the United States, the government's role in controlling financial institutions, and list the advantages and disadvantages of using credit.

23 Antitrust laws are designed to promote competition by preventing the formation of

A   monopolies.

B   recessions.

C   externalities.

D   unions.

 SS.7.E.2.3 Identify and describe United States laws and regulations adopted to promote economic competition.

24 The single largest source of federal revenue comes from

F   import taxes.

G   corporate income taxes.

H   payroll taxes.

J   personal income taxes.

 SS.7.E.2.1 Explain how federal, state, and local taxes support the economy as a function of the United States government.

25 An organization that is private, nonpartisan, and works to help people with disabilities by monitoring and influencing the government is best described as

A   a political party.

B   a lobbyist group.

C   a public-interest group.

D   a media company.

 SS.7.C.2.10 Examine the impact of media, individuals, and interest groups on monitoring and influencing government.